Religion in the Media Age

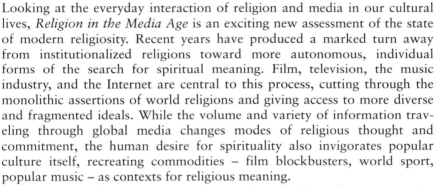

Looking at the everyday interaction of religion and media in our cultural lives, *Religion in the Media Age* is an exciting new assessment of the state of modern religiosity. Recent years have produced a marked turn away from institutionalized religions toward more autonomous, individual forms of the search for spiritual meaning. Film, television, the music industry, and the Internet are central to this process, cutting through the monolithic assertions of world religions and giving access to more diverse and fragmented ideals. While the volume and variety of information traveling through global media changes modes of religious thought and commitment, the human desire for spirituality also invigorates popular culture itself, recreating commodities – film blockbusters, world sport, popular music – as contexts for religious meaning.

Drawing on fascinating research into household media consumption Stewart M. Hoover charts the way in which media and religion intermingle and collide in the cultural experience of media audiences. The result will be essential reading for everyone interested in how today's mass media relate to contemporary religious and spiritual life.

Stewart M. Hoover is Professor of Media Studies in the School of Journalism and Mass Communication, at the University of Colorado, Boulder, where he directs the Center for Media, Religion and Culture. He is a leading authority on media and religion, and has authored, co-authored and co-edited several books, including *Media, Home and Family* (2004), *Practising Religion in the Age of Media* (2002), *Religion in the News* (1998), *Rethinking Media, Religion and Culture* (1997) and *Mass Media Religion* (1989).

Religion, Media and Culture

Edited by Stewart M. Hoover, Jolyon Mitchell and David Morgan

Religion, Media and Culture is an exciting series which analyses the role of media in the history of contemporary practice of religious belief. Books in this series explore the importance of a variety of media in religious practice and highlight the significance of the culture, social and religious setting of such media.

Religion in the Media Age
Stewart M. Hoover

Religion in the Media Age

Stewart M. Hoover

Routledge
Taylor & Francis Group

LONDON AND NEW YORK

First published 2006
by Routledge
2 Park Square, Milton Park, Abingdon, Oxon. OX14 4RN

Simultaneously published in the USA and Canada
by Routledge
270 Madison Avenue, New York, NY 10016

Routledge is an imprint of the Taylor & Francis Group, an informa business

© 2006 Stewart M. Hoover

Typeset in Sabon by Taylor & Francis Books
Printed and bound in Great Britain
by Antony Rowe Ltd, Chippenham, Wiltshire

British Library Cataloguing in Publication Data
A catalogue record for this book is available from the British Library

Library of Congress Cataloging in Publication Data
A catalog record for this book has been requested

ISBN10: 0-415-31422-4   ISBN13: 978-0-415-31422-0 (hbk)
ISBN10: 0-415-31423-2   ISBN13: 978-0-415-31423-7 (pbk)
ISBN10: 0-203-50320-1   ISBN13: 978-0-203-50320-1 (ebk)

Contents

Series editors' preface

Media, Religion, and Culture is a series of interdisciplinary volumes which analyse the role of media in the history and contemporary practice of religious belief. Books in this series scrutinise the importance of a variety of media in religious practice: from lithographs and film to television and the internet. Studies from all over the world highlight the significance of the cultural, social and religious setting of such media.

Rather than thinking of media purely as instruments for information delivery, volumes in this series contribute in various ways to a new paradigm of understanding media as an integral part of lived religion. Employing a variety of methods authors investigate how practices of belief take shape in the production, distribution, and reception of mediated communication.

Stewart Hoover, University of Colorado
Jolyon Mitchell, University of Edinburgh
David Morgan, Valparaiso University

Acknowledgements

No project like this is possible without the support of many people. This is particularly so here both because it is based in a collaborative project and because it has stretched across a longer period than is often the case. While it was underway, I was called upon to serve two terms as Interim Dean of the School of Journalism and Mass Communication at the University of Colorado. This experience reinforced my appreciation of the commitment of our university's leadership to scholarship on our campus.

The research reported here was made possible by a series of grants from the Lilly Endowment, and I want to recognize the advice and support of Dr Craig Dykstra and Dr Chris Coble, and thank the Endowment for its commitment to, and faith in, our efforts. Craig Dykstra became interested in our work at an early stage, and his reflections and encouragement are doubly significant because of his own record as a scholar of lived religious practice.

In these pages, I recognize many of the contributions of our research team to my efforts. Lynn Schofield Clark has been my collaborator and co-investigator in the projects represented here. I thank Lynn for her vital input, advice, and encouragement at various stages of this project, as well as her efforts as director and a member of the research teams. Our approach to research involves team members both in field research and in reflection and analysis. Here I thank Henrik Boes, Diane Alters, Joe Champ, Lee Hood, Denice Walker, Michelle Miles, Christoph Demont-Heinrich, Scott Webber, Anna Maria Russo Lemor, Jin Kyu Park, Monica Emerich, Curtis Coats, and Cari Skogberg for their efforts in the field and in the various aspects of our research process.

Colleagues from across the disciplines of media studies, cultural studies, and religious studies have contributed much to this project in many ways, great and small. For their advice, reflection, reaction, and encouragement, I'd like to thank Catherine Albanese, Nancy Ammerman, Kwabena Asamoah-Gyadu, Liz Bird, Brenda Brasher, Heidi Campbell, Jim Carey, Joy Charlton, Cliff Christians, George Conklin, Nick Couldry, Daniel Dayan, Jay Demerath, Fred Denny, Erika Doss, Mara Einstein, Jan Fernback, John Ferré, Dena Pence Frantz, Faye Ginsburg, Eric Gormly, Ron Grimes, Larry Gross, Ingunn Hagen, Cees Hamelink, Don Handelman, Mary Hess, Birgitta Hoijer, Peter

Horsfield, Janet Jacobs, Klaus Jensen, Elihu Katz, Barbro Klein, Shawn Landres, Brian Larkin, Patty Limerick, Alf Linderman, Sonia Livingstone, Mia Lövheim, Jim Lull, Knut Lundby, Dennis McGilvray, Bill McKinney, Jeffrey Mahan, Martin Marty, Carolyn Marvin, Adán Medrano, Birgit Meyer, Jolyon Mitchell, David Morgan, Horace Newcomb, Thorleif Petterson, Sally Promey, Clark Roof, Michele Rosenthal, Eric Rothenbuhler, Ellen Seiter, Roger Silverstone, Joyce Smith, Judith Stacey, Dan Stout, Rebecca Sullivan, Göran Therborn, Günter Thomas, Pradip Thomas, Sham Thomas, Steve Warner, Hillary Warren, Michael Welker, Diane Winston, Mallory Wober, Linda Woodhead, Bob Wuthnow, Barbie Zelizer, and Angela Zito. I give my apologies to anyone who I have neglected to include. Many of these inputs, and many other helpful conversations, took place at conferences, including the International Communication Association, the International Association for Media and Communication Research, the Association of Internet Researchers, the Association for Education in Journalism and Mass Communication, the American Academy of Religion, and the Society for the Scientific Study of Religion. Specialized venues have been of particular help, and I wish to express gratitude to the planners of conferences on media and religion, including the periodic Conferences on Media, Religion, and Culture in Boulder, Edinburgh, and Louisville, and specialized meetings in Uppsala, Sweden, Heidelberg, Germany, and Jyväskylä, Finland, as well as the International Study Commission on Media, Religion, and Culture, which has been supported by grants from the Stichting Porticus Foundation.

This book is among the first in a new series on Media and Religion, and I wish to thank my series co-editors, David Morgan and Jolyon Mitchell, for their efforts in that series and their helpful reviews of this project. In addition, I want to acknowledge Roger Thorp, the Routledge editor who first envisioned the series and a role for this book in it, and of course our current series editor, Lesley Riddle.

Finally, one's family always has a particular role to play in projects like this one. In an earlier book, I noted that my father, Wilbur R. Hoover (who died while this one was in progress), deserves credit for igniting my interest in media through his own interest in the news, my interest in scholarship through his own scholarly sensibilities, and my interest in religion through his role as my pastor and religious mentor. To my mother, siblings, in-laws, and nieces and nephews, I give my thanks for their eager consumption of the things I write and say. It is good to have those closest to you appreciate what you do. Finally, my wife, Karen, remains my hiking, skiing, and traveling companion, soulmate and partner. Her support throughout this project was essential.

Stewart M. Hoover
Arapaho Ranch, Colorado

Introduction

Religion and the media seem to be ever more connected as we move further into the twenty-first century. It is through the media that much of contemporary religion and spirituality is known. Notable events and icons seem to emerge with increasing frequency. In recent years alone we've seen the mediated events of the September 11, 2001 and July 7, 2005 terror attacks, widely covered scandals in the US and European Catholic Churches, public struggles within religious groups over social values such as gay rights, US political campaigns dominated by mediated discourses of religion, the re-emergence of religion in European political and social life, Mel Gibson's *The Passion of the Christ* and William Arntz's *What the Bleep Do We Know?*,[1] Tom Cruise joining John Travolta as entertainment industry icons of Scientology, Madonna playing the same role in relation to Kabbalah, an increasing number of popular television and film portrayals of gothic, horror, science fiction, magical, mysterious, and conventional religion and spirituality, and controversies over the very presence of religion – of various kinds – in "the media." The realms of "religion" and "media" can no longer be easily separated, and it is the purpose of this book to begin to chart the ways that media and religion intermingle and collide in the cultural experience of media audiences.

It has been easy for us to think of relations between religion and the media in institutional terms. We have thought of religion as a set of traditions, dogmas, practices, and institutions that exist in an autonomous position *vis-à-vis* "the culture." We have thought of culture as merely making communication, interaction, memory, and history possible within social relations by providing the languages and contexts of interaction. In this "received" view, society is the more fixed and hard set of categories within which human beings must learn to function. It provides the structures and boundaries within which things like "culture" and "religion" do their work. And, individual identity is somehow a *result* of these other factors, conditioned – even mostly determined – by them.

This social-theoretical syllogism is being undermined by trends in contemporary social and political life, and by media evolution and change. Media and entertainment figures rival traditional social institutions and their leaders for attention and influence. The marketplace today assumes a determinative role in social and cultural life. Shared, mediated experiences come to define the terms and outlines of social and political discourse. Through such trends, *culture* increasingly functions with a kind of autonomy that is in many ways unprecedented. At the same time, practices of religion are changing, with *individuals* assuming more responsibility for the direction of their own spiritual quests. Through their "seeking," the influence and legitimacy of formal religions of all kinds has increasingly come into question. The *power of legitimation* is more and more in the hands of the seeker as she looks to a wider and wider range of sources and contexts – beyond the traditional ones – for religious or spiritual insight. This has all served to center the media in these trends and in our understanding of them.

A range of observers have contemplated the evolving relations between religion and media. Some have lamented the seeming influence of the media on the more "traditional" and "authentic" forms of religious expression and practice. Others have decried the seeming influence of religious interests in and through the media. Still others have criticized what they see as the "anti-religion bias" of the media. Meanwhile, religion is more and more an object of journalistic scrutiny as religious interests, movements, and individuals have gained a higher profile in contemporary political and social life.

What has been missing from most of the public discourse[2] has been a focus on the role of the reception and meaning-making by media audiences in these trends. Among those who have reflected on the intersection between media and religion is the Korean American video artist Nam June Paik, who has produced several iterations of works that introduce a statue of the Buddha into a conversation about visualization, representation, and reception. In two of these, a Buddha contemplates a video camera and a monitor that displays the image seen by the camera – the Buddha himself[3]. The circularity of the metaphor can be seen either as "closed" or as "open." A "closed" interpretation would center the solipsism of "a religion" focusing on itself through the allure of technology. An "open" interpretation would center on the sense that the dharma – the "teaching" – is idealized and re-presented via the technology, opening the question of which is more "real," the teaching or the image, and the question of whether the representation of the teaching is more or less authentic than the teaching itself. Inserting technology into religion, as Paik's work represents, raises for us a fascinating set of questions about whether representing and receiving tradition in this way somehow fundamentally alters the nature of religion and religious practice. Paik could be read as pointing out that the technology in fact focuses the issue on the fundamental level of the act of seeing, and the way that seeing is the authentic act, not the representation. Thus, rather than threatening tradition by "technologizing" it, or turning tradition's gaze on itself, the argument might be that the fundamental truths, claims, and quests of religion remain in the media age, but in new forms and with a new emphasis.

Paik's rendering thus centers the context and act of reception as the critical point of entry for analysis. To break into the potential circularity of relations between religion and media, we must stand somewhere and take account of ways by which mediated religion is realized in contemporary life. What people do with religious and spiritual resources is the central question, and a standpoint from which to look at the larger contexts of the creation, circulation, and consumption of religious and spiritual resources in an era where such "cultural" practices are fundamentally the province of the media.

To engage in an account of these processes in a deliberate and systematic way involves a certain approach to a set of contexts and trends. These include: the role of culture as an autonomous force, rooted in commodities and markets; the recovery and invigoration of "popular culture" as a valuable context for religious meaning and exploration; the turn to the individual and the individual quest for the self and identity as a central religious project; the redefinition of religion in more anachronistic terms, including "faith," "meaning," and "spirituality"; and the central momentum of media reception becoming a quest for meaning and meaningful cultural and narrative sources.

This view of course runs counter to what one might expect in an exploration of religion in the media age. There is an extent to which "religion" and "the media" exist as institutional forces in the public sphere. Religion is increasingly on the losing side of any struggles that ensue, as the media more and more determine the rules and procedures whereby institutions such as religion find their way into public discourse. There is a long and interesting history there. However, I will contend that looking at such questions ignores the more fundamental social and cultural reality that, on a quite different level, the level of practices of cultural consumption and exchange, individuals and groups have long ago abandoned the larger institutional map. Media and commodity culture are now integrated into practices of meaning and identity in profound and irreversible ways. This book will explore those ways, based on ongoing field research where media households are engaged in discussions about meaning, religion, values, and identity in the media age.

In so doing, we will be pursuing a research direction envisioned in 1988 in a reflection on "next steps" for research in religion and media in the wake of that era's focus on the then-new phenomenon of Televangelism:

I see the need for a "middle level" of analysis, one that understands and builds on what can be known about the aggregate content of the medium *and* that accepts the reality that the process is not instrumental, but rather devolves from the establishment of meaning by an audience in its encounter with mediated texts through which a variety of readings are possible. My middle level of analysis would begin with the simple proposition that not all viewers are the same in social or cultural terms. Not only are there sociocultural dimensions of the audience that can be said to be systematic, and thus (ultimately) quantitatively verifiable, there are also – and this is the critical point – dimensions that help *define* the cultural meaning they derive from television texts.[4]

This book is a major milestone on that research journey, though by no means the last word. The distance from that idea to this reality has been a long and complex one, for significant reasons. The idea of a "middle level" recognized the emergence of a "culturalist" approach to media studies and a turn toward qualitative and ethnographic approaches to media reception. Much progress has been made along those lines and an increasing, substantive literature is developing. Another development critical to this project has been the emerging discourse of a growing network of scholars who have made the intersection between media and religion their primary area of scholarly work. Many of them are credited in these pages for their contributions to this study and to other efforts that are moving our knowledge of these issues ahead.

In order to actually bring about the kind of analysis called for, however, it has been necessary to take on board some critical questions and challenges in theory and methodology. This book addresses the theoretical debates and attempts a way through them. In the process, full justice is not done to their depth, breadth, and complexity. Such an account would have been a book in itself. In the same way, the methodological challenges and turns that have been encountered along the way cannot be fully explored, either. There is an attempt here to describe these in some detail, but reference to the larger project of which this study is a part will be necessary for readers who are primarily interested in method.

The theoretical and methodological roots have received less attention here in part because the intent of this book is to look closely at the experiences and practices of audiences, and decisions have had to be made about how best to move to that level of inquiry, description, and analysis. As will be seen in greater detail in the pages that follow, these studies are rooted in, and result from, the collaborative work of a team of researchers. A good deal of the thinking results from that collective enterprise, and, while I will try to give credit along the way, I cannot fully represent the extent to which interaction and collaboration with colleagues have made this "middle level" of analysis possible. This work would not have been possible as a solo effort. It results from a number of collaborative decisions along the way. In order to look at audience practice it was necessary to go to where that practice is taking place – the domestic sphere of the household and the context of the various types and kinds of families that exist there. In order to understand those practices in their context, it was necessary to make the point of the research interventions a kind of collaboration between researcher and interviewee that did not assume a determinative role for any one element, but assumed interactions between elements in context.

This work also cannot stand completely alone, because it emerges from a larger set of collaborative research efforts focused on meaning-making in the media age. In the process of these inquiries, it became clear that, in order to lay the groundwork for a study such as this one focused on questions of religion and spirituality, it would be necessary first to make a more basic and general account of the processes and practices of media experience in domestic, household, and family life. A previous book, *Media, Home, and Family*,[5] addressed this background, and is referred to at key points in these pages. Beginning with a more general account was necessitated in part by a major learning from the early stages of this research. Alongside the expressed realization that qualitative and interpretive methods were most appropriate to the questions under study stands the realization that the processes and practices whereby people express, represent, and take account of their media experiences are complex and nuanced. In particular, that book lays out a description of the way that expressed "levels of engagement" with media are an important dimension of the meanings made.

Some readers will find that this book does not move in directions they expect. I attempt in the first chapter to describe why this might be the case and the way that this book differs from others. What is most significant about this project is its focus on practices and outcomes of media consumption, and its attempt to bring social theory and analysis to bear on those issues. This focus has determined both the research approach and the range of questions and issues that could be addressed. As will be seen, this study does provide an important set of understandings about the nature of religiously and spiritually inflected media practice, and about the capacities of the media (and of religion and spirituality, too, for that matter) to support certain kinds of meanings and actions. The last chapter of this book draws together some of the larger implications of this work and projects how these learnings might help in other important questions and directions. A book like this simply cannot address all questions. It is a focused piece of social science research that attempts to bring to bear critical and focused theoretical and methodological resources on the central locations of relations between media and religion – the places where people actually interact with, and use, media resources in religious and spiritual ways.

Some momentous events occurred during the course of these studies. It is one of the values of qualitative and interpretive approaches that they are flexible enough to adapt themselves to such historical circumstances. Two of these events – the terrorist attacks of September 2001 and the general elections of 2004 – are specifically addressed in Chapter 9, which attempts to reflect both specific field research related to the events in question, and to reflect the nuanced understandings growing out of this research in analysis of their meanings and potential implications.

So, what the reader will see here is a book that intends to be focused, but that will nonetheless portray a good deal of complexity and breadth. In many ways, it is only a beginning, not a "last word." It stands as a study that is unique for its comprehensive view of media behaviors in the domestic sphere, and its commitment to look at these issues in general terms. This generality is intended, in part, to be *generative* in that it should serve to support the development of a variety of inquiries and reflections on themes, locations, outcomes, and implications. At least that is the intention.

As we move further and further into this century, media and religion will continue to interact and evolve. More than was the case in 1988 we now can see that the interaction between religion and media raises a critical set of public issues and challenges. The implications of this interaction will only grow in importance. A whole new field of inquiry into their relationship is emerging, and should serve to help us understand how best to respond to these developments as scholars, as citizens, as parents, and as people responsible for the spheres of media and of religion. It is my intention that this book serve as a waypoint in that evolving discourse. There already is much more that can be said and that is being said. The ongoing process of scholarly and informed lay inquiry continues and should be the point of efforts such as this. The service of this book in speaking to those discourses and inquiries will be its measure of success.

Chapter 1

What this book *could* be about

A book with the title "Religion in the Media Age" seems ambitious. It also might seem pretty clear and straightforward what it is about. But it could actually be about a number of different things. It could be about the history and future prospects of religions in an era dominated – in the way ours is – by the institutions of the mass media. It could be about the *practice* of religion, the way that religion is *done* in the context of media culture. It could even be a "how to" book of some kind. It is likely, though, that the title also evokes a more particular kind of idea: that the project here is to uncover the *relationship* between religion and the media. If so, it might be assumed that the idea is to look at the kind of *effect* that the media have on religion or *vice versa*.

There is good reason to suspect such a direction. Much of what we know about the worlds of media and religion seems to predict frisson between them. It can be said that they occupy the same "turf," and it is even easy to think of ways that their interests might conflict. Much of our "received" story of the origins of the media in the West – beginning with the development of movable-type printing in Europe in the fifteenth century[1] – carries with it the implication of conflict with religion. Printing, it is thought, ushered in an entirely new era for the established religions of the time because it made it possible for a more "democratic" situation where a reading public could have access to sacred texts and teachings outside the control of clerical authority or the institution of the Church. In fact, the history is much more complex than that. Both Catholic and Protestant churches eventually came to an accommodation with the emerging media realm.

Accommodation was, indeed, inevitable because "the media" were not going away once they came into being. As historian Elizabeth Eisenstein has shown[2] printing was significant not only for the spread of printed works and later the spread of literacy, but also because of a structural realignment that it brought about in the economic and market sphere: the emergence of a new center of social and cultural authority – the publisher. Whereas the Church of Rome (itself already an established institutional, economic, and social power) had enjoyed a good deal of autonomy in the cultural realm prior to printing, afterwards it had to account for an alternative context of cultural autonomy in the form of the publishing industry.[3] This became inevitable because publishing was at the same time an *economic* activity that gradually integrated itself into the emerging mercantile and market economies as early modernity moved through to industrialization. The fact that publishing (and its successor – "the media") was commercial and produced commodities is fundamental to its implications for religion. Its gradual centrality in social, civic, and state affairs is something we accept as a given today, but that has origins going back five centuries.

Our analysis needs to stress that the centrality of the media is rooted and expressed both in their political economy and in their relationship to culture. Their economic basis in capitalism gives them a powerful autonomy and a permanence not enjoyed by all human endeavors. Their cultural location is derived from their capacity – described in a range of ways – to be both *shapers* of culture and *products* of that same culture. This "double articulation" of the media makes their role and impact particularly difficult to pin down, and is one of the reasons that, today, we are still unsure of the nature and extent of their significance.

Some commentators have gone beyond these structural considerations to see the historic relationship between media and religion in more fundamental terms. Marshall McLuhan, for example, famously suggested that the media have radically reoriented the way we perceive and know things.[4] Walter Ong has articulated a more complex and nuanced argument along these same lines, suggesting that successive changes in the dominant mode of communication has shifted human sensorial capacities from the dominance of the eye to the dominance of the ear.[5] Ong and others base their theories very much in realms central to religion, looking at changes in the way social contexts and practices we think of as fundamental to "traditional" religion, such as oral culture, folklore, and storytelling, have been changed and altered, *performatively* as well as *perceptively* in an era dominated by modern mass communication.[6]

These two tendencies – to see the relationship between religion and media in institutional-structural terms on the one hand or in more fundamental, almost organic[7] terms on the other – share in common an implicit *dualism*. They conceive of religion in particular, but also "the media" as coherent, transhistorical, unchanging forms that can be thought of as independent and potentially acting independently upon one another. This dualism holds sway in much of the scholarship that has been devoted to media and religion. From the earliest studies in the 1950s[8] through a flurry of research that followed the emergence of the phenomenon of televangelism in the 1970s,[9] to more recent work on religion and the press,[10] the assumption has been that we can and should look at religion and media as separate realms.[11] This fact has been one of the major reasons that this discourse at the scholarly margins has failed to find much interest nearer the centers. Seen in the context of traditional ideas about secularization, the dimension of religion – as an ideal or inductive category – was of fading interest. In spite of the fact that some of this literature verged on provocative themes and ideas of more central interest to media scholarship[12] the fact that it was about, well – "religion" after all – meant that it could be left at the side. It now emerges, though, that this work was not just about "religion."

It is the major argument of this book that media and religion have come together in fundamental ways. They occupy the same spaces, serve many of the same purposes, and invigorate the same practices in late modernity. Today, it is probably better to think of them as related than to think of them as separate.[13] To some readers, such an argument will seem to be a tall order, and I will spend a number of chapters on it. For now, though, let's look at some of the other things this book *might* have been about. We need to do this because there have been ways to think about religion and media available to us all along, obvious to a project such as this, but less obvious to a media-scholarly discourse that has marginalized religion.[14]

This book, then, might have focused any of a number of questions about media social scientists have addressed. Many of these have obvious connections to religion, and beg asking. It has been suggested that the primary significance of the media lies in their technological arrangements and their ability to transcend space and time.[15] If this is so, then social and cultural practices that are largely rooted in temporal and spatial discourses, such as religious ones, must be implicated. It has been argued that the media are today the most credible sources of social and cultural information, setting the agenda and the context for much of what we think and know about reality.[16] Religion, which addresses itself to such questions, must be expressed and experienced differently today as a result. A number of studies have suggested a central role for the media in community and social solidarity. This has been claimed particularly for youth and young adults.[17] Religion and religious organizations have traditionally been thought to fill this role. What is the implication if that task is now assumed, particularly for younger generations, by the media?

Much has been made of media content and its putative cultural and moral values. Much of this is a critique of media, lamenting the negative and anti-social (even anti-religious) messages that are said to dominate there.[18] What are the prospects for religion and religious values if the dominant sector of public discourse – the media – consistently carries contradictory and antagonistic views? Media have been claimed to be a negative psychological force, deteriorating the quality of individual and social life, tantamount to an addiction.[19] Media have been claimed to structure the flow of daily life, determining when we eat, sleep, socialize, even procreate.[20] These are clear and taken-for-granted roles and functions "traditional" religion is interested in, at least, and are surely profound functions for the media to assume, creating at least a condition or context within which religion must find its place.

A more nuanced view of the media is that they function as a kind of mirror of the culture, or even a "cultural forum" through which important relations in the culture are aired, debated, articulated, and negotiated.[21] This latter view stands in some obvious contrast to much of what I discussed above. Readers who are familiar with the history of mass communication and media theory will recognize the earlier set of issues are consistent with the so-called "dominant" paradigms, the ones that stress media "effects" rather than their relationship to, or embedment in, culture. The idea of the media serving as a "cultural forum" represents a major alternative view in the field of media theory, seeing the media as part of culture, even constituting culture, rather than as somehow separate from it. Such a role for the media would obviously condition the prospects and practices of religion. Religious leaders, institutions, practitioners, symbols, values, practices, and ideas would all find themselves involved in this ongoing discourse, rather than separate from it.

There is also a large and growing body of thought focused on generational differences in media use, significance, and functions. The largest part of this work has been focused on children and the behavioral and value implications of media, including film, television, the Internet, and video games.[22] A substantial body of work has followed a different direction, seeking to understand how media function, are used, and are integrated into the lives of children and particularly adolescents.[23] Important recent work has addressed directly the questions of religion that follow from such a direction. If the media are such a significant source of socialization and acculturation for children, how should religion, which aspires to be directly involved in those processes, respond? Important work on adolescent media use has shown something more profound than such "direct effects" – that media serve to orient and articulate much of teen culture.[24] What are the prospects for religion? How is it adapting or must it adapt to such a situation?

The media have been claimed to be at the center of social and cultural ritual in contemporary life. Some of this is almost commonsensical and taken for granted. We all know and experience the role that the media play in conveying and articulating public events, social conflicts and crises. A more substantive scholarly literature has developed, however, which argues that these processes are articulated, in a fundamental way, into the warp and woof of contemporary common life.[25] In the post-9/11 era, it has even been argued that the media assumed, around that event, a role that can best be described as a "new civil religion of commemoration and mourning."[26] The implications of such a situation for "traditional" and "non-civil" religion are fascinating. Formal religion has always had to contend with the civil variety, particularly in the US. What happens when – as the evidence seems to show – the civil rituals are more widely circulated and participated in than the traditional ones? It is important to point out that most scholars would argue that such rituals play an important social role in developing and maintaining social solidarity, conveying fundamental values and ideals. But to separate those from "religion" (particularly in as "religious" a context as the US) is still an important challenge to our evolving understandings of contemporary religion.

There has also been a great deal written and said about media and *globalization*. We live in an increasingly globalized economic and social environment, and the media are directly implicated in these developments.[27] The world has shrunk, at least for some social sectors and social classes, and our knowledge of the world and of "the other" is a different kind of knowledge than our parents or grandparents had. Religion depends in some fundamental ways on ideas about the world, about difference, about solidarity, and about the conditions of meaning and truth rooted in understandings of place. Scholarship in the world of religion has recognized the effects of globalization for some time,[28] but a more sustained focus on the role and implications of media in these issues awaits doing.[29]

What scholars know as debates over postmodernity and late modernity have also outlined a role for media that has implications for religion. So-called "medium theory"[30] has held that one important implication of the media for social consciousness rests in their tendency to expose both the "frontstage" and "backstage" of social, civic, cultural, and political action. Combined with increasing levels of public knowledge and education, this has led to a situation where the public is far more self-conscious and reflexive about how things work publicly and about their place in those things than in the past.[31] Whether this is empowering or disempowering is a matter of some debate[32] but it obviously conditions a wide range of social contexts, practices, and behaviors. To the extent that religion is rooted in individual consciousness (and, for both commonsensical and more informed reasons, we tend to think that it is) this knowledge and reflexivity clearly has implications. Whether it merely leads to an increased skepticism about institutional authority, makes modern life that much more of a challenge for individuals, or greatly complicates social and structural processes, this media-generated reflexivity is an important issue for our understanding of contemporary religion.

Another claimed effect of the media in late modernity[33] is their role in undermining traditional linguistic truth claims. Postmodernity is supposedly partly rooted in the notion that the relationship between words, symbols, and images, and the things they represent, has been undermined. In an era dominated by the media and their playful deconstruction and reconstruction of traditional meanings, the solidity of the relationships between "signs" and the things they refer to ("referents") comes under suspicion.[34] In a well-known turn of phrase, the French theorist Baudrillard has claimed that today we live, interact, and communicate at a surface level derived from commodified, mediated images, a level he calls the "simulacrum."[35] Whether we accept the totalistic notion that we live in a postmodernity defined only by surfaces, or merely observe that such semiotic or linguistic superficiality does seem to be commonplace in our time, the implications for religion are clear. Many religions are grounded in doctrines and pieties that specify *precisely* the relationship between signs and referents, between metaphors and concrete meanings, and between words and ideas. If today such claims are increasingly undermined, that is an important issue for those religions and particularly for their legitimacy and authority.

Another claim about the media that is inflected with discourses of late modernity and postmodernity is related to the issues of globalization, and has to do with the capacity of media to blur the boundaries between "private" and "public" spaces. Just as globalization is partly defined by an increasing fungability between the "local," the "national," and the "global," rooted in the capacities of modern media to bring those three contexts together, so too the media make the private sphere public and vice versa. Leaving aside for the moment an important argument over whether this is a valuable distinction in late modernity, it is still worth considering what it means for religion that such a distinction would no longer be viable. In the US and most of Western Europe, for example, the consensus that has surrounded accommodation to religious difference in public discourse through the crafting of a set of putative "common religious values" has allowed for a significant degree of latitude to religion in private.[36] When the distinction between those two "spheres" is no longer recognized, what happens to that accommodation? The "culture wars" that have raged on the US political landscape for the last two decades could be described, for example, as a result of the blurring of that boundary; of the resistance of once-private religion to staying "private" in a media context where a range of "private" perspectives are relentlessly made "public."[37]

This can all be put in a larger context, of course. To the extent that the media are among the root conditions of either postmodernity or late modernity, they are therefore fundamental to the historical context within which religion today finds itself. They condition the way knowledge is produced and shared, the way symbols, ideas, and values are encountered in private life, and the senses we have of the nature of late modernity. A large and complex project awaits, and this book can be seen as part of that project.

The media today have evolved in economic terms to the point that they are increasingly closely linked to global capital. Media corporations are among the largest and most influential companies there are. They carry immense economic and cultural influence at the same time that an increasing array of services, channels, and media devices are available. The effect of this in the context of daily "lived lives" is an increasing commodification of experience through these media. The media are themselves – and they produce – commodities. The symbols and ideas that circulate domestically and globally are mediated, commodified symbols and ideas. Culture is increasingly a *material* culture, and the media are both producers *of* it and produced *by* it.

This means that one way the media age is significant for religion is in the nature of that "media culture." The media today constitute the inventory of symbols, values, and ideas out of which sense is made locally and globally. That material is not something that is idiosyncratically produced by the media (as some would want to claim) but is very much derived from the cultures in which the various media are situated. When I say that the media are produced by culture, that is in part what I mean. The media traffic in the symbols, values, and ideas of their culture(s). The fact that those things become mediated means that they are changed in fundamental ways, certainly, but the integration of the media in and through culture cannot be ignored.

The media can be seen as a source of attractive and salient symbols. The inventory of symbols they provide are in some ways the "raw materials" out of which ideas and values are exchanged in contemporary life. While the media may not originate those symbols, they do reproduce and circulate them, under conditions that are defined by economic, social, and political arrangements. There is thus a certain valence or momentum to these commodified and mediated symbols derived from their provenance in the media sphere. But, as they are experienced in the context of daily lived lives, these mediated symbols have a certain concrete significance and a certain place. They are used in certain ways. For a project interested in the prospects of religion in such an age, the nature of that inventory of symbols, and questions of who uses them and how, become fundamental.

It is worth speculating, further, on the extent to which such mediated symbols might be specifically put to the purposes of contemporary religious practice. I will discuss this in more detail in later chapters, but it is almost a commonplace to say that things are in the media because they "work" on some fundamental level. Commercial, commodified media depend on finding material and ways of articulating it that will be attractive, compelling, and absorbing. There is an increasing tendency for the media to explore a range of sensorial contexts as well. Film and television are often described as the "visual" media and there has been much speculation about the extent to which they have created or changed the "visual culture" or led to increasing "visual literacy" in audiences.[38] The rise of the digital media (the Internet, "web," and personal digital technologies) has extended the range of visual experience, but increasingly auditory experience, too. There has been much experimentation with digital media integration into the sense of touch and smell, and while much of this is still on the horizon, video gaming has already introduced digitally mediated tactile and kinetic experience.

If we expand a bit the definition of "media" to include the publishing, entertainment, marketing, tourism, and service industries, we see even more evidence of the multi-sensory nature of modern communication. It is now more common for us to travel to, and experience the wonders of, places and peoples that we have heretofore only seen in the media. Media industries are increasingly integrated with these other sectors, connecting print and electronic publishing with such things as the "self-help" and "twelve-step" movements through which a wide range of material culture, both objects and experiences directed at the senses, can now be secured. It will continue to be – and increasingly so – that that media we consume will be oriented toward a compelling salience across a range of tactile, kinetic, and sensual domains. This means that media materials are – at the same time – compelling on their own terms as texts and objects, and increasingly significant for interests in the culture that are also about symbols, values, the body, experience, and a range of other modes of experience. The connection to religion is obvious and intriguing.

The purpose of this book is not to explore any – or any combination – of the foregoing issues in and of themselves. It does not propose that the implications of the media for religion are limited to any of these areas. Rather, I want to get behind such questions by looking at the significance of the media for religion in the context of media *consumption* or *reception*. The question, rather than being "*what* is the significance of the media age for religion?" is instead "*where* is that significance to be found?" The difference is a subtle, yet profound one. In a way, the "where" question is the question of an anthropologist[39] who observes a phenomenon in culture, and sets about explaining or interpreting it. In my case here, it is possible to see that the media exist and are ubiquitous, that they traffic in symbolic and cultural material that is significant to what we once thought of as "religion," and that religious institutions and those responsible for religious culture are concerned about this situation. The "what" question presents itself, and it is time to ask "where?" within which is subsumed the also interesting question, "for whom?"

Such an approach is, of course, paradigmatically distinct from much of what has gone before in the way of inquiries into religion and the media. The majority of work, particularly in the fields of mass communication and media studies, seems to revolve around questions of ideology and the influence of media and religion on one another. George Gerbner, who famously declared television "the new state religion," saw the question being one of social and ideological *power*. Where once religion had played a primary role in shaping and enforcing social values and ideas, and conveying the fundamental ideas of the culture, the media can now be seen to be in that role.[40] A concern with ideological or definitive power can be said to underlie critiques such as Malcolm Muggeridge's classic *Christ and the Media*.[41] The idea that media and religion exist in a state of ideological struggle is implicit in more recent works of the same vein, including, for example, Ken Meyers's *All God's Children and Blue Suede Shoes*,[42] *Dancing in the Dark* by Quentin Schultze and his associates,[43] Schultze's more recent *Habits of the High-Tech Heart*,[44] Neil Postman's *Amusing Ourselves to Death*,[45] William Fore's *Television and Religion*,[46] and less scholarly but noteworthy efforts such as Michael Medved's *Hollywood vs. America*[47] and William Bennett's *Book of Virtues*.[48] All of these share in common the idea that we know, inductively, what religion is, and that fundamental questions surround a conflict between that ideal of religion and the reality of contemporary media of various forms. And, most of them lament that "the media" seem to be "winning."

Gerbner was involved in a second, more focused scholarly direction, one that looks at the *effects* of media on religion and vice versa rooted in the dominant "effects" paradigm of US mass-media research. The emergence of televangelism occasioned a significant amount of debate and research when it emerged in the 1970s. Gerbner's "cultural indicators" project at the University of Pennsylvania, in co-operation with researchers from the Gallup Organization and the distinguished religion sociologist Robert Wuthnow, conducted what was to have been the definitive study of the phenomenon.[49] Other significant effects-oriented work includes a series of studies by Judith Buddenbaum on religion journalism and the journalists who cover religion,[50] and other studies of religion and the press.[51]

A third significant school of thought related to religion and media has emerged within media scholarship, that which looks at the media in terms of the religious or quasi-religious functions around rituals of identity and social solidarity. The most important of these is the very influential project by Daniel Dayan and Elihu Katz published as *Media Events: The Live Broadcasting of History*.[52] A more comprehensive review of the solidarity and ritual literature, based in a Durkheimian framework, is Eric Rothenbuhler's *Ritual Communication*.[53] Also from the field of mass communication and media studies are Carolyn Marvin's *Blood Sacrifice and the Nation*[54] and Nick Couldry's critical review of this literature in *Media Rituals*.[55] Implicit in these and other works is the notion fundamental to the work of social theorist Emile Durkheim, that religion is integral to the form and shape of society. Further, according to Durkheim, society and religion meet and diverge around questions of identity and social solidarity, with social rituals being the context where these issues are worked out.[56]

A fourth area of research and theory-building in media scholarship related to religion traces its roots to a now classic essay by James Carey, titled "A cultural approach to communication."[57] In it, Carey describes a distinction between "transmission" and "ritual" understandings of communication. The transmission model, he suggested, had inordinately blinded media scholars to the more subtle and profound ways in which communication is integrated into the fabric of daily life. Using the term "ritual" almost metaphorically[58] Carey called for a "ritual" view of communication that would understand it in this more organic, culturally rooted way. Carey's article, and indeed a good deal of his writing, is seen as an important bridge between an emergent culturally oriented media scholarship in the US, and an earlier, and in ways more substantive, scholarly tradition in Europe, particularly in Britain. This so-called "Cultural Studies" approach to media scholarship has found a number of expressions on both sides of the Atlantic, but can be typified in both contexts by certain specific theoretical and methodological directions.

Theoretically, Cultural Studies has been rooted in a concern with culture as a lived context, and has been primarily concerned with materialist and substantive consequences of that context. This is significant in that it contrasts Cultural Studies with approaches that have seen "culture" primarily in terms of its products, and have applied normative categories to those products. For example, it is still common to think of "high culture" (the elite arts – painting, sculpture, "legitimate" theater, classical music, even some films) in contradistinction to "low" or "popular" culture (television, popular music, cheap novels, etc.). Cultural Studies shifts the terms of the debate. It asks the "where" question I raised earlier, and sees culture anthropologically, as it is practiced and experienced. Linked with an emerging literature on media in the field of anthropology[59] this allows for a very different role for media – seeing them as *integrated into* life rather than in their potential *influence on* life.[60] It is still possible to theorize an ideological role for the media in such cultural terms, and this debate is not settled within culturally oriented scholarship. Some scholars stress the autonomy of media audiences, focusing on the ways they make meaning out of media texts and experiences. Others focus on the ideological formations found within those texts and experiences, looking at ways in which those formations are either determinative or contested by audiences.[61]

Methodologically, the "culturalist turn" in media studies has taken scholarship in more anthropological directions as well.[62] Whereas the so-called "dominant paradigm" in media social science has been rooted in positivism and its preferred methods of deduction, testing, and quantitative empiricism, culturalist media scholarship has turned toward qualitative and descriptive methodologies. Culturalist scholars tend to employ more humanistic, ethnographic, observational, and interpretive methods.[63] Case studies and focus groups are more common than surveys with generalizable samples. These "qualitative" methods are more appropriate (and more appropriate for the inquiry we will undertake here) for a number of reasons. First, they do not presume a causal relationship between media-as-instruments and effects in audiences. They allow the audience to speak in its own terms about its relationship to media. They also allow study of phenomena, such as religion, where there is some reason (as I said above) to suspect that relationships may flow in both directions. Second, culturalist scholars are typically interested in questions and issues that are more complex and diffuse than can be easily operationalized in a survey instrument. Religion, as we have seen, certainly invokes such questions. Its relationship to social life may exist and operate on a number of levels, and it is hard to say at the outset where among those levels media might reside. Third, such methods allow for the interpretation of patterns of action and interaction that are recursive as well as sequential. This is significant, for example, if we take seriously the notion that ritual is an important dimension to consider. Fourth, they allow the researcher to identify unexpected patterns both in media texts and in audience practices. As there is much we don't know at this point in our explorations, such openness is a necessity. Fifth, they allow social, cultural, and historical context to be taken into account and to be seen in terms of its contribution to the outcomes of media consumption, something that we can assume will make important differences here. Finally, such methods allow for the investigation of outcomes such as *meaning* and *identity*, themselves highly complex issues, as we will see in later chapters of this book.

The significance of this culturalist turn to the overall burden of this book – questions of media and religion – goes somewhat beyond Carey's metaphoric use of a classic term in religion – ritual – to lay out his new direction. In fact, Carey is precious little help with the matter of religion *per se*. Instead, the contribution of culturalism to our understanding of media and religion lies in its ability to address something as complex, nuanced, diffuse, and changeable as contemporary religion is. We are not easily able to apply a normative definition to contemporary religion. In fact, a prominent religion scholar has argued that the field must instead always be described as the study of *religions*.[64] Other observers of contemporary religion point out that the label "religion" is itself increasingly problematic in describing the contemporary scene. Culturalist media studies allows *both* religion *and* media to be identified and studied in nearer to their "own terms" than has been the case with previous work.

Culturalism has occasioned a developing trend in media studies toward more serious and sustained study of religion and media, and this book is part of that trend. It would be wrong to credit this movement entirely to the fields of communication and media studies, however. Other fields, notably religious studies, history, art history, folklore, and anthropology are each beginning to contribute to a rich and – necessarily – interdisciplinary dialogue about religion and media.[65] This dialogue has been encouraged and nurtured through the kinds of things scholars do: conferences, publications, seminars, research, and teaching. A series of specialized conferences on media, religion, and culture began with a founding event in Uppsala, Sweden, in 1993, followed by meetings in Boulder, Colorado, USA, in 1996, in Edinburgh, Scotland, in 1999, in Louisville, Kentucky, USA, in 2004, again in Sweden in 2006, and planned meetings in Brazil in 2008 and the Netherlands in 2010. The scholarly and professional associations have also contributed, with regular panels and other fora at meetings including the Society for the Scientific Study of Religion, the American Academy of Religion, the International Association for Media and Communication Research, the Association for Education in Journalism and Mass Communication, the International Communication Association, the National Communication Association, and at conferences somewhat more "remote" from the fields of religion studies and media studies.

It is also important to note that in the specific scholarly area of religion and media, much of the progress that has been made has come from younger scholars. Important works in this field such as Diane Winston's *Red Hot and Righteous*,[66] Lynn Schofield Clark's *From Angels to Aliens*,[67] Michele Rosenthal's *Satan and Savior*,[68] Tona Hangen's *Redeeming the Dial: Radio, Religion, and Popular Culture in America*,[69] John Schmalzbaur's *People of Faith*,[70] Sean McCloud's *Making the American Religious Fringe*,[71] Jolyon Mitchell's *Visually Speaking*,[72] Heather Hendershot's *Shaking the World for Jesus*,[73] and David Morgan's edited volume *Icons of American Protestantism*,[74] all emerged early in their careers, and many were closely related to work they had done in their doctoral studies.[75]

Not all of the emerging interest in the connections between media and religion can be credited to scholarship alone. Events have pushed these questions nearer and nearer the center of discourse. At the mid-point of the last century, a kind of easy consensus on questions of religion (and, by extension, its public face in the media realm) seemed to have been reached. In the context of North America, this was described in a classic work by Will Herberg[76] as a time where religion, in the form of the dominant traditions of Christianity and Judaism, was present, but neither too obvious nor too controversial as an element of public culture. That public face of religion – its representation in its institutions – was the index by which religion was known, and as those institutions began to decline in their influence, it was easy to begin to assume that the predictions of some classic versions of secularization theory were being fulfilled. In the same time period a more deeply felt secularization was underway in Europe.

This situation has now changed, and in a very public way. A sea change occurred with the Islamic Revolution in Iran in 1979. That event served to undermine some tried-and-true assumptions in the political, social, cultural, and media realms. Whereas before it had been easy to assume a particular theory of modernity, development, and secularization[77] that saw a relentless march of progress in which religious movements and religiously based ideologies would become less and less important, the Iranian revolution showed that resurgent religion could, indeed, become a force in modernity.[78]

Religiously modulated social and political movements seem to have become more and more obvious in the years since 1979. Resurgent religiously based political parties have drawn increasing attention. Even in the industrialized world, religion has become more obvious. Conservative Christian groups have become a more important feature of American politics over the last two decades (culminating, as we will discuss in Chapter 9, in the November 2004, US General Election). A series of scandals have rocked the Catholic Church, both in North America and in Europe. World Anglicanism has undergone public struggles over gay ordination. The question of religion surfaced in debates over the European constitution. The term "Japanese Doomsday Cult" has become almost a cliché. And, in the most obvious and compelling case, the attacks by Islamicist terror groups around the world, including, of course, those of September 11, 2001 (which we will also consider in more detail in Chapter 9), have put religion on the political and news agendas.

These events in the news have been accompanied by developments in popular culture. Religion and spirituality seem ever more obvious in popular music, television, film, and in books. Media figures have become publicly identified with religious and spiritual ideas of various kinds.[79] Religion seems increasingly "on the agenda" in public culture, though it is often in varieties and forms that seem to defy the label, an issue we will get to in more detail in later chapters.

To better understand the purpose of this book, we should reflect a bit on the challenge of studying the intersection of media and religion in such a historical, social, and scholarly context. The phenomenon of religion, and the institutions of the media, are voluble and dynamic. They do not "stand still" for analysis in the way we might wish them to. Both are complex systems, with a variety of structural, historical, and cultural characteristics that help define and typify them.

It is my argument that audience reception research within the culturalist tradition shows great promise to further our understandings at this point in time. I'll make this argument at this juncture on two grounds. First, as I have said, a more qualitative direction that looks at practices of media consumption within the context of everyday life is particularly well suited to the specific questions around the relationship between religion and media. Much more will be said about this as we move through later chapters devoted specifically to those things.

A second compelling reason for a culturalist look at the context of media and religion practices in daily life lies behind what I see to be the limitations of the other three "paradigms" I discussed earlier.[80] On a fundamental level, if we are to know anything about the ideological or practical or ritual implications of media for religion (or vice versa) shouldn't we first be concerned with how those relations are experienced, consumed, expressed, and negotiated in the lives of individuals? If, for example, we are concerned, along with many observers, about the values conveyed to families in entertainment television (a question infused with religious antecedents and implications) wouldn't it be helpful to take into account how and under what circumstances such messages are seen and consumed by families? If we wish to make an argument that press treatment of religious issues might be becoming determinative of the way religion is understood in contemporary life, should we not want to start by understanding how readers and audiences think about religion when they consume the news? If, as seems obvious, the media are at the center of major public rituals directed at social solidarity, should we not be interested in the extents of audiences' involvement in those rituals, and the ways that they understand them to be meaningful in religious terms?

Beyond these more direct questions, there are a number of issues on either "side" of the acts of reception and consumption of media. How are individuals, families, audiences, readers, etc., conditioned in various ways to consume media? Under what circumstances do they avail themselves of media, and for what implicit and explicit purposes? Moving in the other direction, what do they do with the media they consume? How are their media practices embedded in their social relations both within domestic contexts and beyond? In each of these areas, it seems important to be able to establish the capacities of media practices to articulate with the lives of viewers and audiences. These are questions that are best addressed by going to where people are, and "looking back" with them – as it were – at the cultural context within which they live, and along with them, understanding how the various elements of that context: media, symbols, social relations, identities, meanings, etc., relate to one another.

This is obviously a large and complex agenda but I want to argue as well for a more focused and refined way of doing this, a way that is rooted in the ongoing projects of life we expect to encounter as we go and look. The particular approach I take here is to try and understand people's efforts at making meaningful, coherent narratives of themselves as active participants in their social and cultural surrounds, and the extent to which media and religion, individually and in interaction, are resources to that narrative-building. This provides both a theoretical and methodological standpoint from which to study and interpret these complex relations. Further, it gets us nearer to the perspectives and particular ways of seeing and doing that exist in daily life. It presumes that, on some level, we can learn a lot by talking with people. At the same time, it provides a way of understanding that talk in relation to ideas about meaning, value, and practice.

No one method or approach can answer everything, and, as we will see as we move along, many questions remain. However, there is much we can know this way. The central motif of the book, then, is accounting for, recounting, and interpreting these narratives of the self, of family (broadly defined), and social relations, and attempting to see where we can go and what we can do with that information and those interpretations.

This strategy is rooted in an implied limitation of such descriptive, qualitative work,[81] namely that we can only know the accounts people construct of themselves and that they are willing or able to share in the contexts where we encounter them. I hold that it is possible to see, through these "presented identities," how those identities are 1) modulated by or inflected with religious impulses and meanings, and 2) so modulated or inflected through or with reference to media experience and practice. I will discuss the methodological extents and limits of this approach in more detail in later chapters. I will argue, further, that these constructions have significance beyond the particular intervention of an interview or observation, and that they are important in relation to other questions, approaches, and methods as well.

As I have said, some of the claims that have been made about the relationship of media to religion are rather large, grand, and epochal in nature. There are some practical reasons that support the field-theoretical approach I am outlining here, particularly when we think about these things in relationship to the "larger" questions addressed by others. An important one is the fact that we can never actually know very much definitively about some of those larger questions, anyway. The whole question of whether media technologies have come to fundamentally alter our perceptual and social capacities, or whether, historically, cultures can be defined by their media, can't be answered because we don't have a "parallel universe" without media to which we can compare this one. In the industrialized West, for all practical purposes, no one does not have media, and those who might not are so different in other ways so as to make empirical comparison problematic. Many opportunities to conduct panel-like studies of societies "before" and "after" television (in South Africa, where it was introduced rather late, for example, or in Fiji)[82] were largely missed. So, what we have instead are the faint tracings of the more gradual introduction of media into the context of daily, domestic life, tracings that are probably more amenable to the kind of close descriptive analysis proposed here than to some other approaches.

Another argument for going to the field, to the context of media reception, is the obvious one that it is accessible. There is, of course, a large and important scholarly and conceptual legacy that addresses itself to this kind of study, one that I acknowledge and will refer to at important points along the way.

The field material I will discuss comes from a larger and more comprehensive set of studies. The accounts in later chapters were developed out of studies undertaken by a team of researchers working collaboratively.[83] This

collaboration involves methodology and theory as well as the more practical aspects of conducting the field research and getting the interviews and
observations done. A good deal of the insight I will share here was thus
developed collaboratively, too, and I will endeavor to credit my colleagues
as I go along, both for their fieldwork and for their insights and ideas. The
larger project is devoted to understanding meaning-making in the media
age, of which religious meaning-making is thought to be a central component. We wanted, throughout our studies, to model an approach to social
and cultural analysis that gives religion its due in a way that much
previous work in media studies (and in interpretive sociology, for that
matter) has not. A description of this project and its methodology appears
as the Appendix of this book.

Before I conclude, it is important to say a few things about the central
themes of this discussion: religion and media. It is conventional in a work
such as this to begin with a definition of terms, and these are, of course,
the big terms here. I intend my working definitions to become clearer as
we proceed through the book, but there are a few things I should say at
this point. First is my definition of "religion." Do I mean the specific religions of the West, of monotheism? Do I mean the established religions in
other contexts? Do I mean "new" or "emerging" religions? Do I mean the
received traditions of those religions? Do I mean "traditional" religions
such as those studied by anthropologists "over there"? Do I mean explicit
or implicit religious practice? Do I mean those things that are sometimes
called "quasi-religions"? "Religion" as a label has lately become problematic. Do I mean "spirituality" or "transcendence," terms that are more
current? Do I mean "effervescence" (a term from Durkheim), or do I
mean the kind of religion William James (and, more recently, Charles
Taylor) wrote of? Do I mean "substantive" or "functional" religion (terms
from Peter Berger)? Do I mean a "sacred canopy" or a "golden bough," or
"bliss," or the numinous, or the *axis mundi*? Do I mean more mundane,
"religion-like" practices, or the "dry rituals" of religion decried in many
critiques of late modern bourgeois culture? Do I mean "*the* Madonna" or
Madonna?

Well, I guess I mean all of these things, and this is not an intellectual
dodge. There is, of course, a danger in claiming so many things as "religious," that it becomes a meaningless category. On one level, it is
important for a project such as this one to open itself to the varieties of
religious, and quasi-religious, and implicitly religious, experiences as they
are expressed and experienced by the people with whom we will talk. One
of the advantages of such interventions is that we can come to understand
how *they* are defining these things in personal contexts where those definitions are undoubtedly changing along with the definitions in the larger
culture. It is important, also, to be able to account for the ways those definitions and understandings are interacting with such resources as media.

The problem of defining religion is not a new one to social scientists and to anthropologists in particular. Religious essentialists and formalists have been critical of Clifford Geertz, a scholar to whom much of the conceptual and theoretical legacy here can be traced, for adopting a definition of religion that is too deductive and too inclined to see anything as "religion" as long as informants say it is. In fact, Geertz's definition of religion is one that provides precisely the kind of foundation needed by the kind of exploration I am undertaking here. Geertz describes religion as

> (1) a system of symbols which acts to (2) establish a powerful, pervasive, and long-lasting moods and motivations in men by (3) formulating conceptions of a general order of existence and (4) clothing these conceptions with such an aura of factuality that (5) the moods and motivations seem uniquely realistic.[84]

The way this works practically is that, for a social meaning or practice to be significant of what we want to understand as "religious," it must be something that – in the perspective of the individuals involved – moves beyond the mundane to the level of particular significance and is something that she herself sees in those terms. There is, of course, debate about whether this is an unequivocal definition, and things we encounter that are attributed to religion (or "spirituality," a term of emerging social significance) will also avail themselves of further exploration. This is one of the values of the kind of embedded, descriptive research we will be doing. We are able to look at the ways people describe themselves and their practices as religious. This will tell us things not just about the particular media-centered practices of concern to our explorations here, but also about the nature of contemporary religious evolution. The point is not to "validate" what they say about religion in relation to media culture; it is to embed these ideas in the larger context of their social lives and (by extension) the broader culture. So, for better or worse, it will be Geertz's definition that will be the working definition of religion employed as we proceed with this study.

While it might be thought that a definition of "media" is probably a more straightforward matter than a definition of "religion," there is still some complexity here. Traditionally, and in common discourse, media are thought of primarily in technological terms. "Media" are devices, services, publications, and channels. I'd like to suggest instead that we begin to think of media as *practices*, not just as *institutions, texts, or objects*. First, there is a range of things that are significant to our inquiries here that transcend "media" as traditionally understood. For example, public performances of various kinds, as well as sacred spaces, rituals, encounter groups, classes, seminars, objects such as paintings, sculptures, and what have been called "religious kitsch" items all appear in our interviews and in other studies as religiously significant. That these may be *religious* is probably less difficult to understand than that they are also *media*. As I will discuss in more detail in the next chapter, one of the things that typifies late modernity is the increasing array of social and cultural objects and practices that have become commodified, and, almost by definition, part of the mediated cultural environment. Thus, I want to maintain a definition of religion that is also quite open, and in a way parallels our definition of religion. To the extent that a social context or practice is part of public culture, involves technological or social intervention, and is made accessible to the contexts where we will be looking, I will keep open the option of thinking of it as an example of "media."

What I will be attempting to argue in this study is the notion that many of the approaches, ideas, and criticisms that have been leveled at the nexus of religion and media in late modernity derive from unexamined and untested assumptions about the fundamental interaction between the media and the religiously or spiritually inflected experiences of individuals and audiences. Much of what we think we know about the way media and religion interact and relate is based on ideas about this interaction that may or may not be relevant to the situation "on the ground." It is as if there is a piece of the chain of meanings and consequences missing until we are able to take a closer, more careful look at actual experience.

By extension, then, I expect what we will be doing here is to provide important resources, ideas, and tests to some of the received assumptions. Once we know more about how people use media in religious and spiritual ways, and about the kinds of things they find religiously and spiritually significant there, we will be able to say more, with more confidence, about the kinds of larger effects, implications, and possibilities. On the most fundamental level, I see the project here as establishing what the capacities are of the systematic relationship that exists between medium and reception to support what kinds of religious and spiritual meanings and outcomes. It may make sense in some ways to describe "effects" that emerge in those contexts. It may make sense in other ways to talk about negotiations and representations. For now, though, there is much we don't know. And, as we will see, some of the most widely held received assumptions we will enter the field with will be the first to fall.

There is a limitation to the work we will do here that is rooted in the timeliness of this project. I will argue in the coming chapters that this study in many ways represents an interaction between emerging paradigms in media studies, cultural studies, and religious studies. The conceptual and theoretical resources available from those fields to our inquiries here are invaluable in establishing the terms and outlines of what we will do. But with those resources come a responsibility to also bring them to bear in a concrete way in our analyses. As we will see, what we may find at times is that these scholarly assumptions are also not supported or supportable in the field. That, too, will be a finding, of course, but will be significant of the fact that all research is always transitional. This book should be seen to be at the beginning, not near the end, of the debate on relations between religion and media.

In the next chapter, we will move to a consideration of the issues of the contemporary media and religious contexts in more detail. It is important to understand how the evolution of these domains is creating the conditions under which meaning-making – around "religion" and around social meaning in general – is taking place.

Chapter 2

From medium to meaning

The evolution of theories about media, religion, and culture

Most historians date the origins of modern mass communication to the nineteenth century. The eighteenth century ended with a media sphere pretty much defined, technologically, by the printed word – books, journals, pamphlets, and posters. And – more importantly, perhaps – in spite of innovations in production and distribution, access to the media was still limited by geography, social class, and economic prospects. It is an important lesson, therefore, that to understand the significance of any given medium, or "the media" in general, we need to look beyond the devices themselves, to their contexts, practices, and audiences. Media are, in a very fundamental way, social practices, both in their production and in their consumption. As such, it is important to understand where they are being consumed, by whom, and with what results.

In the case of the eighteenth and nineteenth centuries, a culture of *reception*[1] emerged and developed around publishing. Jürgen Habermas has described this with reference to the realm of politics and elite culture.[2] David Nord and Doug Underwood have done so in areas nearer the theme of this book – *religious* publishing and journalism.[3] There is also evidence that a vibrant "popular" reception was emerging, described more substantively with reference to later in the century by Laurence Moore and others.[4] Tocqueville's classic account from the same period found in the emerging American nation a concrete and vibrant religious culture that was in many ways the basis of social, political, and religious relations.[5] Thus, it might be reasonable to have thought all along about how the media of religion and the media of the rest of society and culture interact and should be related. However, from the earliest days, a distinction between the two held sway.[6]

Great technological change typified the nineteenth century, though, and it was this change that set the stage for the evolution of modern mass communication. Several technologies stand out. Photography had been developed in Europe in the late eighteenth century, but remained in limited circulation until the middle of the nineteenth. Like many of the media that followed, photography found its way into broader public consciousness through singular public events. The US Civil War was a watershed in this, becoming the first really "visual" war through photography, most famously that of Matthew Brady. We should remember that the linkage between Brady, photographs, and the war moves in several directions. Photography allowed the war to be experienced in unprecedented ways, and to achieve a purchase on the national consciousness in which the pictures themselves were inscribed. Thus the singularity of this development arose from the technology, from the historical circumstances, from social practices of consumption, and from the integration of these dimensions.

The nineteenth century also saw the first exponential advancement in the *speed* of communication since the domestication of the horse: the invention of the telegraph, the first "electric" medium. Before telegraphy, the swiftest forms of communication were carrier pigeons and semaphores. The semaphore was fast, but its speed declined with distance. Carrier pigeons could cover impressive distances very accurately, but could not carry large volumes of information. Telegraphy involved the kind of systematic infrastructure that had made the Roman postal system such an important element of that empire. Rapid communication became dependable and – more importantly – public with the development of the Roman road and postal systems. Telegraphy added incredible advances in speed and volume to these systems, changing forever the way communities, nations, and indeed the world thought of itself.

In a feat of engineering that must still stand as one of the great technological achievements of the modern era, Cyrus Field succeeded in laying a telegraph cable across the Atlantic Ocean in 1866. It is hard to imagine the conceptual change this brought about in worldview among the elites who could have access to this development – through the near instantaneity of overseas news in their daily papers, for example. One day, the most current news from across the ocean is ten days to two weeks old. The next day, currency is defined in terms of hours – and the limitation is not the transmission of the raw news; it is in the compiling, editing, and distributing of it. The difference was even more profound with the completion of the first cable to Australia in the 1870s. The time gap for London news shrank from over a month to a few hours, again overnight.

A third major technology of the nineteenth century was the telephone. Most of us would today probably think of it as the most important of all, because it is such a ubiquitous part of our lives. It was not a major advancement over the telegraph in terms of speed, but it had great utility in daily life and daily commerce due to its ease and transparency of use. The fact that it also seemed – on a *prima-facie* basis – more "human" (what you heard was a voice at the other end) was also an important factor. The telephone was clearly the most "domestic" of these technologies, and became the most quickly integrated into daily life. It radically reorganized a range of social and cultural relations,[7] and forever altered patterns in areas such as dating, parenting, and the delivery of a variety of commercial and social services.

The final significant communication-technological development of the eighteenth century was the high-speed printing press. Beginning in London in the 1860s, new ideas of mass production, rooted in the textile industries, were merged with publishing, and with the introduction of steam and then electric power, the volume of printing that could be accomplished increased exponentially. Papers such as the *Illustrated London News* demonstrated the effect that such a technological change could have on publishing by introducing new forms of content and distribution. Suddenly, a medium could become a "mass" medium, available to a much larger readership than ever before. The so-called "mass press" era that ensued introduced three elements that define modern mass communication. First, high-volume, low unit-cost production allowed individual newspapers, pamphlets, or books to be sold much more cheaply than previously. This led to a sea change in the nature of the reading audience. Whereas newspapers had been consumed primarily by the middle and elite classes, they were now available to the masses, ushering in what some have called a more "democratic" era in news distribution.[8] Second, this had far-reaching consequences in the nature of news content, as everything from the kinds of stories covered to the reading level of the reader changed. And third, the "massification" of the media also changed forever the way media are capitalized and financed. Previously, newspapers had to rely on their "cover price" for income. With the evolution of the mass press, advertising could be a significant source of revenue, and, indeed, is today the dominant source in the media.[9]

Each of these features of the mass media era that more or less dawned with the twentieth century – the massification of the audience, the "popularization" of content, and the prominence of advertising as a source of income – has become a dimension of significance, and significant debate, in the century since. Each is, more specifically, significant to our discussion here of relations between religion and media. With the development of the broadcast, visual, and digital media of the twentieth century, the idea of a "mass audience" is still relevant in some ways, but these media have become an integral part of, and contributor to, the larger cultural environment in a very concrete and organic way.[10] Thus, their capacity to challenge, reconstruct, or replace those institutions and practices once typical of "religion" is rooted in this fact. The taste cultures that have emerged in the various media are a point of continuing controversy as well. The so-called "popular media" of television, film, and popular music are implicated in important debates about cultural norms and social relations, having come to represent – for some – the very definition of the kind of culture and cultural values that must be confronted and contested in any project that is interested in normative values, as religion is.[11]

The role of advertising in media is significant, too. First and foremost, advertising gave the new media that emerged in the twentieth century a kind of autonomy not enjoyed by the published media before that time. The dominant media of the nineteenth century were beholden to other organizations: in the case of Britain and the US, to governments, political parties, social organizations, and institutions, including religiously motivated ones. With advertising, media could become independent of those ties, while it of course can and should be argued that advertising support itself carries with it certain obligations and expectations.[12] A perhaps more important consequence (and significant to our discussions here) of the integration of advertising into mass media is the fact that all aspects of the media over the course of the twentieth century became increasingly *commodified*, and the boundary between non-media "commodities" and media images, programs, icons, content, and services became increasingly blurred.

In the case of American broadcasting, for example, traditions of "public service" and other obligations of broadcasting gave way, by the end of the century, to an orientation toward "markets" and "marketplace forces."[13] Product cross-promotion in children's television programming, the increasing practice of "product placement" in film and television, and the cross-promotion of films, television, and popular music are all examples of this blurring of traditional boundaries.[14] The media have become integrated into – and are in many ways the basis of – the larger economic project of the creation, marketing, and consumption of cultural commodities.

The turn of the twentieth century, though, witnessed the adolescence (and some of the excesses)[15] of an emergent mass-media sphere. Emerging along with the media were a set of *social ideas* and *social understandings* of their force, effect, and significance. As the media rose to prominence in new ways as the century progressed, they were increasingly identified with technologies and with technological developments. The telephone, the motion picture, the record-player, the radio, the "dime novel," and later television – the devices themselves – came to embody whatever social and cultural transformation was being wrought by their development. It is not surprising, then, that the focus of popular – and later scientific – discourse was in the first instance on "*the medium*" itself, or rather on "the *media*" *them*selves. There were some distinct strains to this discourse. On the popular level, public discourse came to know the media in terms of their assumed "power" or influence. Radio came to broad public attention during the Titanic disaster of 1917. For the first time, radio played a role in bringing news of a major event to the public. The public imagination was also captured by the 1937 *War of the Worlds* broadcast, where radio was thought to have led to widespread panic and mayhem through its power to lead and mislead.

The evolution of media research and theory

More serious and scholarly consideration of these emerging media came in several different – though related – forms. A significant school of thought, rooted in what is now identified in scholarly circles as "the Frankfurt School,"[16] focused on the role of media in the development of what came to be called "mass society." Behind this notion was the influential idea in social theory that the evolution to modernity in the industrialized West needed to be seen against the backdrop of an ideal (and idealized) social life that preceded it. This was most influentially put by Ferdinand Tönnies in his classic work *Gemeinschaft und Gesellschaft*.[17] Tönnies contended that pre-industrial society was defined by a set of social relations closely connected to place, family, and worldview. With the increasing rationalization of society under industrialization came social dislocations that undermined this original, ideal, situation.

Mass-society theory held that among these dislocations was the concentration of populations organized around the manufacturing centers of the Industrial Revolution. This led to migrations of labor from the farm and village to the cities, and even to cities abroad. The new population centers – the industrial cities – were places which lacked the kind of social connectedness and sense of location that are important to human social consciousness and social stability. Thus *a* "mass society" replaced the numerous settled *societies* from which this labor force had come. In such a mass society, factors of difference such as language, culture, religion, etc., that had traditionally provided the foundations of identity and worldview for individuals would become less and less effective. This is where mass media were thought to come in, replacing those lost ties with new ones that would link individuals to their new location. Mass-society theory in fact feared the consequences of this situation, supposing that the media were at the same time incapable of authentically carrying out such functions and potentially involved in ideological domination of various kinds as a result.[18]

The second scholarly direction taken in the mid-twentieth century also focused on the media themselves, but proposed to study their assumed "effects" in a more individual and psychological sense. This developed into what is now called the "dominant paradigm" in American media research. The idea was that the various media were to be best understood and studied in terms of their intended consequences on readers, viewers, and audiences. A newspaper was intended to inform, for example, so research and scholarship needed to undertake the task of seeing whether it was successful in doing so. Unintended and negative consequences of media exposure were also studied. The most prominent example of this was the extensive research project that, over a number of decades, focused on the question of the effects of media violence on viewers, particularly on younger viewers.[19]

Other topics have also been addressed by the "effects" tradition, including individual psychological effects,[20] political and civic engagement,[21] adolescent socialization,[22] and ethnic and gender roles and identities.[23] It is important to my argument here to see that a given medium and its presumed effects are assumed in most of this work. The focus is very much on the devices, their messages, and investigations of outcomes in audiences that are consonant with the intended effects of those devices and messages. The effects tradition is called the "dominant" tradition in part because of its breadth and its longevity. Major scientific studies of the effects of motion pictures on youth audiences were published in the 1920s.[24] Since then, it has been widely observed that each new development in media technology has seemed to stimulate its own set of questions and concerns, resulting in calls for research on its effects.[25] The effects tradition has also been broadly influential due to the fact that it is so intuitively persuasive. It simply makes sense to think of media as having instrumental effects. The media themselves make such claims. Advertising is assumed to be able to "sell," newspapers to "inform," entertainment television to help us "escape," documentary films to "take us new places," etc. There is also the tendency to think (along with the mass-society theorists) of these media as somehow foreign to authentic and normative community and domestic life. They are always, to some extent, "from the outside." In Habermas's distinction between "lifeworld" and "system world,"[26] the media carry telltale characteristics of the latter, even as they evoke symbols and values of the former. As we will see in later chapters, the notion of the media as distinct from authentic, expressive living is always there, just beneath the surface.[27] It therefore made sense for much attention to be paid to media effects.

In both scholarly and popular discourse, the media seem also to be somehow always "new." This is one of the implications of their emergence in the nineteenth and early twentieth centuries as part of the process of industrialization and the march of modernity. Because we can draw a clear line of temporal demarcation around them that connects them (in most industrialized countries in the West) with the large-scale social transformations of industrialization, they are placed in cultural "memory" in a certain category, and again this makes it logical to think in terms of their effects.

Marshall McLuhan and others who engage in "grand theory" of the media age represent a different kind of effort to account for the evolution of media in modernity. As with the effects tradition, they see these devices as new and embedded in a certain place in the grand sweep of modernity, and attempt to unlock the secrets of their significance for individuals and societies. And, consistent with the effects tradition, there is the assumption that it is something about these media *as media* that is at the root of their significance.[28]

Looking at mass communication in terms of its technologies and technological arrangements alone proved to be unsatisfying rather early in the development of mass communication and media theory. The effects tradition was soon joined by a set of "limited effects" traditions that saw the questions in more nuanced ways. A major turning point was the "People's Choice" studies of the 1950s conducted by Paul Lazersfeld and Elihu Katz.[29] These studies of voting behavior found, rather than a leading role in affecting political attitudes, a rather limited effect for the media. The key conceptual shift was away from an assumption that the media would play some sort of autonomous, determinitive role, to a view that the media should be seen as one element of a larger set of social dynamics that explained voting behavior. In one key turn, Katz proposed that determination in voting preferences should be seen in other *people*, called "opinion leaders," with media being used by those opinion leaders as an information source. This led to the notion that media "effects," to the extent they could be demonstrated in this area at least, would follow a "multi-step" pattern, flowing through *social networks* rather than directly from medium to individual. A variety of theoretical perspectives followed in succeeding decades, including work that focused on the uses to which people put media, and the satisfactions or gratifications they achieved as a result. The shift in perspective is, again, important. Many of these new evolutions of theory began to think differently about the social position of medium, message, and reception. It became more common to think in terms of what audiences, individuals, or communities *did with* the media they consumed than what the media *did to* those audiences, individuals, and communities.

These perspectives still relied on a kind of objectification of *medium* and of *audience or receiver*. These two participants were conceived of as independent of one another, with certain resources or potential for influence implicit in the concept of the medium, and certain needs, wants, or functions relevant to those resources or influences implicit in the actions of receivers. And, again, the "medium" was thought to be determinative, at least to the extent that the given media seem to have given "purposes."

Research on media and religion

Much research and scholarship on religion and media tended to follow predictable patterns within the "medium" paradigms. It was possible to conceive of various media in terms of their capacities to convey religious messages to audiences. A certain amount of effects-oriented research has gone on, looking at such things as the effect of religious television viewing on church attendance and giving, and more marketing-oriented work on various religious messages and religious content in specifically "religious" media.[30] But such research was unsatisfying when applied to questions of religion because of something implicit – a theory of the psychology or sociology of religion – that religion could be in effect "caused" by something like "media."[31]

That the relationship between medium and audience could be seen differently, however, was available in some accounts of religion and media

from the very earliest days. Historian Joel Carpenter, in a study of fundamentalist radio broadcasting in the 1920s, found evidence that some of
these broadcasters had a different objective in mind than a direct effect in
the salvation of sinners via the airwaves. He quotes one promoter of
fundamentalist radio as noting that the most important effect of radio
broadcasting was not in projecting or promoting the Christian message to
believers and non-believers, but to aid in the cultural ascendancy of
Fundamentalism and later Evangelicalism. Radio, he said, would project
them into "the show windows of modern publicity."[32]

Thus, there was a self-consciousness that the media might function in a
way beyond the mere direct transmission of a message. There was a
cultural-symbolic project as well: that, in the era of the Scopes trial and the
general marginalization of Fundamentalism as a social movement in the US,
radio could serve to recover some lost ground for the movement by positioning it within a specific cultural realm of emerging and growing
significance, that of the modern mass media, entertainment, and marketing.

The landmark 1954 Parker, Barry, and Smythe study of religious broadcasting[33] included evidence beyond "effects" as well. While interested in
the success of various religious broadcasts, an effects-oriented task, Parker
and his colleagues also noted the many ways in which the meaning and
significance of given broadcasts needed to be seen in social, class, and
sectarian contexts. Media were significant to the extent that they
connected with these other things. The significant issue at the time of the
Parker et al. study, for instance, was the emergence of Bishop Fulton Sheen
as a major figure on national television. As a Roman Catholic, Sheen's
prominence had significant implications in two directions. There was the
rather straightforward question of the force and effect of his message.
More interesting and significant, perhaps, was what his presence represented for American Catholicism: its emergence from marginality to
cultural centrality. As Parker, Barry, and Smythe themselves noted, it was
increasingly clear it was more important to understand the various ways
such broadcasts were interpreted and used than to assume some sort of
unitary "effect" of them on audience beliefs or behaviors.[34]

Similar perspectives emerged in the great wave of research that followed
the emergence of televangelism in the 1970s. In the first scholarly article
about the phenomenon to appear in a major media studies journal,
Quentin Schultze explored the notion that these ministries should be
understood in terms of the mythology of media power that lay behind
them rather than just in relation to their claimed or assumed effects on
audiences.[35] In the first scholarly book on the subject to be published, Peter
Horsfield analyzed these new religious broadcasts in historical and denominational context, demonstrating that the only way to assess their
significance was in the interaction between their claims and symbols and
the larger religious culture at that moment in time.[36]

In my own work on televangelism,[37] I came to understand that the significance of these ministries went beyond any reliable evidence that they actually reached the size and kinds of audiences they claimed. Rather, what was important about the reception of these broadcasts was how they helped the viewers I interviewed understand and account for themselves and their religious worldviews in contexts where they often felt like outsiders. In the work that was in many ways the scholarly "last word" on televangelism, Janice Peck proposed that these programs be seen as complex arguments about the nature and significance of their contrasting worldviews and cultural surrounds. Again, Peck suggested that questions of their effectiveness at doing what they claimed to do – reach great numbers of unconvinced viewers – was beside the point.[38]

These various approaches in effect "changed the subject" of research on media and religion away from the medium and toward other things: the audience, the larger social context of meanings and symbols, relations of power and ideology in modernity, and in so doing exposed the limitations of approaches that look at medium and effect. First among those limitations was an implicit theory of the religious individual – that he or she is a "blank slate" on to which meaning and significance could be written with the right combination of medium and message. Not only does such a notion defy our received commonsensical understandings of religion (that is, we want to think of religion as something deeper and more significant), but it also defies much received and current scholarship on the package of symbols, values, structures, practices, and ideas that we call "religion."

Much of what I described in Chapter 1 as the "culturalist" turn in work on media and religion emerged in recognition of this complexity and subtlety. The culturalist solution described there involves refocusing attention on audience reception and away from the processes and products of production. It does not necessarily address two issues implicit in the history we've been discussing in this chapter, though. These issues are the social-structural relationships between individuals, society, and the media – the ways that media may be integrated in social life – and the individual – even psychological – motivations and meaning practices that constitute media reception.

Alternatives to the "medium" orientation that dominated much of the twentieth century provide some potential resources. A particularly intriguing notion comes from Latin America in the thought of Jesus Martin-Barbero and his notion of "mediation." Martin-Barbero holds that the persuasive alternative to "medium theories" is the idea that, rather than being objectifiable resources and influences on the culture, the media play a role of mediating *between* the individual and her culture.[39] In fact, a series of "mediations" enable individuals to locate themselves in social and cultural space and time. We assume that such things as language, ideology, received history, social and cultural values, mythology, and consciousness of location serve to enculturate us and provide means of solidarity, binding us to our place and time. These shared ideas mediate our experience of the physical world, enabling us to interact, develop psychologically and socially, learn, and achieve the kind of social autonomy that is at the base of human-ness and freedom.

The idea of "mediation" when applied to the mass media suggests a role for these devices and processes in social and cultural life and consciousness that is more integral to, less distinct from, that social and cultural life. They become a part of the fabric of social consciousness, not just an influence on that consciousness.

Another kind of research and theory that contrasts with approaches which focus on the medium has also come to importance in questions of media and religion: a more humanistic orientation to seeing religion and spirituality in terms of the *cultural artifacts* that support them and give them meaning. Work such as Laurence Moore's study of nineteenth-century religious commodities,[40] Colleen McDannell's influential work on "Material Christianity,"[41] David Morgan's studies of the visual culture of nineteenth- and twentieth-century American Protestantism,[42] Leigh Schmidt's history of the process of gifting,[43] Diane Winston's history of the Salvation Army as a public commodity,[44] and Heather Hendershot's history of Evangelical media[45] are examples which illustrate that there is much to be learned by focusing attention on the practices which emerge around the artifacts of religion.[46]

From medium to meaning

In the last chapter I argued that, across a range of ideas about media and society, there exists an important set of questions about what actually goes on when people encounter and consume media. I presented this as radically alternative to the more "medium"-oriented approaches that have dominated the field. At the core of the problem is recognition that there is a fundamental interaction or interrrelationship between practices of mediation and practices of religion. As Hent De Vries put it in the introduction to his collection on religion and media,

> We should no longer reflect exclusively on the meaning, historically and in the present, of religion – of faith and belief and their supposed opposites such as knowledge and technology – but concentrate on the significance of the processes of mediation and mediatization without and outside of which no religion would be able to manifest or reveal itself in the first place. In contradistinction to Heidegger's analysis, mediatization and the technology it entails form the condition of possibility for all revelation – for its revealability, so to speak. An element of technicity belongs to the realm of the "transcendental" and vice versa.[47]

Theories of "mediation" and of artifacts and commodities help get us part way there, helping us understand that, as people interact with media artifacts, they will be involved in a process that at the same time connects them with their various cultures and with remembered and imagined pasts and sources of insight and meaning. But a gap in our knowledge will remain. We still want to know how that mediation is felt, understood, and used in the various contexts of daily life. More specifically, we want to know what *social meanings* the media have in those contexts.

A focus on meaning is both a contrast with other approaches, and a potential complement to them. It enables us to see how the various media and messages that are accessible to individuals in the private sphere are received, understood, and potentially used in other spheres of social and cultural life. More importantly, though, a focus on meaning gets to the heart of the relationship of media to culture. The burden of culturalist theory, after all, is to understand how cultural meanings are produced and reproduced through the instruments and contexts of the culture. What meanings are made through mediated sources are an important component of that larger process, of course. More fundamentally, though, looking at the process of meaning-making should allow interpretive purchase on the specific role that media culture, in particular, plays.

For the specific questions of concern to us here, those surrounding media and religion, a focus on meaning-making has additional benefits. We assume that a good deal of what we will encounter in addressing questions of religion, spirituality, faith, transcendence, and "deeper meaning" will be subtle, diffuse, and nuanced. Religion and spirituality are assumed to be highly subjective, complex, and subjunctive components of life. What we know about contemporary religion from religion scholarship further holds that many of the concrete formal, inductive, and structural dimensions that have traditionally defined religion, religious difference, and religious meaning are changing and evolving in late modernity. Thus, the measurement of that which is intrinsically religious, spiritual, transcendent, or deeply meaningful has become more difficult as time has gone on. The indicia that once worked do so no longer. Indeed, as I will discuss in more detail later in the book, much of the definition of these things is now itself lodged in subjective processes of self- and cultural exploration. This means that analysis and interpretation of contemporary religion depends more and more on accounting for both the practices individuals engage in, and their own definition of the object of their engagement in cultural meaning.

Given the nature of our exploration here – that we are looking at issues related to religion – it is important to note that not all "meaning" is the same. And, not all meaning is *religious* meaning. As should be clear from this discussion, it is axiomatic of culturalist scholarship that meanings are connected with cultures, and that meaning is, in fact, a broad category that encompasses a variety of contexts, of which religion is one. So, in a way, we will be thinking here of religious meaning as a subset – a particular kind – of cultural meaning. This makes our quest in this book one that will be focused on those meanings among the ones we encounter that are, or are thought to be, or can be argued to be, *religious* meanings.

It is conceivable that through an exploration of religious meaning we may come to understand other meanings as they are related to media culture as well. It is certainly the case that a contextual exploration of *religious* meaning-making in the media age must necessarily be seen in the context of the cultural meaning practice of which it is a subset. That religious meaning is – presumably – *about* something, suggests it might well be a valuable heuristic for broader processes of meaning-making.

This is not to argue that religious meaning is not, in and of itself, important and significant. Religion, and the whole range of social and cultural resources, commitments, and symbols that we identify with religion (whether they today carry the label or not), has always been an important feature of the social and cultural landscape. Even in highly "secularized" societies, religion plays an important role. The fact that secularization has not exactly worked out the way it was predicted[48] makes it more important than ever to understand religion and to study the thing in itself. Religion is an ever more prominent feature of the political landscape in the industrialized West and beyond. It is an important – even determinitive – dimension of globalization. It is a motivator of social movements. Most specifically to our task here, religion continues to be an important element of the modern quest for the self. As we will discuss in more detail presently, a good deal of contemporary social practice can be seen as oriented toward the self and self-identity. This is an age where individuals increasingly pursue meaning quests directed at autonomy through self-perfection and self-awareness. Observers of this situation note that religion, spirituality, transcendence, and the other dimensions we have typically identified with "religion" continue to be important (and even growing in importance) elements of the "quest culture."

The kind of meanings we will be interested in is a subset of all meanings in another way as well. We will be interested not just in meaning *per se*, but in that which is meaning*ful* to specific people in specific places and at specific times. This gets at the commonplace sense of meaning as being potentially about something "beyond" simple social knowledge. Typically, such meanings will be marked by a sense of utility – they will be meanings that are to be put to some *use*. This notion is deeply rooted in the traditions of cultural studies. Raymond Williams, an intellectual leader in that discipline, contended that social life involved the articulation of the individual into a "structure of feeling," or a set of emotions, understandings, and cultural meanings which identified that individual with his context.[49] This notion was intended to be distinct from more purely rational or pragmatic motivations and actions in social life. Meaning*ful* knowledge or experience would among other things be that which effectively serves the connection of individuals to their structures of feeling. Foucault's idea of "*episteme*" and Bourdieu's notion of "*habitus*" address similar ideas and functions in the social and cultural world.

An important project for individuals in modernity is the construction of the self. Influential theorists of late modernity hold that the conditions of contemporary social life enforce on individuals a set of responsibilities they did not have in the past. Whereas once social and cultural structures and other arrangements could be depended on to provide plausible and compelling ideals, values, and resources for social life, today those same arrangements have broken down, for a number of reasons, some of which are rooted in the emergence of the media age. This leaves individuals increasingly on their own devices to construct meaningful and functional ways of understanding themselves as social beings. Anthony Giddens, perhaps the most prominent of these theorists, suggests that, as a result, a focus on the self and on the perfection of the self has replaced earlier pathways to the achievement of social knowledge.[50] What will be meaningful in media practice then should bear some relationship to this emerging concept and project of self.

There is, at the same time, some controversy over the role of media in the project of the self. One of the causes of this new situation, to Giddens, is very much a phenomenon of the media age; Giddens contends that the existence of modern mass communication and its broad circulation of knowledge about the nature of daily life has directly supported the development of a new kind of social and cultural consciousness, which he calls "reflexivity."[51] Individuals today are more "reflexive" in the sense that they know and understand the web of social and cultural relations – and their place in that web – in a more sophisticated way than would have been typical earlier. This knowledge has both positive and negative consequences of course,[52] but is simply a fact of late modern life. Psychologist Kenneth Gergen, in contrast, sees a very different – and more negative – role for media culture in the contemporary project of the self. To Gergen, the self is under assault from the range and sophistication of cultural symbols, appeals, and contexts to which we have access today. He calls this the "saturated self," unable to find a standpoint or position of reference that might have been available to the formation of a stable self in times past.[53] Giddens and Gergen thus present quite different views of the individual's relationship to media culture. For Giddens, while there are challenges to social life and social consciousness in the media age, the practices of the self are about individuals relating to culture with a certain autonomy. Gergen also sees this cultural practice in the hands of individuals, but at the same time is convinced that the sheer weight and volume of cultural contexts and material places the individual and her project of the self at a disadvantage.[54]

Meaning and identity

These sources, along with many from the field of culturalist media studies,[55] contend that a central object of meaning around the self is the formation and maintenance of *identity*. As an aspect of the self, the identity is the self's *description*. As such, it is necessarily a presentation of a kind, and necessarily articulated in such a way that it is accessible to others in the same context or milieu, that is, *culture*.[56] There is much anecdotal evidence that the media play an important role in identity. Popular music, film, and television all provide material that is relevant to identity. Research – on young people and youth culture in particular – has established that media culture is integral to providing resources, contexts, and practices to youth identity.[57]

Making identity the focus of inquiry is a refinement in direction that serves a number of purposes. I have been arguing that much is to be gained by a research project that looks at the *where* of the relationship between media and religion. Identity is an important location, though not the only location, where media and religion interact in human experience. But, as a kind of heuristic device for guiding our inquiry, identity presents itself as an important category.

This can be seen when we look at the nature of contemporary work on contemporary religion. In his influential essay on new paradigms in the study of religion,[58] Stephen Warner has suggested that, to account for contemporary religion, we must shift our thinking away from religion "as ascribed," toward religion "as achieved." By this he means that, in late modernity, religion has not faded away, but its nature has changed. It can no longer be defined only in terms of its historical, structural, or doctrinal attributes. Religion-as-institution, as we will discuss in more detail in later chapters, is in decline or at least under some stress. Instead, Warner posits, we must see religion as something that is generated in the experience, practice, and aspirations of "lived lives." The focus on identity that I am advocating argues what adherents to this new form of religion "achieve" is – in part, at least – a new sense of themselves as religious or spiritual beings; thus their religious or spiritual *identities*.

In his comprehensive account of the late modern religiosity of the "baby boom" generation,[59] Wade Clark Roof notes that this practice of identity-construction (as we might call it) is an articulation between the context of individual experience and broader contexts of social and cultural life, including claims made by the culture about symbolic meanings. The rough and tumble of twentieth-century religious change and evolution has resulted in the formation of clear and distinct religious ideological claims,[60] and, as Roof notes, these "ideological labels" are increasingly encountered *reflexively*. That is, people articulate for themselves a range of symbols, claims, and ideas from a variety of contexts (personal as well as public) into an achieved (though always under construction) identity.[61] As Roof notes, such practices were anticipated decades ago by Eric Hobsbawm's notion of "invented tradition."

An important nuance in Roof's (and other) work is the notion that the resources that the individual brings to bear on his spirituality or religiosity are largely encountered *as objects*. By this I do not mean to say that they are "things" in the sense of material culture, though such things are indeed part of what we encounter in culture that relates to religion and spirituality. Instead, I want to argue that we think of cultural symbols and resources as objects in relation to each other and to the range of things we encounter in our subjective experience of daily life. Again, this is a bit of a heuristic, a way of separating out this kind of practice from the ways we have typically thought of media. Thus, I tend to think of media as "objects," not as "texts" or "messages," or "environments," or "ideological systems" at least as they are encountered by selves in the lived environment. In the following chapters, we will explore how this works in the context of individual meaning-making.

Symbolic-interactionist theory provides a way of thinking about individuals and their relationship to culture and cultural objects, particularly around questions of identity and meaning, which may be of some use here. On the most basic level, interactionism holds that we develop as social beings through our interactions with others, and that those interactions involve a kind of conscious self-construction and self-representation.[62] We learn who we are, how we act, what is valued, and what is appropriate through interactions with others. Over time, we develop an idealized sense of self that is relevant to our specific place, time, and web of social relations. This supports a logic of social and cultural life as the construction of identities that we understand to make sense because they reflect our understandings of the cultural logics of the contexts we live in and because they contain the cultural objects, including symbols, values, and languages, that help constitute and make sense in those contexts.[63] The approach I am arguing for here assumes a role for media practices and media objects in such constructions of self and identity. How limited, extensive, determinative, or passive the role of such objects is, is in a way an empirical question that will be tested in later chapters. For now, though, it is important to see that, for some good reasons, we can expect there to be a role for media in meaning and identity.

This becomes a more subtle and nuanced contrast with traditional "effects"-oriented media theory in a number of ways. Along with the various valences of culturalist media studies in general, it wants to look at the media from the perspective of media audiences and individual and collective meaning-making, rather than from the perspective media institutions or texts. It wants to understand things in terms of the media objects as symbolic resources rather than as determinative ideological constructions. It wants to propose that the important questions may be in the realm of meaning-making rather than the "impact" of media on *behavior*. There is also a more fundamental, and interesting, contrast in that what I am developing here – a view that sees media in terms of their *integration into daily life* rather than in terms of their *effects on it*.

Much of the so-called "dominant" effects paradigm of media thinks of media in relation to various pathologies. From the early twentieth-century studies of the impact of films and novels on children and youth through the "mass society" theories of mid-century, to the studies of the impact of television on violent behavior later in the century, there has been a consistent tendency for media to be thought of in terms of how they might impact the otherwise-well-socialized pre-teen, the smooth-functioning social network, or the functional family. Interactionism in a way (and – it might be argued – the pragmatist social-theoretical tradition out of which it grew) focuses on the opposite. It wishes to understand and explain the way we come to be socialized, the way we make meaningful sense of ourselves in the social worlds we inhabit and the social and cultural resources we use for these purposes. It further assumes that, on important levels, this is a conscious, cognitive process. Not denying that there is much that is not fully self-conscious about individual psychological development, even much that is latent and subconscious, interactionism nonetheless wishes to look at how we make sense of our world and take action to inhabit it.

The approach here has much in common with a relatively recent development in the field of psychology called "positive psychology." According to its proponents, it has arisen in part in response to the same general issue I've raised here: that the measurement tools available have too often assumed pathology rather than integration.[64] One of the proponents of the positive approach, Mihaly Csikszentmihalyi, has provided valuable insights to an approach that would look at media objects in a germinal essay titled "Why we need things." In it, he suggests that physical (and, by extension, cultural) objects serve important functions in grounding us in space, time, and history.[65]

I am not arguing that the whole point of social analysis of media and religion is to see stability and functioning totalized systems. Indeed, culturalist media analysis is most helpfully directed at issues of difference, distinction, resistance, alternative readings, contrasting interpretations, social critique, and social change. It does this through critiques and interpretations that foreground the conditions under which certain systems of meaning and meaning practice make sense or do not make sense. Thus, it foregrounds the social system and its attributes rather than assumed "effects" on it. It is possible to see such systems happily functioning, but also to see ways in which there are contradictions and stresses within them. The focus is on culture. Even though much of what we will discuss in later chapters involves individuals and their experiences, meanings, and practices, the point is really to look at the cultures within which they find themselves, and to understand how the various resources of those cultures, particularly those in the media sphere and related to religion and spirituality, are made sense of.

This is, once again, in contrast with the received paradigms in mass-communication research, and in contrast with much of our "lay theory" about media as well. We all know – on some level – the history of the development and integration of media technologies into social space. We are aware of, and even participate in, discourses about the nature and effects of these developments. For many reasons, it makes sense for us to think in terms of how these media – which are, after all, technologies – are or are not to be integrated in authentic ways into our lives. There has been a good deal of scholarship devoted to these issues, most of which illustrates that the integration of media into the context of daily life has been a process of negotiation rather than a tacit, easy, transparent thing.[66] It thus makes some sense that we would continue to think of the media as somewhat artificial "influences" on life, and focus on those influences in terms of their potential pathological effects, rather than think of them as the taken-for-granted aspects of our lives that they have become. This has had particular purchase with regard to religion because it is a commonplace to identify religion with values, with the inculcation of values and normative behaviors, and with the raising of children. A religious lens or framework directed at the media in daily life has thus been even more likely to think in terms of pathologies or effects.

None of this is to argue that there are not media effects, even on or related to religion. It is to argue instead that to understand the nature of those effects, we must look more carefully at how and where and in what contexts they are produced. And, as will be described in the next chapter, there is good reason to believe that many of the questions we have had regarding the religious implications of the media are simply misplaced – that media and religion have come to function together in the context of contemporary culture in subtle and some not-so-subtle ways.

Looking at culture and meaning-making in the context of daily life also addresses an issue that emerges when we again pick up the narrative of the development of the media in the US in the twentieth century. The effects paradigm in a way made more sense in an earlier media era, one typified by a relatively small number of dominant media. By the 1930s, the electronic media landscape in the US had settled into a situation that for many came to be thought of as "natural": a public media sphere that seemed to play a large and unifying role in defining the terms of the culture. For much of the century, the dominant media of radio and then television were provided by three large private companies, and there was arguably little difference between them. In that context, it made some sense to think in terms of small variations on that theme. Effects of media were seen in terms of relatively unequivocal and unitary characteristics of content, with the interesting questions being where and for whom different kinds of outcomes could be seen. There was little awareness, for example, that different audiences, different communities of interpretation, and different cosmologies might make the experience of these media radically different in different contexts. The dominant assumption was that there was one national media market, and that its needs, interests, and motivations were more or less universal, and that the role of broadcasting, for example, as a cultural authority, was more or less unquestioned.

In terms of religion, the centrality and seeming unity of the media of that era (roughly the middle third of the twentieth century) coincided with the self-understanding of an era described by Will Herberg[67] as one of sectarian simplicity and unity in his famous aphorism, "to be Catholic, Protestant, or Jew are simply various ways of being American." The question became one of access for these dominant religious institutions to a public sphere determined by the media. Elaborate systems of access emerged that in a way gave the major television networks in both the US and the UK the authority to confirm the legitimacy of the institutions of the religious establishment.[68] The effect of this was in fact an early – and profound – articulation of religion and the public media, a linkage that was somewhat opaque at the time but today appears as only the beginning of a growing integration between these two realms.

But certain voices in the world of religion began to realize that the times had changed in important ways – that religion could no longer ignore the media.[69] This point was driven home more forcefully in the 1970s with the emergence of televangelism. This development was important in several ways. It constituted a seeming challenge to the cultural hegemony of the established religions (in both the US and elsewhere), a challenge confirmed by much of the discourse about it at the time. It was one of the first examples of the fracturing and multiplication of media channels that would typify the last quarter of the century, as technologies such as satellite and cable broadcasting broke the hold of the dominant networks over the mediated public sphere. In the early days of satellite and cable television, many – even in the media industries – could not quite envision the possibilities for the multiplication of channels and services directed at discrete taste cultures. The socialization of the dominant "network" era was very strong. Televangelism and the hugely successful premium-cable service Home Box Office both emerged around the same time, and served to illustrate what was possible. Televangelism further stimulated new directions in research and reflection on religion and media (as discussed earlier) that pointed to more culturalist and audience-centered ways of explaining its implications.

By the end of the century, the media industries were becoming more and more complex and multifaceted. Whereas, in the "network era" of US broadcasting, it had been common to think of the media as a kind of national "hearth" around which the whole nation gathered, by the millennium it was no longer common to think of the media in those terms. Cable television brought dozens, then hundreds, of channels into the home. The Internet, the World Wide Web, and other advancements in digital communication provided still more sources of media experience and more competition for the previously dominant media. Other technologies, including video games, hand-held devices, and cellular phones, as well as new software services such as instant messaging and pod-casting, made the media sphere increasingly complex and multifaceted. An important implication of this for research was that it became increasingly difficult to study "the media" as a whole. Even the relatively straightforward task of measuring audience sizes for marketing and advertising purposes became more difficult.

This has served to reinforce approaches to audience research that have at the same time made the study of religion in media more central. At mid-century, the questions seemed simpler, but that simplicity hid a range of important questions that could not be answered by the available means. Religion is a complex, subtle, and nuanced phenomenon, and, as we will see in the next chapter, is becoming more complex all the time. The simplicity of earlier times hid the fact that it was not clear precisely what effects media content might be having on religious meaning and religious practice. The large trends were available, but there were many questions that could not be answered without different methods, methods more sensitive to the nuances of religion and spirituality.

Where the nineteenth century ended with the emergence of the entirely new cultural and social reality of mass communication, the twentieth ended with mass communication changing in ways that made the whole notion of the "mass" problematic. Technological change has thus made culturalist questions inevitable and necessary, a matter we will explore in more detail in the next chapter.

Chapter 3

Media and religion in transition

In the last chapter I argued that, by the end of the twentieth century, the world of the media was changing in significant ways. Whereas the century began with the emergence of what we came to know as "the mass media," and the middle of the period saw the formation of those media into centralized and dominant social and cultural forces, by the end, the whole notion of those media being about "masses" was coming under question. That "the media" are now well established as central to social and cultural life is not in very much dispute. What is under review is the question of how we are to look at them.

A variety of metaphors for the media have been proposed. Are they an "environment"? a "vast wasteland"? the "fourth estate"? the "cultural environment"? the "family hearth"? "Satanic"? "technologies of freedom"? "technologies of domination or hegemony"? "the video altar"? Each of these is rooted in the more universal, totalizing version of the media typical of the mid-twentieth century. While I won't propose any particular new metaphor for media, it is important to understand a few things that are significant issues of definition as we abandon the view of media as primarily a "mass" phenomenon. Audiences are today smaller, more fractured, more specialized, and more homogeneous than was the case in the past, so the adjective "mass" seems no longer to apply. This is a matter of significance meriting further consideration, though, as many would argue that large, "mass" audiences continue to gather for many television programs, which is true. What we have seen is a *relative* "de-massification" of audiences, accompanied by a rethinking of our ideas about what the significance of a mass audience would be, anyway. Several other characteristics of the media today are also worth rethinking.[1]

Changes in the media

It is true that even though the media are no longer "mass" media in quite the way they once were, they still are, in fundamental ways, *public*. In fact, the nature of their being "public" is probably also the most important dimension of their "mass-ness". The sheer size of media audiences matters only in a restricted range of contexts and discourses. What is far more significant is the notion that, in important ways, they are open and available beyond a restricted audience. Of course there *are* private media, but the media we will talk about here derive a major part of their significance from the fact that they are public and open. Negotiations over *who is part of the discussion, who is watching, who is asking*, and *who has access* become important questions as audiences negotiate themselves into and out of participation in various media, but they all rely on the fundamental characteristic or assumption of "public-ness."

This public-ness is also rooted in the characteristic that originally made the mass media "mass" – that their political economy relies on as broad an audience as can be assembled, something that today is still of great concern to the advertisers who support most of these media. The label "democratic," first applied to the mass press over a century ago, now seems quaint to us but obscures a more ideological assumption: that these media, open to "the masses," were necessarily something for lower-class taste cultures, and would reflect that class location in their content and consumption. This remains a matter of interest today. The changes in the media have allowed a demographic and class–taste targeting of electronic media, something that was less possible before, but the questions of which media are available to which audiences, which are "appropriate" taste cultures and which are not, and questions of the relationship between the assumed "quality" of various media and the national, ethnic, and social classes typical of their audiences remain matters of meaning-making and negotiation.[2]

Some other characteristics of what we once thought of as the "mass media" also continue to be important. Their instantaneity or timeliness is also significant. The mass-media era accustomed us to the notion that much of what we encountered in the media was at least intended to be consumed with a known "sell-by date." It had a sense of its time, even though we have become accustomed to consuming media at our leisure, collecting and re-consuming films and television programs years after their original release, and enjoying nostalgic re-consumption on channels and in places intended for that purpose. The timeliness of news programming is taken for granted for most audiences.

Another significant characteristic of the media has to do with their origins or sources. Traditional definitions of the mass media highlighted the characteristic of their being "one to many," that is that there was a centralized source attended to by a larger audience. This bears much in common with the notion of their being public. But this is contested today on a number of fronts, while it remains an important issue. It is contested because a variety of audience practices and technological arrangements today present themselves as being "interactive" or "bottom up." It is common to think of the Internet in this way, for example, and the advertising and marketing industries have talked for years now about a shift from "push" to "pull" marketing, where the Internet and the general self-oriented social consciousness of today's consumers has them, rather than the advertiser or the marketer, in the "driver's seat." And, as we will see in later chapters, there is much about contemporary media consumption that thinks of itself as interactive and self-generating.[3]

At the same time, though, we should not lose sight of the fact that the mass media are complex and capital-intensive industries, and that they are, in fact, centrally organized and function according to centralized and centralizing logics. They are, as a prominent literary theorist has labeled them, "consciousness industries,"[4] devoted to the production of cultural artifacts intended to shape consciousness, if for no other reasons than economic ones. Their economic logic moves toward centralization, even monopoly, with fewer and fewer corporations now controlling more and more of the media landscape.[5] The artifacts they produce are systematic representations. An impressive scholarly enterprise has been directed at revealing the nature of these representations, and has made a convincing case that there are clear ideological themes identifiable in them.[6] Thus, while we might want to move away from the too-facile assumption that the media are monolithic processes responsible for the ideological subjugation of undifferentiated masses, it would also be incorrect to say that the processes of media production, representation, and consumption operate in a totally free and unfettered way. The truth is somewhere in between, and it is the task of contemporary media studies to work toward more complex interpretations at that boundary.

We look at the media differently today in part because of changes in their technologies, structures, and patterns of consumption. The decline of the era of "dominant" media has by definition coincided with the emergence of a multiplicity of sources. In magazine publishing, for example, there has been an explosion in new titles over the past few decades. In the face of widespread predictions of the end of magazines as a consequence of television and other new media, what has occurred instead is a diversification, with an increasing number of titles, each directed at smaller and narrower "niche" markets.

The same phenomenon has occurred in television. Cable and satellite television have produced a multiplicity of channels and services unthinkable in the "network" era. These range from those directed at relatively large, heterogeneous interests (in news, for example) to those focusing on relatively narrow interests or demographics. And within these channels, it now makes economic sense, in a way it did not before, to present individual programs with very discretely focused interests. The diversification unleashed by cable television has also influenced the development of new over-the-air networks.[7] In both the US and the UK, television companies targeting smaller markets and taste cultures are surviving and even flourishing.

In the Internet and World Wide Web, the situation is even more fluid and multifaceted. Many scholars have observed and detailed the plethora of new services available along the "information superhighway." A stunning array of websites have emerged, specifically focused on religion and spirituality. These range from those directed self-consciously at traditional religious movements (including many sponsored by institutions or congregations themselves), to those such as the prominent and influential *Beliefnet*, intended to be pan-religious or meta-institutional, to those focused on new, "fringe," or emerging religious or spiritual movements or sensibilities, to those that seemingly intend to *become* new religious movements themselves, to sites devoted to religious "pod-casting," to quasi-religious sites such as those for fans and bloggers of various kinds, to sites that are self-consciously "anti-" or "ir-religious."[8] This is particularly significant to the idea that the media may be changing, because Internet and Web-based practices are particularly individualistic, self-directed and generated, and – in the case of the Web in particular – are thought to be fundamentally *interactive*. Further, the character of Web activities such as blogging, gaming, pod-casting, and instant-messaging serves to make acts of *consumption* in that environment also acts of *production* in fundamental ways, an understanding of media practice that is an increasingly important way of understanding *all* media "audience-ing."

These developments have had two specific and direct implications for evolving relations between religion and media. The first of these is that, within the multiplicity of sources available, specifically religious channels and services, and channels and services that can accommodate religious and spiritual interests and uses, are increasingly possible and available. Televangelism, as I noted in the last chapter, helped usher in this era with its pioneering of the concept of the religious channel.[9] Before cable television, religion on television was pretty much confined to the "ghetto" of Sunday mornings or late-night hours, and network policies largely forbade the selling of airtime to religion at any other time. With the development of cable and satellites in the 1970s, this all changed, and religion could suddenly be found across the week, in forms and formats that pushed the envelope.[10] As these channels and sources evolved, they further helped to expand the economic marketplace of religious media materials. The fact that many of these innovators were Evangelicals had a particular impact as well, as Evangelicalism has been observed to be particularly interested in exploring the implications of new media of communication.[11] Implications for religious-cultural-marketing sectors such as the Contemporary Christian Music industry were far-reaching and positive, in terms of reach and growth.

Along with the development of specifically "religious" channels and sources, a more profound and far-reaching effect of this media change came in the way that the so-called "secular" media began to think about religion.

In the network era, it was convenient to think of religion as something that could be contained within a framework of the prerogatives of established religious institutions. Religion has always been problematic for the media, a matter we will get to later.[12] It has been thought of as something that is at the same time inherently controversial and of fading importance and interest (owing to the widespread acceptance of the notion of secularization). Religion defies normal canons of journalistic objectivity, is hard to "source," and is expressed socially and culturally in a dizzying array of forms, movements, interests, and publics. It made sense, then, for the media in the middle of the last century to want to constrain it to defined and limited locations on the TV dial, the magazine rack, and the bookshelf.

In television's "golden era," religion rarely appeared. In the later eras, it remained nearly nonexistent. The major network news operations devoted little attention to it, save for the occasional report from the Vatican. There were, and are, no religion correspondents at any of these major broadcast news outlets,[13] and public broadcasting in the US has traditionally been even less interested in religion.[14] The situation was the same in entertainment media, with few if any characters identified as religious in any network prime-time dramas, and no major series with themes or sub-themes devoted to the topic.

This all changed as the structure and diversity of channels and services in the media began to change and as the world of religion also began to change. The signal event was probably the première, in 1994, of the weekly drama *Touched by an Angel*, on the CBS network.[15] By the 1995 season, *Touched* was in the top-ten programs in terms of ratings, a position it held until shortly before it ended production in 2003. What was so unprecedented about the program was that it was so self-evidently *religious*. While it avoided being identified as a Christian program, it was clearly intended to, and did, speak to a Christian audience.[16] At the same time, however, it straddled to a less devout audience as well, one more attracted to its mysticism surrounding anthropomorphic angels than to its earnest invocations of "God."[17]

Touched was not alone. Over the course of the 1990s, a number of different US programs and series began to more directly explore the religious and spiritual side of life. The popular family drama *7th Heaven* on the WB network, about a Protestant minister's family, outlasted *Touched*. In the 1997 season there was a critically acclaimed, but ratings-deprived, drama about an inner-city Catholic priest, *Nothing Sacred*, which was very popular with Catholics who think of themselves as "lapsed," or "questioning." But the industry and the audience also began to see a good deal of what sociologists would call "implicit" or even "new religion" in television, as well. The hugely popular *The Simpsons* regularly dealt with religion of both the traditional and emerging kinds,[18] as did the *enfant terrible* series *South Park*, and two of the most popular adult dramas of the 1990s, *The X-Files* and *Northern Exposure*, each contained much material relating to transcendent and spiritual, if not religious, themes.[19] These were followed by prominent spirituality-themed series such as *Buffy the Vampire Slayer* and *Joan of Arcadia*.

Similar trends could be seen in film and popular music. As an example, Joan Osborn's 1995 "One of Us" explored the meaning of God in contemporary life, and was accompanied by a provocative music video dense with religious symbolism and imagery. More famously, Madonna's 1989 "Like a Prayer" video pushed new boundaries in bringing traditional religious imagery into the popular music context. Irish singer Sinead O'Connor created an international sensation in 1992 by the act of civil disobedience of tearing up a photo of the Pope on national television.[20] Film has always been an important medium for the exploration of religious themes and images, and recent years have seen this trend continue. In addition to a range of mainstream feature films, alternative films such as *The Fast Runner* and *Whale Rider* pushed the envelope of religiously or spiritually significant film, combining those themes with alternative voices and cultures.[21]

To what can we attribute the sea change of which these trends were emblematic? It is clear that broadcasting – and the media industries more generally – came to be able to imagine religion and spirituality in unprecedented ways. This is due in part to the increasing fragmentation of audiences, channels, media artifacts, and services as the twentieth century ended. As "the media" became less monolithic, they began thinking of themselves in less monolithic ways. Changes in broadcast regulation contributed, as well, as the 1996 Telecommunications Act and later legislation and rulings came to remove many of the "public service" expectations that had applied to broadcasting for most of the century.[22] The assumption that broadcasting was somehow responsible for the presentation of content in the public interest had enforced a sense of responsibility on the part of broadcasters for deciding what was appropriate in the way of religion along with other things. This whole atmosphere has now changed, though there continues to be a vibrant debate over the responsibility broadcasters have to the public for maintaining social and cultural values.[23] In the case of religion, anyway, in the twenty-first century, broadcasters and other media no longer exercise the level of scrutiny once applied to religious and spiritual content. At the same time, the diversification and commodification of the media marketplace has opened the door to a panoply of new programs and services. This, combined with a set of social and cultural trends in the world of religion, has led to the emergence of a new, more vibrant, and more extensive media marketplace of religion.

Changes in religion

A study released in late 2003 attracted a great deal of attention with its finding that the number of Americans who answer "none" when asked what their religion is had doubled in the previous ten years, to 29 million. But, rather than portending the long-awaited secularization of America, this seemed more likely to suggest a further stage in the restructuring of American religion. Just answering "none" does not mean one has no religion. As religion writer Don Lattin noted in his report on these findings,

> Some "nones" identify themselves as atheists or agnostics, but the vast majority believe in God, pray and often describe themselves as "spiritual but not religious." "My sense of God transcends all the different religions," said . . . a clinical supervisor in San Francisco. . . . "It's an energy."[24]

Such religion or spirituality, to the extent it is becoming more common, brings the US into closer alignment with longer-standing traditions in Europe. A letter to the European edition of *Time* responded to the debate over whether to include a reference to God in the new European constitution in this way:

> You asked, where did God go? God does not live in churches alone. He is omnipresent and is the silent witness to all usual and unusual happenings in the universe. Christianity is deeply rooted in Europe. Attendance in churches is not the sole criterion for assessing people's devotion to Christianity.[25]

But change is evident not only outside existing religious structures, but also in their reimagining. A reporter covering the founding of a new church called "All Seasons Chalice" observed,

> The church is one of thousands of "mix and match" or "designer God" communities springing up around the nation as people yearning for a spiritual context seek to build new traditions that incorporate aspects of many belief systems.
>
> All Seasons Chalice founder David Tresemer and Cannon, his wife, who is now president of the small but growing community, say their new tradition emphasizes a connection to the earth and the wisdom of the stars through dance, meditation and music. They offer respect for more traditional belief systems such as Christianity and Buddhism, without the dogma, they say.[26]

Sociologists of religion have been observing for quite some time now that the nature of contemporary religion is undergoing significant change. From the period of relative unity and solidity typified by Will Herberg in the 1950s, religion has gone through a transformation in both its structures and its practices.[27] On the most fundamental level, these changes have been rooted in overall changes in the nature of contemporary social consciousness and social experience. Anthony Giddens, who we discussed in the last chapter, has laid out the theory that, in late modernity, changes in the structure of social relations and more specifically in the sorts of structural supports that once supported individuals in making sense of themselves and their social experience have led to a focus on the self and on perfection of the self as the central social project of the time. We can see evidence of this in – of all places – "the media." The rise of what has come to be called "the culture of therapy" – much of it based in or available through the media and commodity culture – has occurred in part to address the increasing needs of individuals for new, more specific, and particular ways of finding themselves.

Whereas we once might have looked to a network of social relations in home, school, community, church, or family to provide the resources necessary to the making of our "selves," today we think of this as being much more our *own* responsibility. More importantly, we also see it as an essential task. We are much more reflexively self-conscious about it. It is up to us. This means that in our individual practices of meaning-making, we see ourselves as both at the center of the process, and autonomously responsible for generating that process. The culture of therapy has arisen in part to address this new reality.[28] Therapy has come to be an important mode of social practice, a major center of social and cultural articulation, and (not incidentally) a multi-million-dollar industry, with extensive media resources including books, magazines, cassette tapes, television programs, workshops, retreats, really a whole "culture industry" devoted to it.

The kind of religion that emerges in such a social context is also new and different. As the self is the project, the spirituality of the self becomes an important dimension of that project.[29] Individuals today feel much more responsible for their spiritual and religious lives than was the case a generation ago. What Philip Hammond calls "personal autonomy" in matters of faith[30] places the responsibility on the individual to make her own decisions about faith and spirituality without what she is likely to see as intermediaries such as congregational or clerical authority. These dimensions of the process: that it is about the self; that it results from self-conscious autonomous action on the part of individuals, and that it is inherently distrustful of received clerical or institutional authority, combine to support a new religious sensibility that has come to be called "seeking." Wade Clark Roof first identified this in a systematic way a decade ago in his book, *A Generation of Seekers*.[31]

In this work, Roof suggested that the so-called "Baby Boom" generation marked a sea change in the nature of religious experience. This generation was the first to come of age in the late modern era identified by Giddens with its large-scale reorganization of social experience due to radical changes in institutions and culture. The "Boomers" were, in addition, the generation that first came to the reflexive consciousness that Giddens feels supports the kind of autonomy and suspicion of received explanations and authorities that is typical of the quest for the ideal self. As Roof observes,

> The same culture that simplifies and rationalizes religion also alters the very notion of the self. Under contemporary conditions the self becomes fluid, improvable, adaptable, manipulatable, and above all else, something to be satisfied – the assumption being, of course, that the self's appetite is insatiable. Parallels between the self and religion are worth observing. With a more fluid, adaptable, and insatiable self, religious identity becomes less ascribed, and more of a voluntary, subjective, and achieved phenomenon. America's religious pluralism feeds into this "new voluntarism" by demonopolizing any single version as the religious truth and by making a wide variety of religious options open to everyone.[32]

Roof's work is significant in that so much of it was rooted in field research on the evolving ways that this generation looked at religion. Along the way, he laid out the description of "seeking," which seems to typify the rising tide of religiosity and spirituality in American culture. Roof describes this as rooted in some of the same trends noted by Giddens, but at the same time linked to particularities of the American context:

> Today's spiritual quests are the working out of the tendencies deeply rooted in an Emersonian conception of the individual who must find God in herself or himself, and of an experience with the divine affirming that she or he is known and loved in a personal way. Now as in the past, such inclinations have encouraged an assertive self, not necessarily independent of community but one that insists on "working out" the individual's relation to and meaning of such involvement. Americans not only pick and choose what to believe, by and large they also set the terms governing involvement in religious communities. Especially in a time of heightened spiritual activity, we would expect a more rampant subjectivity, but also the possibility of new, emerging forms of community giving expression to personal enhancement.[33]

Fellow sociologist Robert Wuthnow agrees that a religiosity of spirituality of "seeking" is, in fact, a major dimension of the contemporary religious landscape, but also points out that it stands alongside a more traditional spirituality of "dwelling" that can be said to be of continuing significance as well.[34] Wuthnow and Roof in fact argue that the seeking (or sometimes called "questing") sensibility exists in some contexts on its own – that is it is definitive of religious or spiritual action for some people – and in other contexts is a sensibility that defines religion or spirituality for people within more conventional religious bodies, congregations, or traditions. As Roof sees it,

> Three aspects of the situation today particularly stand out. One is the sheer numbers of people involved. . . . Surveys show that large sectors of the American population today are interested in deepening their spirituality. Many who seem to have lost a traditional religious grounding are striving for new and fresh moorings; many with a religious grounding are looking to enrich their lives further. Second, dominant amid all this ferment is an emphasis on self-understanding and self-reflexivity, a product of late modernity with its pluralism, relativism, and ontological uncertainties. Thus my use of the terms *quest*, *seeking* and *searching* arise out of this particular historical and cultural context. Third, and somewhat paradoxically, the spiritual learnings are leading many Americans beyond the self-centered, therapeutic culture in which they grew up. Self-fulfillment as a cultural theme in the 1960s and 1970s set in motion a powerful quest, but now for a generation older and more mature that quest has moved beyond the solutions that were promised in consumption, materialism, and self-absorption. Popular spirituality may appear shallow, indeed flaky; yet its creative currents, under the right conditions, can activate our deepest energies and commitments. Even in its most self-absorbed forms, today's spiritual ferment reflects a deep hunger for a self-transformation that is both genuine and personally satisfying.[35]

And significantly to our discussions here, Roof observes that the generation of which seeking is typical, the Baby Boom generation, is defined in important ways by its relationship to media. It is the first television generation, he notes, and has as well grown up with the mass-marketing and demographic targeting of modern advertising. Its spiritual sensibilities are in important ways, then, both *rooted in* and *represented by* mass media. "All these trends – a more focused spirituality, experience with pluralism, selective mixing of traditions, and new styles of commitment – are deeply entrenched in the popular culture today."[36] In his more recent *Spiritual Marketplace*, Roof explored the media connection to religious seeking in more detail, and observed,

> Of great importance in shaping this more expressive self through symbols and discourses is the mass media. Never before has human life been so caught up in mediated image and symbol. And never before have the people themselves been so aware that ours is such a world of image and symbol. The role of cultural industries and

communication technologies continues to expand, and at the expense of traditional institutions of socialization – the family, the school, and the church.[37]

Beyond the notion of foregrounding media in relation to contemporary religion or spirituality, Roof also notes here an essential dimension of late modern consciousness identified by Giddens, the role that mediated experience plays in establishing a modern self-*reflexivity*. According to Giddens, we know who we are in part by understanding our place in the increasingly complex web of social relations that define modern life.[38] This reflexive self-understanding in part defines the particular challenges of late modernity in that we know much more about the way the social world works than would have been typical of our forebears. As I noted in the previous chapter, this may not be an unparalleled good, with critics such as Kenneth Gergen seeing this type of social consciousness as likely to be disempowering as empowering. Giddens would argue, though, that it is a fact of contemporary life, and as such we must understand it as observers at the same time that we must live it as social actors.

Roof's own view of this tends to coincide with the interactionist position discussed in the last chapter. Interactionism would look to the social practices whereby we make sense of our world (in religious or spiritual or social terms) and would suggest that it is always up to us as social actors to make meaning of the conditions within which we find ourselves. Roof, in fact, contributes to this theoretically by identifying his project as that of looking at and for "lived religion."

> "Lived religion," that is, religion as experienced in everyday life, offers a model for integrating the official, the popular, and the therapeutic modes of religious identity. Lived religion might be thought of as involving three crucial aspects: scripts, or sets of symbols that imaginatively explain what the world and life are about; practices, or the means whereby individuals relate to, and locate themselves within, a symbolic frame of reference; and human agency, or the ability of people to actively engage the religious worlds they help to create.[39]

This provides a rather straightforward model for an exploration of relations between religion and media, locating this exploration radically in the experience of lived religious or spiritual lives as they encounter their social and cultural worlds, of which the media play an ever more important part. Looking at things in this "lived" way gives us a perspective that at the same time reflects emerging trends in religion and media, and enables us to get past some of the problematic ways the interaction between media and religion has been looked at in the past. It radically centers the question on three related parts. First is the question of what *symbols* or *scripts* are available in the media environment, what we might call the *"symbolic inventory"* out of which individuals make religious or spiritual meaning. Second is the *practices of consumption, interaction, and articulation* through which those meanings are accessed, understood, and used. And third is the centering of this in *the experiences of the individuals* who are doing the consuming and the meaning-making.

Chapters 4 through 8 of this book are an exploration of the so-called "symbolic marketplace" of the media as experienced in the daily lives of individuals and families. The orientation is to take seriously the idea that the media today play a central role in providing the symbolic resources through which we make meaning of our social worlds, and that religion and spirituality are important parts of that meaning-making for many of us. Our investigations then begin with the assumption that we can and should go to people where they are, and "look back with them" – as it were – at the symbolic environment they inhabit, attempting to understand how they integrate those symbolic resources into senses of who they are, what they believe, and what they should do.

Media and the "symbolic inventory"

Before we begin those explorations, though, we should take a look at the media landscape with an eye to understanding the nature of the symbolic inventory it offers and its integration into large social and cultural themes and values. The point here is not merely to catalog the self-consciously "religious" material that might be available there, but to understand the ways that patterns of reception, consumption, and meaning-construction today might find material of various kinds and implications available in the media sphere. To do this, we need to be conscious of what we have just reviewed about the changing nature of the media landscape and the changing nature of religion. Thus, we will imagine self-conscious, reflexive individuals encountering a complex and diversifying media landscape, and finding there (or at least looking for) material that relates to their ongoing sense of themselves as religious or spiritual.

A number of sources and contexts of media present themselves as possible locations for these practices to exist in daily life. The sort of "received" ideas discussed in Chapter 1 would have us looking at the locations in the media landscape that we think of as the likely places in a formal sense. That is, places where "religion" as a category might be thought of as likely or at least expected. But, as we discussed there, there is reason to expect that some unexpected sources might well be significant to religious or spiritual "seeking" or "questing" (to use the terms introduced earlier). The media landscape can be divided up in a number of ways, but for our discussion here, for reasons that will become clearer in later chapters, it makes sense to look at things in four rather general categories: news; religious broadcasting; religious publishing; and entertainment. This of course privileges traditional categories of media *vis-á-vis* religion, but at the same time it allows us to look at them in a new way, testing later, by talking with people in the context of their daily lives, how, why, and whether religious or spiritual material is present in these contexts.

News

Journalism has always had a problem with religion.[40] For most of its history, the American press has treated religion in two contradictory ways. On the one hand, when it has dealt with religion, there has been a tendency for it to do so with a kind of deference. This has been particularly so with regard to coverage of the established institutions, including the hierarchy of the Roman Catholic Church, the Protestant denominations, and the regional or national organizations of other faith traditions. When dealing with either "local" religion, or religion as *experienced or practiced* (that is, the kind of religion that we have learned is most significant and typical today), the tendency has been for the stories to be either ignored or under-reported.

It is not difficult to understand some of the reasons for this traditional situation. First, the religion of individuals – religion as experienced – is difficult or impossible to "source." That is, the traditional canons of reporting call for it to be a rational process where sources, motivations, interests, and consequences can be laid out, analyzed, and evaluated. Religion as commonly understood is not thought to be amenable to this kind of treatment. Second, beyond these assumed characteristics, religion has always claimed to be about things beyond the rational sphere of "here and now" – the natural turf on which most journalists see themselves working. Third – and the factor most often cited by media people themselves – journalists, editors, and publishers have tended to see religion as something that is inherently complex. There are many different faiths and truth claims and traditions. Thus, it is a field of inquiry that is inherently much more complicated than US – or even British – politics, where a relatively small number of parties or positions need to be accounted for. Fourth – and also a factor frequently cited by media professionals – is the sense that religion is somehow inherently controversial. Those many different groups also represent an array of advocates, each of which may be offended by coverage they do not like. Most media people can cite telling examples of this.[41]

What this has meant until recently is that religion has been thought of as something that is "not worth the trouble." That is, given the challenges and the potential problems, why cover something that is of fading importance anyway (as the secularization-induced thinking goes)? In the US context, this has been further complicated by the First Amendment to the

Constitution that holds religion, government, and the press at arm's length from one another. This has had two kinds of effects. First, the separation of religion from government has been assumed to be a removal of religion from politics as well, and this has meant that the press could cover government and politics without giving undue attention to religion. Second, the separation has been "read" by many in the press and the media as a separation of religion from the press as well. This has all changed quite dramatically, of course, something I will return to in greater detail in Chapter 9.

In spite of some significant historical examples of religion entering into press coverage,[42] the mid-twentieth-century situation was one of relatively little journalistic treatment of religion beyond a kind of ritualistic attention to the activities of the major religious bodies. Meanwhile, change in the nature and scope of religion both domestically and internationally was beginning to challenge the easy compartmentalization of religion at the margins of press coverage. The singular event was the Islamic Revolution in Iran in 1979, which at the same time revealed that religion could still be central to unfolding global events and that religion needed to be seen in a much broader context than had been typical before that time. The events of 1979 unleashed a period of self-criticism in the media not seen again until after the September 11 attacks of 2001. In both cases, the message was that journalism and the press had been sleeping while important stories were developing under the heading "religion."[43]

Between 1979 and 2001, a number of developments on the domestic front also influenced the priority given to religion by the press. These are seen by some as all falling under the heading of the so-called "culture wars" based in religion or religious values. The signal event on "the right" was the emergence, demonstrated strikingly in the US General Election of 2004, but rooted in trends dating to the 1960s, of a vibrant new politically oriented type of religious conservatism, based on longstanding principles of American Fundamentalism and Pentecostalism, but with new face and new name – Evangelicalism – devoted to having a larger presence in public discourse. A thorough analysis is beyond the scope of our project here.[44] However, two very significant dimensions of this development are the role played in it by the contemporaneous emergence of the phenomenon of televangelism, and the more general sense among the leaders of this new movement that in order to have its desired outcomes it needed to be something that took the public sphere – and particularly the media – seriously.[45] Perhaps as a result, but more probably as a consequence of some characteristics of Evangelicalism and its relationship to culture,[46] this movement has, over the past twenty-five years, moved to the center of American public discourse, eschewing the political quietude that had typified Fundamentalism earlier in the century, and doing so largely in and through the media.

On the "left," American religion (and Western religion more generally) saw the emergence of new religious constructs and movements more typical of the kind of personal and autonomous sensibilities introduced earlier in our discussion of Roof and Wuthnow. A virtual explosion of interest in things religious and spiritual was demonstrated in such things as the trends in entertainment television we've already discussed. Additionally, a range of controversies began to roil the religious establishment from the left. Women became more active in seeking roles for themselves in the institutions of Catholicism and Protestantism. Ethnic-based ferment became prominent as well. And, the century ended with a growing controversy over the role of lesbian, gay, bisexual, and transgendered people in relation to membership and leadership positions in religion, and over the issue of "gay marriage," something that divided major Protestant bodies, and became an important political issue. This was brought to public attention in the autumn of 2004 when the liberal US Protestant denomination the United Church of Christ premièred a television advertisement stressing its openness and inclusion of sexual minorities and people of color. Deemed "too controversial," the ads were refused by two major US networks. The resulting furor brought questions of religious openness to the center of debates about American religion.[47]

These things became news, and the fact that popular culture also began picking up on increasing levels of religious and spiritual interest meant that the news media began increasingly to notice religion.[48] The range of ways religion appears in the news runs a wide spectrum. US general elections generally bring out a spate of stories on religion and politics. Both the 2000 and 2004 presidential races featured a great deal of coverage of the religious leanings of the candidates. In 2004, in particular, questions of religiosity and its relationship to politics came to the fore, with much commentary on the so-called "religion gap," wherein the more religious sectors of the electorate were thought to disproportionately favor conservative candidates, an issue we return to in Chapter 9. Since the September 11 attacks, international news in the US and Britain has focused more and more on trends and developments in what we used to quaintly think of as "world religions," particularly Islam, and on what has come to be called "ethno-religious conflict." Domestically, there are more and more stories relating to the increasing religious diversity resulting from immigration. Also at home, intra-religious battles continue to rage over social values and other "culture wars" issues. The ferment on "the left" also results in coverage, looking at new religious movements, so-called "New Age" practices, "cults," and of course religion and spirituality in popular culture.[49]

Beyond the formal news outlets, there are of course a wide range of sources of information and "news" of religion, particularly through the Internet and on the World Wide Web. Many of these sources are dedicated religion or spirituality "sites," but many others incidentally deal with religion along with other material.[50]

Religious broadcasting and televangelism

Televangelism has faded from public consciousness in recent years. From its emergence in the mid-1970s through most of the 1980s, religious broadcasting achieved a high-profile presence on the airwaves and in public discourse. Its luster faded a good deal as a result of a series of high-profile scandals in the late 1980s leading several important "TV preachers" to leave the air, and led to a general decline in public attention, though audience sizes may not have actually changed that much.

Today, televangelism is more of a "sleeper" in the media landscape, having settled into a comfortable, even significant place at the margins, in combination with a vibrant religious radio market and an emerging and significant Christian music industry. Religious television has actually continued to expand. By the year 2000, there were 245 commercial and fifteen noncommercial religious television stations on the air.[51] In radio, the situation is also one of expansion, with the most recent figures including over 800 stations *each* reporting that at least part of their day is formatted "Christian" or "religious," another 650 calling themselves "Gospel," and thirty-four even self-designating as "New Age."[52] In addition, several cable television channels are devoted to religion, including the (unofficial) Catholic Eternal Word Television Network, which claims 64 million subscribers on 2,275 cable systems in the US, the (also unofficial) National Jewish Television Network, claiming 13 million subscribers on 600 cable systems, and the Trinity Broadcasting Network, the last remaining of the original televangelism networks, claiming 46 million subscribers on 5,230 cable systems as well as 12.5 million direct-broadcast satellite subscribers. The actual viewing numbers for these services are much smaller, most likely a small fraction of claimed subscribers.[53] The Odyssey Channel, a much less controversial service, founded by more mainstream religious interests as an alternative to the televangelists, reached a peak subscriber base in the neighborhood of 28 million homes, but has since been folded into the Hallmark Channel. Pat Robertson's *700 Club* program, once the pre-eminent example of the form, has also undergone a metamorphosis. The Family Channel, which was the final version of the Christian Broadcasting Network founded around Robertson's show, was sold to ABC, and now exists as the ABC Family Channel, where the *Club* can still be seen, though largely no longer in prime-time.

Televangelism is not exclusively a US phenomenon, either. Major religious broadcasters have been actively engaged in exporting programming abroad, and domestically produced programs are available in most countries and regions of the world. One significant exception has been the UK, where while US-style televangelism has long been banned from the domestic airwaves, it has been available via satellite channels, and recent moves by conservative religious groups have attempted to open British terrestrial broadcasting and cable services to this kind of programming at least on radio.[54]

In terms of the media marketplace of religious symbols, then, televangelism and religious broadcasting more generally remain significant elements of the landscape. Their history and prominence over the last quarter-century means that they endure with a certain set of stereotypes, though, and are interpreted within historical frameworks that make them in some ways controversial. If we divide this turf in three parts: the continuing remnants of the televangelism of the 1970s and 1980s; the continuing vibrant religious radio market; and the emergent and growing Christian music industry and its broadcasting outlets, we can see that there continues to be a presence of this type of media in the landscape of media choice. It is important to note, though, that the history of these forms and formats leaves them with a certain legacy that is difficult to overcome. Whereas once it was thought that religious television could find a place in the mix of commercial television, but be a kind of "broadcasting with a difference," that hope has faded. The social and cultural prominence that televangelists sought during their rise has left the genre of religious broadcasting with continuing baggage. Pat Robertson once aspired to create within his Christian Broadcasting Network a schedule of programming that would compete on the same footing with the commercial forms.[55] That is no longer possible, or even necessary. Today, as we have begun to see, and will see in more definition in later chapters, the general commercial marketplace now provides a wider range of religious material than was the case when Robertson started his television ministries. The corner of the marketplace he now occupies is, ironically, as marginal as it was at the beginning, while material such as *Touched by an Angel* is more at the center. At the same time, though, the character and nature of much of this new religious/spiritual material is more significant of the changing face of American religion than those early televangelists would have been comfortable with.

Religious publishing

As we noted earlier, it is important that we understand the media marketplace as something broader than the electronic media alone. Dating back to the eighteenth century, as many historians have shown, a vibrant religious marketplace has existed that has cut across and combined a variety of media and entertainment forms.[56] The consistent medium throughout has been publishing, and as sociologist Anne Borden has demonstrated, it is within the evolution of religious publishing that we can see the trends of gradual expansion in terms of public accessibility, accountability, and purpose that typify much of the rest of the religious media world as well.[57] Borden's study of the central institution of this marketing industry, the Christian Booksellers' Association (CBA), provides interesting insights into the ways in which American religious movements developed in some ways in co-ordination with religious publishing and marketing.

The history of American publishing is deeply rooted in religious publishing.[58] Many major publishing companies began as religious publishers, and the key publishing centers, such as Philadelphia, originally emerged because of that market. The more recent history of religious publishing, however, shows a marked divergence between activities from the more traditional provision of Bibles, Sunday School materials, and tracts (still an important industry in dollar terms) and the activities of independent, or "para-church" publishing, of which the CBA is an example. Borden's history of the CBA demonstrates that, over the course of the twentieth century at least, its members and related organizations gradually began to integrate themselves into the broader media landscape of promotion, marketing, and the mass media. Their independence from the religious establishment became an important marker, but at the same time placed them to take advantage of emerging anti-institutional trends in American religion, at least of the conservative-Christian or Evangelical varieties.

The result has been the emergence of the CBA over the past decades as the central marketplace of religious publishing and a much wider range of media products as well.[59] The significant thing about the industry for our considerations here is its spread and ubiquity. From a relatively small and marginal player on the media landscape, it has grown to a major economic and media force, with CBA-related bookstores now found in all major cities, sitting alongside more conventional "secular" outlets in shopping malls across the country. This means that the books and other resources produced by CBA members are more and more accessible, and have become more and more a commonplace part of the religious and cultural landscape. This "mainstreaming" is similar to that contemplated by religious broadcasting during its rise to prominence.[60]

The CBA and similar activities exist alongside the more "secular" media marketplace, and this has led to a good deal of discussion about such things as the distinct "best-seller lists" that exist for secular and religious publishing. One of the phenomena in this realm has been the *Left Behind* series of books, authored by Tim LeHaye and Jerry Jenkins.[61] Like many other Christian books, these have sold millions of copies, but have found their place on the more marginal "religious" as opposed to "secular" best-seller lists, something that rankles many in the religious world. A film based on these novels failed at the box office, but was an example of attempts to "cross over" between the religious and secular media markets, a project that may face serious obstacles.[62] It serves as an example, though, of the development of a broader religious media market, one that in areas such as cross-promotion resembles the more secular media world.

Perhaps the most significant sector of religious publishing is the religious magazine market. Like book publishing, magazine publishing has diverged from an earlier era where most such journals were directly related to religious groups or denominations, to a situation today where a large and vibrant field of hundreds of independent religious and spiritual publications are available both through religious and secular outlets. The largest-circulation of these, *Christianity Today*, boasts a readership of 330,000.[63] Founded originally as an alternative to the dominant religious publications of the mid-twentieth century, *Christian Century* and *Christianity and Crisis*,[64] by the end of the century this journal had come to prominence as the most widely read such publication, paralleling the growth in independent Evangelicalism, to which it directs itself.[65]

Magazine publishing provides, however, a range of materials across a wide range of interests. Alongside such journals as *Christianity Today* exist a large number of magazines published by, or oriented toward, new religious movements, existing marginal movements, New Age practices of various kinds, and everything in between.

Entertainment media

We've already seen how the media marketplace can be said to have become more religious or spiritual in recent years. A large number of programs both on the major network schedules and within the cable and direct-broadcast satellite industries now regularly deal with religious and spiritual themes and values. It is not my purpose here to establish a set of norms or definitions whereby such material might or might not be *authentically* religious or spiritual, even though that might be a project of some interest. My reluctance is rooted in one of the goals of this project – to lay the groundwork for hearing directly from audiences for this material. To begin with inductive categories of what is or is not religious or spiritual would defeat part of that purpose.

At the same time, though, questions of the definition of what is or is not religious or spiritual in media are important ones, but not because they help us somehow understand the legitimacy or significance of the symbols and values we see there. Rather, they become important ways of defining the cultural landscape in the media, helping us map the cultural environment and our place in it. In the televangelism era, for example, it became clear that a good deal of what was important or salient for supporters of those programs was not discrete elements of the content and what they might learn or be inspired by there, but that the programs represented a kind of cultural space in the media environment with which those supporters were comfortable. As my study of the *700 Club* audience pointed out, the value of that program for its viewers was largely symbolic – representing the presence or even ascendancy of the Evangelical worldview in the important context of the media.[66]

More recent audience research dealing with changing conceptions of home and family in the media era found that a key element or framework of meaning-making in that context is a kind of mapping the self into the cultural context of the media by means of received public scripts that define various programs and media practices in terms of their assumed cultural and social value and significance.[67] In our consideration of televangelism and its aspirations to the "mainstream," we saw exactly this kind of consideration, one that also underlies such cultural-definitional projects as the distinctions between "Christian" and "mainstream" music. The question of which is which is not a simple, straightforward, or tacit one.

Instead, a good deal of negotiation and construction takes place around these questions. While it might seem to make sense for producers of religious material to wish to enter the mainstream, it is clear that a set of concessions make it difficult for them to do so, and very few, if any, examples of successful "crossing over" exist.[68] Instead, there is a kind of reflexive project that intends to achieve such outcomes, and that does so by highlighting the religious origins of religious material. This self-conscious intention becomes ultimately self-defeating, however. As Heather Hendershot has shown in her history of Evangelical cinema in *Shaking the World for Jesus*, cinema or Christian music that intend to cross over face skepticism from believers and secular audiences alike. All media audiences understand the basics of media production well enough to know religious media when they see it. While the believers might support it for the sake of it being there – part of the media mix – they at the same time understand very well that it can probably not compete. For nonbelievers, the signals and signs that mark it as "different" also will likely turn them off.[69]

If we can draw a fairly bright line between the media produced out of religious motivations and that which is more purely "secular," then we might describe some of the media that are responding to new trends in religious and spiritual interest as "crossing over" from the secular side, something that may well be more successful than going the other direction. The success of *Touched*, and other similar shows dealing with spirituality, including *Angel* and *Promised Land*, had much of the television production community looking for similar properties to produce by the 1997 television season.[70] Also that year, an entirely new network of stations was announced that had already secured the rerun rights for *Touched*. Dubbed the PAX network, it was based on a network of seventy-three television stations owned by its founder, Bud Paxon. The idea, according to Paxon, was to found a network based on "wholesome, feel good programming."[71]

By the 2003 season, the PAX network was arguably an economic, if not a cultural, success, having found a place in markets beyond its core through cable television, and continuing to carry Paxon's target mix of programming genres.

Beyond ITV, there exist a number of cable television channels that verge toward similar kinds of programming. The Hallmark Channel, for example, evolved through a relationship with the more mainline Christian-oriented Odyssey network, and the Oxygen and Lifetime networks now carry a good deal of programming that resembles what Heather Hendershot has identified as the ideal programming for "crossing over" between the Christian and secular markets[72] as well as a good representation of therapeutic and even generically "spiritual" programming.

At the same time, the secular or commercial media world also continues to provide material that is much more self-evidently "religious." There has been a consistent output from Hollywood for years, dating to the "bathrobe drama" days of the *Ten Commandments* and *The Robe*, and stretching through significant and critically acclaimed films as disparate as Robert Duvall's 1997 *Apostle*, Kevin Smith's 1999 effort *Dogma*, and Brian Dannelly's 2004 film *Saved*. No film in recent history, though, has achieved the profile of the 2004 film *The Passion of the Christ*, produced and directed by Mel Gibson. *The Passion* unleashed a storm of public, religious, and scholarly commentary.[73] As a marker in the long-term negotiation of relationships between "religion" and "the media," this film stands out. It was produced by a mainstream "star," with a Hollywood blockbuster-sized budget and promotion effort, and with the promise of mainstream production values and star power. At the same time, Gibson saw to it that the film also represented an incursion of "religion" onto the turf of "secular film." He devoted extensive efforts to mobilize millions of Evangelical and Catholic viewers for the film's opening week, ensuring a buzz that carried it into the top-ten initial grossing films of all time. As a film that was self-consciously rooted in conservative, even medieval, conceptions of Catholic piety, it also created important fissures within Catholicism and beyond Catholicism, and was the justifiable target of questions about its position on the age-old question of Jewish guilt for the crucifixion.

There is much more that could be said about the film, but I'll confine myself to two points, leaving the rest to other efforts and projects. First, the film is an example of a very particular "effect" of media (in this case, film) on religion. Much as the *Ten Commandments*' florid visualizations of the Exodus story came to be the visual memory of those events for generations of Christians and Jews, so will *The Passion*'s representation of the passion become the standard visual memory for generations from here on out. Second, this first effect illustrates the extent to which artifacts in the media sphere such as this film have largely become definitive of religious symbolization and representation for the whole culture. In the ongoing negotiation of "turf" between material that is "religiously originated" and that which is "secular," *The Passion* demonstrates that the power is all on the latter side of the ledger. This is particularly and logically so, when we remember that the issue is the definition of terms for the whole culture, and the role that religions may or may not be able to play in the culture.

In sum, then, the media landscape is one that carries within it a wide range of symbolic material relevant to issues of religion and spirituality. This landscape is further defined by history, by aesthetic and religious tradition, and by evolving taste cultures and audience interests. As they encounter the media in their lives, they do not look at a horizontal inventory of symbols so much as they engage in an ongoing conversation with themselves, and with their culture, over the sources, aspirations, and claims of cultural resources, including the media. It is against this complex landscape that evolving religious and spiritual sensibilities today must define themselves and find cultural purchase.

Ways of looking at religion and media

In Chapter 1, we reviewed some key works dealing with religion and media with an eye to understanding where the scholarly study of religion and media is rooted and where it may be going. A set of "lay" or "received" ideas about the relationship between religion and media under-lies these scholarly approaches as well as the broader range of more public and less scholarly theories. I will review some of the most prominent of these briefly here, so as to make clear how the approach we will take in the next chapters differs from them. The point is not to discount these wholesale. Some of them are, in fact, very helpful ways of understanding things. Instead, the point is to differentiate the culturalist/ethnographic approach we will take on from these others.

Archetypes. Theories based on archetypes exist in a number of disciplines from art history to psychology. The underlying idea here is that there exist in the social, cultural, and psychological spheres a set of forms or "archetypes" on which other forms are based. In media studies, structuralist and psychological theories such as those of Lacan and Jung have been variously appropriated to the task of understanding cultural symbolism and media texts. The project is one of uncovering within the media artifacts we have available to us these more fundamental forms.[74] Gregor Goethals's analyses of religious television follow a similar, formalist direction, though less self-consciously rooted in archetypal theory *per se*.[75]

A wider range of critiques of religion in the media also take the approach of looking at underlying forms as a way of analyzing texts and practices. Such formal approaches to cultural analysis make some sense and have some value. It is important, at the same time, to understand that such approaches can become formal*ist*. By this distinction, I mean to say that archetypal or formal approaches become problematic in some ways if they verge from mere formal analysis as description to formal analysis as a route to *legitimating* or *de-legitimating* cultural artifacts. That is, formal or archetypal analysis can be used to say that a certain artifact or text or practice is or is not *authentic* or therefore *legitimate*. This is of a piece with the so-called "Leavisite" tradition in cultural studies, now criticized for its limited utility in understanding or accounting for culture as lived, experienced, and constructed. Much of what we have seen in the evolving shape of American religious experience would lead us to suspect that many people today would question the notion of "legitimate" religious forms or religious expression, making a formalist analysis problematic.

Representational Realism. There is a longstanding tradition of debate over the nature of media artifacts being "real" or "not real." Authenticity and legitimacy are often attributed to cultural products in relation to their "realism." Much clerical critique of media treatments of religion is based on the assumption that such treatments, to be authentic or helpful, must be representational and be "realistic" in order to actually promote religion in positive ways.[76]

An interesting dimension of the debates over Mel Gibson's *The Passion of the Christ* in 2004 was this question of realism. Much of the clerical and lay discourse about the meaning and significance of the film rested on its super-realistic violence. Many viewers took it as a given that this level of violent representation was by its very nature realistic.[77] Representational-realist sensibilities also carry with them a certain class-taste bias as well, being thought of by cultural elites as naïve or vernacular as over against more sophisticated, cultivated tastes.[78]

Instrumentalism. A great deal of commentary and criticism on the nature and effects of the media rely on an assumption of the instrumental efficacy of the media. Fears of the power of media to affect values and spirituality are often connected with the sense that the media are instruments that we encounter and understand primarily in terms of their ability to affect us or affect others. A good deal of religiously based media criticism rests on this notion.

The so-called "media literacy" movement, for example, much of which is rooted in religious sensibilities, assumes that media audience practice should be understood as a project of encountering, interpreting, and ultimately contesting much of what is present in the media. The underlying model of media consumption is one that sees the media as instruments or artifacts that are the sources of cultural action. The momentum is with the media, and audiences must respond or face a kind of subjugation. Conservative critiques of the "anti-religion" of the media agree, seeing a darker, more dangerous project there.[79] In the instrumentalist view, the media are to be understood primarily for their potential to affect and influence audiences, institutions, values, or other sectors of the culture, of which religion is a central one. In the classic study of late-century social life, *Habits of the Heart*, the authors attribute just this sort of influence to the media and popular culture.[80]

Over against instrumentalism stands James Carey's influential essay in which he argues against the instrumentalist "transmission" view of media and for a more culturally articulated "ritual" view. In contrast to an instrumentalist concern with extension across space and time, Carey argued, the ritual view is concerned with communication that "draws persons together in fellowship and commonality."[81]

Totalism/Universalism. A related sensibility looks at media as universals rather than as particulars. Consistent with the received view of the media from the last century, this approach assumes that the media need to be seen not only in terms of their influences, but also as more or less universal in appeal, approach, and effect. This is, of course, consistent with the "mass media" era's understandings of media as large, general, and consensual, rather than the more contemporary view of the media as more diverse, partial, and particular.[82] This is, of course, a case of modernist vs postmodernist cultural understandings. Postmodernism derives a good deal of its interpretive force from its critique of modernism's assumptions regarding cultural universals.[83] It is thought to make little sense today to consider culture in such large terms, when so much of the cultural and interpretive action seems to be taking place in specific communities, by specific cultural and demographic groups and in specific contexts.

Transformationism. The school of thought we called "medium theory" in the first chapter, that associated with McLuhan and the "Toronto School," shares with some other significant observers of the media age the idea that there is within media technology a set of implications for the way we see, hear, and make meanings. McLuhan most famously suggested that the technologies of the media themselves have fundamentally changed the way consciousness is formed by changing the nature of perception.[84] Jacques Ellul saw the media – along with other modern technologies – assuming central, definitive roles in society through a process whereby they have come to regulate the nature of social experience, a view he shares with many modern social critics.[85] Walter Ong connects electronic media with fundamental changes in the way "the word" is understood and shared in modernity.[86]

An impressive and substantive recent collection edited by Hent deVries and Samuel Weber[87] places itself among a number of these perspectives, but most directly in relation to transformationist ideas. While carefully and rightly critiquing some of McLuhan-based "medium theory," the purpose of the collection nonetheless focuses on an assumed central challenge of the media to religion: their role in redefining or transforming the nature of transcendent knowledge. In his introduction, for example, deVries concentrates almost entirely on an issue that also seems to concern many of the others in the collection: the idea that media can, through the manipulations of things like "special effects," radically alter the meaning of religious revelation or insight, specifically in relation to the meaning of "miracles." Weber's essay focuses on the structuration of media experience, on notions of ritual and the relationship of repetition to understandings of truth and the possibility that the media may, in some implicit, yet fundamental, way, be involved in the "return of the religious."[88]

In all of these cases, there is a tendency to invest entirely too much in implicit and assumed characteristics of the media and too little in the wider social and economic contexts within which the media function.[89] Technological determinism has long been discouraged in academic theory-building, and many of those criticisms are relevant when looking at how media technology might be affecting "religion" as well.

Dualism. In contrast to the "transformationist" school, there has also been a tendency for some commentary on religion and media to have within it an implicit dualism dividing the "sacred" from the "secular," and, by implication, dividing "religion" from "the (secular) media" at the same stroke. This has been one of the easy assumptions underlying the secular press's approach to religion, discussed earlier. It has also been at the root of the criticism leveled at the media from critics in the religious world. A good deal of the angst that flows from religious institutions when they are under press scrutiny is based on a sense that the world represented by religion and that represented by the media are – or should be – kept distinct. It has deeper roots, though, going back to Durkheim, who originally theorized a sacred/profane divide, and later social theorists who too quickly connected the sacred with authentic or traditional culture and the profane with the instrumental world of commerce, economy, politics, and social life.[90]

Within mass communication and media studies, there has been a consistent tendency to hold to a separation between those messages and practices of reception that might be construed as "religious" and those which are more "secular" or material in orientation. Recent works on media ritual, for example, have been at pains to keep this distinction in mind.[91] In his influential book, *Television Culture*, John Fiske drew the definition rather starkly, saying that the whole of his analysis on media culture and its audiences should be understood as fundamentally *secular*.[92]

Formalism. There has also been an implicit formalism in some work at the boundary between religion and the media. Daniel Dayan and Elihu Katz's work on "media events,"[93] which we will consider in more detail in Chapter 9, exhibits a tendency to treat religion's presence in public rituals of social meaning by its *absence*. Religion contributes certain forms to the ceremonies, and in keeping with some approaches to the study of "civil religion," Dayan and Katz conceive of these as denatured variations, evoking their original, but lacking their essence. Nick Couldry, in his work on media ritual (also to be discussed in more detail in Chapter 9), also carries this sense of religion's formal "presence by absence."[94]

A more systematic recent example of a formal analysis is Günter Thomas's work on media ritual in the context of television. In a scholarly inquiry that combines a formal analysis with a kind of "transformationism," Thomas seeks to find a standpoint in analysis of media and religion that addresses both the scholarly and public-discursive contexts. Rooted in Luhmann's complex ideas about the nature of contemporary social systems, Thomas's approach begins with the assumption that television is one of society's "functional sub-systems," and its analysis is central to understanding contemporary culture. Taking the "anthropological" approach of looking within the forms of television for practices that evoke, relate to, or function as religious or quasi-religious, he concludes that, "within the stream of television, forms of communication emerge that bear a striking resemblance to well-known religious forms."[95]

Essentialism. In an ironic twist, several of these notions of media and religion share in common the idea of essentialism. That is, they assume that it is possible or desirable to think of there being a category of symbols, artifacts, or practices that we can characterize as *essentially* "religious," "spiritual," or "sacred." The formalist, transformationist, and archetypal projects discussed above, for example – in keeping with the dualist assumption just discussed – assume that it is important to be able to separate things in the cultural realm that are *legitimately religious* from things which are not. This serves different purposes for different critics. For religious or academic authorities, it allows for a position of critique of media in terms of the success or failure of media to authentically convey or serve religion. For media studies scholars who wish to steer clear of the complexities and interstices of religion, it allows religion to be defined "outside" the realm of that which is under study. It can be held to the side, where it will not unnecessarily complicate things, or it can be thought of as beyond the bounds of legitimate scholarly inquiry.

Media and the "new religion scholarship"

The fundamental problem that each of the foregoing approaches share is that they fail to contemplate the *convergence* of religion and the media in the spaces of social practice. As we've seen, it is no longer as relevant to think of the media in large, "mass," or totalizing terms. The media are changing, becoming more diverse, atomized, specialized, targeted, and interactive. This raises serious questions about notions that assume a kind of monopolistic media against which religion must struggle. More importantly, trends in religion now have us questioning whether there *is* such a struggle, anyway.

A good deal of what we've been considering about religious change results from a change in the way religion is *studied* as much as the ways it is *thought about*. This "paradigm shift" in religion scholarship shares much in common with the paradigm shifts in media scholarship we've considered. What we know about these two fields begins to lay out some expectations about what we might find as we delve into meaning-making in the media age in the following chapters. Before we move on, we should look at this new religion scholarship and some of its implications in more detail. In short, there is much in the field of religious studies that can be seen to predict an intriguing, if not substantive, role for the media in the contemporary religious landscape and a similarly provocative role for religion in the media landscape.

Our explorations here are provoked by religious change that has become increasingly obvious to religion scholarship, which is itself undergoing great change. Over recent years, a range of studies of contemporary religion have begun to raise serious questions about the whole way scholarly and lay discourse has thought about religion and spirituality. A leading scholar, Catherine Albanese, has described this change in terms of a shift in understanding religion as a totalizing, or universalizing, reality to an understanding of religion in its multiple forms and locations – from "religion," to "religions."[96]

The paradigm shift here has been most systematically described by R. Stephen Warner in an article that has come to be considered paradigmatic in itself.[97] Warner describes the new religion scholarship as influenced by changes in the nature of religious practice, recognizing a fundamental change in the way we think about religion.

> The conventional social science wisdom is rooted in a paradigm that conceived religion, like politics, to be a property of the whole society, such that the institutionalized separation of state and church in modern society offered religion only two alternatives: either religious values would become increasingly generalized so that they could remain the property of the whole, increasingly pluralistic, society, or, if they remained resolutely particularistic, they would devolve to an inconsequential private sphere. The former alternative was theorized by Talcott Parsons; the latter by Peter Berger. We shall see below that religion in the United States has typically expressed not the culture of the society as a whole but the subcultures of its many constituents; therefore, that it should not be thought of as either the Parsonian conscience of the whole or the Bergerian refuge of the periphery, but as the vital expression of groups.[98]

Thus, what we are seeing in this changing religious landscape is a sensibility that radically contests the received notion that the action in religion is at the level of the whole society or the whole culture. Beginning with the assumption that it is, various versions of secularization theory have looked at religion's retreat to the margins and to the particulars, and have seen its overall decline. Warner's analysis, and the work of most of the "new paradigm," holds that religion instead remains vibrant, though in a radically changed form. It remains "vital," at the same time that its form, location, and practices of meaning-making no longer occupy the traditional spaces. Along with other observers, Warner notes that this type of religion has deep roots in the American context. He notes that "With appropriate complications and qualifications, religion in the United States is and has long been (a) disestablished, (b) culturally pluralistic, (c) structurally adaptable, and (d) empowering."[99] These characteristics define the new religion we have been talking about.

Its connection to the project of the self, which we have seen to be fundamental to contemporary social experience and fundamentally linked to media culture, is seen by Wade Clark Roof, another proponent of the new paradigm, to be one of the most basic logics of this new religious sensibility. The implication for religious or spiritual questing is profound in that focusing on the self necessarily de-emphasizes the role of institutional or clerical authority and at the same time sees the project as one that is open to more or less constant revision.

> A psychological culture encourages definition of the self as open-ended and revisable, and hence a self capable of transcending organizational boundaries and inherited identities. In this respect, even if the psychology within many small groups is overly expansive and potentially misleading in its extreme, such groups will serve an important function for their participants, assisting them in reorganizing their lives and assuring them that they can start over. It is a pattern as old as the United States itself, and one Americans still cherish.[100]

This clearly has the effect of disconnecting the individual from her roots in religion in a rather profound and far-reaching way. In Warner's terms, the shift is from thinking of religion as something that is "ascribed" to thinking of it as something that one "achieves."[101] And, more importantly for our considerations here, it suggests that the self's religious or spiritual project is or can be a more or less constant quest for new insights and resources, and new ways of conceiving of the self in religious or spiritual ways. Consistent with Roof, we can conceive of religious identity as that particular way the self chooses to think of itself in religious or spiritual terms. The other "side" of this sensibility, of course, is its necessary relationship to received symbols, ideas, and authorities. They are simply less important to the quest than would have been the case in the past. And, Warner suggests, significantly, that there is a fundamental level of satisfaction or salience that accompanies this new model of religion.

> What the new religious voluntarism amounts to is a centrifugal process, sorting elemental qualities on the basis of which identities are constructed . . . the breakdown of ascriptive ties to religion can enhance, rather than reduce, the elemental nature that believers attribute to their experiences. From this point of view, social ascription that denies one's true being is seen as arbitrary, while a new-found religion is self-affirming.[102]

But what does this "new volunteerism," what Roof and Wuthnow would call the "seeking" sensibility, look like in actual practice? Both Warner and Roof make the point that, while individual adherents may well see the process as entirely self-generating and self-orienting, it in fact rests on a structure of deep histories of received and socially understood categories of religious experience. An individual's socialization or enculturation to religious practice (remembering what we said in the last chapter about interactionist theories) depends on a connection to culturally specific symbols, resources, practices, and relationships. The difference is in how he *negotiates* his relationships to these things. Does he see them to be *determinative* of his beliefs and actions, or does he consider them to be *resources* to his own construction of meaning and identity? In all of this, Roof sees an interesting dialectic in play on the part of what he calls "the protean self," between the desire to be "fluid" and to be "grounded" at the same time.

> In a highly subjective religious culture, people move back and forth psychologically across what many regard as porous, somewhat artificial, boundaries, wanting at times a stable anchor, and open at other times to more expansive possibilities . . . reminding us of Robert Jay Lifton's comment about the protean self wanting to be both fluid and grounded at the same time, however tenuous that possibility.[103]

The practice that ensues is of particular interest to our considerations here because it places the individual and her practices of cultural consumption at the center of the making of her religious self. Without the firm categories and boundaries of received religion, she feels freed to move beyond them into a cultural/symbolic marketplace increasingly filled with resources relevant to her quest. How she encounters that marketplace and the negotiations through which she brings those resources into her sense of her religious or spiritual "self" (but – as noted above – without being able to fully move beyond received tradition) is the central question. As Roof sees it,

It is the general situation of a person recognizing how deeply embedded he or she may be within a tradition, yet confronting the fact that the inner life may not be fully formed or contained by tradition as received, and that by pulling together from other sources, often resources neglected from within one's own tradition, new and enriched meanings are possible. The believer is thrust into the situation, of the *bricoleur*, who in cobbling together from a variety of imageries, doctrines, symbols, texts, moral codes, and spiritual disciplines finds new religious meaning and in so doing often discovers a nuance, an insight, an angle of vision that is revitalizing in its creativity.[104]

This introduces another dimension to the "quest," and one that is significant to our project here. That is the sense that accompanies these "quests," that there are resources or insights available that may well have been repressed by received tradition. To the extent that these resources might be more available outside those boundaries, or even within the popular-cultural marketplace, gives the project of seeking, understanding, and integrating things from a variety of sources and contexts additionally satisfying. Elsewhere, I have discussed the range of these "repressed modes" of religious experience, suggesting a list that includes *"the visual," the body, objects, ritual, music, and "experience" itself.*[105] There is a wide range of symbolic and other resources available in the media sphere that invoke these modes of experience. For the individual quest that sees itself moving beyond received traditions that may have repressed or underemphasized one or more of these modes, finding cultural resources to right that wrong introduces another level of vitality to that quest.

We need to keep in mind, at the same time, that whatever resources are encountered in the mediated public sphere, they themselves have histories, histories that are often rooted in religious traditions of a variety of kinds. Neither the project, nor its outcome, should be seen as something entirely novel. As Roof cautions us,

the spiritual dynamics of the self are extraordinarily complex. It is even more complex still. For despite all that we have said about spirituality as an individual matter, it involves meanings, symbols, practices, and processes born out of, and shaped by, communal life and the confrontations of modernity and religious tradition; and for this reason, spirituality cannot be thought of simply as a matter of individual choice.[106]

What is novel, though, is the way each individual brings together resources into her own identity, into what I call her "plausible narrative of the self." We will get to this in more detail in the next chapter, but it is important for us to keep straight the difference between the received discourses and resources, the individual's sense of the novelty and uniqueness of her own narratives and constructions growing out of those resources, the role that mediated "secular" contexts may play in making those resources available to her, and the outcome, which will necessarily involve a narrative of self that is a construction involving all of these dimensions.

What the media can do

We have painted a picture of the media context's relationship to this questing that sees the media acting as a kind of "symbolic inventory" of resources available to the quest for the religious or spiritual self in late modernity. As we've seen, there is reason to suspect that what we once thought of as entirely "secular" media have the capacity to provide such resources, and in fact increasingly do. There has been a good deal of concern expressed about certain of these mediated texts and messages, and their potential impact on the religious lives or interests of audiences young and old.[107] In general, these criticisms assume a different role for media in religious lives than we've been developing here. As I've said, such criticisms tend to think of the media instrumentally, and their relationship to religion/spirituality in terms of the effects of media on these things.

As we've seen, there is reason to begin to think of things differently. Against the notion of instrumentalism, for example, there is the idea that the media may well form part of the cultural surround within which we negotiate our religious selves today, and that they may, further, provide important symbolic resources to those negotiations. Critiques that attempt to evaluate religiously or spiritually significant content by means of its legitimacy according to received essentialist or archetypal categories overlook the way that emerging religious questing contests the whole notion of received authority. The idea that the media and their messages should be looked at in terms of large or universal themes and categories is also increasingly problematic, as the emerging religious sensibility tends to focus on the vitality of individualized and localized experience. Dualistic understandings of religion and media are also problematic for two reasons. First, religiously motivated seekers or questers are unlikely to see such categories as determinative of action, as they derive from the same sorts of received authority that they increasingly question. Second, as we've seen, there is much reason to expect that the content of what was once thought of as "secular" media is now increasingly "religious." The line is thus more and more a blurry one.

The development of this new "religious/symbolic marketplace" in the media and its relationship to emerging religious sensibilities has gone on largely "under the radar" of religious and spiritual institutions and authorities. There are a number of reasons for this, but one of the most intriguing has to do with the nature and role of the religious establishment during the last century. At mid-century, as we've noted (and this situation was most straightforward in the case of broadcasting), the established religions and the established media existed in a convenient relationship whereby the media accepted responsibility for providing access and coverage for religious programming of the religious establishment.[108]

This programming was by definition of a certain kind. It fit with the self-understanding of religion as a central, stable, and significant force on the cultural landscape. The same went for the kind of journalistic treatment of religion thought to be most appropriate, and the sorts of religious material that would appear in the other media as well. Appropriate media, it was thought, were that which supported the highest aspirations and ideals of religion in late modernity. These ideals were consistent with more general notions about cultural hierarchy among the educational and cultural establishment. Just as educational leaders in Britain and the US had long held to the view that "high art" could be uplifting, inspirational, and positive, while "low," or "popular," art ran the risk of at least wasting time if not actually misleading people morally, the religious establishment at mid-century took the same view of the relationship of art (and culture generally) to religion.

Art historian Sally Promey has shown a fundamental link between the mass-culture debates of the academy familiar to media scholars and the thought of influential leaders in the neo-orthodox establishment that dominated the Protestant theological academy for much of the twentieth century. The central figure was the theologian Paul Tillich who, according to Promey, promoted ideas about elite culture and mass culture derived from the influential "Frankfurt School" and its ideas about ideological domination by the mass media.[109] In Tillich's view, only "high art" should be thought of as playing a normative role in religious or spiritual exploration. The "low art" of the mass media was to be avoided. As with the Frankfurt School, Tillich's critique rested on two notions: that the profane art of the masses – of which mass media were the embodiment – was at least a distraction, if not actually misleading to true faith, and that the mass media were at the center of a "mass culture" that always had the capacity for ideological domination and would by its nature verge toward fascism, as it had in Europe before the Second World War.[110] This kind of thinking about media coincided with a general tendency in the academy (theological as well as secular) to eschew, even denigrate, "popular" or "low" culture as imperfect, immature, and trivial to true enlightenment.

It goes without saying that the kind of religious sensibility and religious practice envisioned by Tillich and his colleagues is very different from the emerging religious sensibility we've been discussing. The new religious volunteerism (to use Warner's term) sees itself as fully capable of separating the religious wheat from the religious chaff, and further would want to explore a wide range of cultural resources, hoping to find nuggets of authenticity or truth therein. Further, where the older, received understandings of religious enlightenment thought of it as a practice that would always on some level separate itself from the culture, the seekers of the new volunteerism seem to be always on a quest for enlightenment and will simply get it where they can, in popular culture or not, according to the logic of their own quest for self.

The seeming solipsism of this is troubling for many observers. In *Habits of the Heart*,[111] Robert Bellah and his colleagues were among the first to identify this seeking or questing at the center of religious/spiritual identity for some. Yet, they expressed strong reservations about the phenomenon, worrying that such individualized practice would fail to deliver a wholesome religious worldview; that it would amount to a kind of narcissism. Warner addressed this concern, noting,

> The authors of *Habits of the Heart* . . . have most eloquently lamented these individualistic trends. Although they recognize that Americans, no matter how individualistic, seek out like-minded others, they fear that the resulting associations are only "lifestyle enclaves," a term they intend to connote shallowness and mutual narcissism . . . "there is a givenness about the community and the tradition. They are not normally a matter of individual choice. I do not wish to dismiss the concerns of Bellah and his colleagues, but there is considerable evidence that religious switchers are morally serious."[112]

Instead of a situation where religious questing is to be feared for its potential to lead individual seekers toward isolation and irrelevance, Warner suggests that there is much in the record of the new religion scholarship that sees individuals engaging in practices which remake tradition, understanding, and ultimately identity. And, it is our task here to try to understand how these practices take place in the context of media culture.

Seeking through the media

While there is good reason to believe that the emerging religious sensibility we have been calling "seeking" will be more attuned to culture, and thus to the media, than would have been the case in earlier eras, we probably should at the same time not expect this to be a monolithic or monotonic phenomenon. The argument I've been making is in part an argument that all of contemporary religious practice could be expected to take on aspects of a seeking sensibility, particularly as regards its relationship to cultural materials available in the media. At the same time, though, we should expect there to be differences between individuals and interpretive communities within the whole field, defined by social and religious demographics as well as by different life trajectories and histories.

Roof provides a taxonomy of religious sensibilities he has identified within the boomer generation, for example, and we might begin to move to the next step in analysis by considering how these various categories might be positioned *vis-à-vis* religious history, religious practice, religious and social experience, orientation toward religious tradition and authority, and religion/spirituality in media culture. We will look at each in turn.

Born-Again Christians. Roof found within the boom generation a significant subset who identify themselves religiously primarily through their having had an experience of personal salvation. This has long and deep roots in American religious culture, of course, but the label "born again" came to be significant as a reflexive label in the latter part of the twentieth century, coinciding with the rise of Evangelicalism. As Roof notes, this is a "highly personal" type of faith, and in that sense shares much in common with the overall trend toward individualism in matters of faith. For many "born agains," membership or participation in conventional churches is less important than their experience of faith. "Where" is less important to them than "what." This means that people who think of themselves in this way might readily be members of even denominationally related congregations.

As Roof notes, while this sensibility can be traced to old-line Fundamentalism, it today shares much more in common with the "introverted self" and reflexive "self-oriented" dynamic as articulated in the broader American culture. They exhibit greater reflexivity than was the case with conservative religion before the boom generation came along. The "typical" churches of this group – the "seeker" or "apostolic" churches – are more "dialogical" than was the case with Fundamentalism.[113]

What kind of relationship to media might we expect from this group? It can be argued that, as a movement, Evangelicalism has historically been more media-oriented than either Catholicism or Mainline Protestantism as we have noted. For the Evangelical movement, this has derived from a theology that focuses on the act of evangelism or "sharing the word" and sees modern media of communication as logical tools for this process.[114] The neo-orthodox critique of media culture discussed earlier, as well as establishment ideas in general, had traditionally recognized this tendency, and has found it convenient to be able to conflate its ideas about the immature and unsophisticated nature of popular culture with Evangelicalism's use of it.[115] For Evangelicals "in the pew" as it were, we might expect there to be a greater affinity to mediated imagery as a result, though with an important twist. Evangelicalism in general has been typified by sociologists for its rootedness in a kind of "strictness."[116] As Heather Hendershot and Lynn Schofield Clark have shown in their analyses of Evangelicals and the media in the context of "quest" culture, a sense of judgment about culture and media artifacts, rooted in the legacy of "strictness," may be the important factor.[117]

This would lead us to expect relations to media among this cohort to be complex. On the one hand, there would be a general acceptance of the notion that media can be an appropriate context for religion and spirituality. There would be a class-taste dimension to this, as well. Traditionally, Evangelicalism has tended, demographically, to be a lower-class phenomenon (though this has changed in recent years). At the same time, though, Evangelicals would be more likely than others to be critical of the values present in "secular media," and more likely to be suspicious of the idea that non-Christian media might be an appropriate place to look for religious or spiritual insight.

Mainstream Believers. According to Roof, this group is most centrally defined by the fact that they continue to identify with the Mainline or "Oldline" faith groups that were at the center of the religious landscape at the mid-point of the last century. They tend to think of themselves *as* "mainstream."[118] Continuity in religious history is important to them, with religion important as a "shared tradition." Unlike the "born-agains," *where* they are is more important than *what* they are. They often identify their religion with family heritage, and like their worship traditional. Importantly, Roof contends that they often identify themselves by "negative reference." That is, they are *not* "born again."

Tolerance is also an important value for this group, a "mainstream" that can transcend traditional barriers, and include Jews, Catholics, Protestants, and the "new" immigrant religions such as Buddhism and Islam. Distinctions are less important to them, and they are more likely than "born-agains" to look across faith boundaries for cultural resources. As with others, the "self" is an important project here, and they tend to agree with others that the traditional resources of religious institutions are inadequate to the task of the religious self. They tend to be unfamiliar with religious symbolism and language, particularly the Protestants, and see their position as one of "practical reason and responsibility." This is in contrast (in their view) to the extremes of "born-agains" and "traditionalists" (who we will get to presently) who they see as too inflexible and dogmatic, and the "metaphysical seekers," who they see to be "too flaky" or indifferent to religious values.[119]

Roof describes mainstreamers as "straddling," thinking of Jesus as a savior and a teacher, redeemer, and moral teacher. They represent an interesting contrast with the "born-agains," according to Roof. Whereas "born-agains"

> have a personal language, but must "work at" connecting with a viable cultural and religious past, mainstreamers search for a fresh vocabulary but must "work at" distancing themselves from either an

Evangelical past or even the older cultural or religious establishment in which many of them grew up.[120]

There are several things we might predict about how this group would relate to media culture. First, they are the group that is most linked, theologically, to the neo-orthodox "mass-culture" critique discussed earlier. The religious context with which they identify, then, has traditionally been skeptical of the value and substance of the media sphere.[121] This would be likely to have class-taste dimensions, with some members of this group at least valuing "high" or "elite" culture over "popular" or "low" culture. This might even emerge as a self-conscious term of differentiation for them as they compare themselves with other groups, especially the "born agains." At the same time, though, their reflexive self-consciousness of difference might well have them eschewing the kind of judgmentalism about the "values" of the mass media we suggested might be more likely among "born-agains." Further, to the extent that we might expect the media to represent in some way an evolving "cultural mainstream" in terms of its overall textual output, this group would be the group that would most identify with that "mainstream" in religious terms.

Like others, they would likely be motivated to look in some corners of media culture, at least, for resources relevant to their religious/spiritual quests of the self. If, as Roof suggests, they would also be less judgmental about cultures beyond their own, even accepting of them, we would expect them to be particularly drawn to media materials that bring them resources and insights from beyond their immediate cultural surrounds.

Metaphysical Believers and Seekers. This is the core group of the "seeking" sensibility, the one most self-consciously disconnected from tradition. According to Roof, they often have a narrative of "bridge-burning" with a former faith group to share that is parallel to the "born-again's" narrative of salvation. They can be identified by labels, according to Roof, including identifications with Wicca, Zen Buddhism, channeling, "New Age," various "masters" or "paths," and feminist spirituality. At the same time, some defy labels, according to Roof. They tend to reject the label "religion," favoring "spirituality" or "spiritual exploration" instead. They share with "mainstreamers" a sense of adaptability to shifting realities.

As other scholars have, Roof notes that this sensibility has deep roots in the nineteenth-century "new thought" and metaphysical movements. They reject the old dualisms, however, thinking of them as outmoded categories. They favor a kinetic and holistic conceptions of human existence and action. Roof suggests that this is the most Gnostic of the categories, believing in an intuitive sense of religion and spirituality without the mediation of institutional or clerical authority. Roof presents them as the central group of exemplars of the religious project of the self as predicted by Giddens. They are reflexive, self-conscious, and very much about perfection, but they are also – more significantly – protean in that their adaptability is both a characteristic that defines them and a self-conscious or reflexive self-assessment.

We might argue that this group would also be the central category with reference to religious exploration and meaning-making in media culture. If, as we have been arguing, media culture might come to function as an alternative to traditional religion in important ways, this would be the group we would expect to be most actively involved. In fact, there is a great deal of evidence of media culture moving in this direction. Many of the recent waves of spiritually oriented entertainment television programs have explored spiritualities such as those of most interest to these "seekers." The ensuing criticisms from conservative religious circles would make such programs additionally salient for this group. And, the fact that such resources are available in an open marketplace outside the control of traditional institutions or authorities would also make them more attractive and salient.

Commodified media culture also provides a range of resources to these various sensibilities in the new media and specialized "niche" media such as magazine publishing. What remains to be seen is whether the provision of material connects with these sensibilities in terms of consumption and reception. A perhaps more interesting question, though, relates to the "mainstreamers" discussed earlier. They should be attracted to many of the same resources that define this group. The extent to which these media are salient for which group becomes an important question.

Dogmatists. Whereas the group above would be likely to describe themselves as "spiritual but not religious," this group would be likely to say the opposite. In Roof's classification, they are the most concerned with the "external forms of religion" and are "rigidly religious." He describes them as supporting institutional religion, "encrusted institutions frozen in a nostalgic past." This group is perhaps best understood in contrast with the three foregoing groups, who each articulated an approach to religion that questions the prerogatives and powers of received authority. These people are more interested in that authority, but, more precisely, in an imagined, remembered past, for which they are nostalgic. Indirectly accepting the critique that the institutions today struggle to remain relevant to lived lives, they wish to return to a more stable, sensible past.

Roof describes the narratives of this group as "formulaic in character, rather lifeless and closed." Most were raised Catholic or in conservative Protestant groups, and their social networks tend to revolve around their places of worship. They also tend to be lower-educated and lower in socioeconomic status.

It seems rather straightforward to suggest that the relationship of this group to media culture would be rather strict and judgmental. It is hard to imagine them going anywhere outside their traditions or institutions for insights, inspiration, or resources related to religion or spirituality (a term they are unlikely to use). They'd be unlikely to connect their media lives to their religious lives, and unlikely to attend to media related to "secular" or "mainstream" culture.

Secularists. This group would be likely to describe themselves as being neither "religious" nor "spiritual." Most likely to have been raised in Mainline Protestant contexts, this group is also likely to be higher in socioeconomic status and education, and to be members of the so-called "knowledge class." Like the Mainstream group, their narratives are most likely to be stated in negative terms. It is easier for them to describe themselves in terms of what they are *not* as what they *are*. Tradition is distant and of little importance to them. Roof describes them as being a-religious or ir-religious rather than anti-religious. But, along with most of the other groups, they share a self-consciousness and reflexivity regarding religion, expressed by their defining themselves in terms distinct from other categories of religious meaning practice.

What would the secularists' media-cultural diets be? Most likely, given their educational level, they would eschew most popular media, likely favoring public broadcasting to commercial broadcasting. Because of their relationship to religion and spirituality, they'd be unlikely to seek out or consume material in the media sphere related to religion.

It is important to reaffirm here that these categories result from a specific set of studies, and are presented as applying most precisely there and more generally to the Baby Boom generation at that point in history. Their relationship to succeeding generations deserves some reflection. Roof would argue (as would I) that his studies describe a transitional moment in the evolution of religious culture, and that post-Boomer religiosity can be expected to bear some important resemblances to what we see here. We might as well expect a different classification to emerge in our study, as the questions are different. We are interested, more than Roof was, in the way that religious identity is created in relation to cultural resources such as the commodities of the media sphere. As we will discuss in later chapters, we will also be looking at these matters in the context of the domestic spaces of private life, which introduces other questions and considerations into interviews and observations. A value of Roof's approach to "data gathering" is that it is possible for us to unpack important dimensions of his analysis, to deconstruct them and reconstruct them in relation to our own project as it is itself deconstructed and reconstructed. The test of the success of this will be in the doing, of course.

Of all the categories, as we noted earlier, the metaphysical believers and seekers might well be the group most likely to seek out and consume religious or spiritual material in the media sphere. Their interest in religious and spiritual matters beyond the received categories, as well as their eschewal of such traditions, might well put them in the position to look to sources in the broader culture for resources. But, interestingly, they share some significant sensibilities with other of the categories as well. The metaphysical group shares with the mainstreamers, and to an extent the born-agains, an orientation toward individual – and away from institutional or clerical – logics for organizing their spiritual lives.

As we move on to an investigation of religious or spiritual meaning-making in the media age, we will use Roof's categories, though not only as an inductive structure against which to classify our interviews and the results from those interviews. Instead, they may help us look at the narratives of self we will encounter and understand the evolving religious cultures they represent. As Roof himself does, we will try to understand how these narratives result from a mixture of history, self-consciousness, identity-building, aspiration, and practices in daily life and daily experience. We will look for what is intended and aspired to in terms of the religious and spiritual lives we will encounter here, and, in keeping with Roof and Warner, be most interested in what is achieved as well as what is ascribed by received categories. In the next chapter, we will begin this process by reflecting on the challenges of engaging in this kind of research into meaning-making in the media age.

Chapter 4

Articulating life and culture in the media age
Plausible narratives of the self

This should be a simple task. We are interested in charting the way that religious lives and religious identities are formed in relation to media culture. We began with what seemed a rather straightforward question, that of how the emergence of the media as a fundamental condition of modern and late-modern life has affected religion. And, as we have seen, much of the received thought and scholarship about the relationship of media and religion presents itself as straightforward as well. At the same time, though, the rather simple question of what "effect" the media may have had on "religion" raises a plethora of complex and fascinating issues. We have set the stage, though, for a more focused approach: we will "go and ask." Or, more precisely, we will engage in conversations with real people about the way they use media, about the way they think about religion and spirituality, and about the relationships between these things in their lives.

In this chapter, I will lay out a strategy for researching the relationship between religion and media at this most basic and provocative level: where individuals and groups in the various media audiences encounter media texts and engage in media practices. Following Wade Clark Roof's suggestion in the last chapter, we will want to look at the symbolic resources or the "symbolic inventory" available in the media sphere, the practices of consumption, interaction, and articulation through which those resources are accessed, and the experiences of the individuals who are active in this process of reception.

Earlier, we explored some of the history and complexity of researching media audiences and their reception of media. We looked first at how media and mass communication scholarship developed along with the emergence of the media sphere as a technological and social phenomenon. What we saw there was a gradual evolution away from the initial idea that the media should be looked at as large, monolithic social forces and toward the notion that they are better understood in terms of their use and reception in lived lives. We also considered the argument that questions of religion, spirituality, transcendence, etc., are particularly apt topics for a reception-oriented, qualitative, ethnographic approach.

Studying media on the larger scale, of course, has certain advantages. It enables social research to describe with some confidence how people in larger social and demographic categories relate to the media they consume. At the same time, the approach is limited in the kinds of questions it can address. Research on media audiences conducted through survey or other large-sample techniques suffers a relative inability to look at fine, detailed, and complex social phenomena. Put in technical terms, the "measures" that such research deals with must be "operationalized," that is, the large questions must be reduced to measurable data. For some kinds of questions, this is not a problem. For example, there is much to learn that is interesting and significant in looking at gender and age differences in media consumption. These are easily operationalized and can be studied readily using quantitative techniques.[1]

However, how would we measure the meanings that these various groups derive from the media they consume? How would we formulate questions focused on such meanings, without first understanding how and where such meanings are made with reference to media? Do we assume that media "creates" such meanings, or that meanings are made out of a number of social and cultural resources, including those in the media? As I have argued in previous chapters, there is reason to believe that media reception is much more a matter of such meaning-making by its audiences than it is a question of the media "creating" meaning. This is particularly the case if what we are interested in are questions of identity and values (social *and* cultural), in which the leading social theories would suggest the matter is in the hands of the individual rather than social forces such as the media, doing the "work" of identity.

It is important to recognize, further, that the reception of the symbolic marketplace takes place in a specific context: the domestic sphere. We like to think of the home and the family as bounded, protected spaces within which the most fundamental and authentic relationships are formed and shaped, the basic work of socialization and enculturation takes place, and thus as the foundation of meaning, values, and identity. Further, we like to think of the domestic sphere as – in Christopher Lasch's well-known book title – a "haven in a heartless world,"[2] a space whose boundaries protect us, and particularly children, from the potential influences of a world "outside" that does not always have their – or our – best interests at heart. The question about this domestic map has always been "where are the media?" Are they *outside* the boundary, thus a potential influence on the authentic articulation of love, care, values, meanings, and identities that naturally occur within, or are they *inside* the boundary, part of the local network of influences and resources for the making of meanings there?

A number of recent studies of television and other media have demonstrated that, in important ways, the "boundary" between the domestic sphere and the wider world is not really a relevant distinction in relation to media. In a large qualitative study of the British television audience, for example, David Gauntlett and Annette Hill found that, in the most fundamental ways, television is integrated into the context of daily life in the home. It is structured into the tempos and patterns of the day, regulating some, being regulated by others. At the same time, its content is a matter of both pleasure and guilt for them.[3] In a more recent study of media in the domestic sphere, my colleagues and I found that the media are integrated into the way parents *think* about themselves as parents, forming an important element of family identity.[4] That research found parents in a way mapping their practices of parenting and their children's progress through socialization by means of the media, the kind of media consumed in the home and the means by which the media were or were not regulated.[5]

Talking about media

On the most basic level our task now is to move to the context of daily, domestic, and social life, to find out how people there negotiate media into their spiritual and religious lives. This involves talking with them about media, about religion and spirituality, and about values. One of the criticisms I've leveled at traditional approaches to media research is that they assume too much about the power and prerogatives of the media and too little about what people do with those media texts and other resources when they encounter them. This criticism is, as we've seen, consistent with general trends in culturalist media studies. It moves toward in-depth qualitative interpretation and description, and away from more superficial, large-context issues and questions. It enables us to talk about how media are received and used within the flow of daily life in relation to the other resources, activities, relationships, and influences available there.

In another context, my colleagues and I have described the approach we take as "constructivist." By this, we mean that it recognizes that the knowledge we produce through research such as this is *constructed* in a series of steps and contexts, including the design of research, the interviews and their outcomes, the analysis of those interviews, the writing of interpretations and findings, and, finally, the reception of the research by readers.[6] That second step, the interviews themselves, is of course key, as it is our source of insights – as researchers and as readers – into the processes, practices, and meanings we seek to understand more fully.

So, how are we to think about these interviews? What kind of knowledge and process do they represent? It is important to understand how informants represent the social and cultural contexts that they inhabit. Because of our interest in contextualizing the meanings they make, we want to hold the conversation at the borderline between the individual and the social levels. These questions are not only a matter of individual motivation and psychology, and nor are they a matter of what the social and cultural order make people do and think. Because we want to bring into descriptive definition the way that specific resources from the culture (i.e. including in the "symbolic inventory" of media texts, symbols, and messages), we want to be able to see how the individual and the sociocultural interact, and inter-relate in the meaning-making process. The best way of describing this is as the *individual* seen on the *social* level. The purpose is not to generalize from these individuals to other individuals, but to say how these individuals represent the range of cultural and social contexts and influences that have produced them as social and cultural beings. My colleagues and I have described the implication of this "shift" in focus this way:

> We believe it enabled us to move away from a position in which we sought to explore how individuals are relatively close or distant from an imagined "core" of society. We could approach each person as a "universal singular," to use Jean-Paul Sartre's term. Each person's story becomes important, for it is simultaneously the story of a unique individual and the embodiment of the social world that has produced her or him.[7]

Thus, when we talk with people we open the possibility of learning much about the various cultural and social elements that go into making their view of the world and their sense of self. This grounding in the self, as I noted in an earlier chapter, is the fundamental project of late modernity, and a reflexive engagement in that project typifies late-modern social consciousness. Thus when we engage people in conversations about these things, we can imagine that what they are telling us is a reflexive account related in some way to what they actually think about who they are and where they fit in the cultures they inhabit.

My colleagues and I have become convinced that the way the media enter into such accounts is itself structured in important ways, ways that are rooted in the reflexivity of the late-modern moment. We describe this in terms of three "levels of engagement" with the media that we have observed in our conversations with our informants.

The first of these levels is *experiences in the media*. These are our informants' first-order relations to media texts. They recount the pleasures, the irritations, the satisfactions, the boredom, the revulsions, etc., that we all express related to the media we encounter. These are familiar to us in relation to our own viewing of media. They are also the core of what used to be called "uses and gratifications" media research, the reasons and satisfactions that people express for the various media they consume. They speak to the more direct salience of various kinds of media for various needs and interests. Much of this talk relates to specific *genres* of media. It is on this level that viewers and audiences can and do express their most direct reactions to the media they consume, and on this level that they are most comfortable talking about their news viewing and reading, for example.

The second level of engagement is *interactions about the media*. These are those occasions and practices through which we bring our media experiences to bear in our social relationships. This category is familiar in the media studies literature as the kind of material detailed in the work of James Lull,[8] David Morley,[9] and Elihu Katz and Tamar Liebes.[10] In important ways, as these and other scholars have shown, media became important cultural "currencies of exchange" in daily interactions with peers and other groups.[11] While this is most obvious in relation to youth, it is also a common experience with adults. As David Gauntlett and Annette Hill observe in their book,

> Ann Gray previously found that "a very important part of the pleasure of television serials is to gossip about them the following day," and in the present study we similarly identified the social activity which derives from watching television as an important aspect of TV's place in everyday life. When some respondents consider what they would miss about watching television, being able to talk to other people about what was watched last night is high on the list.[12]

Thus, the "interactions about" level of engagement functions along at least two dimensions. First, there is the direct sharing or "passing along" of information, anecdotes, and stories, the sort of thing that the classic "multi-step flow" theories of media influence used to concentrate on. Second, there is a social salience in the relationship formation and maintenance that media knowledge allows. Knowing about media provides the occasion for social interaction, almost regardless of the original "experiences in" media on the part of the individuals involved.

Finally, the third level, *accounts of the media*, is a category unique to our work. These are the received public scripts according to which we position ourselves as media audiences. These scripts are – in the area of media – what James Carey has called the "publicly available stock" of images and ideas through which we understand ourselves in our social and cultural contexts,[13] and what Ellen Seiter has called "lay theories of media effects."[14] Television is bad for children. It is better to watch public television. Too much time spent on the Internet or playing video games is bad. Learning to use a computer is good. The media are anti-religious or at least ir-religious.

We first encountered these "accounts of" media in the form of what seemed to be a mismatch between people's descriptions of their media behaviors and their actual behaviors. This personal anecdote is illustrative. Several years ago, in a ski-area hotel, I had to knock on the door of the next room one night to ask that the television set be turned down. They graciously obliged. The next day, I encountered the mother from next door in the spa *après-ski*. In making small-talk, she said she was an ordained Protestant minister. In learning that I research television, she responded, as if by reflex, "You know what our approach to television is in our family? We just don't allow it." In our book, *Media, Home, and Family*,[15] my colleagues and I present a large number of such accounts from a range of families and in a range of contexts. As we've proceeded, it has interested us a great deal to learn how consistent such received ideas about the media are, how deeply rooted they are, how they cut across class and cultural lines, and how extensively articulated they are. The most interesting thing about them to us initially was the curious phenomenon of the contrasts between belief about the media – these expressed accounts – and media behaviors, as with the skiing family next door.

While we might be tempted to begin an investigation of this phenomenon as an example of the social-psychological phenomenon of cognitive dissonance[16] or an example of how people are poor informants of their own behaviors, or to try to get behind their misleading talk to understand what they "really" do, I think a better approach is to *theorize* this phenomenon, to try to understand it. Why does it make sense for people to say the things they do about the media, and, further, what is sensical about the particular ways particular people choose to describe their media lives? As my colleagues and I argued with regard to media, home, and family, these self-presentations regarding media are important elements of overall self-presentations, and thus are identity statements. And, as I said, we found a great deal of consistency from interview to interview in the public scripts people referred to in crafting their "accounts of media." At the same time, though, there were and are important variations, and it is in the interpretation of these variations and their relation to the contexts of specific lives and specific locations that we can learn important things about how the media relate to identity and meaning.

Gauntlett and Hill describe this phenomenon in terms of the guilt that the British television viewers in their study felt about their viewing lives.

> We saw that the more television people watched, the more they were likely to feel guilty for not doing other things, such as household chores, homework, or socialising, or any number of other things that people don't do if they're watching television. If we looked at the responses about TV guilt in isolation, it would be easy to form the impression that the British public is fundamentally uncomfortable with watching television, and is somewhat annoyed that TV has come to settle so easily into their living rooms and everyday lives. However, taking into account the context in which these responses were written, and looking at how much pleasure people get from watching

television – even when they only have daytime TV for company – we can see that these respondents are well able to "cope" with whatever guilt their viewing may bring, and in fact would be most reluctant to part with their TVs.[17]

To these people, television is a "guilty pleasure," but it is more than that. As Gauntlett and Hill, Ellen Seiter, and our studies in *Media, Home, and Family* showed, television and the other media are integrated into the warp and woof of daily life in a way that is both pleasurable and unsettling, both isolating and connecting, both trivial and deeply meaningful. The point is that it is there, it is "settled" and integrated, and people have found ways of living their lives with it, around it, through it, and without it.

Our inquiries into the particular role that media play depend then on accounts from informants that have a purpose for them. They are a certain kind of talk. They are directed at the larger project of the creation of the ideal self, inflected with a reflexivity about their social location and about societal and cultural sources of the self. Their motive is to make a particular kind of self-presentation. That "accounts of media" fit so tacitly into such self-presentations means that they are integrated into ideal and normative ideals of self, the self that informants want to present in a particular setting and to a particular listener. They are meant for publication, in a way, and the meanings and knowledge we derive from them must take account of the settings in which they were derived. Thus the method we must use is itself a reflexive method. We understand where we are and who they are, and who they think is asking.

It remains, though, to describe the nature of the presentations they make. I would like to propose that we think of them as *narratives*.[18] In the context of an inquiry into religious and spiritual meaning, values, and symbols, the sense that these are narratives enables us to connect them with the larger project of the family and of normative ideals. Wade Clark Roof describes the role of such narratives in this way:

> Put into narrative terms, families are the settings where great stories embodying trust, respect, love, honesty, integrity, fairness, responsibility, and other values are shared and practiced. Here children first learn what it means to belong and to be loyal, to relate to others, to share in ritual practices, to celebrate the values of families and loved ones, all crucial to personal identity and social life. Here parents not only teach moral virtues and faith but model them, setting examples that children may follow. We might even go so far as to assert that the link between parents and children rests to a considerable extent on storytelling itself.[19]

There is, of course, a growing body of social research based on narrative. There are two broad approaches, one more psychological and clinically oriented,[20] and the other more oriented to culture and identity. In the latter category, there is a further difference between those studies that conceive of narratives as *evidence* of deeper dispositions and meanings "beyond"[21] and those that, in a more postmodern turn, conceive of narratives as social and cultural *constructions* that reveal important things about the nature of meaning and identity.[22] There is also an emerging tradition of "autoethnography" within cultural studies, where researchers interrogate their own biographies as a way of understanding culture.[23]

It may be obvious that the way I intend to use the term narrative in the context of our inquiries here is consistent with thinking of them as constructions. At the same time, though, the point is not to use the narratives as data in an exploration of identity as a fixed psycho-social category, but as constructions drawing on the resources of the culture. Rather than thinking of "life narratives" in the way that a psychological or therapeutic intervention might, I want to think of these self-descriptions more as identity statements within which we can read the contributions of various elements, from life history to the symbolic resources of media culture to the way our interviewees think about and describe their own experiences and actions. While this is not necessarily the totality of what some psychologists might think of as "identity," these are "identity statements" that are central to the way people negotiate and construct meanings.

Identity and narrative

This approach bears much in common with Paul Ricoeur's ideas about narrative and identity. Ricoeur argued that *mediation* is essential to personal identity, that our self-understandings necessarily are mediated by symbols, signs, language, texts, and the whole range of cultural-symbolic resources we encounter.[24] This would suggest an integration of cultural resources into identity at a very basic and profound level, and therefore that media commodities that are the primary focus of our project here can be expected to be among them.

Ricoeur's ideas are even more relevant to our inquiries in what he has to say about the narrative basis of identity. Personal identity, he argued, is a *narrative* identity. By that he meant to say that identity is neither static nor discontinuous with our ongoing experience of life, culture, and history. Narratives strive for *coherence*, drawing together sometimes contradictory elements into a coherent trajectory through time. They unite experiential elements that are "contingencies," meaning that they do not necessarily work in a determined, coherent form, but must be brought into coherence through the narrative. They also unite *disparate* elements such as people, experiences, symbols, events, weaving them into a form that makes them seem necessary or rational.[25]

Ricoeur further contended that there is an element of reflexive self-evaluation in the way we make senses of ourselves. We do this by telling ourselves stories about our lives. These identities are fluid and mobile, not fixed, and continue to be woven over time. They also involve others, with our individual stories also bound up with stories of our families and others in our lives. Each element of our identity narratives – including the other participants, elements, and experiences – comes from a particular place and time, and thus these do not float freely, but are culturally, historically, and experientially grounded. Our narratives are thus not "fictive." Ricoeur also contends that these narratives necessarily have a *normative* dimension. They are about values, and are evaluative. We say, through our narratives of self, not only who we are but also who and what we want to be.[26]

The way I will use the term narrative here is consistent with Ricoeur's conception. Narratives are a process whereby we weave together sometimes disparate, contingent elements of life into a story that at least aspires to coherence. Identity narratives are the stories we tell ourselves and tell about ourselves. They involve a variety of elements, including life experience, symbolic resources, and (most importantly to Ricoeur) other persons and our relationships with and to them. They have a normative or value-laden dimension, in that they tell about who we are in terms of what we aspire to be. We want to describe ourselves in terms of what we value. At the same time they are necessarily grounded, because on some level they involve real persons, real experiences, real languages, texts, and symbols.

Narratives as a research tool

The interviews we will examine here resulted from a long-term study of religion and meaning in the media age. I have described the approach of this research as interpretive and constructivist. We have been interested in understanding how people make meanings in the media age, and how the symbolic resources of the media sphere relate to those meanings that are oriented to faith, spirituality, religion, and transcendent meaning. The interviews are in-depth and based on semi-structured interview agendas. They are thus intended to have some consistency across time and across interviews, but also are flexible to account for new information and new experiences. This flexibility results from an ongoing interpretive process whereby the interviewers meet regularly with the whole research team to discuss what we are finding.[27]

It probably goes without saying that a good deal of care and deliberation is necessary because it is not really possible to just "go and ask" people what they do with media that is religiously or spiritually significant. As we will see, the responses we get are complex and elusive. What we have already seen about the contrast between the various "levels of engagement" with media also determines, in important ways, the extents and limits of what we are able to learn in the field context.

We will make some assumptions about these interviews. First, the assumption of constructivism will have us looking at these interviews themselves in context, and seeing them as fluid and mobile negotiations of the various elements and resources that constitute them. Second, rooted in the pragmatist and Interactionist assumptions we discussed earlier, we will think of these interviews as purposive. Interactionism would have us expect people to want to make meaningful senses of themselves and their world, and the concrete mode by which they will do this is a *self-represen-tation*. This is, of course, consistent with what we have seen earlier about the self in late modernity. The project of constructing an ideal self will be a motivating factor in the lives, experiences, and representations of people in their daily lives, and it is through narratives of self that they tell themselves and others how this is working out.

We should not underplay the extent to which these narratives are about ideals and what is aspired to. In his germinal work, *Sources of the Self*, Charles Taylor put it this way:

> To know who I am is a species of knowing where I stand. My identity is defined by the commitments and identifications which provide the frame or horizon within which I can try to determine from case to case what is good, or valuable, or what ought to be done, or what I endorse or oppose.[28]

And, as we have seen, it is through representations of these ideals that we both confirm and endorse them for ourselves, and share that self with others.

The idea that we know and share identity through representation is familiar from the theory of the pragmatist/Interactionist of Erving Goffman. In his *Presentation of Self in Everyday Life*,[29] he laid out a "dramaturgical" theory of social interaction. By this he meant that we engage in social life self-consciously and reflexively, and that we are aware of what our language and actions symbolize about who we are, and we consciously engage in presentations that reflect that knowledge. This is, of course, consistent with the more fundamental Interactionist ideas about socialization and social learning, which hold that it is through a self-conscious role-taking that we come to know our proper place in the social and cultural order.[30] Goffman's dramaturgic perspective, like Ricoeur's ideas, suggests that this self-conscious representation is something that we engage in more or less continuously, that it is one of the essential elements of our social lives and of our human-ness.

What I want to suggest, then, is that within these interviews we can detect self-narratives.[31] This draws on the pragmatist/Interactionist idea that people will more or less self-consciously use the opportunity of the interview to share these narratives in whole or in part, and that what we come away with is material that can most helpfully be seen in this way. We should expect, further, that they will to some extent reflect that late-modern project of the self, and will be about the struggle to construct such a self. They will thus carry evidence of the challenges and contradictions to the self that our interviewees have encountered, and evidence of their strategies for crafting a coherent sense of self in response. They are also normative in that they represent the ideals and aspirations of their speakers, again consistent with Ricoeur's as well as with Giddens's ideas.

It is helpful as well to think of these narratives as "plausible." This is rooted in the Interactionist idea that these constructions of self involve a logic that they are fitted to certain contexts and certain "others" for which and for whom they must "make sense." It is in this sense that our interpretations of them most reflect constructivist ideas about reflexivity. This point can be clarified by means of the earlier discussion of "accounts of media." To the extent that media resources are brought to bear in narratives of self, they necessarily carry with them a certain set of culturally determined ideas about the nature and status of those resources. It could be said that what my friend at the ski area was doing was making an account of media that she intended to "make sense" – that is, to be "plausible" – to a university professor who studies media. It is likely that she would have made the same account of television to many other categories of people as well, given the generalized opprobrium the culture attaches to television viewing.

The purpose of the interviews is not to "collect" these narratives as such. The interviews collect discourses, interactions among informants, and interactions between informants and interviewers. The agenda of the interview is to talk about media, home, family, religion, spirituality, and values. What results, as we will see, are in fact elements of the larger, more comprehensive narratives of self through which these informants make sense of themselves for themselves and for others.

I want to argue that the notion of the "plausible narrative of the self," then, is less *evidentiary* than it is *heuristic*. It provides us an opportunity to understand how all of the elements of life experience are drawn into these narratives, how they relate, what is struggled over, what is negotiated "in" and what is negotiated "out." The point is thus not the narrative itself and what it results in. The point is what goes into the narrative.

Consistent with the reflexive and postmodern turns in ethnography and cultural studies, I further want to suggest that we think of these narratives as a particular kind of *work* for our informants, and a particular kind of *account* for us as observers and interpreters.

For our informants, these narratives are, as I have said, a "representation," a description of self and of the lifecourse. They are also a "history" of a kind, lodged in space and time, as well as an account of expectations about the future. As Ricoeur would say, the lodgment in space and time integrates into the narrative a range of social and material factors that are socially and culturally significant. They seek to represent coherence, binding together sometimes distinct and contradictory elements into what the informant would like to see as a seamless whole. As Ricoeur claims, they necessarily encompass aspirations toward normative ideals. As a project of social representation, they are rooted in subjective ideas about norms and values, and about what is socially desirable and in what contexts. Finally, they are an opportunity to make a certain kind of representation, one that is focused on accountability in a location between "the personal" and "the public." These representations are the ones that these informants chose to make in a context where some kind of normative authority (in the form of a university-based researcher) is "listening." Thus, what we see in our transcripts is what these informants are willing to say or want to say in that context. Which contradictions they choose to address, to ignore, and to resolve in that context is significant. It is valuable information.

For us as observers, interpreters, and researchers, these narratives should provide insights into a number of different things. First, as we discussed in the last chapter, one of the most important ways we expect the media to contribute to individuals' religious and spiritual identities is through mediated provision of symbols and resources. These narratives can therefore be expected to contain evidence of that "symbolic inventory," seen from the perspective of the individuals and groups in the media audience. Further, they can help us understand how the media symbols and resources are or are not embedded in the overall symbolic environment out of which meanings are made.

Second, these narratives should contain evidence of the ways that individuals negotiate with those symbols and resources, what they think of them, how they use them, and how they construct worlds of meaning out of them. They can also tell us how those resources are articulated, understood, and used by particular people in particular locations.

Third, they should provide some evidence of actual practice or behavior, but we should expect that they will also represent attempts to integrate practice into the larger context of social and cultural relations. As I suggested earlier, it is far less important to understand actual behavior or to chart the distance between belief and behavior or self-description and behavior than it is to understand why claims about behavior make sense at certain times and in certain contexts.

Fourth, these narratives should be a kind of *unobtrusive* measure of whatever contradictions informants perceive between belief and behavior, between contrasting beliefs, and between various claims on their time, attention, beliefs, and values. Fifth, they should also provide a kind of unobtrusive measure of the capacities of symbols, discourses, and other resources to be put to work in meaning-making.

As a heuristic device, these narratives should in a way "hold constant" the structural location and purpose of the field material through which they are seen. They can provide a touchpoint in the midst of the complex and potentially contradictory material that naturally appears in such interviews, asking the question, "What was this informant interested in saying or willing to say in the context of our interview, and what does that mean?" They should thus allow interpretation of complex and contradictory relations of at least two kinds. First, there are the complex, subtle, and contradictory negotiations between what Habermas called the "lifeworld" and "system world," or between the material sphere and the more sensaic, sentimental, and emotional realm Raymond Williams called the "structure of feeling." How does media culture contribute to these contradictions and potential coherences, as expressed in informant narratives? Second, there are the negotiations that are more central to our overall quest here, those surrounding religion, spirituality, effervescence, "the sacred," enchantment, everyday and exceptional ritualization, the nonrational, and the ludic. And again, the question is, how does media culture relate to these issues?

What might we expect?

We ended the last chapter by reviewing what we might expect in the way of specific, religiously/spiritually inflected uses of media. As we begin thinking about these "plausible narratives of the self," in the broader context of overall media use and media behavior, we should also back away a bit and consider some of the elements of media experience in general that might impinge on the lives we will encounter through our interviews. There are, simply, a number of things we might wish to assume but that we probably should not assume. For example, we will learn a good deal about the way people relate to and consume media in the context of daily life. We have already seen that there is good reason to see media as integrated into life in some fundamental ways. While people might wish to adopt "accounts of media" that distance media from what they seem to value at the center of their lives, at the same time, they seem not to be able to do without media, and thus the media are, in Gauntlett and Hill's term, "settled." We might wish to think of media in a way that is discontinuous with daily life, but there is reason to doubt that this is a very helpful direction to take.

Another assumption we might make but about which we should probably withhold judgment is the question of the continuous or discontinuous nature of daily life in relation to media. It has been claimed by some to be a "flow," into which media experience and media behaviors intrude to a greater or lesser extent and with positive or negative consequences.[32] Since I have argued that it is problematic to think of interviews such as ours as evidence of behavior or practice *per se*, we will not be drawing many conclusions about how media relate to the flow of daily life. However, we will be able to draw some inferences about how our informants think about these questions, and therefore about the capacities of media practice to relate in transparent or opaque ways to daily life.

Another larger question relates to a matter we discussed in Chapters 2 and 3: how optimistic or pessimistic to be about the reflexivity and self-consciousness of contemporary life, and the extent to which media culture contributes to these conditions. As we noted there, observers such as Kenneth Gergen have suggested that the cultural and conceptual suffusion of contemporary life – in which the media are centrally implicated – so overwhelms contemporary consciousness that the "self" has little room to maneuver. Gergen puts it this way:

> we are now bombarded with ever-increasing intensity by the images and actions of others; our range of social participation is expanding exponentially. As we absorb the views, values, and visions of others, and live out the multiple plots in which we are enmeshed, we enter a postmodern consciousness. It is a world in which we no longer experience a secure sense of self, and in which doubt is increasingly placed on the very assumption of a bounded identity with palpable attributes. What are the consequences? How are we to respond to the coming conditions?[33]

As we saw there, other observers follow the influential lead of Anthony Giddens, who holds that there is reason to suspect that this condition leads to a sense of cultural autonomy in the crafting of the self as readily as it leads to *anomie*. The difference may reside in how identity and self are conceptualized. Giddens, for example, holds that the self and identity are fluid rather than fixed, and are in the hands of individual social actors in a more or less constant process of construction and reconstruction.

> Self-identity . . . is not something that is just given, as a result of the continuities of the individual's action-system, but something that has to be routinely created and sustained in the reflexive activities of the individual. . . . Self-identity is not a distinctive trait, or even a collection of traits, possessed by the individual. It is *the self as reflexively understood by the person in terms of her or his biography.*[34]

To Giddens, then, something very much like our plausible narratives of the self are at the core of the creation and maintenance of the self and identity. The question of whether we are to see these processes as evidence of the reflexive autonomy of the self or as something darker and more disempowering is an issue we may well hope to address through our investigations. It is, in any case, part of the contextual surround of the culturally appropriative practices we will be attempting to assess through these interviews.

Interviews and narratives

As a way of considering how interviews may reveal or relate to the notion of the "plausible narrative of the self," let's look at a particularly interesting and complex interview. On the most straightforward level, these interviews involve simple questions. We "go and ask" people how they use media, what they think of media, about their religious and spiritual lives, and about how media might or do relate to their lives as individuals, parents, members of groups, and as religious and spiritual beings. What then remains is to try to account for their responses. This becomes a complex task because their answers are far from systematic and straightforward, as we will see. Having a heuristic through which to understand what is going on in their accounts is a virtual necessity.

Glenn Donegal is 47 and is a self-employed contractor. He lives in the suburbs of a large midwestern city with his wife, Liz, age 50, and their two sons, Robbie, 16, and Quinn, 12.[35] Glenn was raised Catholic, but is now an Evangelical Protestant, and an active member of the Evangelical "Promise Keepers" men's organization. His religious conversion is linked with his recovery from alcoholism, which he attributes to finding a strong and focused faith. He is a regular reader of "Christian" literature, including from the "Focus on the Family" organization and the popular *Left Behind* series of novels discussed in Chapter 3.

At one point in the interview he notes that he believes that fathers should be the spiritual heads of their households. The interviewer follows up:

Interviewer: Okay. When you say you see yourself as the spiritual head of the house, is that because of your gender or because you are more knowledgeable than other members of the family about Christianity or what does that role mean to you?
Glenn: It really has nothing to do with masculinity. It has more to do biblically. We are called out as men to be heads of our households and spiritual leaders. Now that may translate into masculinity for someone else but for me personally, there is a big difference between being a man and a woman and I am not by any means a male chauvinist but I firmly believe there is a place for a male in his role in the family and as a spiritual leader I am biblically responsible for my kids and my wife and our family as far as what the Bible tells me I am supposed to

do. . . . It is not egotistical like I am the man and that's it and you're going to live by my rules. We share that relationship, my wife and I. That is very well balanced in how we deal with that. But when it comes to [the] spirituality part of it, we are to be leaders in the household but unfortunately in today's society, I think women are the spiritual leaders in most households. They are the ones doing all the praying, doing all the "let's get to church, c'mon, guys." You know. Whereas, it is just not supposed to be that way.

Interviewer: What do you think has caused that?

Glenn: I think men are more driven, at least in my eyes, I know a lot of men that are driven by success and money. Some are driven by being self-centered and being selfish. . . . I think most men, unfortunately, have lost sight of who we really are. I say that because I think a lot of men are not in touch with their – can I say this – their *feminine* side. And, without having that balance, not to get too charismatic, *yin and yang* here, but I do believe that there is a balance in all of us and there is an emotional side in all of us that men don't touch and really deal with. Well, tied into that emotional side is the spirituality. And, if you are not in touch with the spirit in deep and the emotion that is in there then you are really not balanced as a man, at least in my eyes. So, I firmly believe that most men don't go there because it is too touchy feely for them. Whereas I believe that a true man . . . I believe in Lord Jesus Christ as my Lord and Savior, a true man, and I use Him as an example, that he was very compassionate, very loving, very understanding, yet he was very, very strong. Not only physically, but also mentally and when it came to self-denial, and all those things. So, I think He shows me that there is a balance and you need to have that balance.

Interviewer: Do you have any male Bible groups that you do with your men friends?

Glenn: I'm trying to get a men's ministry started in our church. We don't have a men's ministry *per se*.

Interviewer: Ministry meaning . . . ?

Glenn: Ministry meaning where men meet with men. And men hold men accountable for what they do in their lives. Men can go and sit and meet once a week and have coffee together and you talk about this, that, and the other thing. Whatever it is men do. And I had that in California, an accountability group where I would meet on a regular basis and we were involved with men's ministry and all that. Promise Keepers, I'm involved with.

The conversation about Glenn's own beliefs and spirituality moves quickly to his ideas about how men's spirituality is formed and shaped in childhood. He sees a particular kind of need in this area.

Glenn: . . . the biggest problem I see today in our society when it comes to men mentoring boys is that we do not have . . . as an Aboriginal family would . . . a tradition. Aborigines have a coming out party like a bar mitzvah. They say, "Son, you are going to be a man if you do this walk . . . and you do this." . . . I think the problem is for Americans that we do not have something like a rite of passage that teaches our boys. . . . Most boys don't know they are men until their dad says, "I'm really proud of you son, now you are a man." A lot of those boys do not get that affirmation ever or their dad is passed away or they are still searching for that "Dad, am I a man? You never really told me I was a man?"

One of the challenges of this research is to get people to begin talking about media in relation to religion and values. Glenn's fundamental position on media is to be critical, saying at one point that the media are entirely secular and therefore only about "the almighty dollar." He feels they have "a tremendous role in how kids look at where they are in society." And, "I think the media is very slanted in their politics, their views. They have an agenda they want to push and they are so . . . just out there. I firmly believe they are not in touch with reality."

In an earlier interview, Glenn has said some things about one television program in particular, and the interviewer raises this with him, particularly the fact that he has identified *Touched by an Angel* as a good program, but not "in terms of actual spirituality." She asks him what he means by this.

Glenn: Well, I think what the show did was that it gave you the sense that there was a greater, higher being and that there are ways to make moral, good decisions. But that isn't all there is to spirituality. Spirituality is multiplicity. I think the show itself didn't go that deep. It was an overview that would give you an indication. If you were sitting on the fence you might go "Gosh, there are good people out there and maybe I can find that peace that comes from making a decision." . . . It is almost "goody-two-shoes." There is a big difference between that and spirituality. Spirituality is very, very, to me, deep and exudes from the inside out and it is something you don't get from a TV or a book. To me, it is a relationship with the Lord. It is a personal relationship with Him. . . . I feel good when I read some books that are along those lines, but true spirituality is a relationship that you share with Him that really penetrates you inside in the deepest parts of you. Whereas the book can only give me book knowledge and say, you can look at life this way and that is kind of spiritual or here's some spiritual notes for you to take and keep in mind.

The clear indication is that, for Glenn, faith and spirituality are deeply connected with "a decision" (indicative of his Evangelical faith) and with a kind of "depth" as over against media superficiality. To Glenn, then, a program like *Touched* is to be evaluated for its spiritual or religious significance not in terms of the symbols and values it contains but how those are put to the purpose of convincing people of the need for an intense and personal salvation.

Perhaps because Glenn has been somewhat fluid in his own religious trajectory, having made a rather large change in his own religious identification (from Catholic to Evangelical Protestant) he maintains something of an interest in religious diversity, and reports having sought information about a variety of religions, at least while he was on his own religious quest. In response to a question about whether he'd ever explored non-Christian traditions, and which ones, Glenn responds:

Glenn: Taoism, Buddhism, and the Koran. I've read a lot of information about a lot of different religions and how they operate and I looked at why the Baptists are the Baptists, why Evangelicals are Evangelical, why Lutherans are Lutherans, Mormons. I was very interested in all that. What is this all about? What is their search? Why are they looking?

Interviewer: So, why did you stop exploring non-traditional paths?

Glenn: I stopped exploring non-traditional paths because I found that there was so much diversity in all those paths that there was something that was not right for me in all that. . . . And the conclusion I came to is that we are all searching. We all have that spiritual hole that needs to be filled and it is a matter of where you choose to plug in but what I've found is that when I had a relationship with Jesus Christ . . . after that, it was developing a relationship with Jesus. There is only one way, as I see it now today. I was searching in all places but nothing filled me. . . . And, I am very analytical. That is part of my problem that I look at things in that regard. So, what I needed to do was, I said to myself "What's common in all these things?" Well, everyone is searching for God. Okay? But is Buddha a God? No. Because Buddha was dead. Buddha was never resurrected. The only person that was ever truly resurrected that they have proof was Jesus Christ. Jesus Christ had over 600 prophecies come true. What was his name? . . . Nostradamus, right. He was lucky if he got one out of 10 or 1 out of a 100. So to me, I look at the Bible . . . you can pick the Bible apart and say it is this, this, and this, but if you look at the prophecies there are people prophesyzing 400 years before an event happened and that event happened. Isaiah did it. So, what I'm saying to you is when I started seeing that I was like "This is historically correct."

It is perhaps not so clear from this passage that a great deal of the exploration that Glenn has engaged in has involved mediated sources.

He speaks frequently of the books he and Liz have read, have shared with each other and with friends, and have given their children to read. His acquaintance with prophecy is a theme that has found some consonance in the popularity of the *Left Behind* series of books, which he considers to be "tremendous." At the same time, though, it is important for Glenn to be open and questioning – "analytical" as he put it above – and for his children to also be free to make their own choices. He makes a connection between media, particularly books, and what he assumes to be the more coercive and prescriptive practices some parents engage in. The interviewer asks about how Glenn thinks about the religious, spiritual, or values resources his sons may come in contact with through media.

Interviewer: So, for the boys, for instance, do you ask them to be sure they are using different religious stimuli in their daily lives to reinforce these things you have built in them? Do you ask them to listen and watch Christian programming? I know they go to church.

Glenn: Yeah, well that is something that is a good question because I don't, I'm not a firm believer of Bible thumping . . . by that I mean, I don't go in there and say "Are you reading your Bible every day? Are you praying every day? Are you doing this, are you doing that?" Because they see me read my Bible. . . . So, the foundation I laid for them I think is very important but do I actually do that? No, I don't. Because I found that the lessons they learn in life when they run into a situation, then I can say to them, well, did you check that in the Word? Did you look for that in the Bible? Have you prayed over that situation? Where is your Walk now? You seem a little distant. So it's more that than saying "Gosh, you should really read that series *Left Behind*. It's a great series on the Rapture" and all that. I mean, they may decide to read it and they may not . . . but do I put books in their room? No. . . . I really don't because what I found is that until they understand that it is relational . . . those things are really meaningless. . . . So, maybe I should push that a little more but I am a firm believer in planting the seed and letting the Holy Spirit water it. And, by that I mean, they've been given the foundation. They know what it is to be a Christian. They know that they need to be salt and light in the world. . . . And so, I think that is the way that I have developed it . . . more a personal relationship rather than being a teacher and saying "here, you need to read this book or you need to be listening to this radio station." I found music on the Internet that they downloaded and I said "That is not appropriate." So, when I find those things, I bring it to their attention. And, I watch them turn around like that [snaps his fingers] in a heartbeat. He is now downloading all Christian music.

This passage is important in relation to Glenn's ideas about parenting and is significant of what we might call his sense of "parental identity." Consistent with the findings in other studies of family media use, there is a tendency for parents to want to describe themselves in this way. Rather than specifically directing their children's media diets, they would rather think that their role is to equip their children with the skills and values they need to make their own decisions.[36] Interestingly, this holds for someone like Glenn, who we otherwise might have expected to be rather rigid and judgmental in his attitudes about such things.

As for himself, Glenn initially seems reluctant to connect media with anything positive. "What are there?" he asks,

> a few books that are worth giving your kids to read? How many Christian movies are out there? There aren't any Christian moviemakers that I know of. So, you have to take the secular and say, "We sat down and watched a movie. What did you get out of that?"

When the Interviewer mentions the buzz that is beginning to build about Mel Gibson's *The Passion of the Christ*, Glenn – who has apparently not heard about the film yet (this interview took place two months before the film's release) – assumes the worst about the film, and moves from that to an argument about the role that the media play in perpetuating what he sees as social dependency and a culture of victimization, issues he connects directly with faith and spirituality.

Glenn: Oh, I'll bet. Don't get me started on that garbage. Give me a break. No one is willing to assume responsibility for their lives today. Everyone wants to blame everyone else for why their lives are messed up. And I think that is so, so wrong. The media has done that! The media says "Well, it's okay, you poor black people. You were slaves. We just did a terrible thing and we should probably pay you money for what you lived through." Baloney! I'm sorry but . . . that is just the way life was and that is what happened. Get over it! So many people are saying "Well, this happened to me. Poor me." Look, I can say the same thing. I was raised by alcoholics, by service people who moved around constantly. . . . I can sit there and live in that or I can say "Hey, I learned from all that how not to treat my kids or my wife." So we all have an opportunity to change. . . . So, I think what the media says is "Oh, no, it's okay. You were bruised, you were hurt. We will make it better for you."

. . . and the media takes ugly things that happen in life and points fingers. Oh, the police messed up here on this investigation and on and on. You know, they point fingers at everyone without getting to the crux of the matter. . . . You can't just say, at least in my eyes, that society is messed up because society hasn't done anything for its people. It's just the opposite. The people haven't done anything for themselves. They have chosen to stay where they are instead of saying "I'm going to break free and I'm going to break the pattern." . . . Priests were molesting kids. If I was molested I would turn around and say yeah it was ugly. . . . Yeah it was miserable but God has another plan for me. He wants me to take that message. . . . I want to take the message of what happened in my life and show other people that my family is absolutely wonderful now because of Jesus Christ and He turned my life around and I'm not the way I was. In January, I'm 20 years clean and sober.

In a sense, Glenn seems to be saying that his critique of this kind of media is based on his judgment that the media have perpetuated trends in the culture that he disapproves of. These passages tell us more about Glenn and his ideas than they do about the media or about his use of the media, however. In spite of his feelings about the media, though, he is aware of trends in the media, attributing to reality shows, for example, some of the worst motives and effects growing out of the media sphere. "You could put a pulse on society by what the media is showing and promoting," he says. "Listen to the news. How much of the news is garbage and how much is positive?" There is clearly a disconnect between the media and the real, authentic values he sees as missing from contemporary life. He comes back again to his theme that the media are somehow involved in perpetuating values of cultural "victimhood."

I think that is where society has a responsibility to teach our kids these things through the media. I think the media can be a wonderful tool but we are not using it. Look at school. Look at what is happening at school. Books. Are we giving them the right information? People are in there trying to change. . . . "George Washington was not a . . . he had infidelity in his life" or whatever. We got to get George Washington Carver in the books because he was black and we gotta get this, this, and this in the book and before you know it, it gets so muddled up that they are missing the message of what the entire United States was founded on. The United States was founded on Christian beliefs. That is the freedom to worship God. My problem is that we have too many people imposing their views on what we should be and should be. Using the media. Johnny Cochran, the anti-defamation League, you know, all these people come in there and say you can't do, shouldn't be doing this or this.

Glenn's political philosophy is obviously coming through in these passages. He connects the Christian foundation of the nation with certain ideas about race and culture. Interestingly, he seems to assume that there is a natural set of sentiments that children today would be expected to hold that are in turn subverted by the media and the cultural elites whose values are represented in the media.

> The problem is that kids sit there and say "Well, what should I do? If I do this am I going to be an anti-semitist [*sic*], am I going to be a.... " We just get labels. And kids don't really understand who they are.

In Chapter 3, we talked about the implicit Durkheimian boundary between the secular world, represented by the media and a "sacred" world that is the turf of religion and spirituality. Glenn believes in this boundary, and on a rather profound level. In reflecting on the capacities that media might have to contain what he calls "nuggets" of truth, he turns to an anecdote from his own life. At an earlier point in his life, when he was attending a church in California, another parishioner, someone in the film industry, led a discussion group about current films.

> He brought us movies and I can't remember what they were but he said "watch this movie" and I started watching this and there was sex, violence, just nasty language, and then we would go back the next Sunday and he would say "What did you guys get out of that movie?" and I was saying "That was an awful movie, it was terrible." He said, "No, what did you really get out of it?" And then we had to start thinking and he would show clips and he said, "See this clip. See what they are saying here?" They are saying don't do this, yet they are showing everybody to do it. It is okay to drink and get drunk. It is okay to have sex. But he is saying "No, no, no. Look – they are really saying don't do those things because look at the terrible things that happen to the characters." So, we missed the point. It went over our heads. I was blown away. Here we are in a Christian church and the guy has got the blessing of the pastor and I'm going "You have me watch this movie that has the F word every other word and says do this and do that and shows this and shows that." I was offended at first. Then I went back to the class and thought "Wow, he is right. There is a message. There is actually a decent message somewhere here. But do I want to watch all that? I'm not attracted to that! The secular world, they are probably attracted to that. Are they going to see it as a subliminal? I don't know. Is it something they are trying to teach you through all that? I don't think so. But somebody had a nugget and got it in there somehow."

Glenn obviously began by expecting that, to be appropriate, films must be free of the derogated elements of sex, violence, and language. He clearly agrees with the Evangelical taste culture, as described by Hendershot,[37] that to "cross over" from secular to religious, the basic formula calls for secular films or other media to be rather bland and inoffensive in conventional terms. But Glenn encountered in this experience another perspective – that one could look at film more symbolically or metaphorically. He describes himself as gradually coming to the view that there can be a nugget of truth in such films, a nugget that is so profound that the dominant culture – represented in the media – must not have been aware that it was there. Someone sneaked it in, he speculates.

Glenn has a decidedly apocalyptic sense of the world, something that is, as I said earlier, connected with some dominant streams of contemporary Evangelical pop culture. He sees the boundary between the sacred and the profane clearly inscribed in the contrasting media cultures of the secular and Evangelical worlds.

Glenn: When you pick up a magazine off the rack, half of it is just garbage. It really is. There is nothing edifying. You go to a Christian bookstore and find edifying things. . . . Oswald Chambers, all those things that are great literature to read. James Dobson has some wonderful things, Chuck Colson, there are so many people out there but they are just such a small portion. And then if you pass one of those good books to somebody they say "Whew, I'm not reading that crap." So it is our responsibility in society to establish some sort of norm here. We are so sideways. To me it is Sodom and Gomorrah. But, I'm overly critical. But I firmly believe that the Lord is going to be here. I really look at the Bible and I read that the end times are close at hand. I don't think they are that far away. . . . You look at the Temple being rebuilt; you look at what is happening with the common market. The Eurodollar. All those things are really leading to what the Bible says in Revelation about what will happen in the end time. The war, the feast, the famine. It is all happening and it is being accelerated.

At a later point in the interview, Glenn reflects on something specific from the media that he finds to be particularly profound and meaningful: the *Andy Griffith Show*.[38] Glenn connects the character played by Griffith with normative ideals of fatherhood and parenthood, and the character played by Ron Howard (during his days as a child actor) with an ideal of sweet, innocent boyhood. Ironically, Glenn contrasts the character of the son with what he sees to be the profanity of Ron Howard's profession now, as a film director.[39]

Like many of our informants, Glenn initially found it difficult to connect media with his faith and spirituality. As the interview continued, though, it became clear that, in important ways, he sees these issues as integrally related. His views are strongly inflected with "accounts of" media as, first and foremost, a source of negative or anti-social ideas and

values. Further, he assumes the received idea that the media are by definition on the other side of a boundary separating the "sacred" from the
"profane." The connection between media and faith, for him, is further
interconnected with a set of ideas about contemporary social values,
including particularly race, but also gender. This is illustrated by his feelings about the social meaning of the *Andy Griffith Show*, which he
considers to be valid, but it is in the past. For Glenn, there is a natural
order of things that has somehow come to be disrupted in modernity, and
the media are both a cause and a measure of that disruption. They serve it,
but they also are emblematic of it.

At the same time, though, media of certain kinds are integral to
authentic faith and spirituality for Glenn, specifically Christian media such
as the books and other resources of Focus on the Family and the Promise
Keepers, and the books of authors such as Tim LeHaye and Chuck
Colson. He even accepts the notion that the purely "secular" media such
as Hollywood films might have the capacity to convey important
"nuggets" of value. As a whole, the fact that certain media might relate to
authentic faith is a tacit understanding for Glenn. At the same time,
though, he struggles against a taken-for-granted distinction between the
profanity and anti-religion of the secular media (religion linked closely
with social and political ideas as we have seen) and the sacrality of
authentic and faithful life, and the media connected with faith.

Seeing these accounts from Glenn as parts of his larger "plausible narrative of the self" enables us to position his ideas here as representative of a
number of things. First, he strives for coherence and consistency, even
against some contradictions. This is particularly obvious in his discussions
about manhood and spirituality. Consistent with traditional views in
conservative Protestantism, he sees male spirituality as an autonomy
expressed in spiritual "headship" (to use the Evangelical term of art). At
the same time, his narrative reveals a struggle with contemporary gender
roles and gender relations. He further proposes an approach to understanding gender that is no doubt inflected by his experience with the
Promise Keepers organization, which stresses a more balanced view of
manhood. He suggests that men need to develop their "feminine" side.

Second, his descriptions of his views of parenting carry with them sometimes uncomfortable markers of reality and the claims and values of
modernity, with these elements needing to be made coherent and consistent
within his description. On the one hand, he strives to express his spiritual
leadership in the home, but on the other hand is reluctant to be seen as
directive or coercive. He clearly understands media, books, magazines,
television, film, *and* popular music to be important cultural markers and
resources. He is at the same time reluctant to control them. Like many
other parents, as I said, he wants to describe a situation where his spiritual
leadership has educated his children by example, and they therefore make

the "right decisions" more or less on their own. The incident he describes, where his son has downloaded inappropriate media, does show that he intervened, but yet his assessment of the outcome was that the decision was his son's, a decision that happened to coincide with Glenn's own preferences in the matter.

Third, these ideas about parenting are clearly normative, in that what he wishes to project of himself and his ideas he would consider to be models for others. There is also a normative undercurrent; a social philosophy that connects his own "self-help" orientation with a broader culture – influenced by the media – that stresses "victimhood" instead of self-reliance. It is important to see that, for Glenn, this conflict is one that has religious and spiritual overtones. For him, his religious conversion was deeply connected with his triumph over his alcoholism. He sees, then, the question of self-reliance as something that is also deeply spiritual. He cannot disconnect the two. The media are implicated in undermining this spiritual/self-reliance value in a couple of ways. They portray examples of victimization at the social group rather than individual level, and in their attempts to contextualize such things they (to Glenn) perpetuate excuses for individuals not doing anything to better themselves. They further traffic in materialistic as opposed to ascetic values, thus undermining the kind of moral uprightness that Glenn sees as important to spiritual self-reliance.

It is hard to miss that much of Glenn's representations of his social/spiritual philosophy is inflected with race. These statements are not simple statements about issues of victimzation, self-reliance, and self-control in the abstract. The examples he uses are focused on race, and this is clearly an issue for him.

Fourth, his narratives connect him with others, both significant and less significant, binding his sense of who he is in the narrative to a concomitant sense of the others he relates to, specifically his children, Liz, and the men who form his social network at church. One way this is expressed is in terms of his relations with his sons. He aspires to convey to them the essence of true manhood. Invoking one of what I called "the repressed modes" of religious experience in Chapter 3 – *experience* itself – Glenn suggests that what society needs is concrete rites of passage for young men. This works at resolving another contradiction addressed in Glenn's narrative, that exists between an impersonal, media-saturated society, and a personal and individual encounter with what is right, good, and appropriate.

Fifth, a particular normative or ethical dimension enters because Glenn is a recovering alcoholic. He sees himself, and wishes to be seen, as someone who has conquered that disease through a mixture of autonomous action and commitment to his faith. His concentration on his own experience – its centrality in his narrative of self – really dominates most of what we see him talking about here (and, indeed, the whole inter-view).

How then are the media and religion linked in his narrative? It is inter-esting to note that, for Glenn, religious tradition and religious institutions are not particularly important. He has shifted from Catholicism to Evangelical Protestantism, and while he attends church regularly he is far more involved in the Evangelical "para-church," in the form of the Promise Keepers and Focus on the Family organizations, than he is in any church institution. This is also rooted in his own biography and his experi-ence with recovery. It was something he experienced individually, and it enabled a kind of self-reliance that connected him in a strong personal way with faith, thus sidestepping institution and doctrine. For Glenn, his social philosophy serves as "doctrine" for him, inflected of course with his interest in apocalyptic literature.

Glenn's relationship to the media is even more interesting. On the one hand, he is heavily involved in Evangelical popular and media culture. While he eschews religious broadcasting at one point in the interview (not presented here), he and Liz are regular readers of printed literature, including books and magazines, from a variety of sources. The Christian Booksellers Association would consider him to be an ideal market demo-graphic.

On the other hand, he draws a boundary between those media and the secular media. The secular media are "religious" to Glenn – in a sense – because they are so heavily involved in the dark side of what he sees to be the spiritual question of victimhood versus self-reliance. They also carry significant markers of materialism and moral turpitude. They run counter to the upright and ascetic vision of the moral life that he would like to stress. It is problematic, though, because he must at the same time recog-nize the important role that media culture plays in the social lives of his children. He accepts tacitly that they will consume secular media; there is nothing he can do about it. He is further reluctant to be seen as a parent who would direct his children's media lives.

Glenn also sees this boundary operating within the realm of the secular media. There are secular media, such as *Andy Griffith*, that are acceptable. In the anecdote he shares about the film-viewing sessions, though, he recounts having to contend with the idea that even media that carry morally disturbing markers can have a deeper meaning. But, the boundary still functions. He clearly believes that there are larger institutional forces at play – a popular theme in Evangelical pop culture, by the way – and that whatever positive "nuggets" might appear in Hollywood films are probably there by accident.

It almost goes without saying that Glenn Donegal is someone for whom a life narrative will be a normative self-presentation. He wishes to think of himself and present himself in a certain way. Consistent with Ricoeur's ideas, his narrative reveals a range of elements, some synthetic, some contradictory, that he weaves together into a coherent stream. It is a narrative that is dense with normative ideas and aspirations. Further, it reveals much about the relative presence of media and religion in Glenn's social experience and daily life. There is a level on which the media are assumed and religious institutions are not. Certain media, particularly Evangelical media, are an important, even critical element in Glenn's social-spiritual philosophy. Institutional and clerical claims are less important. Consistent with Roof's ideas about "Baby Boom" religion, Glenn demonstrates a deep desire to be "fluid, yet grounded," but to see that as his own quest. He thinks of himself as autonomously responsible for his own faith and his own salvation, and has – in his mind – ample evidence, through his recovery, of the success of this approach.

In a way, Glenn sees the world as a conflict between his normative social and spiritual ideals, ideas that are supported and perfected through his experience with certain media artifacts, and a cultural sphere, also defined by its media, that is in conflict with those ideals. There is a "bright line," for him, but rather than a line between a sacred world defined by a contrast between religious doctrines and a secular media sphere, the boundary is situated elsewhere. Glenn lives in the culture defined by the media. He sees and understands much about the media sphere and is familiar with its outlines. The conflict for him is between his ideal, normative world of spiritually supported self-reliance and an alternative world that preaches victimhood and spiritual *anomie*. There are media on both sides of this gulf. The distinction between them seems to be drawn in two ways. First, there are media that are by definition "good," those media produced by or consonant with the values and symbols he identifies with – the Christian books and other publications he and Liz read and the Christian music he encourages his son to listen to, for example. Second, there are media that are more "secular" in origin, but that are either inoffensive enough (along traditionally understood dimensions) to be acceptable (*Griffith* again), or that contain "nuggets of truth." The politics of this latter world, though, are such that Glenn does not entirely trust the motives of those who would produce and present such "nuggets." His sense of the cultural politics of the times leads him to suspect that the approach that the media take to social and moral philosophy is the result of a worldview that intends to affect the society and culture in certain ways. Thus, there is a cultural struggle afoot, and Glenn is pretty clear on which side of it he stands.

Glenn's is obviously not the simplest case to use in an investigation of religious symbolism in the mass media. As we will see in later chapters, there are more explicit narratives. In a way, Glenn is a type that we would expect to be relatively less interested in or involved in secular media, anyway. In Roof's taxonomy, discussed in the last chapter, he would reside somewhere between two of the cells: "traditionalist," and "born again." In fact, he is a case that problematizes that taxonomy a bit, a matter we will get to in more detail in the next two chapters. As a "traditionalist," he would be less likely to be looking for or finding religious or spiritual resources in the media sphere. As a "born again," he would be likely to orient more toward resources from the extensive marketplace of Evangelical pop culture. As we have seen, this is a pretty good description of him, in terms of his media use, and the relations between media and religion in his narrative. But, this description is a bit superficial at the same time, because we can see that Glenn's notions of the relations between religion/spirituality and the media are rooted not in the inductive categories proposed by Roof, but in Glenn's own synthesis of his personal biography into a social-spiritual philosophy, and it is that social-spiritual philosophy that better defines him and his motivations than his position in Roof's taxonomy.

This is not to argue that we discard Roof's categories. In fact, they will become an important part of our analysis in the next chapters. Instead, it is to say that a taxonomy such as Roof's is valuable at a certain level of analysis. It is particularly helpful in looking at classes of religious identity and religious experience, and tells us much about the cultural and historical moment. Further, such labels make sense in a real way, and can be and are part of people's own narratives. They connect with, and predict action and ideas on a certain level (as they did with reference to Glenn's use of various media). At the same time, though, we need to recognize that on deeper levels, in individual cases and their "plausible narratives of the self," other combinations and consequences will be seen. Which level we look at is part a matter of what we have available, part a matter of what we have the capacity to look at, and part a matter of which questions we are asking. As we shall see, Glenn's case illustrates that by looking at narratives both in their own terms and through the lenses of theory-derived classifications such as Roof's, we can learn a great deal.

In the following chapters, we will of necessity be looking at individual narratives in less detail as we address the question of how media and religion can and do relate in contemporary social experience. We will be looking at a larger number of narratives, and classifying them in ways that aid our interpretations. We should remember, though, that each of these is a "Glenn," with its own unique set of conditions and attributes. What Glenn has helped us see, though, is the status of these narratives. There is good reason to believe that, as we hear from these informants, we are hearing self-descriptions that are significant of the way media and religion relate in their identity constructions.

The next three chapters focus on the presentation and analysis of "plausible narratives of the self." In Chapter 5, we will look at a set of narratives that will help us describe the role that the media play in the culture of daily life, setting the stage for an analysis of their role in relation to religion and spirituality. In Chapters 6 and 7, we will talk about the ways that various narratives express the kinds of things people seek out and find in the media sphere that relate to or serve their religious and spiritual quests. In doing so, we will rely on (and – in a way – test) Roof's taxonomy, looking at how those major categories of identity and action are and can be expressed in relation to media artifacts and symbols. In Chapter 8, we will reflect on the fact that the relations between media and religion are complex and far from straightforward. We will look there at the variety of ways that people relate to media – what the media can "do" for their religious and spiritual lives. The "accounts of media" we will be looking at in these interviews reveal a kind of enigmatic and contradictory role for the media. What does that tell us about the meaning practices that result? In Chapter 9, we will move from the more closely focused level of the household and daily life back toward the larger context of the way the media have come to the center of the formation and expression of religious and spiritual experience in cultural, social, and political life. Chapter 10 will draw the many avenues of inquiry in this book together in an exploration of the contrasts and contradictions we have found along the way, and conclusions we might be able to draw.

Chapter 5

Reception of religion and media

There are a number of ways we might have looked at religion in the media age. There are, admittedly, large structural, political, and social implications of a point in history where the means of communication have become institutionalized, commodified, and routinized. The argument I've been developing here is rooted in two assumptions about the situation that results. First, thinking of religion and media only in institutional-structural terms ignores the way that media and religion are coming together in important ways in contemporary life. Second, those changes militate in favor of a particular kind of analytic strategy: one that focuses on the reception of media, and looks at both the texts and practices of consumption that result.

We have gradually focused on the central task of field research that looks at media texts and media reception related to religion and spirituality. As I've said, it might seem like a rather straightforward task to simply "go and ask" people about the media they see, about what they do with those media, and how those media relate to those moods and motivations we in another time would have called, simply, *religion*. As we will see, this task is not nearly so straightforward.

To begin with, it is important that we ask such questions in such a way as to not "salt the mine."[1] We talked in Chapter 4 about the phenomenon we call "accounts of media," which can be described in certain contexts as an effect of "social desirability," or the tendency to give the "socially desirable" answer. We can then expect our conversations to entail such answers to some extent. This would be particularly so were we to ask a question like, "How do the media affect your religious or spiritual life?" right off the bat. While we do get around to this question at some point in our interview guide, we begin far less obtrusively. This is because the strongest or most convincing evidence of a role for media in religion/spirituality would be from a conversation about religion/spirituality where reference to media simply "comes up" on its own. We'll also see that, in a way, this does happen. Media do appear in conversations about religion/spirituality, and religion/spirituality do appear in conversations about media. Far more often, though, we have to probe to make those connections. We don't *start* there; we go there after first beginning conversation about religion and then about media.

We will think of what we see here as passages from the narratives of the self we discussed in the last chapter. These narratives are self-descriptions that weave together interviewees' experiences, values, ideas, and ideals into what they hope to make a seamless whole. They are not always successful. There are gaps, tensions, ruptures, and struggles, as there are in life. Each of our self-narratives necessarily carries within it the tracings of experiences and relationships that, because they existed in history, need to be accounted for in some way in their roughness and discontinuity. As I said in the last chapter, though, the question for us is not how well our informants are able to weave seamless narratives, or what those narratives reveal about how things "really are." Our project is to understand how symbols, practices, and discourses from the media sphere relate to those meanings and motivations that we and they might identify as "religious" or "spiritual." So, in a way, it is the ingredients or elements that make up these narratives that most interest us, along with how they are brought together, and what they seem to contribute to the project of the whole.

We'll begin by considering one of the fundamental issues we've been discussing all along, the extent to which media are or are not an inevitable dimension of contemporary life, and, by extension, of religious and spiritual meaning quests.

The pervasiveness of media

Brenna Payton is a 12-year-old middle-schooler who lives on the edge of a medium-sized city with her mother, Corrine, and her sister, Sally, who is two years older.[2] Brenna and Corrine have featured in an extensive analysis by my colleague Lynn Schofield Clark, who looked at them as an example of distinctiveness in terms of media consumption.[3] I want to reintroduce them here because they illustrate a point that Clark also made about them – the difficulty all families have in avoiding the pervasive reach of media.[4] Corrine Payton's great passion is ecology and living a balanced, holistic lifestyle, something she tries hard to instill in her daughters. For her, this holism does not include media, which Corrine, who happens to be a Unitarian, considers to be too materialistic and a waste of time. Corrine does not make a clear connection between her Unitarian faith and media use, *per se*, but, rather, her faith interacts with her ideas about holism, and that in turn leads to what she considers to be logical conclusions about what is appropriate in terms of media.[5] Brenna and Sally do watch television at their father's house on weekend visits, but their primary identification is with their mother's place, which is "TV free."

Corrine muses that she might consider getting a television set at some point in the future, in part to address any unintended consequences for Sally and Brenna of her stance on TV.

Corrine: . . . you know, looking at what Sally and Brenna are going through and, we might still get a TV at some point. . . . And they do get TV on the weekends. So as far as the peers, "Hey did you see what was on *ER* last night?" or whatever, you know, they are not totally out of the loop.

Brenna: A lot of people ask "Hey, do you watch South Park?" [The interviewer notes that she has mispronounced "South Park" and her mother corrects her.]

Brenna: . . . I don't even know what it is.

Corrine: Yeah, it must be a TV show.

Brenna: It's a cartoon or something.

Corrine: Yes, that would be my guess.

Brenna: A lot of people at school know that I don't have a TV and they're like "How can you manage without a TV?"

Interviewer: What do you say?

Brenna: I say, "It's easy, I mean I've got lots of other stuff I can do, you know?"

While the lack of a television set at home does not appear to be a big problem for Brenna, her experience here illustrates the extent to which it is really not possible any more to live a life without media, or at least outside the reach of the media. Her family also shows that it requires very concrete and conscious action to maintain a life without television today. In nearly all cases, households without television are like the Paytons': they have made a clear decision to step outside it. And yet, they can't escape it completely. For Brenna and Sally, they can (and do) watch television at their father's house (*Dr Quinn, Medicine Woman* is Brenna's favorite show). But, more pressing for them is the fact that television viewing is such a fundamental reality for Brenna's social network at school that she is seen as different because she is identified as someone who doesn't. Consistent with the level of engagement we have called "interactions about media," knowledge of current television (and presumably other media) becomes a currency of social exchange for young people of all ages.

Brenna is not alone. It is very common among these interviews to find people saying, like Jill Fallon, whose family we'll meet shortly, "people feel sorry for you if you don't have TV." The Paytons and the Fallons are what sociologists might call "outliers" in the landscape of media use, among the relatively few families who, for whatever reason, do not participate in media culture unproblematically but have chosen to separate themselves from it or from aspects of it. And, in both of these cases, it's not that they have no television at all. The Payton girls watch TV at their father's house, and the Fallons are regular, and active, viewers of films on VCR, and have a collection of nearly 200 of them.

Wyonna Fallon, 39, and her two daughters, Jill, 14, and Uta, 12, live in a medium-sized city in a western state. Wyonna works at two jobs while she is finishing an undergraduate degree in social work. The family belongs to the conservative Church of Christ denomination and the girls attend private Christian schools. Their formal involvement in this religion, though, is relatively recent, having evolved after they moved to their current city about four years ago. They are somewhat unusual in that they do not own a conventional television set, only a small combination TV/VCR unit, on which they watch videos regularly. Wyonna attributes her preference for videocassettes to the autonomy it allows. The Interviewer is naturally curious as to whether their video-viewing habits might be related to their relatively conservative religious attitudes (Roof would probably classify this household as "born-again Christian").[6]

Wyonna: I guess I can see a big discrepancy between TV and video. I guess videos, you watch what you want to. TV is just crap.
Interviewer: When you're renting videos – or any of the videos that you own – do they relate to spirituality or religion?
Jill: We had one.
Uta: The (Island?) thing.
Interviewer: The what?
Uta: The Ireland thing.
Jill: There was one. . . .
Wyonna: Oh, *The Secret of Irish Rum* [*The Secret of Roan Inish*].
Jill: Yeah. That wasn't a good one.
Wyonna: It's kind of a folk tale.

The Interviewer notices a more specifically religious videotape sitting on a nearby shelf and asks about it.

Interviewer: What about *Jesus Christ Superstar?*

[Everyone responds at once; general shouting, discussion, laughter.]

Wyonna: Before we started going to church. That [*Jesus Christ Superstar*] was our religious thing. At Easter we'd watch that.
Uta: That's another movie we memorized. We also made up songs.
Wyonna: We started watching that in Florida.
Jill: Plus we tape movies. Like *Monty Python's Holy Grail.*
Wyonna: I'd say that's their all-time favorite.
Uta: [Making funny noises in background; I think in an attempt to imitate parts of *The Holy Grail.*]
Interviewer: That's the family's all-time favorite – *The Holy Grail?*
Wyonna: Yeah. I like it. But those two love it. We taped it off the TV. There's one section of *The Holy Grail* that's a little – it's not bad –

Jill: It's funny.
Uta: But it's really dumb.
Wyonna: It's a little risqué. It's kind of dubbed out, but –
Uta: It's so dumb, it's funny.
Wyonna: But they really like it. I like it too . . . which [*The Holy Grail*], I
    guess, might be considered sacrilegious by some people, *Monty Python
    and the Holy Grail.*

Undoubtedly, a number of their fellow Church of Christ members *would*
find it sacrilegious. Here we have a family that reports no broadcast or
cable television viewing at all. As unusual as this is considered to be by
the girls' friends, the family nonetheless watches a good deal of video
material, and maintains a large collection, watching them together as a
family, usually on Friday nights. Beyond that, they make a number of
explicit connections between religion and their video viewing, at the same
time that they don't seem to reflect, in their video habits, the kinds of
material we would expect of born-again Christians. At an earlier point in
their lives, they used *Jesus Christ Superstar* in a kind of sacramental way,
and, even today, they regularly watch *Monty Python and the Holy Grail*,
and consider it to be one of their favorite films. This "guilty pleasure"
may well define, for them, the kind of autonomy that Wyonna feels is an
important dimension of her self-description. This is her strategy for negotiating between a position that television is somehow bad or a waste of
time, and the natural attractions and pleasures that television and the
other media provide. The Fallons' "experiences in media" and "interactions about media," through which they express a great deal of joy and
satisfaction, and experience family togetherness, are in some conflict with
Wyonna's "account of media" that holds that television is "crap." Their
strategy – watching television by *not* watching television – works for
them.

We might assume that it is a relatively simple matter for individuals and
families to decide not to be part of media culture. We have already
discussed a number of different perspectives on the media in daily life that
assume that a separation is possible, that "bright line" can be drawn
between the media and the more "authentic" or "natural" dimensions of
life, of which religion is an important one. Such distinctions are not as easy
in real life as they are in theory, as we can see here. Particularly for young
people (but really – as we will see – for everyone) the media are more and
more an accepted, tacit part of life and culture, so much so that, when they
are missing, we and others notice.[7]

If separation *were* possible, or if the media could be treated as independent objects in the sociocultural field of everyday experience, it would then
have to be based on a rather direct, straightforward, and intentional set of
understandings and practices. In fact, a great deal of what we say and

think about the media assumes a level of cognitive engagement with media practice. We want to assume that people think about what they do, that they can be reliable interpreters of their own actions and reliable sources about their practices. There is reason to wonder, though, whether these are safe assumptions

Life with media

Dale and Bonnie Johnson are in their early thirties and live with their two sons, Don, 6, and Carson, 5, in a medium-sized city. Dale is completing his undergraduate degree after a change in careers, and Bonnie works part-time. Dale is bilingual in French and English, as his mother was born in France. One of Bonnie's parents also was originally from Europe. They are African American and live in family housing managed by the university Dale attends, which is helpful because their family income is less than $25,000 per year. The apartment is small but comfortable, but there is little spare room available anywhere. They have cable TV through their housing, and also own two television sets, two VCRs (one in the parents' bedroom), and a computer with Internet access. They have a large collection of videocassettes, mostly of popular films, stored on separate racks, one for the kids and one for the parents.[8]

They are devout Christians and attend an independent Baptist church, but the parents are from different religious backgrounds. Dale responds to a question about this: "I grew up as a Protestant I think. No, no a Presbyterian." Bonnie was raised Southern Baptist. Both parents now identify themselves as religious people, and a good deal of what they talk about is inflected with their religious values and religious ideas. When asked what is important to them as a family, for instance, they say both family "quality time" and a "spiritual upbringing." They see themselves as involved parents, and express that in part through the rules they try to maintain for their boys' media exposure.[9]

As is the case with many families, though, their descriptions of media practice in their home are a bit vague. When asked what television programs they regularly watch, Dale and Bonnie respond "news," affirming that they mean, first, *local* news. When asked if they watch "CNN or Tom Brokaw or anything" by the Interviewer, Dale responds "We do watch MSNBC." They then go on, simultaneously saying "*Dateline.*"

Interviewer: So you're watching the news every day?
Dale: We do get news every day.
Interviewer: How long?
Dale: Night time, I guess about two hours.
Interviewer: Two hours of news every day?

Bonnie: Well, not every day.

Dale: But it's pretty close.

Bonnie: Since we work we have the evenings where we're getting lunch or dinner prepared. Ahh . . . I don't watch *Oprah* like I used to (laughs).

Interviewer: So when the news is on, you're not sitting down and watching it?

Bonnie: We do. No that's our time to sit down and watch TV.

Interviewer: And by "our" you mean the kids watch too?

Bonnie: They're in bed by then.

Interviewer: So what time do they go to bed?

Bonnie: We try to get them in bed by eight.

Dale: Yup.

Bonnie: Because that's our quiet time.

Dale: If they (the kids) watch TV, they watch cartoons or something.

This is an interesting passage particularly in light of the great volume of social research on media use that has depended on this sort of "self-report" as a reliable way to assess television viewing. Dale and Bonnie want to say that they are regular news viewers, and name several programs (local news, MSNBC, and *Dateline*) that they watch every day. When the interviewer suggests that what they are describing would add up to two hours a day, that seems like too much. While our purpose here is not to uncover the "truth" of their behavior, it is nonetheless interesting to speculate about what this report may mean about their actual viewing.

What it says about their self-narratives is that news is a value for them, and that they like to think of news as something they should do every day and something that they consume during what they call their "quiet time."

When the conversation moves on to the media habits of their children, Don and Carson, the Johnson parents note that, that day, the boys have been watching *Power Puff Girls*, *Dexter's Laboratory*, and *Courage the Cowardly Dog*.[10] Bonnie jokes with the kids about Courage, the dog, a program she obviously has watched with them. Courage, it seems, uses a computer and the Internet in most plots. Bonnie observes,

Bonnie: That's Dale's source of media – the computer.

Interviewer: So you use it for school?

Dale: For school, yeah. For my internship I get on Word or Microsoft Publisher. Today, I gotta do Excel. And if I'm not doing that and I turn on the computer it's for Minesweeper. I rarely check my e-mail.

Bonnie: And I don't use the computer at all.

Interviewer: [to Bonnie] You don't use it all?

Interviewer: [to Dale] So you're using it every day?

Dale: No, no. I use it probably about three or four times a week to play Minesweeper. And that's, I'd say, about a half hour to 40 minutes if I do play it. But I don't go on the Net. I don't surf the Net.

Interviewer: You do have Internet access though, right?

Dale: Yes we do have Internet access. It's Ethernet I think.

Interviewer: You say that you almost never go on the Internet?

Dale: Rarely. The only thing that I look for actually is Mapquest and that's it.

Bonnie: And I never go on [the Net]. I do not use it. I have no desire for anything. If I want to talk to somebody, I don't e-mail them, I pick up the phone. I am an anti-computer individual.

Dale: The kids will play tank wars on the computer, but that's like once a month. They haven't done it for a while.

So a picture develops of a household where there is Internet access and one parent who does not use the computer while the other one reports using it primarily for word processing and games. The interviewer is curious as to whether the children also go online.

Interviewer: [to Carson and Don] Do you guys go on the Internet?

Dale: [answering for them] The whaaaat!? No, they *never* do. The only thing they go on is, ahh, shockwave.com or tankbattle.

Bonnie: In fact, we have to sign a release tonight if we want our kids to go on the Internet at school. And we're not going to allow them to go on the Internet at school.

Interviewer: Oh really? What are they going to be doing instead then?

Dale: I don't know. . . .

Bonnie: Read, writing. . . .

Dale: They can do whatever. . . .

Dale: As far as the computer goes, there's too many sites that they can get on to. But you know, you can't obviously shield them forever. . . .

Bonnie: Right.

Dale: But as far as school goes, they have no need for it. They have no need for e-mail. They can't read.

It is clear that Bonnie and Dale feel anxiety about the Internet and the computer, and want to limit Don's and Carson's access to them. But, in nearly the same sentence where Dale declares that they never use the Internet, he reveals that, besides the computer game *Tank Battle*,[11] they have also gone online to the commercial site shockwave.com[12] enough that Dale is aware of them having done so. The Interviewer is curious about Dale and Bonnie not approving of the kids having Internet access at school. "Not yet," Dale says. When the Interviewer asks when it will be appropriate, Dale responds,

That's a good question. When it serves a purpose. That's the big thing. Because right now they're five and six. They don't know about the

'Net. If they want to go on the 'Net, then they need to ask the parents and I'll navigate to show them where they need to be. They don't need to go on yet.

This sounds good, except they already go on the 'Net, and it turns out it is not just shockwave.com that they know about. Referring to a site or sites that the kids go to, Bonnie asks Dale, "What is that [site the kids go to] Dale? Disney.com or bluesclues.com?" Don, the 6-year-old, responds for him

Don: Disney.com.
Bonnie: It is Disney.com?
Don: There's Nickjr.com.
Bonnie: Yes, that's it. Thank you Don.
Dale: Yeah, and if they want to go on the computer, they ask us – for just setting the ground rules, OK? Kids nowadays, they can log on to computers and the parents have no clue as to what they're doing. "Oh, they're on the computer? Well, let them go play on the computer." If they want to navigate on the Web to find something, they'll ask us and it'll set precedent for the future. I'm interested, Bonnie's interested in, what our kids look at on a daily basis. So, right now, they have no need for (the Web) unless they want to go to Nickjr.com. But I don't know why they'd want to since we don't buy anything from Nickjr.com or anything like that.

So, there is a bit of a contradictory picture presented here by Bonnie and Dale. Early in the discussion, Bonnie says the boys *never* go online. She also claims to not be a computer user. Then later we find that they use the family computer to play video games, and in fact go online to websites, of which five are named, and not all of these resources are things intended for children. It is clear that Dale and Bonnie intend to be involved in the boys' media use, and their knowledge of where they've been online can be read as a testament to their vigilance in this. The boys are 6 and 5, though, and are already getting started on their Internet journeys, with or without Dale's and Bonnie's continuing intervention. It is hard to predict how this will work out. What is clear, though, is that Dale and Bonnie mean to be – and to be seen as – parents who are involved in this important aspect of their boys' lives, and that this is rooted in how they understand their *religious* identities as parents. They are concerned enough about the Internet to contemplate denying the boys access at school, even though it is likely that the uses they would put it to there would in fact be purposive. Dale and Bonnie "read" the Internet primarily in terms of its entertainment, not its educational value, and in fact have encouraged entertainment use of it by means of the sites they allow – or facilitate – the boys' access to.

The interview takes on a similar feel when the interview moves on to the boys' television use. The interviewer asks "You said they watch?" Dale responds, "Cartoon Network." The interviewer responds "And that's it?" "That's it," Dale replies, but Bonnie has reservations; she begins to answer, and Dale interjects:

Dale: Nickelodeon! Or Nick Junior or something like that.
Bonnie: And PBS or something like that. They watch PBS during the fall because they like – what's that little dog's name? –
Dale: Oh yeah! *Wishbone.*
Bonnie: *Wishbone.* They like *Wishbone.*
Dale: Yeah. And Don was watching *Discovery Channel* yesterday with whales. And other than that, nothing else.
Interviewer: And you guys supervise it pretty closely?
Dale: Yes.
Bonnie: Yeah.
Dale: We always know what they watch.
Bonnie: And like at school, I make sure I know what curriculum they're being taught.
Interviewer: And what kind of curriculum are you interested in them being taught?
Bonnie: They're being taught core knowledge, which is basic. That's what you and I learned when we were little kids and that's really good curriculum. If there's something that they're going to be studying one week and I don't like it, I just let the teacher know and then we'll figure something else out. But that's never happened with the core knowledge, ever. But I try to stay heavily involved as far as volunteering. I'm classroom mom for both of their classes so, you know, I try to stay tight with what they're doing.

One gets the impression that their scrutiny of television viewing is a bit looser than they would like to think. For example, they mention two specific programs here, *Wishbone* and a nature program on the Discovery Channel. We know from earlier in the interview that the boys have probably regularly watched three additional programs on the Cartoon Network, and Nickelodeon's Nickjr morning block of programming. While Bonnie and Dale would like us to think of them as drawing "bright lines" around media for their kids, we find that they and the boys have negotiated their way into television and Internet. Admittedly, the material they have accessed is largely kid-oriented and kid-friendly. Their expressed preference for straightforward, basic knowledge in school, and Dale's idea that the boys' Internet use should be intentional and purposive, are laudable ideas, ideas that echo the perspectives of many religious organizations. In practice, though, the barriers and boundaries are not that clear.

The Johnsons tell us a lot about the nature of family life in the media age. They have clear and laudable aspirations for their children and for the kind of parenting they want to deliver and their children to receive. They perceive the media – both Internet and television – as implicated in this process. They actually don't want to recognize the extent to which Don and Carson are already media-involved. Their experience, though, illustrates several things about the media in family life that are important. First, the media today need to be seen as a package, not as discrete services or experiences. The boys' online activities are articulated into many of the same programs they watch on television.

Second, as we saw earlier with Brenna and Jill, the media sphere is nearly inescapable, even for boys as young as Carson. It is ubiquitous, and is constructive in important ways. *Blue's clues*, for example, one of the websites/programs the boys are familiar with, is an educational program, as is *Wishbone*.[13] The PBS and Discovery shows they watch presumably are probably more helpful than hurtful, too.

Third, this whole landscape is something that exists at a level of social articulation into life that is subtle, tacit, and yet salient in important ways. Neither the parents nor the boys are really clear on which programs are viewed and which websites are visited. At least there is no sense of an actual cataloging or monitoring of these practices. There are clear attractions to these activities, but these media are consumed in a way that is different from the way these parents conceive of education being "consumed." They assume the latter to involve a measure of rational and intentional action. They seem to think about consuming the former as though rationality and intentionality are not really involved.

Finally, there is an extent to which the salience of media drives its consumption, even for parents as seemingly intentional and careful as Dale and Bonnie. In discussing their film-viewing habits, they talk about movies that they will or will not watch with their children. Noting that the boys like war movies, they draw a line between films they consider to be inappropriate, like *Saving Private Ryan*, *Platoon*, and *GI Jane*, and films that are appropriate, such as "John Wayne movies," the *Star Wars* cycle, and "just old things" like *Top Gun*. And, it comes out, the one program they do watch with their children regularly is *ER*.[14]

At a later point in the interview, Bonnie reflects on how the attractions of a specific program came into conflict with her faith, and she describes herself as drawing a line.

Bonnie: I don't like anything that has to deal with, you know, Satan stuff.
    I don't like that. Umm . . . and I used to love – and I've only seen
    South Park once or twice –
Dale: (laughs)
Bonnie: And they made a comment about God, so I refuse to watch
    that anymore.

Interviewer: So. . . .

Bonnie: It was bad comment about God. And you know (almost whispering), it's a really funny cartoon. I mean, a funny, funny cartoon. I can't watch (it) because they insulted God.

Interviewer: Ok. Any TV show or movie that you see that you think is insulting God, that would be something you would. . . .

Bonnie: Insulting God, or me personally as a woman ahh. . . .

Interviewer: You probably get both those things on *South Park*.

Dale: Oh yeah. Geez . . . (laughing)

Bonnie: And it's too bad because it's a really funny cartoon. But I can't compromise my faith.

Interviewer: Do you think there are any kinds of movies or shows that shouldn't be allowed to air at all?

Bonnie: No because that's censorship. You can't have censorship.

Interviewer: So. No matter what the content. . . .

Bonnie: Well, I have that choice. God gave me the choice of either going down this path in life or that path in life and I chose this one. And since we do live in America – which was founded on Christian beliefs – there's the freedom of speech and religion and thought. And God did give us a free will. So, no I don't believe in censorship at all. I just choose not to watch what I don't believe is ethically correct.

One gets the impression that Bonnie is both more attracted to, and more familiar with, *South Park* than she would like to reveal. Whether or not she watches it, it is clear that she sees a line somewhere between the program and her beliefs. That a program like *South Park* can attract someone like Bonnie (a conservative Christian) is a testament to the cultural power and salience of that program. Like the experience her children are having – of the presence and ubiquity of the media as cultural resources – Bonnie finds herself living on a map where she must negotiate her beliefs in relation to media.

Lest we think that it is only media about which people are somewhat fuzzy in recalling and describing their own behaviors, Bonnie and Dale seem also to be a bit vague about their daily religious practice. In the context of their religiosity, they describe themselves as watching one or more televangelists regularly. "Aside from Bible reading, that is it," says Dale, referring to their day-to-day piety. Later, the Interviewer returns to this topic.

Interviewer: And you said spirituality is important too?

Bonnie: Yeah, very important.

Interviewer: So, going to church, what else would you say sort of embodies that . . . Bible (reading)?

Bonnie: Yeah.

Interviewer: You don't do that together as a family?

Dale: Well, right now we each read our Bibles and then we go to bed.

Interviewer: You have prayer, though?

Dale: Yeah, we pray with the boys upstairs, the Lord's Prayer. Well, some-times in the past before I started this internship, we used to read Bible stories to them. We have a couple books of Bible stories.

This comes up at another point in the interview, and this time, the report is slightly different:

Dale: The reading that we do mostly consists of the Bible.

Bonnie: The Bible, at night. . . .

Dale: Before we go to bed.

Interviewer: As a family?

Bonnie: By ourselves. He reads his Bible, I read mine.

Dale: We used to anyway – we need to get back into it – we used to read the kids Bible stories, or just a book before they go to bed. We do say prayers before they go to bed.

The messiness of daily life comes through here. Families such as the Johnsons clearly must constantly negotiate their way through the hurdles that challenge their plans for where to invest time and attention. Most of us can empathize with them, and few of us could probably describe our lives in as straightforward a way as we would like. We strive to be consis-tent and to act in ways that reflect our values. And, like the Johnsons, we would be likely to describe ourselves in the first instance as being successful in doing so. Also like the Johnsons, it would probably become clear the more we talked that we are not always the people and families we wish to describe.

The Johnsons help us understand how the media are integrated into daily life. They are inescapable, troublesome, contradictory, and complex in their role. That is clear. It is also clear that for the Johnsons at least, and for the others we will hear from, the question of the role that the media may play in religion and spirituality will also be inescapable, troublesome, contradictory, and complex. We will now begin looking at the question of the relationship of religion and media in daily life more directly.

We are moving through an analysis that looks within the sociocultural landscape of religion and spirituality for ways in which the cultural resources of the media sphere serve contemporary projects of meaning and identity. In previous chapters, we considered emergent changes in that landscape that substantially alter traditional and received ways of looking at religion. We've seen that contemporary religion scholarship describes religion in terms of its meanings *achieved* more than meanings *ascribed*, and that the relatively autonomous practices of individuals are today more important than the prerogatives of institutions and structures.

We've also reviewed some of the outlines of the landscape, relying particularly on the work of Wade Clark Roof and Robert Wuthnow. The emergent religious/spiritual practice of "seeking" defines a good deal of the momentum in contemporary religion, in their view, while not ignoring the fact that, for many, "seeking" is less important than "dwelling." Roof has helpfully provided a taxonomy of "Baby Boom" religion (discussed in Chapter 3). We will now begin to use this more explicitly in our analysis. The next two cases I'll introduce occupy two separate "poles" of the contemporary religious *Zeitgeist*, and the ways they relate to the media provide some compelling insights into the questions we are concerned with here.

A traditionalist?

Judy Cruz is a 38-year-old single mother living with her son, David, aged 15. Judy is Latina. David's father, from whom she is divorced, was Latino. They live in a two-bedroom apartment in a low-income housing development in the near suburbs of a major city. Though Judy did not finish high school, she has attended community college, with the goal of working as a school para-professional. Having hurt her back, she is now on disability income. David is a sophomore in an alternative high school. Their family income is in the $15–25,000 range.[15]

Judy is an interesting case in light of Roof's taxonomy of religion. From her income and education, we might predict that Judy would be more traditional in religious terms, fitting into either Roof's "mainstream believer" or his "dogmatist" category. However, she's more complicated than that. Judy was raised Catholic, and considers herself Catholic today, but has done quite a bit of moving around, denominationally.

> I've tried other religions . . . Christian, Baptist . . . but I always go back to my own religion because I feel comfortable and because the Catholic religion there's not too much of it shown as far as TV or radio. That's more or less just an out of the home religion.

It is interesting that Judy feels that religions can be classified by this way. She is a regular viewer of a number of programs for their religious content, but sees this "in-home" religion and the "out-of-home" religion of Catholicism as complementary. Interestingly, the kinds of religious and spiritual material she weaves together into her own religious identity is broader than Catholicism or even Christianity.

Interviewer: Do you seek out anything in the media in terms of your spirituality or religiosity? You mentioned the show *Miracles* [the actual name is *It's a Miracle*] and that was the other thing I wanted to ask you about. I know that's a PAX show. Can you tell me a little about that?

Judy: I like *Miracles* from first-hand experiences as far as being saved. Yeah the Miracle station on PAX is interesting and there is another program that is going to be coming out it's for people that have passed on where they speak to this person and that person tells you what they have said.

Interviewer: That's coming up?

Judy: Yeah.

For Judy, the compelling thing about programs like this one and the others she watches is their "reality." She sees them as dealing with life in its concreteness, yet as it is infused with something beyond the concrete. This is her explanation for liking *Touched by an Angel*, for example. "It comes down to life and reality," she says, "as far as what does happen in life. Experiences." The Interviewer asks, "So do you like it because it's about what you think of as real people, or is it the spiritual element that you like?"

Judy: They're combined together.

Interviewer: In what way, in terms of your enjoyment of the show?

David: The mysteries.

Interviewer: The mysteries on that show?

Judy: The angels um . . . what else? I guess the faith.

There is a way that religion and spirituality become compelling for Judy when they are connected with or revealed in "real life." This is, of course, a capacity of the media that makes Judy's "in-home" religious experience what it is, and makes it distinct, for her, from traditional "out-of-home" religion. Where *Touched by an Angel* is rather conventional in its religious referents, other programs she watches are compelling in the same way without being quite so connected with religious categories. The Interviewer asks Judy to talk about what she likes about *It's a Miracle*. Judy describes a recent plot where a van was stolen from a gas station, and there was a child in the van.

Judy: Yeah. And then there were two angels, two people here on earth, that went and chased the van, to get the van back, and they saved the child in the van.

Interviewer: Angels meaning. . . .

Judy: People, just regular people.

Interviewer: When you say angels, what do you. . . .

Judy: Came to their rescue.

Interviewer: Is that what an angel does?

Judy: Yeah. They're just regular people that um. . . . I don't know if some-body talks to them . . . and they right away jumped to . . . something going on and they go and they interact without thinking they might be in danger.

Interviewer: I'm thinking on *Touched by an Angel* the two main charac-ters, and maybe there is a third, are they people on earth or are they brought from somewhere else?

Judy: They are brought from somewhere else, but that's fantasy.

Interviewer: But in the miracle show, they talk about angels on earth, actual people who do good things?

Judy: Actual people, yeah. There's a difference there, yeah.

Interviewer: Is there a difference for you?

Judy: Well, let's see. As far as . . . the fantasy and the reality, yes. But as far as actually doing the purpose, it's about the same.

Interviewer: Do you wish more people watched them?

Judy: Yeah, then they would see more or less what's going on. Kind of like not being so greedy and materialistic. Just more or less an eye-opener, yeah.

Judy thus sees both piety and ethics in these programs. Her sense of the value of the shows connects her piety with what she sees to be their concrete reality. At the same time, they are object lessons for others, effec-tive ways of communicating positive, even Christian, values of justice and other-worldliness. There is a difference, though, in that one of these programs (*Touched*) is "fantasy," while *Miracle* is "reality" in relation to the nature of angels. Both programs are "real" to Judy in that they connect with people's real experiences, and either divine or divinely inspired inter-vention in them.

We learn more about Judy's religious and spiritual proclivities in a discussion about her use of computers. The family has a computer, but it is an older, slower model, and they have normally gone to the library when David wants to play video games or search the Internet. Judy describes herself as not using computers "right now." "I'm not done with them. I just put them to the side for now," she says. The Interviewer asks if there are things on the Internet that interest Judy. She replies, "Stuff like I want to get back into, maybe stuff on healing. I'm more into the healers and the . . . let's say the astrology and the stars and stuff."

Like many other informants, Judy makes a clear distinction between the kinds of media – on television or the Internet – that she is interested in and "religious" programming, which she does not get much out of. It is inter-esting that she interprets the Interviewer's question about seeking inspiration through media to mean this latter kind of programming, which she equates with televangelism.

Interviewer: Do you ever go online or through television or film seek out inspiration?

Judy: As far as spiritual?

Interviewer: Sure.

Judy: No, not really. All of that is about money. They're always asking if you'll pledge money and I don't think it really, through TV or radio it doesn't really get through the waves. You have to do that face-to-face, it's more reality when you do it like that. As far as TV or radio it is hard to concentrate and it seems like a lot of . . . I don't know, too much dancing and music and you just can't get into it. Your thoughts . . . you can't even go there.

Judy is someone for whom spirituality is important, though it is expressed in rather unconventional ways. She divides the world between religious practice that takes place outside of the home – her conventional Catholic practice – and that which can be accessed within the home – including the things that she can get from television, radio, and the Internet. In the latter category, further, there is a difference between the programs and services that really mean something to her, and those which are presented as, self-consciously, "religious."

Interviewer: I know we talked before about *Touched by an Angel* and *It's a Miracle*. Are those different for you from preachers up on the screen or on the radio?

Judy: Yeah, and there is another one that just came out called *Crossing over with John Edward*.[16] That's kind of interesting to me because, I guess because people have had experiences and a person can relate to things like that whether it's miracles or healers or, you experience things like that and you can relate to things like that, but as far as preachers or dancing, it is a little bit more different. It's not as comfortable.

Judy clearly finds meaningful, even spiritually meaningful, material in television (and might well go to the Internet to pursue such interests as well). The thing is, she doesn't go to the expected places. For someone who by other measures (imagine how Judy might answer a telephone survey about her religious preference or beliefs) should be rather traditional, she instead defies easy categorization. This is even more the case when the Interviewer returns to questions of media and religion later in the individual interview with Judy. "Do you think about God or spirituality when you interact with media?" he asks. Judy responds, "Um . . . no I don't. That [spirituality], I do on my own time." She goes on to describe a weekend event she plans to attend where there will be psychics and healers as an example of her doing spirituality "on her own time." This is a fascinating example of the "seeker"-oriented autonomy we spoke of in Chapter 3. Judy presents herself as taking responsibility for her own spirituality. She is the center of the quest, and does not want to cede that role to church or to media.

Still, she sees media as an important context for the working out of her ideas about her beliefs, as is clear when the Interviewer follows her into a discussion of her belief in aliens.[17]

Judy: I believe that there are aliens because where did we get all this knowledge of high-tech equipment and people have found spaceships and they have it on videotape about the, what is that where they did capture an alien?
Interviewer: The autopsy thing?
Judy: Yeah. I have seen, you know, I have seen something but I believe there is life out there in space. There's other things.
Interview: Do you get reminded of that or search things out media-wise for that?
Judy: It's on TV all the time. TV kind of pushes . . . it's kind of pushed. They don't let you find it out on your own. They kind of push it on to you, like the X-Files or like now, Roswell, they kind of push that on you. And also Star Trek. They kind of turn things around. They take fantasy and there's no more reality so they kind of turn things around.

Judy's seeker autonomy is thus offended by what she sees to be the preponderance of alien-oriented programs available in the media. Beyond that, she finds their approach to be less than helpful because it is (a favorite word of hers) "fantasy." The Interviewer asks for a clarification:

Interviewer: I'm just trying to understand this. Are you saying because you take these things [aliens, afterlife, etc.] to be real that the X-Files is kind of a joke because it's playing it for drama or for make-believe?
Judy: Yeah, it's turning more into money because they figure while they . . . [long pause] if they come out with all these stories they have to kind of act, play, and dress up in their little costumes and they kind of, now you're looking into fantasy. It's not reality.
Interviewer: Reality is the things that you believe.
Judy: Yeah.
Interviewer: Is the Crossing over thing closer to reality?
Judy: Yeah, that's a lot closer.
Interviewer: Because they are making the TV show and I think they accept that this isn't what you're calling fantasy, it is real?
Judy: They're actually going into real contact. That's why I said a person has to go and see for themselves. That's the only way you can tell if it's reality or fantasy. You have to go and check it out for yourself. Because there are gifted people out there that can do these certain

things, let alone if people can do that that's fine because they can use their gift into making money and they're not hurting anybody but then you have these programs that come on that are kind of like messing with your head and. . . .

Interviewer: Messing with your head meaning?

Judy: Yeah, they're putting fantasy in your mind and they're projecting you again into what's fantasy and what's reality.

Interviewer: For you, angels, aliens and afterlife, this is what you're calling real?

Judy: Yeah.

Judy is a fascinating case, illustrative of the complexity we've been talking about. While the media play a role in her self-understandings around spirituality and belief, it is a negotiated self-understanding. She sees the media landscape as a place where religious meaning and religious difference are represented. A kind of religion, that she calls "out-of-home," plays an important role for her. She is Catholic, and always has been. She has tried other faiths, but always comes back to Catholicism. But that is not all there is to her beliefs and spirituality.

She is attracted to programs that exist on the boundary between traditional belief and her own sense of existential reality. Angels are important to her, representing values and sentiments that she wishes to identify with, for example. So there is, within media, those media that are authentic and attractive because they are "real." By "real" she means that they deal in episodes that are concrete representations of daily life and perhaps of ordinary people. She has no time for media that present themselves as "religious." Even within the category of media that focus on themes she finds interesting – aliens, for example – she is skeptical of their claims on her attention and beliefs. She wants to make up her own mind. "I do that on my own time," she says. In the end, the "fantasy" that she sees in many programs falls away when she can encounter the "real," put by the Interviewer as "angels, aliens, and afterlife." That is reality, and thus authentic, for Judy.

It is also interesting how Judy defies in a way the earlier characterization of the "symbolic inventory." If, by that, we meant that media symbolism and practices would exist on a shelf to be accessed as resources out of which people might construct new senses of who they are religiously and spiritually, Judy shows us that that description is a bit simplistic. Certainly, there are ways in which Judy does use media as a resource. She would have that intention in seeking things on the Internet, for example. And, there are undoubtedly elements within *It's a Miracle* or *Crossing over* that she would find useful and memorable. Her "experiences in" those programs would result in things that would serve to build and extend her understandings of things. At the same time, though, she clearly sees these media as a field of negotiation over appropriate and inappropriate presentation of such symbolism. She expresses an interesting and subtle "account of" programs like *X-Files* as delving too much into "fantasy" and not enough into "reality" when contemplating aliens from outer space. These media then help her define her own beliefs, they are involved in compelling practice, and they serve identity on more than one level.

As I said, Judy defies some of the categorization we brought into this analysis. As someone who we might have expected – demographically – to be rather conservative or traditional in her religiosity or spirituality, we might also have expected her media tastes and practices to represent that. As a devout Catholic, we would expect that she might not be that interested in media representations of religion, or in specifically Catholic representations if so.[18] We have found something quite different. On one level, she is like we would have expected her to be. She attends services with some regularity, does not like televangelists (though she does watch them), and draws a bright line between her sense of her Catholic faith as "out-of-home" and other things "in-home" that have another status for her. But there is where the great difference lies between what we might have expected and what we found. Her "in-home" practice opens up into an interesting and complex set of beliefs and ideas, a personal sensibility of "seeking" or "questing" (though not described in those terms), and a negotiation with cultural commodities in the achievement of meaning and understanding, and the experience of salience or even *effervescence* (to use a Durkheimian term).

Next is a case that should, on the face of it, provide a contrast. Against Judy, who by conventional measures would fit into Roof's category "mainstream believer" or perhaps even "dogmatic," we'll now go to the other "pole," a family that resembles much more Roof's description of a "metaphysical believer and seeker."

"New Agers?"

Butch and Priscilla Castello live in a large bedroom community outside a major city. Butch, 34, is Latino and Priscilla, 39, is of Italian descent. They have two small children, Leah, aged 5, and Corey, 8, who attend an alternative school nearby. They live in a large, comfortable home in a relatively new neighborhood. Butch works in sales for an international telecommunications firm; Priscilla is a homemaker who writes fiction. Their family income is over $75,000. They were both raised Catholic, but now identify themselves primarily with Buddhism. They are very much like Roof's "metaphysical believers and seekers" in that they describe themselves as still seeking the right religion for them. In some ways, Buddhism seems more like a lifestyle than a spiritual choice for them, both of them agreeing to the Interviewer that they have not yet found the "right" religion or belief. They are able to describe their religious beliefs more in terms of what they are *not*, i.e. "no longer Catholic," than what they *are*. Buddhism, and Asian culture, are distinctive features of their lives, however.[19]

Their religion or spirituality is something very personal to them. They are not involved in religious practice formally, choosing instead to incorporate Buddhist practice into their lives at home. Their self-descriptions, religiously and spiritually, fit the broader category of "seeking" (as – in a way – do Judy Cruz's). Sociologically speaking, we expected Judy Cruz to exhibit media attitudes and behaviors more fitted to her educational and class backgrounds, to have perhaps been more traditional in her religious and spiritual tastes than she was. We found she was more complex than that. Our expectations of the Castellos would also be consistent with their class and educational levels (they are both college graduates). On the face of it, they fit the model of the "seeker," at least in Roof's terms. As with Judy, we then need to ask how their media-related attitudes and behaviors relate to their seeking and to their senses of self.

In fact, their "accounts of media" form an important part of their narratives of self. As with many other parents, this is expressed most clearly with reference to their children's media lives.

Interviewer: Do you have any policies regarding time limits about media use?

Butch: Music is pretty open. If someone turns on the radio, I wouldn't tell them to turn it off unless it was bedtime or dinnertime. (Priscilla echoes "dinnertime.")

Priscilla: Sometimes they (the children) want to watch kids' shows before school but no TV in the morning because we will be later than we already always are. (Laughs.) But in general, our overall rule, always try to find something else to do besides watch TV. Play, instead of watching kids' shows, or go for a walk instead of watching a video. So, we try to take the focus elsewhere because the current in our culture is to always be in front of the TV or on the computer. And, it is very hard when we are with other families in their homes because they tend to be really plugged into the television thing, or videos.

This is a straightforward and quite typical account of parental intentions. Two things are particularly interesting here, though. First, they seem to make a distinction between music and other kinds of media (there are few restrictions on music). Second, they express the same experience we discussed at the beginning of this chapter, the fact that the media are inevitable. If one family eschews media or controls them, another family does not. The children are exposed to media anyway, it is so pervasive. The Castellos are, further, typical of their class and educational level in these preferences. In the case of the Castellos there is a particular distinction they make between what we might call "screen" media (television, film, videos, video games, computers) and other media. There is some insight into this in Butch's recounting of a recent *Nightline* segment on artificial intelligence. Citing his fears about a future where machines come to be in charge and the humans are there to assist them, he says,

> And, they ended the program on a very, very, sort of frightening note in which they said, I don't know that I will say it just right, but to paraphrase, "imagine a day when . . . imagine a force so insidious that it would be able to literally take control of the mind of your child and take over your child's consciousness, control your child's thoughts and therefore control the future of your species in so doing. Subvert your species." Then it showed images of children in front of video games and their eyes (he drags at his lower lids with his fingers). And just this sort of blank look in their faces. I really strongly see it, not necessarily as a conspiracy that is being put upon us, but something that we are unwittingly falling into.

The image of children, glued to screens, is clearly a compelling one for Butch, and an object lesson that resonated with his ideas about television and other screen media. The trope is a powerful one, so powerful that the producers of the *Nightline* segment in question themselves chose to use it as a metaphor for domination by machines. Cultural ideas such as this one are so widespread, it seems, that even members of the media fraternity themselves rather unquestioningly subscribe to them.

Policing media plays an important and definitive role for Butch and Priscilla, as we will see. They connect their ideas about the appropriateness of different kinds of media to their religious and spiritual beliefs and practices. The Interviewer asks Butch if their media policies as a family are related to other aspects of their spirituality or lifestyle.

> Oh yes [he smiles and nods]. These things are very related. Our spiritual beliefs have led us to reduce the noise in our external and internal environments and the media is definitely a part of that. We are macrobiotic. We try to eat slow and make meal times a time of connection. We live in an area that supports that way of being. The kids' school, of course, is a part of that lifestyle choice as well.

The Interviewer asks when and how these lifestyle and spirituality choices entered their lives. Butch replies that while living in Japan for four years, they first encountered esoteric Buddhism, which he describes as "just a calming of the mind . . . a stilling of the sea." He continued,

And then, in addition to that, macrobiotic living, in a sense of *jin* and *jang* balance. TV and the whole ritual around the food and the TV dinners and TV trays don't lend themselves to that.

Interviewer: Right. Does media play into your spiritual life at all in any way?

Butch: If you consider CDs media, then yes. We play calming music. CDs of our choice that create a mood that we want created.

This again reaffirms a distinction Butch wishes to make between certain kinds of media – as typified by television – and other kinds of media, specifically music recordings. But connections between his spirituality and media do not end there for Butch. At a different point in the interview, he is asked, "What is the most important spiritual thing that you have?" His response, in fact, is connected with a major contemporary media enterprise.

I think . . . let me think about this. I have had this experience with Deepak Chopra. I was on a business trip and just was attracted to this book . . . *The Seven Spiritual Laws of Success* and this book is magical. And as a meaningful spiritual experience it seems all I have to do is touch the book. Honestly. If I touch this book something good happens almost invariably. I think it is partly that I'm realizing what is in the book because I have read it and I haven't done all the things he says to do and I don't do them regularly and I wish I did. But when I touch this book or look at it, magical things happen. Good things. It is bizarre.

This is fascinating, as it evokes images of traditional Christian ideas about the capacity of objects to convey spiritual power. More importantly, though, it demonstrates the extent to which media are embedded in daily spiritual life, even for someone like Butch. What we might call his "seeking sensibility," the fact that he is still looking for satisfying spiritual ideas and practices, opens him to things such as commodified therapeutic culture.

As with most people, Butch also carries memories of media from his youth that were both attractive and inspirational.

Oh I enjoyed *Star Wars* and, honestly, even *The Terminator* movie stands as one of my favorite films and not necessarily because, well, I loved the action, the special effects, and the story line . . . what it tells you about your children and the challenges that lay ahead. That is pretty inspirational, that movie at the end. It is almost tear-jerking when the mother is in the desert and she is pregnant and she is determined to help her baby, her unborn child to thrive in what she knew would be a difficult situation in the future.

This at least means that, for Butch, media are a less problematic element of his memories of his own life than he lets on with reference to his children's lives. This might help explain how it is that for most parents and most households where these interviews were conducted, opprobrium about media was also accompanied by an openness to media. Butch finds in *The Terminator* a set of salient cultural values, symbols, and ideals: perseverance, hope for the future, parental love, etc., put in a very compelling and memorable way. That is what media do and do well. They are, as we have seen, fundamentally cultural and fundamental to the culture. There is a tacit taken-for-grantedness in the experience of something like this film, which represents broad cultural values rather than more narrow spiritual ones. It is a very secular kind of inspiration that we find in media like *The Terminator* or the *Star Wars* cycle.

Priscilla Castello shares with Butch a basic parental suspicion of media. Agreeing with him that certain media are inconsistent with the lifestyle and spirituality they hope to cultivate in their home, she is pleased that they have found an alternative school for the children that shares many of these values, particularly around television. At one point, the Interviewer summarizes what she's been hearing from Priscilla about her view of parenting, and the challenges of maintaining a protected space in the home for children. Priscilla responds to the question completely in terms of media, specifically television. Television had not yet come up in the interview.

Interviewer: So, I hear you saying that you are trying . . . you have a very strong idea of how you want to raise your children as people and that you feel that it is sort of you against the world in a way because other people in your circle don't share these values.

Priscilla: Right. And, I know that there are groups, like the Waldorf school system, they're not into TV and if you go to a strict Waldorf school I think you are not even allowed to have a TV in your house. If you interviewed Waldorf families, you would get some interesting . . . and they are really into handicrafts. Like they do this finger knitting and woodwork. They don't even really focus on reading until like third grade, make it a real push, that is (reading). So, they're really working for more . . . it is a spiritual thing, too, that is more, it's Christian but it's sort of . . . I don't know the person whose philosophy it is based on. It is from Germany, I think. Or Austria.

This expresses an extension of the ideals presented by Butch earlier, that there is a kind of holistic lifestyle issue – that he called "stillness" – that the Castellos would like to be the hallmark of their home. And, once again, they see television as particularly antithetical to that settled lifestyle. She pursues this idea about the influence of "outside culture" in response to a question about values. She sees it as important that kids be raised to "have their own mind, to not be influenced by the outside culture," she says, "and maybe just the belief that the outside culture isn't necessarily positive."

Distinction from the outside culture is thus quite important to Priscilla. Its influences are negative, and its vectors into the home (once again, television being the primary one) need to be confronted as much as possible. In describing her own values, Priscilla describes them very much in reflexive, autonomous, metaphysical, "seeker" terms.

> I would describe them [her values] as really functioning from your true self. I guess that is something that I worked on myself, trying to peel off the layers that I've accumulated from people saying how I should be and what is good and what is bad. I was raised Catholic so lots of polarity with good/bad. And, just raising the kids to be aligned with their inner selves and their true being and act from that place and not act because Mom says you should act a certain way. Although, you still have to work within the culture so it is a little tricky to teach them good manners and stuff. But I still allow what I hope is enough of their true being to survive and not get buried. So that is really important. That and the belief in God, the universe, the spiritual energy. That is really important and we talk about that a lot. I try not to make that different. It is just all together. Kind of like when I lived in Japan. You are not separate from the sacred it is just all together.

Typical of the late-modern, autonomous sensibility, she makes a clear distinction between the traditional Catholicism of her roots, and what she sees as a more individual, self-generated spirituality. Spirituality, she says, is not something that one just does on Sunday.

> No, right. It is not something you have to go to church for and you don't have to dress a certain way. It is acting from your core and your heart and your loving being, I guess . . . and respecting nature and other people. I see that with organized religion that does not always happen. To me, it creates separation and judging . . . criticism. To me that breaks off that flow of compassion.

She sees a clear distinction between the traditional ways of church religion and what she finds the more ideal spirituality she has discovered in Buddhism. In the process, she articulates the sort of critique of traditional religion that underlies individuals' interests in what I have called "repressed modes" of religious experience. "I know there were ways of getting [spirituality] through church but it just seems that it was too hard. There are too many layers to peel off. Where in Buddhism it seems like it is more just there . . . here it is," she says. The authenticity of the spirituality she has found is then in part in its immediacy and accessibility. This is, again, a central element to the new "seeking" or "questing" sensibility we have been discussing in these pages. The project of meaning-making is about the "self," and, in the case of children, about helping them refine and develop their own "selves" and their own ideas. Parents should in a sense "step aside" and not make their imposition of rules and explanations the deciding factor; to Priscilla, children should be guided to discover their own true selves instead.

Priscilla, then, presents a narrative of self around children and spirituality that is rooted in distinctions between the protected, perfectable space of the home and the outside world on the one hand and between the authentic and salient spirituality she is striving to craft based on Buddhism and the spirituality proposed by traditional religions such as her childhood Catholicism on the other. Germane to our task here, she and Butch further define and negotiate these distinctions in part by means of media. In Priscilla's case, this comes through in a discussion of her online activities. Interestingly, she sees Internet and Web activities as relatively unproblematic, unlike television.

Priscilla: There are a few websites that I go to now and then and one of them actually is a spiritual site. It is someone named Cealo.[20] He has come to town a few times. I have seen him twice. He is a monk. I guess he is Buddhist but he breaks some of the rules sometimes. Like, you are not supposed to touch women and he does. His assistant, the person who travels with him, is a woman. He is from a monastery in Burma. He was a Japanese businessman. So, he just had a life change.

Interviewer: Have you heard him speak?

Priscilla: Yes, I heard him speak and I had a private session with him.

So, for Priscilla, the Web is an unproblematic context for her own spiritual exploration (she does not approve of her children going online and the Castellos do not have a computer at home – she must go online elsewhere). It is a context that is interconnected with real-life spiritual experience. Spiritual commodities and resources, such as those offered by Gayuna Cealo, effectively blur boundaries between the "real" local and personal life and the "artificial" outside and mediated life. One can move from the website to an actual encounter with him. This particular Web-based "ministry" is further interesting in the way it seemingly embodies the kind of exploratory spirituality that seekers such as Priscilla find attractive and salient. Buddhist tradition is less important than the authenticity of this particular monk, and his accessibility through the Internet adds a measure of connection for her. In response to further exploration by the Interviewer on her Internet habits, Priscilla describes in a relaxed way her encounters with this website.

Interviewer: Tell me, what do you do at his site. Do you go there to get information, to look up schedules or is there inspiration there?

Priscilla: It is pretty simple. Actually I was babysitting my friend's daughter and she said I could use her computer so I was looking. It just had a calendar of his upcoming things. It wasn't even filled in entirely. I think it had the January stuff but not the future stuff. And then they have a little market where they are selling some bags and things to raise money. And then it had a page that told about, a letter, to Americans after Sept. 11. I'm trying to think if there are any other sites I visit. There are some others I want to go to. They are spiritual or sort of . . . like Mothers Acting Up. It is a site for . . . it could be anyone not just mothers . . . working for children to have a better life in this country and also in the world. So, it is just a lot of letter writing to not support war because children suffer so much during wartime and women, too. I don't know the details because I have not been to the website but they are really big on everyone writing a letter to the president . . . they had the Mother's Day parade [here in town] last year where everyone dressed up really silly. Two or three people were on really tall stilts. It is also light, not real heavy, and that is an interesting aspect of it.

This is an enlightening description of how the Internet/Web can function so effectively to connect with beliefs and values. In marketing terms, the Internet is called a "pull medium" (where individuals can "pull" material out that is meaningful to them) rather than a "push medium" (where things are pushed at them). Priscilla's experience shows that these terms are not exactly descriptive. It is probably better to think of websites as "associative" media, where people associate themselves and their ideas with the symbols and values available there. To an extent, information is important, but there is also symbolic value in what these various websites and links represent. They represent things that are important to Priscilla, and are negotiable into her sense of self and self-description, as she describes here. It is undoubtedly important to her that such a website exists, for information about upcoming public events, for content such as teachings and reflections, and for the symbolic values represented by the site and its links.

Even though Priscilla has a particular website (and commodity) with which she identifies in a specific medium – the Internet – later in the interview she seemingly makes a distinction between her own practice there and what she identifies as "media" – publishing and broadcasting. The Interviewer puts the question about "screen media" rather directly.

Interviewer: Do you think there is anything in the media that is actually helpful for your spirituality?

Priscilla: There is the *Nexus* magazine. So, I guess there are publications
that do help with that.

Interviewer: So, mostly for you it seems like the media of choice for spirituality is print and when we talk about screen media, like television,
you are less inclined to find spiritual growth and inspiration there.

Priscilla: Right. Unless it is public TV. I know PBS does interesting things.
There is something on Tibet coming up in a couple of days. And Butch
is the one who checks it out. I don't know what is on ever. But sometimes he will be watching and something will look interesting and I
will watch, about people or. . . . So, I do see how it is possible. I'm sure
if we had cable there must be cable stations.

Priscilla and Butch thus have very different media diets than Judy Cruz.
Significant of their respective social demographics, the Castellos eschew
the kind of so-called "trash TV" that Judy finds interesting. Judy, in
contrast, does not read *Nexus* magazine and is less interested in public
television. More significant, perhaps, is the distinction between the two
households in terms of this issue of "screen" media versus other kinds of
media. Judy simply does not think of screen media as problematic in the
same way the Castellos do. There is a difference, as well, in Judy's readi-
ness and ability to discuss specific programs. The Castellos, who also use
media to chart relations in the cultural sphere and to define distinctions
there, are less capable of talking specifics.

As I observed earlier, there are ways that Judy and the Castellos share
some things in common, most particularly, their seeking sensibility,
autonomy of the self, and suspicion of traditional religion as over against
more authentic, "in-home," and lived religion. Where they really differ is
in their media diets, and how they use media in the context of what we
might call their "core" beliefs. For Judy, her interests were really piqued by
programs dealing with "angels, aliens, and afterlife." Priscilla is asked,
"Do you ever seek out anything related to spirituality on television or in
the movies?"

Priscilla: Sometimes at movie theaters. I only usually see art films or something like that. Yes, videos too. I haven't done this for a long time but I
like to get videos about religion. Mostly it is goddess stuff or
Buddhism.

Interviewer: How about music and spirituality?

Priscilla: Music! Oh, yeah. I don't have a huge collection of music but I do
go to the library. I like to get Celtic music. They have such great
music. I hear music and I think "Where did they get that music"! I try
to explore and find new music, mostly at the library. If we had more
money to spend in that direction I probably would buy more CDs or if
I found one I really like, I will go buy it.

Like Butch, she finds music a much closer connection to her spirituality than other media (another example of one of the "repressed modes" of religious expression). When seeking out screen media, her equivalent to Judy's "angels, aliens, and afterlife" is "goddess stuff or Buddhism." When pushed further by the Interviewer to describe any characters or roles in TV or the movies that are most like her spiritually, Priscilla cannot think of specifics, responding that "I do like a lot of movies that are about people, just snapshots of culture . . . mostly foreign films are so full of life and color and music."

The distinction between Judy and Priscilla is provocative. These tastes and interests are definitive on a number of levels. They reveal class and educational tastes. They reveal the possibilities of spirituality in contemporary culture. The fact that the only screen medium Priscilla is able to see unproblematically is film – and preferably *foreign* film – reveals a real distinction on that level, as well. A key difference is in how media relate to their respective spiritualities. Judy's voluble spirituality is engaged and supported (and negotiated) with reference to screen media. Priscilla and Butch see their autonomous, seeking Buddhism as very much in *contrast* to most of screen media. For Judy, media are part of daily life; for the Castellos, the media undermine their normative ideal of daily life. Thus, these two "poles" illustrate some important and provocative capacities of the media sphere to support contemporary religiosity. The extents and limits of the various media are not as straightforward and clear as we might have expected. Importantly, it is in some ways through these accounts of media that we can draw important distinctions between the Castellos and Judy Cruz. There are some other insights here, as well.

Negotiating media in everyday spirituality

These conversations reveal the challenge of asking people about media and religion. Our interviews attempt to get at these questions in a number of different ways, and we can see here the utility of such an approach. We learned more each time we circle back to questions of relations between religion and media, no matter how we asked the questions. As I said before, part of the reason for this is to be unobtrusive, to let these relations emerge in the narratives as they unfold. The interviewer's role is to follow the narrative in a way, guiding it and guiding it back, as necessary. It is important to emphasize that what results from these interviews are narratives that tell us some very provocative things about media, religion, and culture in general, and provocative things about these individuals and families in particular. The point is not to generalize from these individuals as representative of their demographic categories, but instead to understand what their stories tell us about how people in those categories use media, think about religion, and bring the two together. They tell us about the capacities of these things to *relate* in the context of domestic life.

So, what have we learned? I will summarize in terms of what we've seen and heard in these accounts that are indicative and provocative.

We began by observing that the media are a necessary and inescapable dimension of modern life. Each of the cases we saw demonstrated this to a greater or lesser degree. Children and young people tend to experience this most directly, and parents feel it at least indirectly. Even for the parents in these interviews, there is a way that the media are taken-for-granted, something that is a tacit fixture of modern life, through which and about which a good deal of discourse and meaning-making is made possible. We saw that they play a tacit and subtle role in these households and lives. I've also described the role as a complex one, a matter that has a number of dimensions.

It is interesting that for most of these interviewees, "the media" are a "package," not necessarily discrete channels or services. Differences between kinds of media do make a difference, but, at the same time, it is a technological fact (experienced in these homes) that we are in an era of "multi-media." This means that the program on Cartoon Network or the PAX network also has a website, and a magazine, and perhaps a video game, and other "spin-offs" as well. Importantly, there is a tacitness to the way people consume these media across these platforms. What they know and what they do from one bleeds over to the other.

Even though much of what we want to know about is the way that the media may or may not be "religious" or "spiritual," they do seem clearly to be "culturally" meaningful, too. They make sense in the culture that produces them (not surprisingly). This is most clearly expressed by Butch Castello's reflections on his youthful attraction to *The Terminator*. He got what he described as "inspiration" from that film, but it is a "secular" or "cultural" inspiration, not a spiritual one, that he is talking about. The media are successful because they are able to invoke and trade on tropes, values, symbols, and ideas that are salient in the culture. They are attractive, even pleasurable.[21] On the most basic level, then, it makes sense for us to think of them as articulated into the culture in fundamental ways.

On the question that brought us here, the media do contain religiously and spiritually significant material. Consistent with the arguments in Chapter 3, there is a good deal of material in what we otherwise would call "secular" media that connects with the religious and spiritual quests expressed in these narratives. This is most interestingly found in Judy Cruz's consumption of material related to "angels, aliens, and afterlife." We might expect Judy, as someone who demographically looks more traditional or conservative in her religious views, to be particularly unlikely to venture into territories like these. Instead, she rejects the derogated category of traditional religious broadcasting (even though she watches enough of it to critique it) and finds the more "secular" programming more interesting, even intriguing and spiritually satisfying. In her view, she sees these programs as actually evangelizing about a kind of "theology" of aliens and miracles. Even more interesting, she makes a distinction within these programs, finding some of them excessively commodified and fantastic, and others more satisfying because they are more "real."

Judy further makes a distinction between "in-home" practice and "out-of-home" practice. In a way that is reminiscent of some of Roof's and Wuthnow's ideas about the dynamism of the autonomous, seeking, self, she wants to see her more authentic spiritual practice as something that is closer to home, that is more domestic. Like the Castellos (as well as Wyonna Fallon and the Johnsons), autonomy and seeking are important – even vital – to her, and she shares with the others a concomitant suspicion of clerical and institutional religious authority. There is a good deal of evidence here, then, for the notion that a "seeking" sensibility around religion and spirituality transcends the expected or received social or cultural categories. It has been a too easy assumption that "seeking" is more of a phenomenon of upper-socioeconomic status households and individuals within them who are interested in practices such as the so-called "New Age." That is, people like the Castellos.

Another prediction from Chapter 3 was that the evolving religious/symbolic marketplace would be a place where new, more focused mediated symbolic and practical material would be made accessible to interested receivers. There is much evidence of this in these interviews. Judy, Butch, and Priscilla each have their own favorite media-based spiritual commodity. Each of them is "multi-media." For Judy, the best example is John Edward and his program *Crossing over*. While primarily a television program, Edward has an extensive Web presence, and a set of commodified media services and materials available. For Priscilla, it is the ministry of Gayuna Cealo, which she has accessed both online and in person, finding the online version an intriguing confirmation of her larger self-narrative. For Butch, it is Deepak Chopra, who he experiences most tactilely in the form of his book, which seems to have an almost mystical inspirational power for him. For Priscilla and Butch, Cealo and Chopra evoke symbols and ideas that are loosely related to their quasi-Buddhist practice. Chopra, Cealo, and Edward are, further, extensively commodified, and really "media phenomena" in the sense that they could not exist in anywhere near their present forms without the media. Their accessibility in the Cruz and Castello households demonstrates the value of mediation in bringing specialized symbols such as these within reach of the domestic sphere.

There is also a sense in which these secular media-based programs and services constitute a kind of necessary challenge to more traditional ways of looking at things. The cultural salience of *Monty Python's Holy Grail* for the Fallons, for example, drew them into consumption of a film that, on its face, would be found to be antithetical to the traditional ideas about Christianity that we'd assume would be conventional in the church they attend. For all seekers, there is an additional attraction to anything that challenges received, institutional religion, and there is reason to suspect that this would make such "resistant" media as *Holy Grail* additionally pleasurable.

There is much evidence in these interviews as well that the salience of these media tends to drive consumption. Bonnie Johnson's viewing of *South Park* and the Fallons' viewing of *Holy Grail* seem to show that there is a kind of attractiveness to media, something that we think of as a commonplace. But it is important in this context to reflect on the fact that the received assumptions we have tended to bring to questions of media and religion presume a different kind of viewing behavior, one driven by spiritual or religious values or interests that are satisfied by certain media in a more-or-less rational and cognitive process. At least some of the consumption we've seen talked about here does not exactly move in that direction. It seems like the media are just "there," they are consumed, and the religious or spiritual implications either follow on later or exist in a kind of dialectical relationship with audience choice. As I said earlier, this also raises questions about our notion of the "symbolic inventory."

The accessibility of media is also probably part of the story here. The fact that the media have become settled in the domestic sphere is a point of some concern and anxiety, but we see here some evidence that for these individuals, at least, the fact that certain of the media are *there* means that they will be consumed. This is a matter of some importance. Judy Cruz finds the Web unproblematic in part because it is there. I've also argued that we need to think of the media as tacit and subtle at the same time they are salient. People don't focus on them, instead taking them for granted in some ways, contextualizing them in other ways.

At the same time, though, the media are not so tacit that they are completely transparent. The autonomous project of the self has these narratives integrating media practice in ways that are an expression of that autonomy. Judy resists the imposition of media-derived ideas about aliens, for example. Autonomy is not surrendered to anyone, including the media. Parents such as the Johnsons want their children to develop their self-autonomy as well, and see media choice as an important element of that. For most of them, but the Fallons in particular, the idea that the media are something you can and should control also contributes to this project of autonomy. It goes without saying that, for each of them, *spiritual* autonomy is also a value, expressed in the context of the seeker sensibility, and expressed over against received authority.

The "accounts of media" we see here are also significant for the distinctions the media help make in the cultural, religious, and spiritual spheres. The media inscribe maps on which interviewees place their narrative selves. We've already talked about Judy Cruz's distinction between "in-home" and "out-of-home" religion, and her distinction between traditional religious broadcasting and the spiritually significant "secular" media she consumes. Judy's distinction between "reality" and "fantasy" in these latter programs is another interesting classification. For her, the "in-home" religion and the media that she negotiates into that spirituality are particularly meaningful because they are rooted and grounded in historical experience and in what she sees to be "real life."

Distinctions for the Castellos, the Johnsons, and Wyonna Fallon are more technological. The Johnsons are concerned about the Internet, seeing it as particularly portentous for their children. Wyonna likes being able to program her own media diet using a VCR, and has even made video viewing a central ritual of family life. The Castellos' distinctions are more typically class-oriented. They have a clear suspicion of "screen media," based on both their potential as persuasive media, and on their feeling that time spent in front of a screen is wasted time. They much prefer print media, the Internet, popular music, and film. And, it is important to add, for all their class-relevant distaste for media, they do find spiritually meaningful material there. The media are classified and made distinct in these accounts, and these distinctions are, in part, statements about religious and spiritual meaning and value.

The naturalization of media in these homes is also significant. For Judy Cruz and the Johnsons, there is a sense that the media are part of the home environment and that they are more or less unproblematic there. For the Castellos, there is a more fundamental map, one that draws a line between media and their *lifestyle*. All media, but particularly television, are simply antithetical to the kind of holistic atmosphere they are attempting to create in the home. This is a sentiment shared broadly among their social networks, apparently, and is taken-for-granted at their children's school.

When any of these interviewees moves to the level of accounting for their own engagement with specific media, they recount a certain kind of practice. As they negotiate media material into their spiritual and religious lives, *playfulness* rather than *deliberation* is the best description. Consistent with ideas about media practice such as Henry Jenkins's well-known notion of "textual poaching,"[22] these interviewees can be seen to approach media with a sense of experiment, testing, and appropriation. That is not to say that this is not a serious matter for them. Butch's encounter with Deepak Chopra's book has clearly been very significant in his life. But this playfulness takes on another meaning in a context where people are using these media-based resources to negotiate against the more rigid orthodoxies of received religious practice. In Butch's case, his seeking sensibility thus allowed him to negotiate around the hard realities of traditional faith (including – in his case – "orthodox" Buddhism), finding a "playful margin" where he encountered Chopra and the inspiration he found there. For Judy, the harder, more solid, structural/institutional claims of traditional Catholicism are held at a distance, while the more voluble meaning-making around angels, aliens, and afterlife can flourish "in the home."

Like Butch, Priscilla and Judy also recognize the extent to which these spiritually meaningful media contrast with the claims of authority and orthodoxy. For each of them, there are saliencies to the media that invoke various of the "repressed modes" of religious experience I introduced in the previous chapters. For the Castellos, this is clearly music; for all of them, it is the notion of "experience" itself, as well as ideas of voluble spirituality.

We've seen here that the media are an inescapable, even pervasive, dimension of modern life. We've further seen evidence of how the media relate to spiritual and religious lives in these households. The differences and the commonalities between what should have been quite distinct contexts – the Castello and Cruz households – are provocative. In the next chapter, we will look at a larger number of households using Roof's classification more directly. In this way, we'll hope to further elaborate the ways that media are coming to significance in daily spiritual and religious lives.

Chapter 6

Cultural objects and religious identity among born-agains and mainstream believers

American and Western religiosity is currently undergoing great change. Many of the received and remembered ways of thinking about religion no longer hold sway, while these shared memories of religion continue to determine much of what we consider to be normatively "religious" or "spiritual." The newer ways of looking at religion represented by the work of scholars including Robert Wuthnow, Steven Warner, Nancy Ammerman, Catherine Albanese, and Wade Clark Roof provide important markers of the changing face of religious experience and expression. The families and individuals we heard from in the last chapter illustrated some of the significant characteristics of religious and spiritual expression today. There is reason to believe that much of this new religiosity should be particularly connected with culture and with media culture, as I have argued along the way.

We will now turn to a more direct appraisal of contemporary religious experience and its connection to media. In order to do so in the context of current thought about religion, we'll turn again to the taxonomy of "Baby-Boom" religiosity developed by Wade Clark Roof. It is important to keep in mind that Roof's analyses, described in two influential books, have derived a classification of religious practice out of surveys and in-depth interviews. They were not inductive categories for him, but rather ways that his informants thought and talked about religion and spirituality, grouped according to commonalities of perception, identity, self-description, and practice. They are rooted in the religious sensibility that Roof identified in his work in the 1990s, one defined not only by a concern with identity, but also with authenticating that identity in a particular way. As Roof puts it, "the emerging forces arise out of quests not so much for group identity and social location as for an authentic inner life and personhood."[1]

Roof suggests that this situation has three significant dimensions. First, the numbers of people involved. It is, in fact, a widespread movement toward "questing" or "searching" that transcends demographically the social and religious categories where we might have expected it to be strongest. Second, according to Roof, is the self-consciousness and self-reflexivity of these practices, rooted as they are in a postmodern moment described by Giddens and others as an era where the self and self-under-standing are dominant modes of consciousness. Third, Roof wishes to emphasize that these trends are not self-centered or self-absorbed, but are about "a deep hunger for a self-transformation that is both genuine and personally satisfying."[2]

As I suggested earlier, these emerging ways of doing religion and spiritu-ality are rooted in a "new paradigm" that combines a number of dimensions into a frame of reference centered on *practice*. Roof calls this a "lived religion" of everyday life[3] that combines novel symbols, practices that locate individuals in symbolic frames of reference, with the more-or-less autonomous self that is both the active agent and the object of this religion or spirituality. The larger societal context is also an important factor, with traditional religion now having to compete with a media-saturated and pluralistic society where mixing of religious traditions and symbols is the norm.[4] Roof sees the agency of the individual as a logical consequence of the conditions of religion in late modernity. As he puts it,

> To emphasize quest is to make the point that in an age when bound-aries are especially permeable, when exchanges freely occur, spiritual searching should come as no surprise. Flexibility and movement encourage creative, soul-searching processes; the actual practice of religion in a context of overlapping religious cultures and blurred boundaries encourages a degree of self-scrutiny and reflection. Both faith as traditionally conceived within religious communities and spiri-tuality conceived in its extreme as its alternative require deliberation and a sustained act of will, certainly under conditions where no single *type* of religious institution or spiritual activity monopolizes symbol-ization of the sacred.[5]

While such self-orientation might raise anxieties in the absence of a sense of form or grounding, Roof refers to Robert Jay Lifton's notion of "the protean self." The object is to be *fluid* in that the individual moves freely between contexts, locations, and symbolic resources, but yet *grounded* in that what is sought is an explanation or a framework for understanding or action.[6] This desire to be "fluid, yet grounded" is in fact one of the most difficult things for many to understand abut quest culture. It helps to keep in mind that the whole practice circulates around the reflexive agency and autonomy of the individual. A given set of symbols or practices derived from a specific religious tradition need not depend for legitimacy on the formal characteristics of that tradition. What matters is that they are meaningful to the individual in her negotiation between traditions (fluidity) and within traditions (grounded). As Roof notes, most of his informants (and many we present in these pages) legitimate their quest very pragmatically, "following one and then another strategy 'works' for them."[7]

To review the key dimensions of these arguments about the nature of questing or seeking spirituality today, the following seem most important. First, religion and spirituality are *everyday* things. They are pursued, constructed, and experienced in the context of daily life. Second, the practices are *reflexive*, meaning that they involve a level of complex self-consciousness and orientation toward self-identity. Third, they involve *agency* on the part of the individual, a sense of autonomy in the quest and in the construction. Finally, the object does have to do with *integration* of these various symbols, practices, and values into an *ideal construction of self*.

The importance of Roof's work to our project of understanding religious and spiritual meaning-making in the media age lies in its nuanced interpretations of contemporary religious culture and how that culture is expressible and expressed in the lives and accounts of individuals, families, and groups as they encounter religious and spiritual culture. The fact that his categories are not formal or inductive should further serve to connect our conversations about religion, spirituality, and media to larger themes in the study of religious culture. As Roof, Warner, Albanese, and other "new-paradigm" religion scholars argue, it no longer makes sense to look for religion in received, formal, inductive, or essentialized categories. Roof's religious "types" thus provide us with a way of organizing and interpreting expressed experiences of daily life in a way that reflects what we think we know about how religion today is reorganizing itself.

Roof's categories

I introduced Roof's categories in Chapter 3, including there some proposals about what kind of media practice we might expect to find among the various types. We'll look at each of his categories in turn, beginning with a review of what we speculated we might find in terms of media practices in each category. From there, we'll proceed to see what we can say about the individuals and families we've interviewed that seem to most closely fit Roof's definitions. We'll then move on to some overall conclusions about what we've seen here.

This project of placing our interviewees into these categories is a bit more difficult than we might have expected. As we already saw with Glenn Donegal in Chapter 4 and will be seen in other cases as we proceed, interviewees here do not fall neatly into Roof's taxonomy. Instead, it is necessary to use his classifications somewhat formally at times, other times making assignments to the various categories using a combination of his descriptions, received labels, and self-descriptions.

There are some clues to this challenge in the interviews we looked at in the last chapter. One thing that typifies many of the narratives there is a kind of playfulness. People like Judy Cruz and the Castellos engage media in spiritual terms through a style of appropriation (consistent with ideas about reflexivity in modernity) that is experimental, voluble, and effervescent. What may result for Judy is a *bricolage* to a certain extent, but one that is both "fluid *and* grounded." This means that her religiosity and spirituality are not static in a way that makes them easily amenable to classification. There is a further complexity in the place that media play in Judy's (and others') seeking and questing. For her, the media are also a playful context in that they seem to provide a relatively "low-stakes" place to explore. For her and the others we will look at in more detail in this chapter, media meaning-making thus varies from what we might expect to see in encounters with the symbolic resources of the culture. Judy and other of our interviewees treat the media as a *context* as well as a *symbolic inventory*, thus its contribution to their identities and meanings may well be less formal than we might have expected.

Born-again Christians

I noted in Chapter 3 that Evangelicalism has been more oriented toward media than other traditions. I suggested that we might therefore find more acceptance among our born-again informants of the idea that at least certain kinds of media would be appropriate to religious meaning and questing. We might also expect that they would draw clear distinctions between various media, seeing the "secular" media as less appropriate than "religious" media as conveyors of normative ideas and values. I also suggested that we might see class tastes represented in their interpretations due to the traditional tendency for Evangelicals and "born-again Christians" to be over-represented among lower social and economic strata (though that distinction has eroded in recent years). At the same time, though, Roof makes the point that even among born-again Christians there exists a dimension of autonomous seeking and suspicion of religious authority. Thus received categories of "good" and "bad" media might make less sense to them than would be the case with more traditional or dogmatic interviewees.

The Milliken family

The Milliken family live in the suburbs of a major city. They are a two-parent family, and both parents, Lynn and Jay, work outside the home.[8] They think of themselves as born-again Christians, but had joined an independent Pentecostal church through baptism shortly before our interview. Lynn and Jay had been raised in Mainline churches, but recently began a quest that resulted in their finding their current church. Lynn and the children attend more than once a week; Jay is not able to attend that frequently because of his work schedule. Both Lynn and Jay hold junior college degrees. She works in daycare; he is a truck driver. They moved to their current location from out-of-state a little over a year ago.

Their social activities are centered on their church, with the exception of the "Young Marines" organization that 13-year-old Ray belongs to and 7-year-old Laura plans to join when she is old enough. Lynn is the mother of all three children, but Ray and Laura have different fathers. Four-year-old Rich is Jay's son, but Jay wants very much to be considered a father to the two older children, though Lynn is the custodial parent for each. Their family income is just over $35,000.

Like many families, the Millikens contend with the presence of media in their homes. While we might expect their habits and behaviors to represent a strict – or perhaps moralistic – approach to media, they experience the ubiquity and presence of these technologies in their lives. At one point, they begin talking about Ray's media habits:

Lynn: He bought this one tape, CD, that was called Baby . . .
Interviewer: Babyface?
Lynn: Baby something . . .
Interviewer: Was that the artist or was that the title?
Lynn: The title. It was an Afro-American. . . .
Jay: Well, we heard the lyrics, and then. . . .
Lynn: So what we did was we looked at it and listened to it first, you know checked it out. And then we told Ray he had to go choose another one.
Interviewer: Is that a common thing?
Lynn: Well, it's just like the games on the computer. We have the parental.
Jay: The parental filter.
Interviewer: Oh on the Internet?
Lynn: Yeah, on him, we do. But he knows how to access ours.
Jay: He knows how to get around everything.
Lynn: He tries, but you know what? We pretty much . . . [to Ray] I think we monitor you on the computer, don't we?
Jay: I think we ought to turn it [the computer] the other way, actually, because when I walk up sometimes I see him go "click" and I don't know if he got rid of the screen or what. I have no idea.

This is the universal parental experience with teens and media. The inroads of culture into the home via the tastes and choices of the household's children is a fundamental fact of life in the media age, as we saw in Chapter 5. For the Millikens, it is clearly something they think about and care about, but yet they find themselves dealing with conditions over which they have less control than they would like. The Millikens are thus like many other parents in terms of the role of media in their lives. It is also interesting that here, as with many other points in the interview where they talk about their strategies for dealing with media, they do not obviously or self-consciously refer to religion or to values or ideas derived from their "born-again" faith as normative tools for addressing problems of the media.

We should really not expect any individual family to be fully representative of an "ideal type" labeled "born-again believer." The Millikens, though, like many of the interview families that fit in that category, actually resist some received stereotypes of what that label should mean in terms of values or behaviors. Lynn, for example, argues against the notion that her religion, or any religion, should be seen as determinative of practice.

> I think there's a difference between religion and a relationship with God. That's how I personally feel. You can go to church, you can have your religion, you can do your thing, but there's a big difference between religion and relationship with the Lord.

This is typical of born-again individualism. The powerful, voluble edge of the religious or spiritual experience is the relationship one has with God and Jesus, not with an organized group or body. Religious institutions, histories, or doctrines do not intervene or mediate the religious or spiritual experience. For example, Lynn expresses this independence from authoritative structures in one key area: her attitudes about sex education for her children. While she might be seen as more liberal than other parents, she's talked openly with her children about sex, and used a video produced by the Evangelical organization Focus on the Family that is pretty explicit about childbirth. She reports this in such a way that it is clear she sees herself differentiated from other, more conservative parents in this way. The explicit or implicit notion that those who call themselves "born again" might be expected to look to clerical or institutional authority for signals on social values clearly does not apply to Lynn or Jay, who see themselves charting their own course *vis-à-vis* the broader culture.

What about the media in their lives? Like many of our Evangelical or born-again informants, the Millikens make a clear distinction between secular media and religious media, and they are not particularly attracted to the latter. When asked about media that would relate to their faith, Jay says:

Jay: Actually, we try not to watch . . . TBN, is that what it's called?
Interviewer: Trinity Broadcasting Network?
Jay: There's a little too much hocus-pocus on that channel.

While Lynn admits to a bit more openness to religious programs such as *Trinity Broadcasting Network* and *Benny Hinn*, she is cautious.

There has to be a balance, I would think. Sometimes people go over-board on stuff like that. And where can it fall . . . there has to be a balance. You can either go the other way and go fanatic about it or you can go this way and be wishy-washy, you know what I mean?

This once again seems to be rooted in her belief, shared by Jay, that ulti-mately it is the individual's responsibility to make sense of faith and to craft a sensible and meaningful set of ideas and practices. This is not some-thing that one surrenders to another or to a center of authority, religious or otherwise. The Millikens own a range of video and audio tapes distributed by the Focus on the Family organization, but they see these as resources to their own meaning-making and sense-making, more like a reference library than materials that would dictate belief and action to them. Besides their library of Focus materials, the Millikens also own a number of religious CDs, including some from the "Contemporary Christian Music" genre, and are fairly regular listeners to Christian radio stations in their market area.

Ray, the 13-year-old, is the focus of a good bit of the family's attention in media use. While he likes Contemporary Christian Music, Ray also has a penchant for Internet and video games that his parents sometimes find questionable. This has led to the withdrawal of Internet and gaming privileges in the past as punishment. Beyond this, however, the Millikens are not a family that holds to a strict sent of media "dos" and "don'ts." Ray clearly has different media preferences from his parents. At one point, speculating about what he might watch if and when the family would get cable television at their new home, he says he'll watch Nickelodeon and the Cartoon Network, to which his father adds the Learning Channel and the History Channel. Ray, in fact, is at the age where he often verges into the dark edges of the media marketplace, enjoying videogames such as *Starcraft* and *Carnivore*, and going online to play games at the Shockware site.

Like many families in our (and others') studies, the Millikens exhibit some conflict between their beliefs about media and their behaviors. For example, while they express dislike for the "reality TV" genre, they nonetheless seem to watch *Survivor*, one of the originators of the form, as well as some others. In this passage, the Interviewer has asked the family if there are programs they regularly watch together. Laura, age 7, begins to answer.

Laura: Me and Ray watched that movie that these kids like they have a partner and it's like they have races and stuff on red teams and blue teams. And the last one. . . .
Jay: What's it called Ray?
Ray: I don't know what she's talking about.

Laura: It's like this thing where there's like five people having a race. And after. . . .

Interviewer: Is it on at night?

Laura: It's in that Hawaiian place on TV Ray. What is it?

Ray: I don't know what you're talking about.

Laura: Remember when they eat like bugs and stuff those things? Or how they win like a thousand dollars and stuff?

Ray: *Survivor*?

Laura: Yeah. *Survivor.*

Interviewer: *Survivor* . . . you two watch that? Did you guys watch that when it was on?

Lynn: We watched it together a couple of times up here.

Jay: I didn't really watch the whole series.

Lynn: He's always, what do you call it?

Interviewer: Flippin'?

Lynn: Flippin' the channels. Right Jay?

Jay: Yep.

Interviewer: Are you going to watch the new *Survivor* that starts this week as a matter of fact?

Jay: I don't really like those reality TV shows.

Lynn: So we watch a little bit of it and then he'll turn it.

Jay: I mean probably an episode of every one of them and made a determination that this is, you know. . . .

Interviewer: Have you not seen one yet that you'd like to watch? Are you open to the possibility, like, hey this looks interesting . . . or is it just that the reality shows are not for you?

Jay: They're not for me.

Lynn: You watch one. The reality one where they were on that island.

Jay: Yeah, I've seen episodes.

This is an approach to television we saw and discussed earlier. The "account of media" that reality television is inappropriate is common in discourse about contemporary media, and this seems evident here. At the same time, we see in this family a style of television viewing that does not readily lend itself to intervention that might specifically address limiting this kind of programming. Not only have the children apparently viewed *Survivor*, Lynn agrees that they have all seen it a few times. This excerpt also reveals a bit about the style of viewing in the Milliken household, particularly when Jay has control of the remote control device. But, significantly, Jay reveals that, in spite of saying they're "not for him," he admits to watching reality shows.

We get the clear impression that a good deal of the television viewing in the Milliken household is driven by things other than selectivity and choice, whether based on values or other criteria. When asked about programs that the family does not watch, Lynn identifies *Married with*

Children. But, as with the reality genre, not liking or not approving of something does not necessarily mean that it is not watched.

Interviewer: Are there TV shows that anybody doesn't like?

Lynn: What's that marriage family show?

Jay: *Married with Children*?

Lynn: Yeah, you like that one.

Jay: I'll turn it on, 'cause maybe I want to watch the news that day. We only really get two or three channels on this TV, so I'm limited to what I can watch.

Interviewer: Are there shows . . . let's not call you the biggest fan of *Married with Children*, but okay, you can watch it. Are there things that one person likes that other people just don't? I mean do you not like *Married with Children*?

Lynn: I don't like it.

Interviewer: How come?

Lynn: Some of the things . . . it doesn't set a very good example in some areas.

Interviewer: What areas?

Jay: Respect for each other. They're always chopping each other down.

Lynn: They just . . . I don't know. It just doesn't set a very good example I guess. I'm not saying that it's wrong or anything. . . .

So what explains Jay's viewing of this program? It is on near a news program he wants to watch. But, more important than that as an explanation is the simple fact of television's attraction *per se*. To Jay, the fact that they cannot receive more than two channels justifies their viewing choices. Television viewing is simply assumed; the specific programs or content are less important. Beyond that, what he or they end up watching as a result seems to be almost a matter of expectation, or right. When Lynn observes that *Married with Children* might not set the best example, and Jay agrees, she does draw back from full condemnation of the program, stating "I'm not saying that it's wrong or anything."

There are some programs that Jay and Lynn do intentionally watch. "There are some shows that I try never to miss," Jay says. When asked which ones, he answers, "I'm a big *Star Trek* fan" and then adds that they also watch *X-Files* regularly. It turns out that the whole family watches *X-Files*, including Laura, the youngest. It is a bit of an uncomfortable pleasure for them, though. Lynn reveals with some seeming discomfort that Laura had "told her Dad in California that she watches it."

Jay: You're watching it because you're interested in it and all of a sudden something will come on and you'll go, "Oh, maybe I shouldn't have let the kids see that."

Interviewer: What are those things?

Jay: Just the gruesome.

Interviewer: Like the monsters gruesome? Or the . . . I don't watch it a
ton, but there are monster episodes. . . .

Lynn: Well, there's, you know, dead people.

Ray: Dead people and like, flesh-eating stuff.

Beyond concern about gruesome violence, there is little more they have to
add about implicit or explicit standards for appropriate content. Jay has
stopped watching pro wrestling because he thought Ray was imitating
what he saw there. When asked directly if he understands there to be limits
or rules on what he can watch, Ray replies that he is not to watch "bad
videos." When the Interviewer asks what constitutes such a bad video, Ray
replies, "A videotape with cursing, stuff like that." This evokes an idea we
raised earlier, that acceptable media may merely be those which are simply
"inoffensive" in some vague way.

The Millikens also watch one of the most popular of all television
shows (and one that has been the subject of a good bit of controversy):
The Simpsons.

Interviewer: So, *The Simpsons* . . . do the kids watch it?

Jay: Yeah, they'll sit and watch it. It's a cartoon so they'll sit and watch it.

Interviewer: What do you think about that? Either one of you.

Ray: Sometimes I'll watch it.

Lynn: It's not all the time though.

Interviewer: Do you like it?

Ray: Yeah, it's okay.

Interviewer: [to Lynn] Do you like it? Do you like them watching it?

Lynn: I'll sit and watch with them for a little bit and then if I don't like
what's happening, I'll just say, "Let's turn it."

Interviewer: What kinds of things prompt you to turn the channel? When
it's *The Simpsons*.

Ray: When they say bad words and stuff.

Jay: Well, they don't really say. . . .

Lynn: I don't know they [Jay and the children] watch it.

Ray: It's another dysfunctional family.

Lynn: Yeah, really.

Interviewer: You say that and you all laugh.

Lynn: Because it's true.

Jay: We think we're dysfunctional sometimes.

Like millions of other Americans, the Milliken family watches, enjoys, and
identifies with *The Simpsons*. It is a pleasure for them, and something that
ties them together with others' practices of meaning-making in media

culture. In spite of the fact that this program has, over the course of its run on the air, repeatedly been the object of severe criticism particularly from conservative and so-called "pro family" voices in the culture, this family of born-again believers rather unproblematically watches it. Our expectations about the way such families would relate to television probably would have been for particular and focused religious or spiritual meanings and values to be brought into play in viewing choices and in reception of television programs. We might ask, with reference to the Millikens, "What is essentially 'religious' or 'spiritual' about their consumption of television?" The answer is really "nothing," and that is interesting. Their "accounts of media" are thus less complex and articulated to their faith than we expected.

We might explore some possible reasons why the Millikens don't apply categories of value out of their religious lives directly to the media they consume. We saw that Lynn, at least, does not identify strongly with institutional or doctrinal authority in her religious and values self-understandings, and there is little evidence that those sources mean much for Jay, either. Where might a values discourse focused on television emerge from in that case? In addition to the possibility that the Millikens might lack the "moral compass" we'd expected to find because of their relative distance from institutional authority (not forgetting, of course, the evidence that such institutional suspicion is a more general feature of contemporary Evangelicalism, and thus they may be more typical than we'd prepared ourselves to think), there may be another factor. The Millikens seem to be rather unfocused and unreflective about their media behaviors. Jay's seeming notion that television viewing is somehow a commonplace behavior that is simply "expected" evokes the kind of stereotype commonly identified with the label "couch potato."[9] In order to pursue this further, let's turn to a family that seems on its face to be somewhat different from the Millikens in some important ways.

The Callahan family

The Callahans are a two-parent family living in the suburbs of a major city.[10] Karl, 45, and Dinah, 37, have three children, twins Lisa and Cathy, age 8, and young Brent, age four. Karl and Dinah are registered Republicans, and readily describe themselves as both politically and religiously "conservative." They are a solidly middle-class, two-income family, though Dinah works half-time as a registered nurse. They are rather emphatic about identifying themselves as born-again Evangelicals, though they are in the process of moving from a Presbyterian to a Baptist church. "We're going to a Baptist church – that's really of secondary importance to the overall church offering – but it is a Baptist church," Karl notes.

They consider their church their primary social involvement, though Dinah belongs to a mothers' prayer group and they both participate in the volunteer management of the community swimming pool in their neighborhood. Karl describes his faith history as moving "from nonreligious to religious," though, like many Evangelicals, he recounts a faith history that began in a denominational church, then fell away during college, but became "born again" as the result of contact with the Young Life organization. Dinah reports that she has not made a major change in her religious beliefs during her lifetime. They are more eloquent and direct about their beliefs and the relationship of those beliefs to social practice than are the Millikens. With regard to media, they see their beliefs as at least in part informing attitudes about social and political discourse they encounter there, thus seeing media more as "context" than as a "symbolic inventory." In fact, much of what they have to say about media is about such religiously inflected values and political issues. In a reflection that combines awareness of media and values conflicts with a critique of local news, Karl observes,

> We usually watch the local news. I think it tends to be sensationalized and ever-increasingly appeals to tabloidish kind of things. And I think they're more into ratings than truly what's newsworthy, so they gear their content towards what will get ratings and be more entertaining as opposed to truly informational and newsworthy. The Disney boycott, for instance, I think they like those kind of things because it sensationalizes and stereotypes religion and religious people in a negative way.

Karl's reflections on media values tend to be focused in this way, on questions that we might describe as almost more "political" than they are "religious." When asked about situations where they feel moved to discuss questionable media content with their children, Karl and Dinah give examples that reflect current debates over religious politics.

Karl: If something, it seems to me, we may comment about something if it's grossly politically correct.
Interviewer: What do you mean by grossly politically correct?
Karl: Well, if there's just so much plurality and so much diversity that it's atypical of a life situation. And it's not something we discuss so much as point out and probably make light of.
Dinah: Like, there is a TV show they used to watch called *The Puzzle Place*. And it's very pluralistic. And I just don't believe in a lot of that. And I would frequently talk about the topics that they would bring up and why we don't subscribe to it or how our values and beliefs are different from that.

Karl: In my opinion, it's rather gushy and unrealistic, relativistic.

Dinah: And it has to do with family structures and whether you have moms and dads, and religious differences. . . . *Wishbone*'s the same way, and actually I have talked to them a lot about *Wishbone*'s subjects, and *Kratt's Creatures*. *Kratt's Creatures* comes from a very ecological save the earth, animals are misunderstood. That's their philosophy. That's not what I think. I mean, I'll talk about that. That doesn't mean they can't watch it. There's some good things there, but I don't agree with their presentation. And also on *Wishbone* it's the same thing. You've got the divorced parents and the child living with the mom. They just always bring these different lifestyles out, which is the way life is, but I just want them to know that that's not necessarily the *best* way for life to be, so we'll talk about those kind of things.

Clearly Dinah and Karl are particularly sensitive to media content that addresses issues in family and social values. In a way, it seems that they see media as a central site of struggle between their values and what has been otherwise called the "secular humanism" of the broader culture. Pluralism and diversity seem to be almost *negative* values to them, again reflecting discourses about "values" in the public sphere.

Dinah: They had every . . . they had the Jewish girl and the African American boy and the Indian who . . . the whole Indian philosophy was in there, and the Mexican girl. I mean, it had every racial culture. I do believe that we need to accept other people, but just the way it was presented was too much for me.

The Callahans thus "get it" that the messages of openness and diversity in this public television program are intended to represent as well as to teach diversity, and they resist and negotiate with those messages and intentions. "Why do they have to deal with it when they're 3 years old? Just present Barney, you know . . . " says Dinah.

Like the Millikens, the Callahans are well aware of religious television, and Dinah even reports watching a bit of the local Christian station. This does not seem to be a major interest for her, and Karl is dismissive of it. Saying it seems "contrived and stereotypical" of "televangelism stuff," Karl goes on,

> it seems to me that a lot of the preaching there is health and wealth gospel kinds of stuff: God's a big Sugar Daddy and if you are really walking with God things will go well, etc., etc. and that's not necessarily the case. It seems to be to me very superficial, popularly oriented that I don't think is the real full package, genuine article, walk in relationship with God.

Karl does have some interesting responses to questions about his favorite films, though, identifying both the very traditional American values of the warhorse *It's a Wonderful Life*, and Woody Allen films. He's quick to point out, though, that it is the "earlier" Allen films he has in mind, those that deal with "big questions" and represent "darker existentialism." Like many others, he sees the Jimmy Stewart character in *It's a Wonderful Life* representing positive American values of character and resilience, and also likes it because it has a happy ending. Karl claims not to be very interested in television, or a very regular viewer of television, except for sports. He is quick to point out that his opinions about television derive from his exposure to promotions and advertising he sees while watching sports. His assessment of most of television? Consistent with the idea that for many, appropriate television is that which is "inoffensive," Karl sees it is entirely too oriented toward sex and titillation. Television programs and advertisements "appeal to my baser side, as opposed to the side that would want to uplift or inform" he observes. Everything has a "hook" of sex or violence, in his view.

Karl also expresses a distrust of what he sees to be the primarily *visual* experience of media like television and film (and presumably the Internet and World Wide Web). Proposing that a primary role of visual media should be *entertainment*, he observes,

> [visual media] also shapes our understanding of the world and education. It shapes our understanding of the world and issues, it helps to think about things. You can watch something on the TV or go to a movie and it makes you think about it and what your values are in relation. And it's still kind of entertaining in that because you're talking and sharing ideas. [extending his comments to music and computers] I think music can really speak to your soul, and I don't get that so much from visual . . . visual media but from hearing and music can really calm your spirit and, you know, uplift you or maybe make you feel sad. [Computers are also] a little bit different from just the visual media. [They] should educate and inform us and be something that we can use to get entertainment but to make things easier by doing your bookkeeping or computer or writing letters.

The Callahans do watch television, though. Cathy and Lisa possess an extensive knowledge of the television schedule both for weekday evenings and weekends, but do not go into much detail about their viewing preferences. Prohibited shows, particularly *Beavis and Butthead* and *Ren and Stimpy*, come up frequently in their discussions and answers. In their individual interviews, each describes a wide range of children's programs they are familiar with, and Cathy even reports having watched the prohibited shows while visiting friends.

Viewing together as a family seems to be important, and they report doing so when they can. Like most families we've spoken with, their ideas about what is appropriate are then rooted in their notions of what is best for their children, the kind of role models they are in terms of viewing, and the kinds of content they are exposing themselves and their family to.

Karl: To me, it's ultimately a quality of entertainment kind of decision. I don't think there are any big-time prohibitions. We just . . . we prefer other things. For instance, Dinah and I used to watch *ER*. And maybe now that the new season's rolled around. . . . That's really the only thing we settled into intentionally in the way of network TV. Otherwise, life doesn't gravitate around watching TV that much. I enjoy watching sports on weekends, especially now that football season's starting. But, again, I'd say what we watch is not so much rooted in prohibitions as a preference for stuff that's truly entertaining, as opposed to gratuitous in terms of language, sexual content, violence. And I'm not even sure we know what they are.

Dinah: No. We just feel like we . . . I'd say our rule is, when we spend time watching TV it's going to be uplifting and something worthwhile and we're going to learn from it, or it's humorous. That's why we don't watch Saturday morning cartoons, because hardly any of them have anything worthwhile or profitable, and I don't care for that. I don't care for ridiculous silliness, and a lot of them are just slapstick stupid. A lot of the things on PBS have good moral lessons or they're about reading. So I'd rather we use our time for things that are worthwhile. The main rule is limiting the time that we are in front of the TV, and so really, I try to keep it to about an hour a day. Sometimes it's more than that. That would be my general guideline. A lot of time we'll watch our videos as opposed to watching TV. And they need to make their own decisions when they watch at other kids' houses. But at our house, I know what's on TV.

We see here an interesting contradiction that we see in many families. On the one hand, the Callahans want to present an "account of media" in their home that is clear on questions of the qualities and values of appropriate media content and media viewing behavior. At the same time, their particular choices in these regards are not that different from those of other families. Worthwhile television behavior is intentional and focused, and worthwhile content is that which does not stress sex and violence. At the same time, they want very much to not be seen as "prohibiting" anything. "We want them to see that life is full of choices," Karl says, "and some are more beneficial than others." It's a better approach to managing people, he observes, than trying to tell them what whey cannot do. They seem to want to trust their children to make appropriate choices for themselves, based on the choices they have seen their parents make for them when they watch together.

Agreeing with many others among our interview families, Dinah believes older television programs to be less offensive and problematic than current ones. The Nickelodeon cable channel provides a selection of such programs, and Dinah reports that much of their family viewing is concentrated on its fare. She lists some examples of the kinds of programs they watch together there, listing re-run programs like the *Dick Van Dyke Show* and *Mary Tyler Moore*. Some of their choices, like re-runs of *Taxi*, do border on the kind of salacious programs they would otherwise want to be seen to eschew, having been somewhat "racy" at the time they were originally aired.

When asked if they have watched network programs with religious themes or plots, such as the long-running *Touched by an Angel* or *Seventh Heaven*, they respond,

Karl: Every once in a while we kind of stumbled into – is it, *Touched by an Angel*?

Dinah: Yeah, and then *Seventh Heaven*. I've seen that once. But no, we don't search them out and watch them

But then, Karl goes on,

Karl: Again, the only intentional network watching we've done that I can remember in five years is *ER*. It's a function of schedule and doing other things and the fact that really TV is kind of an unimportant entertainment outlet. It's not all that intentional, except for me to see sports on the weekends and when we watch a video.

This is interesting, and comes up in such a way as to suggest it has been an important program, at least for Karl and Dinah. Their explanation for their interest in *ER* and the way they began watching it is interesting. "I never watched it until all these people that I really respect said they really liked it," says Dinah. Asked if it was people at the hospital where she worked, Dinah replies, "Well actually it was more people in my family who really liked it and said that I should check it out, and I'd been wanting to because they'd talk about it."

This suggests that *ER*, which is clearly in a different category for Dinah and Karl than the shows they watch with their children, has a level of social and personal currency for them. It is the one program they identify as something they watch together. It was something they began to watch as the result of recommendations from family and friends. It is pleasing and satisfying for them, and it is, significantly, not a program that we would put in that category of sentimental or inoffensive television. Instead, it is a commonplace experience of secular American culture, rife with the kinds of secular humanist values that the Callahans otherwise criticize. There is a sense in which the Callahans' most precious television experience embeds them in secular culture more readily than it does in sectarian or religious culture. They do not engage in a religiously based values critique of *ER*. Instead, they view it, and could be argued to therefore participate in a generalized American cultural experience of a rather fundamental kind. In that way they are not that different from the Millikens, and do experience the pull to participate in the cultural experience of television viewing much as their non-born-again neighbors do.

The Alberts

A third family, the Alberts,[11] present an interesting contrast and comparison with the Millikens and the Callahans. Describing themselves in a way that seems much more restrictive of their children's viewing than the others,[12] the Alberts nonetheless agree that their role is not to dictate what their children's moral choices should be, but to give them tools to make those choices on their own. Like others, Rachel Albert, the mother, sees a fundamental conflict between "the media" and "Christian values." Like the Callahans, she and Terry, her husband, illustrate this point primarily by means of references to politically charged "moral values" like diversity and environmental awareness. Like the others, they identify as "acceptable" programs that are sentimental or inoffensive like the Callahans but, unlike the Millikens, find *The Simpsons* to be an unacceptable program. Among the sentimental and inoffensive programming they find acceptable, they regularly view *Home Improvement* and *Seventh Heaven* as a family. Also like the others, the Alberts express a view that is critical of received, traditional "religion," even denying that they are in any way "religious." And yet they are clearly and proudly "born-again Christians."

For the Alberts as with others, the focus on the perfection of the religious self separates them from institutional authority, and makes them critical or suspicious of it. To Terry, this means that it is up to him to exercise his own moral choices, "to make my own walk."

> [T]he longer I go . . . the longer that I walk with Christ, the more I realize that religion . . . well, it just stymies the growth of the human being, and I think there's a lot of taboos that the Christian church – quote, unquote – would say permeates our society, but I don't know that they're all as important or as radically harmful to us as it would be portrayed or be thought of within the Christian realm. Meaning, by watching *Dawson's Creek* with my children. I can say, "See, they're havin' sex. Sex is good. But sex with 18-year-olds, not married, having no idea what they're doing, is not good." So basically using things

more as a teachable tool. And plus helping them learn what life is about. 'Cause they're gonna make mistakes. My daughters all could go out and get pregnant out of wedlock, and I'm not gonna throw 'em out of the house or anything like that.

It is important to Terry and Rachel that they not then appear to be moralistic and prohibitive in their attitudes toward media. They would expect such an approach to be typical of the "religion" that they see themselves transcending. Religions are "moralistic" and the Alberts are finding the prohibitions of traditional religion less and less valid. They want to control their children's access to certain things, but at the same time do not see themselves as determining their children's attitudes for them. Terry is particularly concerned that such an approach could appear – or be – "hypocritical." Interestingly, one of the programs they watch together as a family actually describes for them the struggles they feel between traditional religiosity and what they see to be their authentic faith. On a fundamental level, *Seventh Heaven* is too preachy and judgmental for Rachel.

> Yeah, they portray basically the traditional pastor, his wife, and their kids and the way they're supposed to live their lives. It's just kind of the judgmentalness of it all. I don't like that aspect as a label of Christianity. This goes back to my strong feelings against what I call "Churchianity."

When the conversation gets around to the kinds of media Terry and Rachel Albert find spiritually and morally meaningful, it is not "Christian" or "religious" media they refer to, but "secular." In Terry's case, he found *Braveheart* to be a fully acceptable film for even his 8-year-old to watch – because "it really happened" – in spite of its violence and his and Rachel's criticism of overly violent entertainment. What Rachel and Terry choose to watch together is also interesting and significant. Rachel finds science fiction media to be particularly compelling, even in spiritual terms. They watched the *X-Files* regularly.

Rachel: Well, we actually watch TV . . . Terry and I watch the *X-Files* on Sunday nights, so we pretty much plan, everybody knows they're supposed to be in their beds looking at books while we watch TV. (laughs) And that's a new thing. And we used to watch *Star Trek* after the kids went to bed, but we're kind of not into that right now.

Star Trek had been a particularly meaningful show for Rachel, even though she clearly identified within it values that "the religious right, whoever they are" would label "liberal." At the same time, though, the program was "spiritual" for her, "because I think when you're talking about higher powers and higher beings and that type of thing, that there's an undercurrent of spiritualism in that." The same goes for the *X-Files*, but in describing it Rachel goes beyond merely attributing religion-like qualities to the program, and struggles with her own attraction to something about it that she resists and can't quite define.

> Yeah, [*X-Files*] is like another kind of religion, basically. People can really get involved with . . . but I don't look at it that way. "Well, the truth is out there." Well, what truth? It's a whole different branch . . . the hereafter, the here and now. It's out there, I guess. I don't know. It could be. I guess you could say it's spiritual, or you could just say it's science fiction. I don't know. I don't really watch the shows based on that.

Like the others, then, the Alberts do not inscribe a bright line between religious and secular media. In important ways, they live more on the "secular" media map than they live separately from it. They implicitly recognize that their role as parents is not to cordon their children off from the influence of profane secular-humanist culture, but to learn to negotiate with it. And, they find important symbolic, cultural, and even religious "capital" within it.

The Alberts illustrate more clearly than the others something that all three families seem to have in common. The choices they make in the media sphere – the "accounts of media" through which they describe their relationship to media, the practices of media consumption they engage in and attempt to educate their children about, and the meanings they negotiate and derive from media content – all serve as important markers of their negotiations between the various worlds they inhabit. These contexts – their faith; religious symbols, claims, and traditions; the symbols, claims, and traditions of the broader culture; and the media – all insist on certain kinds of identifications, practices, and loyalties. Each has its own saliencies and its own dangers. Significantly, though, it can be seen that the media sphere is active in providing both pointers to the other contexts, and ways of navigating them, and is in some ways the "home base" from which this all takes place.

We can see that much of what we expected to find among families that fit Roof's "born-again" category was a bit off the mark. Each of the families we've seen here, as well as others in our sample and ones we met in previous chapters, endorses some of the most basic "accounts of media" shared by the culture at large. In terms of parenting, there is a consensual expectation that parenting involves a kind of "media education" for the children. Some media are good and some are bad. These born-again families agree that education and enlightenment are important values of the media (with Karl Callahan going so far as to say that "entertainment" is also a positive value of the "visual" or "screen" media as well).

At the same time, even though they are identified with a side of the American religious landscape that is generally seen as conservative and moralistic, all of them fight that stereotype, and recognize that their judgments and behaviors around media are commonly understood markers of their place on that map. That is, they understand that conservative Christians are expected to be restrictive and moralistic about media, and they resist that role. They know that it is important to make distinctions, yet they are reluctant on some levels to do so. On reflection, this makes some sense. Contemporary religion, as we have seen, is oriented toward the autonomous self. Born-again Christians express their own version of this, as was clearly said by a number of our interviewees among these families. Traditional institutional and clerical authority is resisted, and, within the home, traditional parental authority is to be felt in teachable moments about and through media. No one wants to raise automatons. Everyone wants their children to think for themselves, and these families exhibit that sentiment, rather than a "prohibitive" one.

Interestingly, none of these families showed a particular interest in religious television. In fact, several interviewees were actually critical of that genre. Most of these families were familiar with, and many used, religious media of a variety of kinds, including Contemporary Christian Music, cassettes, videos, and books distributed by religious producers and publishers, etc. These media do provide an alternative to the "secular" media for many of them. At the same time, however, these alternatives do not substitute for what they all accept is a commonplace of American cultural participation, watching television, listening to radio, going to movies, and surfing the Internet. Their choices within secular media are in part defined by notions such as the idea that sentimental or "inoffensive" or "traditional" television programs are by definition good. There is also some evidence of the kind of class tastes represented by Karl Callahan's ideas about the problems with "visual" or "screen" media. Thus, some of our expectations for our "born-again" believers" were met and some were not.

Mainstream believers

Those people Roof calls "mainstream believers" are more closely identified with religious institutions than are born-again believers. As he points out, they think of themselves *as* mainstream in important ways, and identify with religious traditions both as matters of their own identity and through extended family associations with those traditions. In Chapter 3, I speculated that they might well be the group most likely to identify with the so-called "mass-culture critique" of the media, being thus more oriented toward "high culture" than to "popular culture," and more suspicious than born-again believers of mass culture more generally. As the mainstream or establishment churches have been less involved than Evangelical groups in producing their own media, we might expect this group not to identify readily with self-consciously "religious media," and to even be suspicious of such media. Whereas we might have expected a kind of moralistic cultural critique of media content from the born-again Christians, mainstream believers might be expected to be less involved in such critiques. Because of their identification *as* "mainstream," I also suggested that they might well identify with aspects of media culture that could be typified as themselves "mainstream," commonplace, or "consensual."

The Boswell family

Dan and Laura Boswell, both in their mid-forties, live in the suburbs of a major western city with their three children, Catherine, 15, Emily, 13, and Ryan, 8. Laura was raised Roman Catholic, and the family continues to regularly attend, and identify with, a local Catholic church. Dan was raised in a Congregational church, but has since converted to Catholicism. The Boswells lack the kind of focused story of personal salvation typical of the born-again believer. To them, religion is something they expect to participate in, and something that is authentically experienced through the institution of the church. Weekly attendance is important, though Laura reports that the children typically resist this practice.[13]

Our conversation with the Boswells about the connection between their faith and their media focused on three media in particular: magazines, the library of videotapes they maintain, and their online and Internet activities. They are less explicit about any regular viewing of broadcast television. Consistent with many of our other interviews, questions of the children, child-rearing, and media values dominated these discussions. Values are clearly on Laura's and Dan's minds when they think about media and their children. A discussion of the values of *YM* magazine was typical:

Emily: It's just kind of like a teen magazine, but sometimes they have bad stuff in it. We don't read the bad stuff. We just read the fashion columns.
Interviewer: What do you mean by "bad stuff"?
Emily: Well. . . .
Laura: It talks about how to kiss your boyfriend when you're 14, you know . . . how to start relationships, and it just seems like it's a little more than early teenagers need to know. I mean, I think even for Catherine it's just kind of . . . (something) . . . where probably *Seventeen* or something like that would have been a better choice. I think even they get into some of that, but not quite so graphically. [to

the girls] Isn't it *YM* that had that article about that girl on that *Seventh Heaven* show? I mean, that's the neatest show and then it talked about how much . . . stuff about her boyfriend and how much she hated her mother. I mean, it kind of took this nice character and . . . it was weird. But I'm sure that's what she really is.

Laura is clearly aware of the content of the magazine, and it is now banned, in favor of more appropriate fare, such as *Seventeen*. The television program *Seventh Heaven* is a regular part of the family's television diet, and she and the girls were surprised to find one of its actresses in the context of such a magazine.

The children go to films regularly, and the family as a whole goes to a movie about once a month, according to Laura. The family is not too specific about the kinds of films they attend or want the children to watch when they go alone. The girls report that they are allowed to attend PG-13 films. The family does own a large library of videos, though, and those tend to be the viewing of choice for the most part. They think they watch fifty to seventy of them regularly, including films like *It's a Bug's Life*, "lots of Disney," and *Apollo 13*. Also in this library are what Laura calls her "ironing movies," mentioning specifically *Sleepless in Seattle* and taped re-runs of *The Phil Silvers Show*. There seems to be a value in the idea of being able to control the content of the family's diet through these taped programs.

The children, particularly young Ryan, saw the family's going "online" after the Christmastime purchase of a new computer as a major watershed in their media diets. This was particularly significant for the kids, who saw their pre-Internet lives as a kind of cultural and social isolation.

Emily: Until we got our new computer, we were like the only people who didn't have the Internet. We had like a typewriter.
Ryan: Amish.
Emily: We were like technologically impaired.
Ryan: Amish.
Interviewer: Did that feel strange?
Catherine: Yea, kind of
Interviewer: Is it something you didn't tell your friends about, or how did you handle that?
Catherine: Well, they would always talk about what they would do on the Internet.
Emily: They'd be like, "Oh, get on it at 5:30 and we'll all talk." And we're like, "What's the Internet?"
Laura: (sarcastically) Pretty sad, isn't it?

For this family, the ubiquity and pervasiveness of media in the home is felt most keenly around Internet and Internet access. Dan and Laura had resisted going online out of a generalized sense that it would only be a waste of time for the kids, deciding in the end that its value as an information source justified this decision. The children keep current on MTV programs, and the family reports regular viewing of two programs, *Home Improvement* when it was on, and, subsequent to that, the domestic situation program about a clergy family, *Seventh Heaven*. Asked which programs they regularly watch as a family, Laura identifies *Seventh Heaven*, and a discussion of its value ensues.

Interviewer: You described that as a really neat show earlier. What do you like about that show?

Ryan: Uh, I don't know.

Laura: It's realistic. (Both girls say, "Yeah.") It's not too goody-goody. It's a nice family show, but it's realistic for the times, with the things they look at – drugs and sex, but they handle it nicely.

Dan: And I think the kids can relate to probably each one of the characters.

Laura: There's somebody their age. . . .

Dan: Kind of their age that they can identify with.

Interestingly, the implicit religiosity of the program does not appear to be a major value for the Boswell family. They do not readily connect their faith and beliefs with media in other areas, and its absence here is interesting (though not unusual – many of our families who do view *Seventh Heaven* identify it much more readily as a model family drama than they do as the story of a clergy family). As with our born-again believers earlier, and Evangelicals more generally, the notion that this program is merely inoffensive is an important value, along with the idea that it somehow models positive family relations.

The picture the Boswells paint of their media viewing is unremarkable. Their accounts of media connect with their professed viewing choices and their ability to plan and program their media diets through their video library (and to an extent through their Internet access) seems to be important to them. However, as with many other households, that is not all there is to the story. When the Interviewer asks if they have rules governing media viewing, a discussion ensues that reveals a very similar situation to that encountered in some of the other households.

Interviewer: Do you have any policies about media use in your house, policies or rules?

Ryan: Umm. . . .

Catherine: We can't watch talk shows.

Ryan: What's talk shows? Oh, yeah. *Jerry Springer*.

Laura: I mean, *Oprah* would be OK, but some of those. . . .

Dan: *Judge Judy.*
Ryan: Oh, yeah. Me and Dad watch that a lot.
Laura: And I hate it. It just drives me nuts when they watch stuff like that.
Interviewer: (to Ryan) You and your dad watch *Judge Judy*?
Dan: Not very often. About once a month.
Ryan: And we watch . . . what's that one, that cop show?
Dan: Oh, *Top Cops.*
Ryan: Yeah. That's what we watch.
Laura: If I'm around I won't let them watch it.
Dan: I think the big one is we don't let them watch the *Jerry Springers* and some of those kinds of shows.
Laura: I think the girls police themselves pretty well, and if they're uncomfortable they'll usually shut it off.
Interviewer: What do you not like about the talk shows?
Laura: They're just so dumb.
Dan: All the general crap on 'em that's just . . . they're such far-fetched topics that it's just not worth your time to turn it on.
Interviewer: And has that always been a rule, no talk shows?
(Several answer "yes")

The similarities to other families are striking here. While the Boswells express some fairly clear understandings and accounts of media, some variations in viewing behavior from expressed preferences do take place. It is further not clear how the distinctions between types of talk format programs are made. It is not clear what Laura means by "dumb," and exploration of this issue with her does not result in any more enlightenment on that point. In addition, Ryan and Dan seem to enjoy the guilty pleasure of some programs of which Laura does not approve. The Boswells, in short, are not that different from many other families in many of the ways they consume media.

The Allen family

Jill Allen, 37, lives in the inner suburbs of a major city with her two daughters, Laura, 16, and Melissa, 10. She is divorced from the girls' father, and has had on-again/off-again relationships in the years since. Jill is Anglo, the girls' father Hispanic. They do not maintain close contact, and he does not contribute to the maintenance of the family. Jill has a high-school education and works at a nearby manufacturing plant on the assembly line. The family income is low, and life is a constant financial struggle. The family is fortunate to be able to live in a neat, clean, and well-maintained three-bedroom home, subsidized by a local non-profit housing organization. Laura, the 16-year-old, plans to begin after-school work soon to help support the family.[14]

Jill was raised in a Baptist church, but at age 16 her mother began taking the family to a Lutheran church and the family has been Lutheran ever since. Jill and the girls attend regularly, usually with Jill's mother, who lives nearby. Church is thus an important point of family identification for them, and the family tradition is one of the major reasons for their loyalty to it. The girls attend youth programs at the church regularly, and Laura is in confirmation class there. Laura sings in the youth choir at church and Jill sings in the adult choir. Church is also the major social involvement for the family. Laura has participated in fund raisers at the church, and is presently working on a summer trip that the youth group will make to Washington, DC.

Media are pretty important in the Allen household. They own three television sets, a large one in an entertainment center in the living room, and one in each of the girls' rooms. However, those are primarily for playing video games. The living room set is the common set where they view together. They subscribe to a satellite television service that brings in 120 channels of television. Jill objects to the preponderance of sports on the service, but they like being able to watch a variety of channels, and do subscribe to one cable movie channel. "I can't afford more than that," Jill says. The Allens do not regularly tape programs to watch later and do not maintain a library of videotapes. Music is also not a major medium for them. Television is much more important.

For them, it seems, television is something they share. During the interview, they all participate in the conversation about television choices and viewing. Unlike many other parents, who seemingly speak from a position of oversight over the children's viewing habits, Jill participates more directly in describing her and her daughters' television tastes and behaviors as a sort of common family practice. Their favorite channels seem to be those carrying re-runs of older and classic programs. For instance, they have had a family ritual of watching re-runs of the classic *I Love Lucy* on one of those channels, and talk about it with some interest and excitement.

Interviewer: You two watch a lot of *I Love Lucy* [to the kids], do you
    watch that with them [to Jill]?
Jill: Oh yeah.
Interviewer: When is it on?
Laura: It's on Monday nights all night and so we watch it Monday night.
Interviewer: All night?
Laura: Until 11 o'clock.
Interviewer: When does it start?
Laura: Seven.
Interviewer: What do you like about the show? I think this is the 50-year
    anniversary of the first airing of the show.
Jill: Lucy just cracks me up. She always makes us laugh.

Melissa: Like Lucy, she tries to figure out everything to get something back or do something back that somebody did to her so she like thinks of an idea and she says, I got an idea and then she goes into the house and then she hears somebody coming and she hides somewhere.

Compared to other families, the Allens seem to have few explicit standards for appropriate media content. When asked about this, Jill's ideas seem less focused and more general than is often the case, and few specific programs are mentioned.

Interviewer: Are there any TV shows or video games that aren't allowed?
Laura: [nods no].
Interviewer: You could buy any video game you wanted and you wouldn't have a problem with it?
Jill: Unless it's . . . no sexual. That's all. But they both know.
Interviewer: For the TV also . . . ?
Jill: Right.
Interviewer: But are there things that you don't let them watch?
Jill: No, I just say we can't watch that and we watch something else.
Interviewer: And what would that be? What are some examples of things that aren't allowed?
Jill: Like a violent movie or something like that. And she knows pretty good and I just don't want her to see that most of the time, so young.
Interviewer: So violence and sex?
[Melissa puts her hands over her eyes]
Interviewer: Is that what you do, cover your eyes?
Melissa: Yeah.
Interviewer: How do you know when to cover your eyes?
Melissa: My mom tells me.

For Jill, it seems that the fact that she typically watches with them is a check on her daughters' viewing. But, beyond that, there is a sense that television is a tacit and normal aspect of the family's daily life. Thus, for Jill, the threshold of concern or suspicion about it is rarely reached, except for vague concerns about sex and violence. These seem rather empty and meaningless, though, when the majority of viewing they do is of inoffensive family sitcoms and dramas anyway. Beyond the re-runs of classic programs such as *I Love Lucy*, their television diet includes more contemporary programs such as *Seventh Heaven* and *Home Improvement*. *Seventh Heaven*, as we have seen, is a program that can be read for its religious content (the lead character is a clergyman, but the program's plots tend to focus on family issues rather than his career). The Allens, though, identify a bit more with the program's religious content than others we've spoken with. Laura notes that, while the father is a "preacher," the program shows her that all families are basically the same. "You can tell how different their life is from ours because he is a preacher and it's not really different. It's the same," she observes. There are, however, programs that they describe as more religiously or spiritually significant, specifically *Touched by an Angel* and *It's a Miracle*. They actually see these as guides to spirituality or religiosity.

For Jill and the girls, these programs' religious or spiritual content is rooted in the mysterious – even mystical – conditions through which lives are touched and people changed. While the girls can only observe that these programs are "very cool," Jill tries to explain it more concretely, suggesting that she shares the kinds of feelings of prescience that are in *It's a Miracle*. "I like that show because um . . . when someone . . . like me, I can feel it that something is going to happen and then . . . that somebody is going to help you get it," she says. Referring to *It's a Miracle*, *Seventh Heaven*, and *Touched by an Angel*, the Interviewer asks if watching these programs "helps in relation to your church or makes connections for you."

Laura: Sometimes.
Jill: Yeah . . . yeah, when I go to church and I pray, then I can feel it.
Interviewer: When you say you can feel it, do you feel in relation to those shows, or are there other shows also, or other media. . . .
Jill: No, the way I feel is . . . he's telling me . . . that I'm doing the best I can. To be a good mom and a hard worker. To be the best I can. That's what he's telling me. In the future time something will come up, but I just don't know what it is. But when it hits then I know. I just don't know when.
Interviewer: You feel when you watch these shows?
Laura: Yeah. And it feels like it's actually like true and it feels like well . . . it is kind of hard to explain. Like . . . like he's actually watching over us. Like he was over them and it feels like we're in relation somehow.

For the Allens, then, there is a kind of spiritual connection to the themes of these programs, something that they consciously refer to in their religious practices at church, and a kind of identification with the experiences and expectations of the characters in these programs. There is a way in which the programs are almost a guide for spiritual life of a kind, as well as a comforting reminder that the lives they see there are not that different from their own.

Life in the mainstream

In *A Generation of Seekers*, Roof makes the point that the mainstream believers are significant because they are "mainstream" and think of themselves that way. My colleague Diane F. Alters considered the idea of religious "mainstream-ness" and its relationship to household media practice in our book *Media, Home, and Family*.[15] In it, she introduced a family we called the Roelofs. While they were not regular church-goers, and had done quite a bit of shopping around, this family felt quite strongly that they were religious, not denominationally identified, but simply "Christian." The father, Ryan, insisted that they wanted their children to lead a "Christian, moral" life, but was rather vague about the nature of that life, and its relationship to religiously rooted values. As Alters noted, his explanation of what that meant evoked the kind of "golden-rule" Christianity we might expect in a "mainstream" household. As Ryan put it, "You know, love-thy-neighbor-as-thyself type of attitude, do-unto-others-as-you-would-have-them-do-unto-you type of situation."[16]

The Roelofs' religiosity and its relationship to media were complex, as Alters noted.[17] However, some commonalities and contrasts with the Allens and Boswells are apt here. Like the others, the Roelofs valued the idea of families viewing media together (though they rarely did). They also stressed the importance of parents using media to help their children learn about values. Like the others, the Roelofs expressed a vague set of media prohibitions, focused mostly around sex and violence. They expressed a rather more focused set of accounts of media than these other families, though, specifically criticizing daytime talk shows and rap music. Like the Boswells, the Roelofs focused on the issue of time, expressing an intention to limit the amount of time their children spent with media of all kinds. Also like both the Boswells and the Allens, the Roelofs seemed to be embedded in media. In spite of the parents' claims that they attempted to set limits on the kinds of programs viewed by their children, they found that the reality did not exactly fit the aspiration in that regard.

One of the most important ways that these mainstream families seem to differ from the born-again believers is in the sense on the part of the latter group that their religious or spiritual beliefs necessarily put them at odds with the broader culture and its claims. In contrast, these mainstream believers rarely expressed such a notion of difference. As Alters put it in describing the Roelofs, "They believed that they shared with other people in the society certain morals that helped them judge media products."[18] Commonality with the rest of the culture, rather than difference from it, seemed to define their view. Whereas the born-again believers seemed to accept and express a received view that they were necessarily more moralistic, sectarian, and partisan, these mainstream believers did not express as developed and extensive received stereotype of their beliefs and attitudes about media. In addition, their accounts lacked much if any reference to contemporary issues in religious politics, matters that were more common in our discussions with born-again believers.

A broad center

The narratives here raise some themes and values that seem common between "born-again" and "mainstream" believers. First of all, most of those we've heard from so far seem comfortable with the idea that their values and their expectations should somehow be represented or expressed through the media they consume and through their families' practices of reception. There is an idea here that the media represent some sort of a broad cultural surround to which they should be expected to relate on some level. It is the legacy of their location on the cultural landscape that they should have an opinion about the media that are available in their homes. In this context, they seem also to share the perspective that issues of choice and control should be central to their responses to media. There is a kind of shared idea that the media demand a response and that response is expressed either through control, through choice, or through some combination of the two.

For most of these interviewees, ideas of choice and control imply a kind of autonomy in relation to the media. No one wants to be a passive viewer; everyone wants to think of himself as critically and dynamically involved in his media viewing. It is also common across these interviews that the concern parents have for children, and the way that children are to come to consume media, are important distinctions as well. We will consider this in more detail in the next chapter, but few of the parents here want to think of themselves as exercising direct control over their family's viewing habits. Instead, most of them preferred to wish for their children what they saw in themselves – autonomous action in careful choice as to what is viewed or consumed.

The distance between the aspiration and the reality here is an important and fascinating dimension of these interviews. As we noted earlier, a set of received ideas or "accounts of media" play a role in the way people think about and represent media practice for themselves in their households. What we begin to see here, and will discuss in more detail later, is a growing sense that these received ideas are at odds with the realities of media consumption on some rather fundamental and determinative levels. It is not a trivial matter such as a lack of moral will that keeps a parent from being the kind of media consumer they present themselves as being. There are a broader set of social and cultural forces at play.

We will gain some additional insight into these and other dimensions of media practice vis-à-vis religion and spirituality in the next chapter, where we will move on to consider interviewees who represent the rest of Roof's categories. That chapter will end with an overall assessment of what we have learned by looking at matters in this way.

Chapter 7

Cultural objects and religious identity among metaphysical believers, dogmatists, and secularists

The categories we considered in the last chapter represent the two most significant "poles" of (at least) American religious history. The evolution of the Evangelical movement in the middle of the twentieth century left Protestantism with two important "faces": those individuals and movements that came to identify with Evangelicalism (those likely to describe themselves as "born again"); and those who did not. As Roof has suggested, what may form the core of identity for the *latter* group is that they are not part of the *former*. At the same time, people on both sides share a great deal in common, particularly as regards an identification with Christian and Protestant tradition in some specific and formal way, and a general Protestant sensibility to be open to the culture, though the two "sides" do so in different ways.

They also seem to share a good deal in common in terms of their approaches to media culture, which is our central concern here. Issues of choice and control, as I have said, are major themes of their self-reflection on their relationship to the media sphere. They also seem to share a particular focus on the idea of parenthood and the objectification of the experience of their children or others' children as important dimensions defining media practice. For all of them, there is a shared implicit sense that they are, or should be, at the center of the religious landscape. The people we will hear from here do not share that view.

In this chapter, we move a bit more to the "sides" of the religious/cultural current. The differing flows of Evangelicalism and mainstream identity derive from a sense of relationship to tradition, yet, for the categories we will see here, tradition itself becomes the important issue. For the first category below, the "metaphysical believers and seekers," contestation of the notion of traditional religion becomes an important point of identity, as it does for the "secularists" we will end with. For the "dogmatists," in the middle, tradition is something that absolutely must be embraced and honored. What we see here, then, are categories of practice for whom the idea that there are received religious histories and traditions is probably more important than it was for the people we heard from in the last chapter. We will end with an overall review of all five categories and what we seem to have learned along the way.

Metaphysical believers and seekers

In discussing this category of contemporary religiosity earlier, I suggested that their relationship to media might differ markedly from the others. As the Roof category that most centrally represents the practices and sensibilities of autonomy and "seeking" or "questing," we might expect that the metaphysical believers and seekers would be the most open to the range of symbolic and spiritual resources available in the media sphere. Characteristic of this group is a deep separation from, even a critique of, traditional religious institutions and religious culture. Thus, there is reason to look for them to be more active in acquiring and assembling religious and spiritual senses of themselves using resources from a variety of sources, most of which are available to them through the media. Without the intervening frame of clerical or institutional authority, they should be the group most active at the boundary between "media" and "religion."

The Stevens-Van Gelder family

Vicky Stevens, age 46, and Jan Van Gelder, age 44, are a lesbian couple who have celebrated a commitment ceremony and are the parents of Brett, age 9. They live in a small city in the west, in a two-story frame house.[1] Vicky and Jan are both social workers, and Jan also invests in real estate. They are a solidly middle-class two-income family. Brett attends a non-traditional elementary school, but also goes to religious school weekly at the local Jewish Renewal Community, where Jan is a member. Vicky attends a Church of Religious Science. In spite of their holding memberships in religious organizations, Vicky and Jan are decidedly "seekers," and are not clearly identified with any such body. It is Brett who observes to the Interviewer how unusual it must seem to have one of them identify with a Jewish center and the other with a Christian one. Vicky admits to having also identified with Judaism from time to time. "Yes, I'm eclectic in my spirituality," she says. All three of them seem very comfortable talking about their religious lives, using the language of "spirituality," which they prefer to "religion." Their views about the relationship between their spirituality and their religious organizations show a negotiation between their autonomous seeking and a taste for some sort of religious grounding or structure, however limited. They attend, as a family, both the Renewal Community (which meets once a month) and the Church of Religious Science (which meets weekly).

Vicky: We all kind of go to all of it. Because they don't contradict each other at all. The Jewish Renewal is like the most very liberal end of Judaism and Religious Science is probably the most liberal end of . . .
Brett: Christianity.
Vicky: Yeah. So they don't contradict each other at all.

Brett: What do you mean, contradict?

Vicky: Well, for instance, Religious Science doesn't really talk about Jesus. They talk about the God within, and they just talk about Jesus as a teacher. They don't believe Jesus was the only son of God, and so it doesn't contradict Judaism, who also sees Jesus as a wise person . . .

Brett: but not . . .

Vicky: not having special status, other than somebody who knew a lot.

Jan: They don't talk about Jesus in their services, but if you talk to Jewish people about Jesus, they feel that he was a very spiritual and wise teacher but just not the Messiah, which is similar to. . . .

It is important for them that both their Judaism and their Christianity come from the "liberal" end of the spectrum. The fact that both traditions distance themselves from traditional Christianity is also important. Thus, the notion that Jesus could be a great teacher, but not the exclusive source of insight, is an important marker for them. It is interesting that, at such a young age, Brett seems to have absorbed some of his mothers' language about these issues. Vicky provides the most extensive explanation of their religiosity. She was raised Catholic but left that church in her twenties and felt no need for any religious affiliation until a decade later. The openness she finds in Religious Science is, for her, a critical difference in comparison to the Catholicism of her youth and most other religions.

Vicky: They have a very open approach. Their whole thing is that God lives in each of us, and there's no one savior or one particular anything . . . they sort of see Jesus as a very wise teacher, and there are many other wise teachers, and that no one is particularly the son of God, rather that we're all children of God. And I like that kind of openness. I really have gotten very turned off by, "This is the way" kind of thing. So at the Church of Religious Science, there are people from a lot of religious backgrounds. There are some people who were raised Jewish there, there's all different Christian denominations, because it is very open that way. . . . I went to some workshops and gatherings that were talking about Native American spirituality and that whole kind of concept of what they call "the all that is," the spirit that lives in everything that lives. And I thought, "Oh, that's really open. I like that!" And then I studied some of the earth religions who have that same kind of openness, about honoring the God in all of us. And then Jan started really wanting us to be involved in learning about Judaism, so we started going in that direction. (Brett, from the dining table nearby, interjects that they celebrate the Winter Solstice.)

Interviewer: And so do you consider yourself part of that, as well?

Vicky: Yeah, that's what Jan's main interest is, but we all go to the Shabbat services, and then they both go with me to Religious Science on Sundays. So we kind of all do it all, because none of it precludes the other. Like, the Jewish Renewal movement is very open and very liberal, and so is the Religious Science. [She says she goes to the Religious Science services every Sunday, and frequently also goes to the Jewish services.]

Vicky's orientation away from strict religions and toward "open" ones seems clearly to be a fundamental issue for her – one that defines both her religious identity and the kinds of religious involvements she wants for herself and for her family. It is common in our interviews to find our meta-physical believers and seekers to be more aware of the landscape of contemporary "culture wars" and religious politics than are the main-stream believers. In this way, they are a counterpoint to many of the born-again believers, who recognize media culture as a context where their distinctiveness can be expressed and charted. Seeing the same difference from the other direction, Vicky identifies her religiosity in part by means of what it is *not*: not "born again." When asked if she makes a distinction between religion and spirituality, Vicky replies,

> Yeah, I do. I think spirituality has to do with our own relationship with spirit and how we see that in the world, and I think religion is a set of rules and dogma and ritual that people use – hopefully for their spirituality, but not necessarily. A lot of the right-wing, born-again Christians that I know are . . . I don't think there's anything spiritual about it at all. It's very cruel, a lot of the ones I've come across. My sister, for instance. I have a sister who's awful. And she constantly wants to tell me how bad I am and condemn my lifestyle, all that kind of stuff. There's nothing spiritual about that. I think spirituality is inclusive and honors everyone equally, and I don't think religion.

This stereotype of born-again believers includes two distinctions that are important to Vicky. First, the notion that spirituality itself is a positive value: the most appropriate way to express autonomous seeking. Second, she identifies spirituality as she describes it as more open and inclusive than religions, which are necessarily judgmental and exclusive.

The family is asked about their current media viewing habits. Brett responds that currently the television and VCR are off limits, unplugged by Vicky.

Interviewer: Why did you do that?
Brett: Because we thought . . . (turns to Vicky) Why don't you say? 'Cause you decided it.
Vicky: Well, I just thought . . . not just TV *per se*, but one of the things connected to the TV is Nintendo, SuperNintendo for Brett, and we

were feeling like he was so focused on being in front of the TV playing SuperNintendo. . . . We don't watch a lot of regular TV, but we just decided we would turn it off for a month and see what else we would do instead, if we didn't have that for a month.

They do talk about their general media behaviors, however, noting that they tend to favor what they call "family movies," and they own a small library of videotapes that they watch together on a regular basis. It turns out that television viewing is an important family ritual for them, something they do (usually – but not always – a Disney movie) on Sunday evenings. They think of it as a "nice family time," Brett observes.

Vicky: Yeah, we eat dinner in the living room, which is unusual. We sort of have dinner while we're watching it. And then after we eat we sort of all snuggle on the couch to watch it. And it's usually something fun, a fun movie. It just seems like a cozy family time.
Jan: It's a time that you can generally also assume that it's going to be appropriate for a kid to watch. I mean, there's so much violence and stuff, you know, on TV, and we usually stay away from that. And there's only been one time that we turned it off.

The Stevens-Van Gelder family is hardly skeptical about television and other media. They do have standards for what they watch, though, and want to make it clear that it is violence more than sex that bothers them about television and movies. This prohibition has even prevented them from taking Brett to see some popular animated films. As with other families who wish to distinguish themselves from those on the right bank of the cultural mainstream, they are careful to hold to this view of media violence, though they admit their exposure to sexually suggestive material is limited because they do not have cable television. When asked about these standards, Brett refers to nudity and bad language, but Jan and Vicky quickly bring the discussion back to violence.

Brett: But like, if it was an X-rated movie and everyone was walking around without wearing any clothes . . . or the ones that are rated R because they have bad language in them.
Jan: He's never seen it, but Chuck Norris's *Texas Ranger*, I really object to that one. I don't know, there's a number of just really violent, I think, shows on.
Interviewer: So is violence then the main reason that you'll avoid the show? (Jan and Brett both say yes.)
Jan: I certainly don't think that kids this age should be presented with sexual material, but since we don't have cable – and that's one of the reasons we don't have cable is, I think there is a lot of R-rated movies on cable.

Brett: There's like three good shows, and the rest are R-rated.

Vicky: Plus we don't watch TV enough to justify cable. I mean, we watch the news and a movie once in a while that might be on the TV, we do the Sunday night thing, and other than that we don't watch much TV.

Their concern about violent media even extends to local news programs, which they view nearly every night to "stay updated," Vicky says.[2] But they watch the late news in part because it comes on after Brett's bedtime.

Jan: Part of why I don't want him to see the news at this point is that I don't like him to feel like the world is as violent as it's portrayed. I mean, sometimes you turn on the news and it's like, well there was a murder . . . where three kids were shot, and then two kids were in a drunk driving accident . . .

Vicky: and there's a rapist . . . who's doing this.

Jan: Sometimes it's like, God, it's three murders and three acts of violence (in a row), and certainly those things are out there, but we try to also say – a lot – that most people are good. The news doesn't look like most people are good or doing positive things. It's real skewed.

Their preferred reading of media violence then is based not on a fear of Brett imitating violent behavior, which is the theme of much of the research on the topic, but on a social learning about values in contemporary human relations. They are concerned that he not learn to think of the world as a violent place, or a place where violence is accepted as normative. Jan and Vicky are also concerned about an issue with television that is not as common a concern, the sex-role stereotyping found in many programs. Asked specifically about sexism in the content of the Disney films they like to watch as a family, Jan observes,

Jan: I don't watch them as much as Brett and Vicky do. Oh, like *The Beauty and the Beast*, that was on recently. I hate that movie because of that. I mean, it's just . . . you know, the idea of this woman being captured and then falling in love with those men that seems abusive. We've talked a lot about that theme with *Beauty and the Beast*, and how . . . just kind of how ridiculous that is, to me.

Jan clearly thinks of herself as being more strict and vigilant about Brett's media life. She actively pre-screens films and other videos they buy, and describes herself as paying more attention than Vicky to the content of films they might attend with Brett. While she is reluctant to say that she and Vicky differ on fundamentals, she nonetheless sees Vicky and Brett as much more the media consumers in the household. Reflecting on the overall question, Jan echoes a sentiment we encountered in the born-again

Milliken and mainstream Allen households: the idea that parenting should be about equipping children to make their own choices about media rather than acting as censors or controllers of content. The difference, of course, is the kind of content that is of concern.

Jan: I get really . . . I wish there were more movies that would be productive and positive. There seems to be such a focus on violence. I mean, I don't think it's appropriate for Brett to watch movies that are sexual, but I'd much rather he be exposed to that than violence . . . I think . . . I mean, he doesn't just want to turn on the TV and watch something violent, but I get . . . I think that it's going to be more of an issue in a few years, when his friends are going to the high-action movies, that that may become more of an issue. Maybe not. I mean, his value around non-violence is pretty secure.

The one medium they are the most concerned about with reference to Brett is video games. Brett is a heavy Nintendo user. He is limited to three and one-half hours of "non-educational" computer use a week. This is clearly a point of tension in the household, but Jan intends to hold fast. Where she and Vicky prefer to think of Brett's relationship to media in terms of his developing skills at selectivity, Jan feels that video games are one medium that has had a direct influence *on* him.

Jan is more concerned about the family's relationship to the broader culture than Vicky, and shares in common with the born-again believers we interviewed the sense that her family is somehow out of the mainstream of American culture, and not just because they are a gay family. Her ideas here actually sound a good bit like those we heard from religiously strict households. She sees media culture and choice to participate in it as a major marker of the way individuality and individual values come into conflict with a seemingly coercive media-cultural environment.

Jan: I certainly don't want to embrace what I feel like is out there. It seems like there needs to be a huge change in that way, and would really like to get involved in some sort of organization to make changes. Because I feel like, I can do what I can in terms of my own family, but I think that there's a much broader issue that I would like to see something be done about. So I think that there's a lot of people who are in agreement with that, but none of us know what to do. And I'm not really sure how much of the culture really likes what's out there, but I think that an awful lot of 'em certainly participate – in going to the movies or buying the video games or whatever. So, I think that there's much greater acceptance than I'm comfortable with, so in that way I feel like I stand apart and don't really want to embrace what the general public is doing.

Like more socially conservative parents, then, Jan feels the pressure of the ubiquitous, pervasive media, and wishes to see herself standing outside its influence. In a certain way, Jan understands that her family is not that different from many others in either their attitudes about media or their media behaviors. In a way, there may even be a comfort for her in this identification. When asked whether she thought others would find anything to be uncomfortable about her family's media behaviors, she responds that, with the possible exceptions of films they might watch with gay or lesbian themes, she doesn't think so.

Jan: Some of the people I work with . . . have a more religious orientation, and for some of them, I think any gay and lesbian issue is uncomfortable for them. And so watching a movie, even though it's not sexual or anything like that, would be uncomfortable for them. But generally, most of the things we watch, most people wouldn't have a problem with that.

Interviewer: Do you feel that your spiritual beliefs influence your choices about what you watch in the media and your rules for media use?

Jan: Do my beliefs influence what I watch? Yeah. I mean, I don't tend to like a lot of violence, and have a pretty non-violent approach and belief system, and certainly don't choose to watch those things. (Also) I'm not likely to turn on Billy Graham or anything like that. (chuckles)

Vicky agrees with Jan about the general bent of media (dismissing most of it as bad, negative, violent, and exploitative) and about the notion that their values, if gauged by the media, are out of step with the majority of the culture. "Our society is going off the deep end," she concludes. She also believes that the fact that they are a lesbian family does not make much of a difference in their attitudes about media culture.

> I think it has to do with more just our values in general. I think if we were a heterosexual family, we'd have the same values and hopefully the same sensitivities . . . we have friends who are heterosexual who are very similar to me. We have the same kinds of discussions, and they're very aware of discrimination issues and they watch the same kind of shows and don't watch other kinds and that kind of stuff.

As evidence of this, Vicky notes that she and her born-again sister, while they can agree on little else, can agree that violent television is bad for their children. For both Jan and Vicky, there is a sense that their beliefs and practices around media connect them with larger discourses about parenting and family values in the society. "I think we just want to see ourselves as part of the larger community, and we want to be accepted as we are," she says. Both Jan and Vicky have a hard time identifying specific media that have been religiously or spiritually meaningful to them. Like many others among our interviews, that is simply a hard connection for them to make. Vicky does think that their beliefs influence the kinds of movies they attend, however. Asked if they select films or other media because of their spirituality, she says,

> I like movies that have that theme to it, and we'll look for movies that have that kind of theme to it if we're going to rent a video or something, or we'll see a movie. I mean, the movies we go to are about people's relationships and about – whether it's relationships with each other or with the earth or with spirituality or whatever – those are the kind of things that we're more interested in. But yeah, we like movies like that.

The Stevens-Van Gelder family has some clear ideas about the media. They avoid violent media, they see media choice and content through the frame of religiously based "culture wars," and yet they enjoy media as a family, even ritually consuming it weekly. They think of their attitudes about media as pretty conventional for parents of a young child. At the same time, they do agree with families in other of Roof's categories that there is a media-based cultural mainstream out there that is at some variance from their own values. Jan and Vicky want their son to develop his own skills of media consumption, and to guide him toward that end. There is one area, though, that concerns them, and that is simply the amount of time media take away from other, more positive or "educational" pursuits. They are critical of parents who seem not to be concerned about this issue.

Jan: Boy, I think for a lot of people, for most people, it [media] has a huge role in people's life. I think people watch a lot of TV.
Interviewer: Do you know some people like that?
Jan: Most of the people I know do try to set some limits around TV-watching in their households. . . . Brett, there was a time when he really liked *Wishbone*, and it would be on three times a day, and it's like, "That's an hour-and-a-half." And most of them, he had already seen. It's like, the same ones over and over. And so I think that it's very enticing for people to just sit in front of the TV and be entertained and not have to be creative.
Interviewer: So with *Wishbone*, was the show itself OK? Was it just the amount of time?
Jan: Yeah, I think it's a great show. But he would come in and just turn on the TV, and it's like, "Wait a minute. This doesn't make sense."

This sets up an account of media for this family that sees media use – whether an educational show like *Wishbone* or Brett's playing of video games – as a potential distraction from education, enlightenment, and creativity. While they do not make a great matter of it, there is also a sense that these "screen" media are somehow less valuable and more distracting than other media, specifically books, would be. Both parents speak approvingly of books and reading, and reflect on books as more spiritually significant in their own lives than either films or television. In this way, they are more like others among their social and educational class, where it has always been more common to accept such culturally hierarchical attitudes about media.

The Tabor-Collins family

Sarah Tabor, age 41, lives in a medium-sized city in the western US with her three daughters, Samantha Collins, 17, Christine Collins, 14, and Chloe Collins, 13.[3] Their annual income is less than $25,000, but they live comfortably in a split-level home. They are Buddhist, and their home includes a shrine and other symbols of their faith. When asked if she would describe herself as a convert to Buddhism from another religion, Sarah responds that she was raised in a household that had very little, if any, religiosity. "I was pretty much raised as an atheist," she says. "My father was an atheist so I was pretty much agnostic." She offers that, for her, Buddhism is not really a "religion,"

Sarah: I mean I see it more of a daily practice than I do as a religion. I guess it is a religion, is an organization but . . . it's you know, the organization is very quite spread all over the world and it's a very strong peace organization . . . critical of violence, you know really supportive people, and just what it takes to be a human being.
Interviewer: But if somebody would ask you. . . .
Sarah: If I was very religious?
Interviewer: What kind of religion would you say. . . .
Sarah: Then I would probably say Buddhism.

The girls, by contrast, "go back and forth," Sarah says. Their paternal grandmother is a "strong Christian woman" so they are coming under Christian influence, too. The family, however, goes to a local Buddhist center weekly for meditation, so that is their most regular religious or spiritual involvement. While they are in a way conventional in their practices as American Buddhists, they nonetheless fit most appropriately in the "metaphysical believer and seeker" category.[4]

Based on our reading of Roof, we expect families in this category to be somewhat unconventional in their media tastes and behaviors. If the media sphere does provide commodified resources to seeking, as it seems to, these families should be the ones that express that through the way they interact with, and use, the media. When asked if there are any programs they watch regularly, the girls respond,

Chloe: *Friends* on Thursday.
Samantha: And *The Simpsons*.
Chloe: And *The Simpsons* and . . . *Will and Grace*.
Samantha: Yeah, *Will and Grace*. We watch MTV sometimes and BET and Comedy Central.
Interviewer: BET [Black Entertainment Television], the channel?
Christine: Sometimes, there are some shows that all want to watch, some music videos or something that I will watch.
Interviewer: Is there anything that you tape, because you don't want to miss it?
Chloe: *Friends*.
Interviewer: You tape it?
Chloe: Yeah, when we can't watch it that night, we tape it.

In addition to these more ritualized television-viewing experiences, they own a collection of videotapes, reporting that the film *Fried Green Tomatoes* is their all-time favorite among those. Similar to many mainstream believers and differing from many born-again believers, Sarah believes that the single most concerning thing about television or other media is violence. Like other parents, Sarah reports that her ideas about appropriate media are codified in a set of rules or practices that her daughters understand and follow. She specifically recalls having to control access to *Buffy the Vampire Slayer* not so much because of its sexuality, but more because of its "gore." Asked for other examples, she responds,

Sarah: *X-Files* I didn't like either. That was awful.
Chloe: And *Angel*.
Interviewer: So is it the ones that are kind of sci-fiction?
Sarah: No, no just more violent mixed with a lot of sexual connotations.
Interviewer: Did that disturb you, you know talking about the Devil, angels, vampire things, supernatural things?
Sarah: No, it's kind of kind of gore type stuff. I mean that does nothing for me. I don't really personally agree with what they do so.

At the same time, though, Sarah does not want to be thought of as someone who is too restrictive about media content. This coincides with a sense that the family is, in fact, happily a television- and media-consuming family.

Sarah: I mean there are some things that I put limit to, but not very much. You know, I would probably . . . you know most R-rated movies I wanna know what they are watching for but I'd say yeah to with these two [referring to Christine and Chloe]. Samantha, she is pretty much . . . I feel she is grown up enough to make good decisions for herself so.

Interviewer: OK. So are there any TV shows that all of you guys hate?

Samantha: No.

The Tabor-Collins family does watch television with some frequency. The girls were able to provide a list of programs and channels they regularly watch. For them and for Sarah, though, it is important to say that, in comparison with others, their family is not a media-saturated one.

Interviewer: So from an outsider's point of view your family is kind of low key on media in general?

Sarah: Uh [yes].

Interviewer: [to the girls] Is that what you think too, compared to your friends?

Samantha: Oh, yeah by far. 'Cause a lot of my friends go home and watch TV for hours. I mean we have had surveys at school on how much TV we watch, some kids watch like four hours of TV everyday and like I watch four hours maybe every two weeks. Like I hardly watch TV at all, I get bored when I watch TV.

Interviewer: What about you? [to Christine] Your friends are the same watch a lot of TV? Use computer a lot more than you?

Chloe: Yeah, our friends do.

This family wishes to present an account of media as something that they can take or leave. They consume media regularly, but it is important for them to think of themselves as distinct from other, more media-saturated, families. Sarah does not express the kind of concern about media content (except for violent content) that we hear elsewhere. Like the Stevens-Van Gelder family, the concern is more about the time used in watching television than it is about the effects of content or the values found there. This is a more intellectualized than moralized vision, something that is not too surprising in a non-traditional "seeking" household.

Some other families

Several of these themes are echoed in interviews with other families in the "metaphysical believer and seeker" category. Mark Price and Gabriel Benoit are a gay couple who live in a suburban neighborhood with their 11-year-old daughter, Lisette.[5] All three of them express views of religion and spirituality consistent with Roof's "metaphysical seeking" category. Mark observes that religion is choosing a denominational identity, and then, "you have all kinds of beliefs around that. That's religion to me. Spirituality is your relationship with God, and to me that means my relationship with the world." Lisette agrees. "Spirituality is, you know, believing in yourself, and your belief's not necessarily in religion," she says.

Media uses and behaviors are an important part of family identity for the Price-Benoits. Media play an important role in their family life and in their narratives of who they are as a family. It is important for them, at the same time, to describe themselves as a family that is less restrictive than other families. In an analysis of this family's media behaviors, my colleague Lee Hood noted that, while they described themselves as relatively infrequent viewers of television and other media, it seemed that media were nonetheless an important way for them to see themselves within the mainstream of American family culture.[6] Within that mainstream, though, they wanted to be seen on its "left bank," distinct from moralistic or restrictive families. "We have very few rules," Mark told Hood, "Lisette has more rules for herself than we have for her." Lisette continued,

> In the movies that are bloody or news shows that are bloody and gory, I can watch it, but if it's getting too bad then I'll just stop myself. My parents don't really care what I watch as long as I'm willing to talk to them about it if I have questions. And I can get up and leave. I don't feel like I have to stay there. So I kind of have the discipline, so they trust me with it.

The idea that she can be trusted to make her own wise choices regarding media content is an important element of the family's self-description. "My whole thing, though, is she knows it's there, she knows we don't do it, and you can't shelter 'em from everything," Gabriel observes. Almost more important than the question of what specific choices Lisette makes is the sense of social distinction they wish to confirm through their use of media. This seems to be more of a class-based distinction than one that is related to their being a same-gender couple. "Other people might do something, we don't," Gabriel says. "It might be appropriate for one person . . . that doesn't mean it is for us."

Their religious self-understandings give the Price-Benoits a particular kind of understanding of how and when religion enters into media and media consumption. When asked whether they ever think about religion or spirituality when they are watching television, Gabriel suggests that only those programs that are self-consciously "religious" would invoke such ideas.

> [I]t would have to spark something with religion or that type of thing for me to bring God into it. If it was a movie about some lunatic

minister, then of course I'd be sitting there thinking about God. Or if it's some news show about a religious sect, it would bring my spiritual thoughts into it. But other than that, no.

Mark's and Gabriel's ideas here seem to be related to a number of important issues of identity for them. They feel that it is important for them and Lisette to make their own decisions about things without the intervention of history, doctrine, or clerical authority. The media should not be more authoritative than one's own judgment, Gabriel asserts. "Just because you read it or hear it, you don't have to swallow it, and to form your opinion. It's just kind of a tool, it's not written in stone, that type of a thing," he says. Their feelings about religion are similar, that it is something about which they need to form their own opinions. Because they assume that the media need to be greeted with a kind of skepticism, it is hard for them to see how they could provide any sort of authentic or meaningful resources to religion or spirituality, which also require a good deal of personal autonomy to work out. Where religion or spirituality enter into media in significant ways is in cases where a given program or source is self-consciously labeled "religious," or where news programs cover themes or topics that can be straightforwardly labeled "religion."

The fact that they are a gay couple may make Mark and Gabriel particularly attuned to distinctions in the realm of religion and media. As an example, Mark describes his interactions with Lisette over a conservative Christian magazine she receives, subscribed for her by one of her aunts.

Mark: She'll get it in the mail and she'll read it, and I'll say, "What are you thinking about this stuff?" And she'll say, "Oh, that's silly. Don't bother me with that." So I'll read it and there's all this stuff. It's very anti-gay, very, very conservative. And so I'll wanna talk about it with her, and she just says, "Well, don't worry about it." And so then I try not to worry.

The overarching theme for them, then, is the parent–child relationship and the ideal that Lisette come to take responsibility for her own choices. What is important is not the specifics of the content that Lisette consumes or avoids, but the fact that she can and does make such choices for herself. Religion and media interact for them in the way that media with religious themes or ideas are an important and consistent dimension of the media marketplace. There is no sense in which they religiously seek "through" the media. Instead, it is important for them, as seekers, to maintain the same sort of critical distance from media that they do from religion.

Butch and Priscilla Castello are in their thirties and the parents of 8-year-old Corey and 5-year-old Leah.[7] Both Butch and Priscilla were raised Catholic, but now identify much more with Buddhism, after having lived in

Japan for a few years. Like the other "metaphysical seeker" families among our interviews, they stress the issue of time use more than content as an issue in media practices in their homes. Also like the others, they resist the idea that parental rules about media use would be restrictive or moralistic, and think of this as making them distinct from other families that are either more moralistic or less restrictive. When asked about media use, Priscilla says,

Priscilla: . . . our overall rule, always try to find something else to do besides watch TV. Play instead of watching kids' shows, or go for a walk instead of watching a video. So, we try to take the focus elsewhere because the current in our culture is to always be in front of the TV or on the computer. And, it is very hard when we are with other families in their homes because they tend to be really plugged into the television thing, or videos.

Interviewer: And you have made a conscious choice to really limit television and interaction with media?

Priscilla: Yes . . . we also try to make it . . . umm . . . not so . . . there is the feeling that . . . for us it is, I don't know how the kids feel . . . but to try and make it feel natural. . . . Like, in our household, it isn't that we are trying not to watch TV, but rather . . . we just don't. That's just not part of our daily thing.

Others among both our mainstream believer and metaphysical seeker households wished to separate themselves from the "typical" parental complaints regarding "media sex and violence." For some, of these more liberal or progressive parents, it was important that it was violence, not sex, that concerned them. For the Castellos, it is neither sex nor violence, but monopolization of time and materialism that are the issues.

Butch: I think if there is one advantage that we can provide to our children, it really is an advantage for them, I think, not to be controlled by the computers, TVs, the media.

Priscilla: Well, you are also being controlled by consumerism. That is the other thing. You know, our kids never say, "I want this brand of clothing or that toy."

We have seen that for many of our interviewees, it is difficult to make a direct connection between their religion or spirituality and the media they consume. For most of them, it makes the most sense to think in those terms when the media in question are self-consciously and intentionally "religious" or "spiritual" media. For many, however, there are differences in media in this regard, with music and film more likely to evoke authentic religious or spiritual responses, and television less likely to do so, particularly among our mainstreamers and metaphysicians. Kim Anderson is a good example of this.[8] She is a 41-year-old mother. Kim's spirituality is a combination of Christian, Hindu, and Buddhist principles combined in a way that the former is tempered by the two latter.

Kim: I would describe myself as basically being Christian but, you know, not a 100 percent focused on being a Christian like Christian people think I *should* be, and a lot of other spiritual stuff. Because, it's like there's a lot of Buddhist stuff that I can relate to, there's a lot of Hindu stuff I can relate to

Her spirituality is particularly focused on questions of reincarnation. When asked to reflect on the role that media play in her spirituality, Kim immediately moves to a description of kinds of music that serve this function.

Kim: In my music I, ever since I was a kid, I've looked for kind of that combination of the Christian idea but also something more. And so, I also in my music I've always looked for a connection of, like the earth and everything on it, that type of idea, like the Native Americans had of everything being, of interacting with each other. So I've often looked for that kind of thing in my music, too. Of that whole idea of, you know, not just . . . I mean I certainly in my music don't listen to like Christian gospel music . . . you know, when I think about spirituality in my music, that's [gospel music] *certainly* not what I'm thinking. It's more, hearing something in the music that has to do with that whole idea of basically everything. . . . I mean not to the point that everything has a soul like, the trees and whatever. But just the whole idea of everything being, you know, interacting with each other and that being important.

These families, who are describable as "metaphysical believers and seekers" according to Roof's definition, differ markedly from other categories in terms of their religiosity and spirituality. They also differ from the families in the other categories in terms of their ideas about ideal role of media in their lives. However, they seem not to differ from the others so markedly in terms of their acquaintance with contemporary media such as television. Most of them have watched the most popular contemporary programs and genres, and have clear ideas about their content. There are issues beyond content, though, with most of them also articulating a concern not about the content of television but about its tendency to dominate the time and attention of children and families.

Dogmatists

Based on our reading of Roof's description of this category, I speculated in Chapter 3 that we'd expect them to be the most "dualist" in their understanding of media. Where some of the interviewees we've just heard from very much want to separate themselves from the idea that judgmental or moralistic restriction is the appropriate way to deal with media in the home, these families would be expected to feel that such an approach is precisely appropriate. As people who believe in the authority of tradition over belief and action, they should be expected to look to such sources for guidance on how to deal with the media. Unlike some of the others, we'd expect that they would be able to make clear connections between their beliefs and the media, but that would generally be a *negative* connection.

The Mueller family

Kathy and David Mueller, both in their late twenties, live in a smaller city in the west with their three children, Cody, age 6, Reese, age 3, and Brian, 10 months.[9] They are devout Mormons,[10] active in their local stake, and their neat and tidy double-wide mobile home is decorated with family photos and a picture of the Temple in Salt Lake City. They are middle income, and describe themselves as "on the way up" economically. Media are also prominent in their home, with a large collection of videotapes on a bookshelf in the living room, and a home entertainment center with a TV and VCR. Their ideas about Church authority come up in a discussion of their Internet use. Kathy and David both use their computer to access Mormon-related sites, both having to do with genealogy and things such as daily inspiration or prayer. Distinct from many of the other accounts of Internet religion/spirituality "surfing" we've encountered, the Muellers clearly feel that the authority of the Church is behind these sites, and that is a valuable thing for them.

Interviewer: Now do you [go online] more for information, or do you do it sort of to connect with the church?
Kathy: The church. . . .
David: The spiritual enlightenment and it's just kind of like knowing that . . . it's more to know we're not just *stuck* here, you've got all these world problems that are like that . . . you know, you want to make sure your kids grow up in, (laughs), you know, or good citizens and stuff. . . .
Kathy: They give you . . . ways to live . . .
David: . . . and it's more with spiritual enlightenment and kind of a boost that, "Hey, we are here, you know, after he died, there is a purpose to life," and, you know, stuff like that. Without getting into a lot of reli-gious doctrine and things because this way it's . . . I mean, we believe in, you know, direct revelation. There is a prophet. So, this is the direc-tion that's given to us from our prophet that speaks with our heavenly father, or higher deity. And so, it's just as important as scripture. . . .

The Muellers feel uncomfortable with television. They much prefer their children to spend time playing with toys to watching television, and see media in hierarchical terms, seeing reading as much better for the children than television or other media. Yet, at the same time, they seem to view television rather unproblematically (like some others). In response to a question about how frequently they watch television, Kathy responds,

Kathy: I don't think we watch a whole lot . . . no . . . not really. Sometimes Disney, we'll sit and watch, or, like . . . they want to watch, oh, we do watch . . . on Friday night . . . what do we watch on Friday night?
Cody: *Crocodile Hunter?*
Kathy: We like *Crocodile Hunter.* What's the other one with the *great* big trucks?
Cody: [pause . . . thinks]
Kathy: "Grave Digger."
Cody: [recognition] Oh!
Kathy: Monster trucks.
Reese: We watch *Monster Jam*!
Kathy: *Monster Jam.*
Interviewer: *Monster Jam*, and that's on Friday nights. It's sort of the *Allstar Wrestling* of trucks.
Kathy: Yeah. They *jump*, they go through obstacle courses. . . .
Cody: Oh, tell him about "Mr Muscle."
Kathy: "Mr Muscle," he knows the. . . .
David: We'll watch *Monster Jam* and then we'll watch the *PBR*, the bull-riding.
Kathy: The *PBR Rodeo* afterwards. So we watch the *Monster* . . . that is our Friday night, we watch that and the rodeo. That's our Friday night, sitting home, we look forward to at 5:00. [Kathy and David both laugh at how silly it sounds]

The Muellers do report that some of their media are chosen with direct reference to "what the church advises." When asked to describe some of those choices, they seem not to differ too markedly from those made by people such as the Boswells and Millikens. The Muellers avoid offensive and troubling programming containing sex, violence, and strong language. They do report having seen some "R" rated films, though. David and Kathy also differ between themselves. David tends not to be as strict as Kathy in either his choices or his negotiations with television or film content. For instance, Kathy is very critical of the popular animated program *The Simpsons.* "You can make a positive thing out of nearly anything," David says. Agreeing with others that the point for parents is to instill in their children the ability to make the right choices, rather than try to protect them from anything troubling, David explains,

David: . . . that's something that we're trying to instill in our kids is
that . . . that there is good things out there and if you look at the good
things, or look for the good . . . that's what you need to be looking for.
I mean, you can find, I was just telling you about the bad things about
all these shows and stuff, but, and there's good . . . in the same
amount there's as much good and things that way. I'm not as, you
know, as far as *The Simpsons*, I . . . I'm like, you can find good there
too if you really look hard enough. I mean, they're cartoons, if you
don't take them to heart [laughs] you know, but they're not kids'
cartoons. A lot of cartoons are not.

Interviewer: So you have less of a problem with *The Simpsons* than . . .

David: Than what she (Kathy) does, yeah. And the *Rugrats* do not bother
me. [laughs] I just, but, you know, it's the thing, but it's, you know, it's
the same thing with, whatever, scary movies, or whatever. . . .

There is an echo of others we've heard from in David's assertion that
media use should be about individual ideas and responsibility. Unlike
many, though, he suspects that the so-called "mainstream media" are not
trustworthy sources of news or information. He looks to a multiplicity of
sources to avoid being ideologically misled.

David: I don't like *Dateline* and *20/20* shows because most of them are a
crock, I mean, they're one person's opinion, um, and it's the same with
any news article that you read in the newspaper, or radio, or whatever,
it's one person's opinion that's bringing you that story. And . . . that's
why I like, you know, the Internet newspaper news because then you
can read six different reporters on the same subject, and. . . .

There is some of what we expected to find among dogmatists in the
Muellers. They make some clear distinctions between the world represented by the media and the world represented by the Mormon faith. They
tend to refer to the Church and its ideas in relation to their media choices,
though it is hard to see how the resulting behavior actually represents
those ideas in any systematic way. They don't at the same time see their
role as prohibiting things as much as helping their children learn to make
their own choices.

The Donegals

Glenn Donegal, who we met in Chapter 4, exhibits many of the characteristics of what Roof would call "dogmatism." He has left Catholicism for
Evangelical Protestantism, but treats the latter more as a set of codes or
doctrines than is the case with the "born-again believers" we've met.
Glenn seems "dualist" in his understanding of the media, speaking from

the assumption that most media, most of the time, are involved in supporting ideas and values that he disapproves of. While he believes with most others that it is the role of parenthood to equip children more than it is to protect them from negative media, Glenn has some pretty extensive critiques of media content. Unlike others, then, it is *content* more than *time* that concerns him.

Glenn and Liz Donegal limit their television viewing to inoffensive "clean" programming. When asked what they specifically avoid watching, Liz stresses sex more than violence.

Liz: MTV. We have that blocked. Anything that is kind of, you know, extreme sexual content, or . . .

Glenn: Not even extreme.

Liz: Yeah, well, I just read a thing today that on prime-time TV they are going to start showing more and more sexual content. We just try to remind the kids to discern. We can't get away from all of it, that is for sure. And it depends on the level of violence. I mean there are movies that we do like that have violence in them, *Braveheart. The Green Mile.*

Glenn: There are some movies like *Shawshank Redemption* . . . there is a lot of profanity but it was a very poignant movie so those are things we will allow the kids to watch with us if we preview them primarily. But I think it is important that there is a strong message sent in those movies. And if you can kind of filter out the not so good ones, which is hard. There is an intense level of discernment that needs to go on.

While Liz and Glenn express some pretty clear ideas about what is and is not appropriate in television, particularly with reference to their children, they do watch regularly themselves. They are fans of a situation comedy that they watch regularly, and say that it is their practice to watch television (usually the late-night comedy-talk shows) in bed for an hour each night. For them like others, media seem to be more or less inevitable.

Secularists

I suggested in Chapter 3 that "secularists" according to Roof's classification would be typified by two characteristics. First, because of their tendency to be over-represented in the upper-income and educational strata, they'd be likely to be infrequent consumers of popular media. They also might be more selective and targeted in their media diets, preferring things like public broadcasting over commercial broadcasting. Because of their relative uninterest in religion, they'd also be unlikely to be attracted to religious or spiritual content in media.

The Murphy-Gordon family

Sheryl Murphy, age 49, and Lanny Gordon, age 56, are professors on the same faculty. They live in a major city with their son Paul, 13, and daughter Erin, 10.[11] They do not belong to a parish or attend religious services, though the children attend a Catholic school that their parents see to be their best option for a private school nearby. They stress that this school does not engage in very much religious instruction. Sheryl, who was raised in a Protestant household, says that her religious background has contributed to her "secular humanist" values today. Lanny and Sheryl do not want to be thought of as puritanical in their attitudes toward media, but, at the same time, they think it is important to be selective about media. For them, that means that they do have preferences about what the children watch. "We used to have a kind of rule that all they could watch was PBS and the videos we had," Sheryl says. This rule has faded as the children have gotten older.

The Murphy-Gordon family sees the practice of distinguishing between acceptable and unacceptable media as an important way of marking themselves in contemporary culture. They are aware of the means by which movie ratings are established and how those ratings relate to commonplace or mainstream social values.

Lanny: We basically don't let the kids see anything that's R-level, unless it's very selective. But we've noticed that the way those ratings go are very misleading. 'Cause they'll let PG-13's have violence, but if they have any kind of language or sex, then they go to R. But you can go to R with very little violence, but there's sex and language. So it's a little misleading how the ratings go.
Sheryl: In fact, this summer Paul watched two R movies with us.
Paul: Three.

They speak with some pride about their difference from other families in this regard. Like others, they want their children to develop their own skills at selecting and viewing media, but they are more willing than most to expose them to material that is "on the edge."[12]

They do make distinctions between media. Film and reading are clearly preferred over television. They have chosen not to subscribe to cable television, for example, because they are "not a TV family." In spite of that self-understanding, they nonetheless view a good deal of television. They are able to name a number of series and genres that they have regularly watched as individuals or as a family, noting that, when it was on the air, they habitually viewed the situation comedy *Home Improvement* together and have fond memories of bonding around that show. Sheryl also notes that she watches one of the late-night talk shows daily.

Sheryl and Lanny are among the few parents we've interviewed who specifically point out the problem of sex-role stereotyping in media and culture.

Sheryl: And I think the other thing we have tried to avoid is sexual stereotyping. We clearly don't fit it, and we don't want our daughter to be
compartmentalized.

Interviewer: Is that why no Barbie dolls?

Sheryl: That's right. No bimbos. She has dolls, she's loved dolls since she
was little. But they're American Girl dolls.

Lanny: Dolls with a story. You know, those have a story . . . that have a
humanity. Rather than just fitting a certain stereotypical image of
what a beautiful woman is supposed to be.

The distinction between their concerns about violence and their perceived
sense that sex or strong language are more of concern to the typical household is an important issue. Pursuing this, Sheryl is asked to confirm that
violence is really the thing that concerns them the most. She confirms,

Sheryl: Violence is the big one. It's absolutely high on my list.

Interviewer: More so than other things like . . .

Sheryl: Yeah, I don't care about language, probably because I have a
terrible mouth myself. Also that I don't think hearing a swear word is
going to alter their personality or give them a terrible model. I mean,
most of the words they hear aren't that. And the other thing is sex,
and frankly, as far as I can tell . . . especially boys are not intrigued
with mush at an early age. So there has been no desire on their part to
see anything that was sexually explicit. . . . And so that left violence,
which for me does have an effect of corroding people's sensibilities.
And often the violence is against women.

She goes on to elaborate about the problem with screen violence.

[I]n the media . . . in movies, it's unrealistic. It never explores the repercussions of violence, at least the kind of things these kids are prone to
see. There are profound movies about violence that I would like them
to see some day, but they don't . . . I mean, I'd like them to see
Schindler's List or *Gandhi* or something like that, but that's not what
they wanna see. They wanna see *Robocop*. And, you know, by the time
you're 10 you've seen 25,000 murders? Well, I have to say that by the
time Paul was 10 he had not seen even a small fraction of that number
of murders. So it's the lack of realism, it's the lack of exploring repercussions, it's totally the lack of any kind of response . . . I mean,
violence is glorified in these things, especially in the movies. . . . And
the glorification of violence in a violent society, to me is obscene.

Lanny and Sheryl do have familiarity with a good deal of television
programming, and are even able to name programs that they particularly

enjoy or identify with. For Sheryl, that is the British crime series *Prime Suspect*, where the lead character is a strong, professional woman. "I relate to all woman detectives," she says, noting that crime novels are one of her guilty pleasures.

Along with their idea that they are distinct because of their attitudes about media content, Sheryl and Lanny also see a difference between themselves and other families in terms of their consciousness of the dangers of that content.

Sheryl: I think in lots of families, it's not so much that they're family values versus media values. If I see anything, it's an indifference among families about the values their kids are getting. And I see the same thing with a lot of Paul's friends. I mean, I'm sure there are values. And if you said, "Are you for violence?" they would say, "No, I'm not for violence." But they think they survived seeing movies, so their kids will survive seeing movies.

The Murphy-Gordons are among the most self-conscious about relations between media, parenting, and family identity of any family we've interviewed. They articulate clear and complex accounts of media in their lives, and use media as a way of making distinctions between themselves and other families. They disagree with others, including the dogmatists we just heard from, on questions of which kind of television and film content are acceptable and which are not. They clearly do not place a high value on the kind of inoffensive television that others identify as good programming. For them, that would be too bland. They want their children to be exposed to significant films, books, and (to the extent such things exist – in their view) television. Religious belief is related to their feelings about media, but only through the pathway that links their religious backgrounds with their present values. There is such a linkage, but it flows through their own autonomously established independence in values and ideals.

The Abraham family

A second "secularist" family, the Abrahams, share a good deal in common with the Murphy-Gordons. Susan and Joseph Abraham, both 50, live in the suburbs of a major western city with their son, Zed, 16.[13] The Abrahams both have graduate degrees, and work in professional capacities. Both Susan and Joseph were raised Jewish, and still belong to a synagogue today, but do not go frequently, and do not identify with it to the extent Roof's "mainstream believers" would. When their sons (an older son has now left home) were of the appropriate age, they did celebrate bar mitzvahs for them, wanting to give them the option of connecting with their Jewish backgrounds. They describe themselves as religiously liberal. Religion is not an "external way of coping" for them, Joseph says.

Like the Murphy-Gordons, there is little if any connection between religion or spirituality and media for the Abrahams. At the same time, they also have some clear ideas about what is and is not appropriate media fare. They have never had a system of rules for what the boys could watch on TV or what films they could go to. Like the Murphy-Gordons, they are less concerned about sex than they are about violence in screen media. Susan recounts a time when they rented an art film that contained nudity and felt that it was perfectly appropriate for Zed, who was 8 at the time, to watch it.

Susan: . . . the *Baghdad Café* had that old woman, she was having her
    portrait, and she was bared from the top? Remember?
Zed: I don't remember that.
Susan: [laughs]
Zed: I must've blocked that out.
Joseph: Susan remembers that. I wasn't home.

The matter-of-fact way in which this is recounted suggests that, for the Abrahams, the value of the artistic nature of the film is more important than incidental nudity, and that the overall question of monitoring such things is a low priority for them. Violence is a more important problem for them. Like the Murphy-Gordons and others, the Abrahams wish to make a distinction between media. For them, there is a clear hierarchy of media. Reading is at the top, and, for screen media, news is preferred over entertainment.

Joseph: Literate people read the paper. Well, I don't think that's very
    common among kids anymore.
Zed: When did you start reading the paper? College?
Joseph: No, I got the paper in college, as a matter of fact, I got the
    Chicago paper sent to me. . . . TV was much less important and intru-
    sive thirty-five years ago. More people really did read the paper. I
    mean, we didn't have a TV in our college room till I was a junior or
    senior, and then it was just a little bitty black and white. So I mean,
    the world was different then. It's not a criticism as much as a state-
    ment of fact. But I'd like the kids to read as well as watch TV. And the
    kids, really the older one, looks at CNN. Adam [their older son] does.
Zed: I do, too. And CNBC, and MSNBC.

It should of course not be surprising to learn that people who are basically secularist in their outlook would not think very much about relations between media and religion or spirituality. The fact that these secularists are so similar to the others we've interviewed is therefore striking. We might have expected that families like the Murphy-Gordons and the Abrahams would differ markedly from other, more religious families in both their media behaviors and their self-descriptions. These secularist families do clearly understand themselves to be different from mainstream media households, and are proud to describe those differences. They see their approach to media as self-consciously less judgmental than they see others to be, and they report with some pride that they are less moralistic in their media choices. They also seem to analyze and critique media using categories and ideas drawn from art and film criticism. Where other families seem to interpret media more through the lens of parenthood and a kind of prescriptive parental practice, these families are more distant and evaluative in their orientation.

Conclusions and reflections on all five categories

There seem to be more similarities than differences here. We began this review expecting to find some clear distinctions between the various categories that we might be able to describe as approaches "typical" of those categories. Instead, there are striking *commonalities*. The most important of these commonalities derives from the idea that the media – and particularly television – seem to constitute a "common culture" in which all of these families live and to which all of them – on some level – wish to subscribe. We saw evidence of this in earlier chapters where we discussed the transparency, ubiquity, and pervasiveness of the media as everyday social practices in the home. For most families, even ones who clearly identify themselves as distinct in religious terms, there is a powerful set of motivations to consume the same media everyone else is.

In these interviews the idea of television being a taken-for-granted "common culture" expresses itself on three levels. First, there is the notion, expressed most clearly by Jay Milliken, that television is a kind of *expectation* or *right*. He simply assumed that he would watch television, with his specific choices determined by the fact that the family could only receive two channels. Television seems to be something that, on a very fundamental level of practice, is simply expected and done. This is even more obvious with children, of course, with many of our families (and many other studies) showing that, for children and teens, television and other media are simply a fact of life.

The second level on which media constitute a "common culture" is in the idea that they are a common set of languages, symbols, and ideas that our families want to participate in in order to be culturally "current." Even our most dogmatic and anti-media couple (the Donegals) watch the late-night talk shows before they retire for the night. Most of our interviewees are interested in the latest trends and genres of television, and even watch them regularly, across all of the categories here. The born-again believers express clear ideas of distinction between their faith and the faiths of others – even with regard to tastes in media – but nonetheless seem much more like others in their media attitudes and behaviors.

The final level on which media are a "common culture" is in the capacity media have to present culturally relevant and significant ideas and symbols in a powerful and attractive way. The media are the public media in part due to their ability to do this, and to center themselves aesthetically within broad cultural norms and ideas. Nearly all the people we spoke to here recognize and respond to this capacity of the media. At the same time, this seems to be a capacity particularly of the so-called "secular" media, with even Evangelical and born-again informants preferring secular over "religious" media.

The intra-household dynamics of the media as "common culture" are also important. There are clearly generational and gender dynamics at work. As has been widely noted elsewhere as well as within these pages, children and youth consume media in very different ways than their parents do. And the common *youth* culture seems even more important than is the case in general. There are also interesting distinctions between men and women. While men and women share common interests in media, men tend to consume their own media in a less self-critical way than do women, and women tend to more commonly see and think of media through the lens of parenthood than do men, at least among these interviews.

Another area of similarity between these categories is in a broad agreement on what we have been calling "accounts of media." The greatest area of agreement seems to be that it is important for children to develop their own skills at media consumption rather than having their choices permanently determined for them. With the exception of the dogmatists, who seemed to be the most interested in actually controlling their children's media, all others wanted for their children what they valued for themselves: the ability to make their own autonomous choices about what they watch and what they do. There is less agreement on accounts of specific kinds of programs, genres, and values in media.

For all categories, "accounts of media" seemed to be important turf on which to draw important and clear distinctions between their religious or spiritual identities and the identities of "others." The nature of these accounts vary, however. For the secularists and metaphysical seekers, it was important to distance themselves from the moralistic critiques of media content on such issues as sexuality and profanity. Predictably, dogmatists and born-again believers seemed to be the most concerned about those latter issues. For mainstream believers, seekers, and secularists, violence was mentioned as a more important concern, but it was also a concern of the born-again believers.

The broader agreement on the issue of violence was not the only area where there was more commonality, either. Nearly all of the families expressed the idea of a "hierarchy" of acceptable media that saw the so-called "screen" media (with the exception of film for some) as lower in the hierarchy than reading or the use of the Internet for information-gathering purposes. Among the households we saw here, all but the dogmatists seemed to feel that some of the problems with media behavior and content are mediated by autonomous choice. Many maintain video libraries and talk about those as their major media involvements (though there is much evidence that even those households also consume a great deal of out-of-home media, too). There was also some agreement among some of the households that the problem with the derogated screen media is almost as much their impact on time (distracting from more worthy pursuits) as their conveyance of values.

Nearly all the families have a difficult time directly connecting media with their religious or spiritual values, beliefs, and behaviors. It is as if there is an "account of media" that stipulates those to be contradictory realms. Few could easily or facilely talk about media that influenced or expressed their faith, religious beliefs, or spirituality. The born-again believers and dogmatists had the most to say about media and religion. For families in both of those categories, there was a clear and focused sense that there *should* be clear connections and distinctions between media and faith. That did not seem to result in distinctive or necessary ways of encountering, using, or interpreting media. Born-again believers, for example, eschewed specifically "religious" media,[14] and, as I noted earlier, did not make assessments of media that seemed directly significant of their beliefs or faith. As I noted, when asked for examples of acceptable programming, the typical responses were shows that were merely "inoffensive" in some way, judgments that were not really different from those made by parents in other categories. This aspect of media judgment thus seemed to be more related to their roles as *parents* than to their roles as *born-again parents*.

We should note, of course, that media other than television were more often connected with religion and spirituality for many of our interviewees across all five categories. Music seemed to be the media form most often mentioned as the most powerfully connected to authentic faith and belief. Others mentioned significant films and books. It almost seems that a certain level of media behavior is dominated by an orientation to the mediated common culture through the pervasive media of television, the Internet, and (for young people) video gaming. At other levels of articulation, where deeper and more refined connections are sought or become significant, other media forms come to the fore. What is even more intriguing is that, even for those households with the most focused religious and spiritual sensibilities, media of all of these kinds and on all of these levels are nonetheless encountered, negotiated with, and used.

Distinction seems to be an important element of the judgments and ideas expressed here. Born-again believers and dogmatists see themselves as distinct from mainstream culture in terms of their attitudes about media (while not necessarily behaving in ways that are that distinct). Secularists and metaphysical seekers see themselves as distinct from the moralists on the other bank of the cultural mainstream. Interestingly, the mainstream believers seemed to be the group least able to articulate distinction. It seemed that, for them, it was important to be simply "mainstream" in their attitudes about media as well as their religious beliefs and behaviors. This is important and interesting. There is evidence here that "accounts of media" as expressed in these narratives of self are significant ways that individuals, families, and groups map themselves with reference to the cultural mainstream. While it is not easy to describe ways that media directly relate in authentic ways to articulated senses of religion or spirituality, it is almost a given that self-understood faith, belief, or behavior *should* predict clear attitudes about media.

The fact that we did not find the clear distinctions between religious/spiritual categories we might have expected here warrants some reflection. The primary reason may be in what I've noted above, that, in some important ways, people want to relate to certain media, at least, as resources in a "common culture." Further, from a variety of religious perspectives, they do not easily relate media to central facets of their religious lives. This is not to say that there is no connection, because we have seen (and will see) that there is a connection. It is to say that for a variety of reasons related to the received public scripts out of which we derive our accounts of media, we do not easily recognize or articulate a connection. We do not want to think of ourselves as subject to the influence of media (or – interestingly – of clerical or institutional religious authority, either). This means that the received understanding that media are primarily significant for their *effects* makes it difficult for us to think of media "affecting" our religious or spiritual lives. At the same time, we don't want to think of ourselves as needing to slavishly follow the dictates of others, so it is also difficult to think of religion or spirituality "affecting" media, too.

We also saw here that some of the easy assumptions about the basic taxonomy and our expectations need some critique. In one way very important to our considerations here, there is less difference than we expected. That is in the area of the self-conscious autonomy with which people today think of themselves with respect to cultural and social practice. Nearly all of the individuals and families we saw here want on some fundamental level to think of themselves as having primary responsibility for their religious lives. This language was nearly as common among the households we'd typified as born-again believers as for the metaphysical believers and seekers. This means that one of the essential dynamics I'd suggested would be at work here – that of autonomous "seeking" – is present across categories rather than limited to one or two of them.

In the next chapter, we will look at interviews in a different way that is more closely related to how media might relate to deeper and more fundamental narratives of the religious or spiritual "self." This is a different way of looking at these issues. Rather than the inductive approach in this chapter, the next one will look at things more deductively. As I've noted earlier, many of our interviewees have had a difficult time describing the ways that media relate in a fundamental way to their religious or spiritual lives. In many interviews, though, there comes a point when they finally are able to make such an articulation. In Chapter 8, we will look at those moments and others in which interviewees describe the range of ways that they see media relating to their lives.

Representing outcomes

One of the persistent ideas about the way media and religion relate to one another is rooted in broader social conceptions of the power and influence of "the media" on social life. Much more common than ideas of how religion might be influencing media are ideas about how influence might flow in the opposite direction.[1] A good deal of the discourse in this direction has lamented potential negative impacts of an irreligious "secular" media on religious belief and behavior. As I have said, our explorations in this book are a way of testing such ideas, and in this chapter we'll address questions of how media might be leading to religious outcomes or being used in religious ways or ways that bear a resemblance to religion.[2]

In Chapter 3 we reviewed a diverse set of ways that the relationship between religion and media has been conceived. These included essentialist, archetypal, formal, realist, transformationist, and other approaches. The notion of "effect" or "outcome" of media exposure is implicit in many of these views, relying on an assumption that the media are able to compel action or to engage or articulate beliefs, symbols, or ideas in powerful ways. It should be clear from our discussions to this point that the paradigm here does not assume "function" or "effect," but instead has found more evidence of, and insight into, how individuals interact with, and use, media to represent themselves and their lives. This holds in reserve questions of outcome or effect, wishing to lodge questions of outcome in a complex and nuanced understanding of the preconditions of where, when, and how interactions with media occur and meanings are made. And, as we have seen, there is a good deal of distance between "text" and "reception." One of the most significant aspects of this distance is the ways that people position themselves and their lives *vis-à-vis* media, the "accounts of media" we have seen in these interviews. But we are able to explore beyond these accounts to ways that people's "experiences in" and "interactions about" media are also significant in their lives.

We've seen how our interviewees' "narratives of self" relate media and religion/spirituality in some fundamental ways. Certain media seem to form an important basis for participation in culture and society. There is a kind of expectation that, to be part of the culture, we need to be involved in the media. This holds even for people whose religious and spiritual beliefs and practices might be expected to place them at some distance from the values of the so-called "secular media." For families with children, there is a kind of relentless pressure supporting media consumption that is rooted both in children's natural attraction to media and in the way that media serve to articulate child and youth culture in contemporary life. At the same time, though, adults seem also to be attracted to media and to want to be part of a larger mediated cultural discourse.

This means that, as a kind of baseline, we can expect to see media to be a taken-for-granted and tacit reality in most homes across a range of religious traditions and backgrounds. It also seems that people have some difficulty making a clear and straightforward connection between their media lives and their religious or spiritual lives. Their accounts of media reflect a commonplace assumption that the media should not have a positive relationship to spirituality or religion. This is confounded by the seeming tendency for these accounts to also assume that only those media that are self-consciously religious or spiritual to be obviously involved (or alternatively *not* involved) in individual, family, or collective religious or spiritual experience.

The effect of all this is that, in most of our interviews, people have not readily described a role for their media lives in relation to religion or spirituality in their narratives of self. At the same time, though, media are such a common and pervasive aspect of those lives, that some kind of connection seems inevitable. What appears to happen is that, for most of them, what we have been calling their "accounts of media" intervene between their media use and their understanding of the ways that media connect with their religious and spiritual lives. This means that, in most cases, we have had to get at these questions in a more indirect way. As we saw with Glenn Donegal in Chapter 4, for instance, there are often a number of ways that people can and do describe media in relation to their religious lives, but that deeper and more directly meaningful connections come only after some reflection and conversation. In Glenn's case, for example, the classic television series *The Andy Griffith Show* represented for him senses of his religious, spiritual, and moral selves in a fundamental and meaningful way. He was able to articulate a complex and meaningful account of how the program connected him with vital senses of self, identity, and normative values. And yet, this did not come easily. He and the Interviewer needed to cover a great deal of narrative "turf" before *Andy* came up. And when the program did come up, it clearly served important ideas and meanings for Glenn.

We saw in the last chapter that received categories of contemporary religious experience and practice do not readily correlate with ways of thinking about and using media. The commonalities there seemed to be more important than the differences. In this chapter, we'll look at some of our interviewees from a very different perspective. In the last chapter, we assumed that there would be differences in media practices and beliefs based on people's expressed religiosity or spirituality. The assumption there focused on the associations and identifications that might exist. Here, we will turn things around, and look at those accounts where informants express ways that the media actually contribute something to their senses of self, identity, or meaning. This approach is actually much more like the traditional way that we've looked at media: in terms of its "effects" on audiences. As I've said, such effects are only part (and in many cases a relatively insignificant part) of the story. But there is always the expectation in our thinking and talking about the media, that there should be times and ways that the momentum is with the media. We'll explore those here, by proposing a set of categories of meaning, effect, or function found in our interviews.

As discussions of the effects of media, particularly in relation to religion and spirituality, have proceeded, a range of different ideas about how media might affect religion and vice versa have emerged as central to received "public scripts" in this area. The categories here are derived from that discourse, and represent both our view as analysts and the view of informants as they provide narratives of their own ideas and actions. This interaction between the analytic and self-descriptive is understandable in light of arguments I've made earlier about the nature of discourse about the media. As ideas such as these have become part of a common language regarding the media, they have become both the stuff of expert analysis and the stuff of reflexive parenting and reflexive media "audiencing." It should not surprise us, then, to find within these narratives some of the same ideas about media use and effect that have long been part of expert opinion in the matter. Teachers, opinion writers, clerical voices, religious educators, and media literacy educators have all spoken to the kinds of uses and effects we've been considering in these pages.

The categories we look at here are derived from two sources. First, they come from what we analysts might have expected from reviewing the literature on media and culture, and reflecting on questions of religion, faith, and spirituality. Second, they also emerge from the interviews themselves as we have asked people to reflect on their interactions with and around media. From both of these directions, it made sense to look at the first of the "levels of engagement" we discussed earlier in the book, the level we call "experiences *in* the media." Whereas the issues discussed in Chapters 5, 6, and 7 seemed to more readily invoke the discourses we call "accounts of media," much of what we will see here will be those moments when our interviewees report more direct experiences with specific media texts. At the same time, as we will see, these also invoke the other two levels, "interactions about the media," and "accounts of the media." In most of the narratives we look at, it is difficult to disentangle these levels, and they can be seen to inter-relate and interact in important ways.

The categories we will look at here are described from the perspective of the individual as he or she reflects on media roles and media effects. They are: 1) "It moved me"; 2) "It inspired me"; 3) "It leads me to think or behave"; 4) "It informs me"; 5) "I want to identify with it"; 6) "It describes me"; 7) "I describe myself using it"; 8) "I want to contest/reject/endorse it"; and 9) "I use it to talk with my kids or others about values and morality."

It is important to reiterate the interview approach that has generated these narratives. I said earlier that we try very hard to be as unobtrusive as possible in the ways that we discuss these things with our interviewees. We do not want to lead them to conclusions, or to inordinately define the terms of the discussion or analysis. We prefer that the learnings emerge out of the conversations, not be directed by them. What we'll be looking at here, then, are the results of such a semi-structured and nondirective and (aspirationally, at least) unobtrusive process.

What follow then are a set of ways that seem to emerge from our interviews as people reflect on their more direct experiences with media symbols and products. We have heard from some of these people before, and these accounts are interesting in light of those earlier conversations. What we are seeing here are the ways the people we've interviewed talk about media as active inputs or influences on their experiences.

The first three areas fall generally under the heading of *primary religious or spiritual functions* of media. These are the presumed functions or affects where media might be seen to either influence, compete with, or replace what we think of as the "essential" features of religious piety and practice.

"It moved me"

Much of the received discourse about relations between media and religion has assumed that, on some level, media materials possess unique powers of persuasion and influence. Some of the voices we heard in Chapters 1 and 2 even seemed to suggest that media might have an unparalleled power to compete with spiritual and religious influences in individual lives. We might have expected, then, to find it to be common for our informants to rather easily identify media that had such power. In fact, as we've seen, our interviewees were often reluctant to grant wholesale influence to the media. Here are two examples where such a role for media was identified in the sense that media could be seen to have a kind of emotional force. Fred Kline, a 50-year-old father of two, responded this way to the question of whether he ever saw anything in films that he found spiritual or inspirational.

> . . . the top of the list [would be] *To Kill a Mockingbird*. I saw that when I was actually only 8 years old. . . . I was absolutely enthralled and moved by it. I immediately read the book and part of it was because it was in black and white and it was a simple, moving story

and it has carried all the way through life. I am still moved by it when I see it. It is really wonderful.

Most of us can think of examples like this, where television, films, books, or plays affect us in deep and lasting ways. It is also not surprising that Fred – whose expressed attitudes about media are less moralistic than those of more religiously conservative parents – would identify a primarily "secular" as opposed to "religious" film as particularly moving or inspirational. It is further interesting to note that, for Fred, this film is one that has stuck with him. He continues to think of it as a major influence in his life, and still finds it moving today, as an adult.

Roxanne Connor, like Fred Kline, is more of a "seeker" than a traditionalist, and she also readily identifies film as a source of this kind of "moving" experience.[3]

Interviewer: Do you ever seek out anything related to spirituality on television or in movies, on the Internet, in music or other media?
Roxanne: Not on the Internet, no, but certainly there are movies that have moved me spiritually and music that moves me spiritually, or that I glean a spiritual message from.

Roxanne also readily identifies the moving quality of film and music with her spirituality. It is interesting as well that she excludes the Internet from having this sort of capacity, in her experience. The notable thing here is that it seems to be taken-for-granted that certain media, at least, can easily have emotional impacts on viewers and audiences. Neither Fred nor Roxanne made an easy extension from this media experience to more conventional ideas of religion, faith, or spirituality.

"It inspired me"

To be "moved" by something is a different order than being inspired by it. For Fred Kline, for instance, what he drew from *To Kill a Mockingbird* was a kind of heightened emotional experience, something that continues to this day. Being inspired by something involves a different state of reaction, one where the individual is both emotionally engaged and moved to either identify with or emulate characters or ideas. Chris Chandler is a 35-year-old single father who was raised Catholic, but who has fallen away and become more of a "seeker."[4] Asked to talk about media that might inspire him, he gives the following definition of inspiration, and along the way, gives an example of an "inspirational" film.

Let's just say that there are some movies that are inspirational, you know. Not so much in a real Christian way, but I think that if you are inspired by . . . a movie *Rocky*, you know, that's an inspirational movie and makes you want to try, you know, go for it basically. And I think that in some ways that's kind of a religious type. I think that anything you do really to better yourself is almost spiritual. I think the working out is, that is spiritual in a lot of ways, for me it is.

This is a fascinating idea, given what we've seen about the way most of our interviewees classify "religious" and "secular" media. Chris makes a clear distinction here between those kinds of media. He chooses a secular film as his example of inspiration, though "not in a real Christian way" and yet feels that there is a kind of "religious type" there, meaning that, even though *Rocky* is not a religious film and not about self-consciously religious ideas or motivations, it does deal in a kind of inspiration that is religious in a way.

Rayna Hancock is a 37-year-old Mormon single mother.[5] She was not raised Mormon, but joined as an adult, and still thinks a lot about how to bring this new faith and her life together. When asked about inspirational media, she begins with programs from her childhood, and connects them with the quality of "inoffensiveness" we've seen in a number of our interviews.

Rayna: When I was growing up, there was all these good . . . you know, *Little House on the Prairie*. . . .
Interviewer: Yeah, *Brady Bunch*.
Rayna: [laughs] I don't know if that was such a great show, but. Um, it just seems like there was better quality. Now it's all partying, violence . . . I don't know of a really good . . . other than the things they show on PAX . . . with the *Touched by an Angel* and *It's a Miracle* . . . uplifting . . . um, positive shows.

For Rayna, certain media are markers of a social trajectory she is uncomfortable with. She is aware that the *Brady Bunch* might not have been critically acclaimed, but, somehow, it was just better quality. Combined with some of the more intentionally religious shows on the PAX network, she seems to think she can find a media diet that is inoffensive, even inspirational. More interestingly, Rayna suggests that when she was younger, before her conversion to Mormonism, her media diet did not reflect her faith as much. She finds herself now negotiating between media that she finds inspirational and what she sees to be the Church's self-imposed distance from media.

Interviewer: So when you were younger, you didn't feel like you could be close to the Church and religion and all that.
Rayna: Huh-uh [no]. Right.

Interviewer: I see what you mean. So on PAX ... *Touched by an Angel* ... do those kinds of shows connect then with the way you feel now about religion?

Rayna: Well ... I don't think that the LDS Church would say, "Yeah, that's what we ... believe." But, for me ... it works. You know ... [thinks] ... It's the most positive thing that comes in out of that TV that we can sit and listen to and I enjoy it, so ... it works for me. I don't think that a lot of people in the Church would, [dramatic voice] "Oh yeah, we love *Touched by an Angel*!" I don't think ... but people who have been in the Church forever, and they know a lot more than I do could probably pick out, "Well this isn't right, and that isn't right," but, for me it works.

We've seen this distancing between formal religion and the media from a different direction before. Rayna clearly feels that media inspiration is important to her. She appreciates both inoffensive "secular" programs and self-consciously religious ones like *Touched by an Angel* and *It's a Miracle*. At the same time, she infers that the Church authorities and even her fellow parishioners might not appreciate these shows as much as she does. She's not sure that these media would really represent core beliefs of her Church, but, for her, they "work."

We met Judy Cruz in Chapter 5, and her ideas about the inspirational capacities of media there are relevant to our discussions here. Readers may recall that we called Judy a "traditionalist" there, someone who was very self-conscious about her religious beliefs.[6] While she thinks of herself as a Catholic, she is a "seeker" as well, exploring a range of religious and spiritual ideas and traditions. For her, the "inspiration" of certain television programs lies in a rather traditional religious function: that they give insight into transcendent, even spiritual, aspects of life, of the here and now, and the beyond.

Interviewer: Why do you like that one [*It's a Miracle*]?

Judy: Because it shows life experiences that have happened. I think it's interesting.

When the Interviewer asks her to describe the program, Judy goes into detail about a plot that involves two angels. The Interviewer presses a bit on her understandings about angels, and Judy makes a distinction between shows that present angels as fantasy figures and angels that actually live in the here and now.

Interviewer: Angels meaning. . . .

Judy: People, just regular people . . . came to their rescue.

Interviewer: Is that what an angel does?

Judy: Yeah. . . .

Interviewer: I'm thinking on *Touched by an Angel* the two main characters, and maybe there is a third, are they people on earth or are they
brought from somewhere else?
Judy: They are brought from somewhere else, but that's fantasy.
Interviewer: But in the miracle show, they talk about angels on earth,
actual people who do good things?
Judy: Actual people, yeah. There's a difference there, yeah.

Judy thus sees a real religious or spiritual inspiration in these "angel"
programs. It is interesting how, in each of these cases of inspiration from
media, the relationship to conventional or formal religion is in a way
defined out. For Rayna and Judy, both of whom have a relationship to
conventional, even conservative or traditionalist religious roots and
resources, there is something fundamental and satisfying about the inspiration they achieve from media sources. As we've seen before, the authority
of traditions over the legitimacy of these sources is not really an issue. For
both women, the autonomy to make these choices and judgments rests in
their hands.

"It leads me to think or behave"

We might have expected to find many examples of people who were influenced in one way or another by the media they consume. As I said before,
some of the most seriously held concerns and strident criticisms regarding
the impact of media on religious and spiritual lives is related to the notion
that the media would be able to actually influence the beliefs or behaviors
of viewers. The preponderance of concern about televangelism when it
emerged was centered in such notions. Thus it may be notable that, among
our interviewees, it is difficult to find many examples of people for whom
religious or spiritual material, *per se*, is seen to influence thought or action.
In fact, in most cases, those media materials most likely to act in this way,
the self-consciously "religious" ones, are avoided or contested. The
Milliken family, who we considered at some length in Chapter 6, are born-
again believers who are regular viewers of a range of "secular" television,
including reality shows.[7]

When asked to reflect on the relationship between their religiosity and
their media use, they move immediately to an assumption that the media
in question must be "religious" media, and they are not big fans.

Interviewer: Is there a connection between media use and this spirituality,
your church-going, things like that?
Jay: Actually, we try not to watch . . . TBN (Trinity Broadcasting
Network).
Interviewer: Why?

Jay: There's a little too much hocus-pocus on that channel.

Lynn: For him. . . .

Jay: I've been told, you know, there's healers like Benny Hinn, and it's just. . . .

Interviewer: You've been told by whom?

Jay: Pastors and other people.

Interviewer: At [your present church], or in the past?

Jay: No, in the past. When I first started waking up to God, I was watching it. To tell you the truth, that's what got me interested. But then . . . there are some shows on there that are okay, but some of them. . . .

There appear to be two important and inter-related reasons that Jay distances himself and his faith from ministries such as TBN and *Benny Hinn*. First, there is a general opprobrium that seems to be applied to them by people in his current church, and, second, there is a sense that such programs are more connected with an immature, than a mature, faith. In any case, it is significant that, for one of the most intensely "born-again" families we've interviewed, programming most associated with the Evangelical end of the Christian spectrum is avoided.

The next category differs from the previous three. It is qualitatively different in that it positions media not as integrated into faith or spirituality, but at some distance from these aspects of life. Among the most important functions of the media, at least in our everyday understandings, is their ability to bring us a wealth of *information*. Just as they convey important information about politics, sports, finance, etc., they also can carry information about religion and spirituality. In a post-9/11 world, information about religion, and specifically about religious "others," could be expected to be of increased importance. Information is, of course, something that is qualitatively different from religious or spiritual "experience" as well. It is consumed at some distance, whereas direct experience or expression are more personal and closer to the individual's daily private practice. Information can certainly inform practice, but its contribution is not thought to be as direct.

"It informs me" (about "the other" – and more)

We just met Fred Kline above. He is the father of Stephanie, age 15, who was asked about whether she ever found anything in the media "inspiring," and answered in terms of information instead.

Interviewer: Have you ever watched TV and found something inspiring? How about *Seventh Heaven*?

Steph: I guess. I don't think the main thing is about religion, it is just entertainment. I don't really think I see something religious that I find interesting and then try to follow up on it by seeking information on the media.

Interviewer: Does that include the Internet?

Steph: Oh yeah, I have. I take it back. I just kind of type in certain things and there is always a website that says, "These are our beliefs" and stuff, so I just sort of type in different religions and see what they have to say about different issues and stuff.

She makes an interesting distinction between something being "about religion" and being "just entertainment." This distinction, which we have seen expressed in many different ways by different interviewees, seems important to Steph, who lives in a "metaphysical seeker" household. One way of looking at this would be to say that she has in mind some sort of idealized notion of what something "about religion" would be, and that that is something separate from her experience and her experience with media. It also seems important that Steph is particularly prone to think of the Internet as a place for this sort of "information-seeking." The fact that she initiates and controls an Internet search may well be important to her, rooted in notions of self and personal autonomy. Unlike conventional entertainment media, she can recall having sought out information about religion online.

If we think of this information-seeking behavior as relating to things that are more separate from one's own deeply held beliefs, then it makes sense that such seeking might well be related to religions other than one's own. Bill Baylor is a 41-year-old father of four sons, who lives with them and his wife, Donna, in the suburbs of a major western city.[8] He is a registered nurse, and describes himself as a Presbyterian and a "born-again Christian." He changed faiths as an adult, under Donna's influence. "I was Mormon . . . and converted to Christianity" he says rather unproblematically. The family is seemingly skeptical of "religious" television, making fun of some televangelists during our interview, but at the same time are aware of the Christian stations in their area and of the PAX network. They prefer inoffensive "family" programs, with Bill identifying as a favorite the classic western series, *Gunsmoke*. When asked about what he does when he comes across programs or websites that advocate beliefs other than his own, Bill replies,

Bill: [I] read them for the knowledge. [To] see how different people believe because I have in my life switched major religions. So, in doing so I'm very open – and talking to people also. Like if I see an article. Right now, the guy that's the atheist that wants God taken out of the Pledge of Allegiance, he was on TV, I think it was last month. Because I was flipping through channels. So I paused for a few minutes just to see what his view was. And it was quite interesting, what his view was. I only caught it for two, or three minutes.

Interviewer: So you do a lot of channel surfing?

Bill: I do [laughing]. Donna doesn't like it, but – you know, I didn't just say, "Ah, I'm not hearing this." Yeah, I gave him a few minutes and said, hey, what's his point. What's his fact/counter-fact type of thing. And I said, "That's quite interesting just that little bit that I caught." So I am open to that.

Interviewer: So you won't just switch it when it's something different?

Bill: No. I've made an impression on the kids, even though it's different you still need to keep an open mind to that so you can know how other people believe. So you're not naïve to how they believe and, you know, their stance. Because you can't say to somebody, "I don't believe in what you believe in, if you don't know what they believe in." And I try to tell [the kids] that too.

Bill's view is thus based in ideas we've seen before – that it is important for people to feel that they have the autonomy to make up their own minds about things. The atheist Bill refers to would be someone he'd naturally disagree with, yet he feels it is important to be able to say he's given him a fair hearing – and to model this behavior for his sons. This also introduces the issue of the *kind* of information we might mean when we talk about "information about religion." Bill's examples here seem to relate most to religious controversies or issues that have a public policy or political dimension to them.

There are other kinds of religious information, though, as illustrated by an interview with Megan Sealy. Megan is 40, and a single mother to Dell, age 17.[9] A Southern Baptist, she was raised Catholic, but has also attended a Presbyterian Church. Her parents are now "New Age," she reports, being interested in "very Eastern religion." In a conversation about her use of the Internet, she is asked if she ever seeks out anything related to religion or spirituality there.

Interviewer: Do you ever seek out anything related to religion or spirituality on the Net?

Megan: Yeah. Yeah. I look at different sites and stuff.

Interviewer: Can you give me any examples?

Megan: Ah, well the radio station that I like to listen to [mentions a specific local Christian station], they have a website and so it gives you news about, like there's a missionary couple in – where is it? I wanna say Madagascar, but that's not right. Um, down, in – oh, geez, if I had a map I could figure out what it is. But, ah, it's like Thailand or something like that. They've been basically imprisoned for 14 months. . . . And you don't hear much on TV about them and yet they talk about them because this is something that is happening to them. And, you know, they're being held by Muslim extremists and so, you know, it's just interesting how the media will portray them, the Muslim extremists. But yet I guess I get a bigger picture by checking on that kind of news and seeing what's going on as far as that. Because it's more of a religious issue than anything else. And so they don't portray much of it on the news. So, I can't think of anything else . . . um, you know, I've looked at different church sites and stuff like that. And I have friends in Tennessee and Florida and they'll have me look at different sites and stuff.

Megan's online information-seeking seems thus more closely related to her own faith and religious exploration than Bill's. The capacity of the Internet and Web to provide a wide range of information, and to make it easily accessible to searches, links, and forwards, seems to provide, for Megan at least, an open field of exploration related to her own faith and religious interests. Her favorite Christian station (which is not, incidentally, connected with her own congregation) has a website and other links through which she can connect to a wider network of information sources. The Web is also a context she and distant friends can also share. Even so, her information-seeking is only about information, a commodity that supports, but does not determine, her faith. It is at some distance for her.

There is thus a way that the technology relates to a particular way of thinking about the material which is sought out – in this case, information. Megan moves from a radio station to its website to things linked from there. The autonomy and self-direction implied by these practices is important to her and to Bill, but exists within the limitations of the medium and its protocols. Donna Baylor, Bill's wife, illustrates this during a conversation about her use of the bookmarks in her Internet browser.

Interviewer: Are you going online often to search for things and bookmark them? Or is this something – you have a folder that's already been created and you don't add to it very often? You keep going back to the same places?
Donna: Well, it depends. If I find something new, I'll stick it in there – I've cleaned it out a couple of times because some of the things that I had found previously were gone, were not good anymore. I'd review it and go through it every now and then and put in new things and take out the old. You know, what's relevant and what's not. I have some websites in there on different religions that I've looked at – if I've gotten into a discussion with someone over. Well, I guess my big thing would be Mormonism. Since I have in-laws and relatives that are Mormon and Bill used to be a Mormon. I try and research that a lot so that I have a lot of information to work with that way.

Interviewer: So you don't have anything bookmarked on Islam or Buddhism. . . .

Donna: I haven't found any. I look around for ones that I like and that I can understand, are clear enough for me to get.

This illustrates several capacities of the Web for information-seeking.[10] Where we might have concentrated on the idea that what people do there is primarily to read and digest information, Donna illustrates that it is also possible to "subscribe" to certain sites in a way, by holding them in a bookmark folder as a kind of collection. Donna reports referring to those on a fairly regular basis, keeping current, adding, and deleting. She also seems to use the Web in relation to "interactions about" the media. She reports that she has investigated things online that she has interacted with others about, in a kind of integration between the online context and her context of social relations. Interestingly, though, she is less catholic in her online tastes than some might assume. Where the Web and Internet provide a wide range of materials about a wide range of religious traditions, Donna stays closer to home. She looks online for information about things that she's talked with others about. She seems to say that sites from non-Christian traditions are conceptually inaccessible, and so she avoids them. She also stays close to home in her investigation of Mormonism. It is almost a defensive strategy for her (something we have also heard from other interviewees), to seek information she can use there to better understand or even contest the ideas of a given religion.

We've looked at the ways people talk in terms of media experiences being inspirational and moving, assuming that one of the basic meanings of media materials would be in their abilities to serve such basic religious purposes or meanings. We then moved to a different standpoint, that of the capacity of the media to act as sources of information, something that would be more distant or removed from the individual's or family's religious experience. Now let's look at another possibility: that the media might provide normative models of value and action, either through their plots or through characters that embody such ideals. This, like the other categories we've looked at already, is a common received assumption about the way that the media might be involved in moral or religious life. As we have talked with our interviewees, we've encountered a number of examples of such modeling.

"I want to identify with it"

Television programs and other media can and do provide rich cultural texts with which their audiences can come to identify. Not surprisingly, few people we interviewed seemed to be willing to describe their relationship to such things in terms of the media "affecting" them or the way they think. It is much more common for them to associate themselves with certain symbols, values, and claims. Negotiations over such identification can be seen in the following passage from an interview with the Stein family. Jeff Stein might be classified as a "metaphysical believer and seeker." He is 41 and the single father of Rachel, age 10.[11] Jeff is heavily involved in a "new" or "alternative" religious practice, but is at the same time skeptical of some of the supernaturalism of contemporary television entertainment.

Interviewer: What about supernatural stuff, because you said you don't like *Buffy* [*Buffy the Vampire Slayer*]? You don't like it because of the sexual content or because it's all about witchcraft and. . . .

Jeff: Well, it's just kind of . . . it's just I thought just always kind of intense and scary but it's not. . . .

Interviewer: Not because it's about witchcraft and supernatural . . .

Jeff: No, I mean I think it's silly mostly but [laughs].

Rachel: I believe in witchcraft and stuff.

Jeff: No basically there is witchcraft like they do have on *Buffy* which if you were doing a science fiction show you could do it because it was the future. You know it's all magic, it's just different premise for how you do something that is currently impossible [laughs].

Interviewer: Yeah, ok. So it's an excuse to. . . .

Jeff: [laughs] It's a fictional, it's all a fictional construct.

Interviewer: Yeah, do you believe in witchcraft [to Rachel]?

Rachel: Well, I believe in like . . . I believe in magic and . . . uhm . . . I believe in magical creatures, like dragons and unicorns and Pegasus . . . and different magical creatures like that and to. . . .

Interviewer: So do you believe they existed or exist?

Rachel: I believe they still exist, maybe, and I believe in like in fairies and stuff, I believe that there's other worlds that can be reached by this one that have, and that these creatures live in and but I also believe that some still live in this world.

This reveals an interesting negotiation between Jeff and Rachel over the nature of spirituality, the legitimacy of the representation of the supernatural in popular media, and the nature of such representations. Jeff clearly feels that a level of "truth" or veracity is an important quality in considering media portrayals. He is skeptical of these modes of spirituality, of course, but wants to reserve an openness to them provided they are authentic and real. For Rachel, who is more attracted to such ideas, the media representations are meaningful, and something she wants to associate herself with, in spite of the opprobrium expressed by her father. For her, the mystery and seeming transcendence of media portrayals are salient and significant. She does not use them as sources of insight or even for information so much as she wishes to identify herself with the ideas and values she sees as lying beneath them. It is also interesting to note how and how readily she uses this identification as a way of communicating her difference from her father on these issues.

We met Judy Cruz in Chapter 5, where we saw how, as someone who we would have expected to be rather traditional in her ideas, was nonetheless quite interested in the supernatural, science fiction, and other non-traditional ideas. She is also a good example of now people can use media as a source of association or identity. I'll recall a passage in which she makes a distinction between some traditionalist ideas and traditional religious figures, and television programs. Where she is not as comfortable with television preachers and the entertainments some of them offer, she is drawn much more to miraculous and spiritual programs that are not as self-consciously "religious."

Interviewer: I know we talked before about *Touched by an Angel* and *It's a Miracle*. Are those different for you from preachers up on the screen or on the radio?

Judy: Yeah, and there is another one that just came out called *Crossing over* with John Edward. That's kind of interesting to me because, I guess because people have had experiences and a person can relate to things like that whether it's miracles or healers or, you experience things like that and you can relate to things like that, but as far as preachers or dancing, it is a little bit more different. It's not as comfortable.

Judy and Rachel illustrate an interaction of media with ideas and values that is more precisely "identification" than it is "influence" of some kind. For both of them, certain television programs and films represent a set of commitments and ideas that they feel are important, and articulated in themselves in such a way that they are motivated to associate themselves with them. It is perhaps coincidental that both Judy and Rachel express an interest in some of the same symbols and ideas. For each, this taste is distinct from the expectations of their context, domestically and beyond. Also for each, the specific programs in question do a particularly compelling job of representing the values and ideas in question. And for each, there is a kind of tacit understanding that these materials have a self-fulfilling justification and authenticity about them. They are "real" in some sense, and both Judy and Rachel draw meaning and value from this belief.

"It describes me"

Another relationship between media and audiences we have come across is those places where interviewees talk about media or media practice as describing *them*. We might have assumed that some of the identifications people would make with media would be not because they wanted to identify with something salient there, but because they saw things moving in the other direction. We've encountered such accounts, and on two levels: on the level of "accounts of media," and on the more direct level of individual "experiences in" specific programs and films. As an example of the former, we'll hear again from Jeff Stein. Jeff has become involved in a specific New Age practice[12] that has within it some clear ideas about how individuals can and should gain new knowledge and insight. For Jeff, media are an impediment to such knowledge for a number of reasons. In the following passage, he seems to be saying that he believes that the media represent a kind of insidious influence that seeks to insinuate itself into consciousness, and that care should be exercised.

Interviewer: So in reality for [his religious practice] you shouldn't be exposed too much to media is what you are saying.

Jeff: Well, it's more to say that there are . . . you know there's very powerful and potent um . . . essences and entities available, waiting to get into humans and most of humans are too full and too "don't bother me" to get access . . . but the [practice] is very much about being welcoming to it, to essences, to be a home, to having a dialogue with this intelligence, that can grace your life and you can give it a place to live.

Interviewer: So if you are too busy with the media then you wouldn't have time to listen to the intelligence?

Jeff: Yeah . . . but at the same time you know there is the habit life and there is just . . . enjoying yourself.

Interviewer: Is it a topic in [his practice], in a lot of religions there is a prescription in terms of media use: how much watching, what to watch. . . .

Jeff: No, it's not much prescription like that, it's more a matter of be aware of what you are putting into yourself and exercise common sense.

For Jeff, then, his religious perspective leads him to aspire to an approach to media that he can describe as aware of these dangers and implications. He is, in a sense, described by media, but not by characters, plots, or programs, but by a style of media consumption that is "aware." This is a rather direct, descriptive, "account of media." In Jeff's view, we should want to be known as people who consume media or understand media in certain ways and act accordingly.

There are, of course, examples in our interviews of much more direct examples of ways that media describe individuals and families. In Chapter 6, we met the "born-again" Milliken family. In the following passage, they talk about their love/hate relationship with *The Simpsons*.

Interviewer: What kinds of things prompt you to turn the channel? When it's *The Simpsons*.

Ray: When they say bad things and stuff.

Jay: Well, they don't really say. . . .

Lynn: I don't know they [Jay and the children] watch it.

Ray: It's another dysfunctional family.

Lynn: Yeah, really.

Interviewer: You say that and you all laugh.

Lynn: Because it's true

Jay: We think we're dysfunctional sometimes.

Lynn: Yeah.

Interviewer: Is that why *The Simpsons* is funny sometimes?

Lynn: Just some of the things they do. And that you can relate, you know, with our own family.

Jay: It's hard to say where the humor comes in. When you sit and try to dissect it like that, it's hard to pinpoint where the humor comes from. Because it is a bizarre family . . . bizarre situations that frankly, most people would never get into. . . . Why is it so popular? It's hard to pinpoint. I guess everyone can see a little bit of themselves in it.

Interviewer: You're laughing, Lynn, I see you laughing.

Lynn: Just like *Marriage and Family* . . . I mean *Married with Children*.

This is a clear and self-conscious reflection that *The Simpsons* – a program that they criticize at other points in the interview – conveys ideas and senses of family and family life that the Millikens think of as describing them and their experience of family. It is a guilty pleasure, of course, and Lynn fills the "mother's" role in this passage in distancing herself from some of the program's elements, but yet she herself admits it describes their family to an extent. This is perhaps in part a testament to the nature of television programs like *The Simpsons*. They have their finger on the pulse of contemporary life, and find ways of expressing that pulse that are particularly attractive and real for audiences. *The Simpsons* is a part of the contemporary conversation about family life and family values, and even families like the Millikens, who would like to separate themselves somewhat from the values represented by the media, nonetheless find themselves represented there.

Each of the categories we have looked at so far is linked to the first level of engagement, "experiences in the media." Identifications with certain media and a sense that media can describe individuals and families, as with the Millikens, are characteristics of a direct engagement with media content. Judy Cruz and Rachel Stein seem also to be connecting rather directly with the media in the examples above. The second level of engagement involves the use of media in broader settings. We interact about media in our family, work, and social relationships, and these exchange

relations seem to be an important motivation for many of our interviewees. The next category is representative of this second level, "interactions
about media."

"I describe myself using it"

Megan Sealy, who we've already met, is a Southern Baptist and the single
mother of teenaged Dell. At a point in our interview where she is talking
about ideas and images relevant to her identity as a mother, she is asked
whether the media provide such resources. She responds with a story from
her experience with her son. Dell had begun cutting classes in ninth grade,
and Megan found it necessary to show up at school unannounced to check
on him.

> He was really embarrassed. And I told him if you do it again, I'm
> going to show up in my bathrobe and slippers. You know, because I'd
> seen that on *Roseanne* and I thought, "Oh, that's so cool!" [laughing].
> That would really put him in his place. He'd be so embarrassed.

The Interviewer then refers back to this incident in a question about media
and Megan quickly connects the question with religion and values.

Interviewer: In terms of the roles that you see yourself as having played
and continuing to play in Dell's life, do you use the media in any of
those roles? I mean, you made a joke about *Roseanne*, are there other
cases where you've drawn from media?
Megan: (laughing) Yeah. Um, sometimes. As far as the media, if there was
a lesson to be learned or something like that or if it was a spiritual
lesson. You know, there's a lot of good Christian tapes and stuff like
that we'd watch at home

This judgment of media on Megan's part combines questions of interactions about and accounts of media. While she connects with both
Roseanne and with the Christian tapes she refers to, she sees them as a
way of both connecting with Dell and representing religious values she
endorses. The self-description she invokes both for the Interviewer and for
Dell via these media is specific and rather conventional.

For many of the reasons we discussed in Chapters 2 and 3, we'd expect
young people to be particularly involved in interactions about media and
in the use of media in identity construction. Uta Fallon is the 12-year-old
daughter of Wyonna, who appeared in Chapter 5. She lives with her single
mother and older sister in a small western city. She identifies
Contemporary Christian Music (CCM) as an example of using media for
self-description in social exchange. CCM seems to have the capacity to

provide an opportunity for an alternative identification for young people who, like her, identify themselves with Evangelical or "born-again" faith.

Interviewer: Ah, OK. Do you see any connection between your being a fan of DC Talk and religion or anything like that, spiritually?

Uta: Well, DC Talk is a Christian Group. And, I really don't listen to anything other than Christian (music) because everything else is so stupid. Like N'Sync, the Backstreet Boys. I'm really not into them.

Interviewer: What's stupid about them?

Uta: It's just their songs are pointless. And the Christian songs have an actual meaning. They have a message for you. That God's with you wherever you are.

Uta illustrates how the use of media for self-description works. On one level, she makes a clear distinction between "Christian" and "Not Christian" media, and places DC Talk and the "secular" groups in their proper places on that map. This also, at the same time, places her, by definition. She is a person who makes such distinctions, and who finds within the former music a real "message," the Christian message. Again, it is important to see that the importance of this genre of music can lie, for Uta, both in its intrinsic qualities and in her ability to describe herself as someone who prefers it.

Priscilla Castello, who we identified as a "metaphysical believer and seeker" in the last chapter, lives with her husband Butch and two children in the suburbs of a major city. The Castellos have lived in Japan for extended periods, and are interested in Buddhism and other Asian religions, which they encounter in a classic "seeker" mode, selecting and combining a number of traditions in their home and in their family spiritual practice. It is not surprising, then, that Priscilla is able to identify a wide range of quite disparate sources and kinds of religiously or spiritually significant media.

Interviewer: Do you think there is anything in the media that is actually helpful for your spirituality?

Priscilla: There is the *Nexus* magazine. So, I guess there are publications that do help with that.

Interviewer: So, mostly for you it seems like the media of choice for spirituality is print and when we talk about screen media, like television, you are less inclined to find spiritual growth and inspiration there.

Priscilla: Right. Unless it is public TV. I know PBS does interesting things. There is something on Tibet coming up in a couple of days. And Butch is the one who checks it out. I don't know what is on ever. But sometimes he will be watching and something will look interesting and I will watch, about people or. So, I do see how it is possible. I'm sure if we had cable there must be cable stations.

Priscilla expresses a view that we have heard before: making distinctions between various media in terms of their relevance to those ideas and values that interest her the most. The Interviewer probes by suggesting that it seems that Priscilla's preferences fairly clearly favor other media over television. Priscilla confirms this by suggesting that public television, in particular, is a place where she would expect to find interesting material. Like many others, she makes an exception in her preference for "non-screen" media: films. At another point in the interview, she is asked whether she actively seeks out anything related to her spirituality.

Interviewer: Do you seek out anything related to spirituality on television or in the movies?

Priscilla: Sometimes at movie theaters. I only usually see art films or something like that. Yes, videos too. I haven't done this for a long time but I like to get videos about religion. Mostly it is goddess stuff or Buddhism.

Interviewer: How about music and spirituality?

Priscilla: Music! Oh, yeah. I don't have a huge collection of music but I do go to the library. I like to get Celtic music. They have such great music. I hear music and I think "Where did they get that music"! I try to explore and find new music, mostly at the library. If we had more money to spend in that direction I probably would buy more CDs or if I found one I really like, I will go buy it.

Priscilla shares with many others we've interviewed a preference for film and for music as authentically representing or conveying symbols and values that are important to her. Relevant to our discussion here, which is about how media experience provides opportunities for social presentation, linkage, or exchange, she provides a description of media operating on two levels. She reports a kind of function of these media for her and her sense of her self and a way that media become a set of descriptive associations through which she can make a narrative of who she is in religious and spiritual terms.

"I want to contest/reject/endorse it"

At the same time that people are using the media in various ways for identity and identification, the media also help them make clear distinctions. These negotiations over the meaning, significance, or legitimacy of various media symbols and messages are important to most of the interpretive strategies we've seen, and at their base is an evaluation. There are, of course, many examples of such evaluative statements in our interviews. In the earlier passage where the Millikens talk about their view of televangelism, and other "religious" media, the theme is clearly one of contesting these programs. Let's look at some other examples.

Chris Chandler, we'll recall, is a former Catholic who is now more of a metaphysical seeker. His media tastes and interests related to his spirituality reflect the broad interests of the quest culture. As with most of our interviewees, he has a difficult time thinking of most media as likely contexts for his authentic seeking, but makes a distinction regarding the Internet.

Interviewer: So do you ever seek out anything related to religion or spirituality on TV or on the Internet or on other media, movies?

Chris: Definitely Internet.

Interviewer: . . . where, what about it?

Chris: Uhm, I can't really give sites' names, but definitely I know when I am in those moods where I just search you know and I think to myself well OK I am going . . . I will have a search like . . . I always had a thing for the American Indians, you know. But I can't say definitely that is all religion, but you know . . . but I can't say about TV at all. Do you mean as far as like religious?

Interviewer: Or spirituality, spiritual things or themes.

Chris: Let's say if it's on I see something, but I can't say that I search for it. Maybe we are just using different semantics . . . I don't watch *Touched by an Angel*.

Chris clearly feels the Internet is a better context for seeking out information or other resources than are other media. In a combination of our "experience" and "accounts" levels of engagement, Chris's expectations about media forms and genres determine where he looks for or expects to find relevant or meaningful material. In this passage, he contests the inoffensive genres represented by *Touched by an Angel* and at the same time endorses Internet and websites that provide useful and helpful information about Native American traditions. It is interesting that he is somewhat vague about specific websites. Instead he seems almost to speculate that a range of things would be available to him there, and that if he should decide to engage in a search he'd find appropriate material. This echoes Donna Baylor's, Steph Kline's, and others' assumptions about the Internet, that one of its primary distinctions is its utility as a source of information.

Donna Baylor seems to have clear ideas and standards about the kinds of material she exposes herself to in the media. Earlier, she describe her motivations for seeking out information about other religions in terms of clear distinctions between traditions and a desire to learn information useful to her abilities to relate to believers from those traditions. When asked about her use of the Internet for religious or spiritual information, Donna describes her use in relation to a recent experience at church.

Donna: We did a series at church on different religions and we learned some basics about that. So when we did that, I came home – we did Islam one week and did Seventh Day Adventists. I came home and I would look for some things and see if I could find anything that had more information. And they were all pretty – I didn't have as much time to spend as I would have liked. But they were all pretty similar. So there was nothing at that point that we hadn't talked about.

Interviewer: Would you do the same thing with TV when you're watching? If you come across shows or maybe a movie that advocate beliefs that are different from yours, what do you do? Or a magazine, or whatever?

Donna: I guess it depends on what it is and what the information is. If it's something that I find offensive, I'm gonna just not – I'm really bad about television. I think most of it's pretty much garbage. If I turn it on and watch a couple minutes of a show and it's just yucky, I won't even go back and look at it.

Interviewer: What's a yucky show?

Donna: [laughing] I knew you were going to ask me that. It's not too hard to be yucky in my book. When they get into violence. . . .

Interviewer: Can you give me an example of a yucky show?

Donna: What's a yucky show? This shows you how much I turn on the television. Oh, well it's not on now, but it was on not too long ago. I think it was called *The Bachelor*. It was about this guy who was dating all these women and they were all living in a house together and he –Oh yuck! Oh yuck! That just made me . . . [laughing].

Interviewer: OK. Do you think that some TV programs, websites, and so on are more truthful than others? And if so, how do you make that evaluation?

Donna: Yes, I think that some are more truthful than others. And, boy, to decide that, it's hard. [but I do it by] Talking to other people to see if they've seen it or heard about it or know anything about it. People that I trust. Most of the time . . . well, I guess it depends on what it is again. If I run across something, I try and read through it and I basically go on instinct. And I feel like my instincts are – especially if I pursue them in that manner – are God led. So I feel like there's going to be some kind of leading in either direction. Sometimes there's not. Sometimes you just have to – it depends on what the content is. I mean, if there's something that just doesn't sit right, then. . . . And I guess it just depends on what I'm looking for. If I'm just looking for some information that, you know, you can verify somewhere else, then that's one thing. But if you're looking for religious guidance or something like that you've gotta be a little bit more choosy about your sources.

Donna does not shy away from evaluating the media. She seems to prefer and to endorse those media that are inoffensive (in the case of entertainment media) and informational (in the case of the Internet). Her tastes, values, and instincts in media give her the basis she needs to make these judgments, though she does report depending a bit on others for advice and evaluations of television and the Internet. The significant point, though, is that her evaluations are important to her, and that she describes them as necessary and more or less constant. At least on the level of "accounts of media," most people seem to want to say that they will regularly accept, reject, and contest media in ways that are relevant to their values and their beliefs.

"I use it to talk with my kids or others about values and morality"

Parenting is one of the central contexts of discussion and understanding surrounding media use. In *Media, Home, and Family*, my colleagues and I engaged in a thorough discussion of the ways the people we interviewed came to understand and use television and other media in the context of household life.[13] It is a commonplace to think that parent/child interactions about the media are one of the major themes of contemporary home life, and a major challenge to creative parenting today, and that notion was supported by our research. Thus, it is not a surprise to find many of our interviewees reflecting on the ways that media come into parenting and family life. Often, these accounts are about how the media convey values that are at odds with values parents wish to maintain as normative in their homes. In other cases, there are compelling accounts of families using media as valuable and even positive occasions for family togetherness and interaction. Many of the categories of media use we've talked about in this chapter so far relate to one or the other of these occasions.

However, there is a third category of parental use of media that also appears large in our interviews: the fact that the media – as compelling cultural products – convey cultural and values messages that are tailor-made for parent–child interactions, discourse, and teaching. In a way, the media are seen by many parents as providing the "curriculum" for values and ethics education. Some parents are quite intentional and systematic about this, others more informal. For nearly all of them, though, this capacity of the media seems to be an obvious opportunity. Megan Sealy describes this in reaction to a question about seeking out things related to religion or spirituality on TV or in film.

Interviewer: Do you guys ever seek out anything related to religion or spirituality on TV or in the movies?

Megan: Ahhh . . . sometimes some of those shows on TV, if they show a lot of immorality and stuff like that, I like to make a point of letting Dell know according to my belief system that that's not appropriate.

You know, but usually . . . I can feel him like backing up. I'm like, geez! – [to Dell] Is this making you uncomfortable, Dell?

Dell: No.

Megan: OK.

Megan: But, ah, you know I guess in that way, using the media as a tool to show moral character and behavior. Because, I mean, there's a lot of really bad programs out there.

Interviewer: Any of them on MTV?

Megan: Well, yeah, there's a few. There's a few. You know, but you look for opportunities in anything in life. You know, especially as a parent you want to teach good moral values and things like that. So there's always opportunities, whether it's media or music or just, you know, walking down the street and having people talk rudely to each other. There's always opportunities.

It is interesting that Megan interprets a question that was intended to invoke examples of media portraying religion and spirituality positively in a different way. In fact, her response contrasts with that expectation in two ways. First, she interprets the question as focusing on values and morality rather than spirituality or religion, and, second, she uses examples that are *negative*, rather than *positive*. For Megan, the media are a vast context of negative and problematic portrayals. However, this can be turned to a positive by appropriate parental intervention. Megan thus agrees with many parents and many among our interviewees that, left to their own devices, the media are primarily a negative rather than a positive influence on children and young people. The appropriate stance for parents, then, is to be constantly vigilant about this, and to be prepared to turn troubling portrayals and values into opportunities for positive interaction. It is interesting, too, that she can find few concrete examples to illustrate her point. Where MTV would be an obvious source of such material, she seems not to have interacted with Dell about MTV, at least not recently.

Earlier, we heard from Fred Kline talking about being moved by *To Kill a Mockingbird*. His daughter, Steph, reflected earlier on using the Internet for information about other religions. Fred is more "secular" in his worldview than Megan Sealy, yet he agrees with her about the capacities of media to provide occasions for parental dialogue and intervention. Like Megan, he rather facilely connects media and *negative* values and ideas, ripe for intervention. Fred describes the classic situation comedy *The Andy Griffith Show* as one of his favorite programs for its positive content. Curiously, he agrees with Glenn Donegal, who is very different from Fred in terms of his religiosity and worldview, on the meaning and value of the *Griffith* program. Like Glenn, he connects Andy with simpler times, when life for adults and young people was less complicated, and with what he perceives were simpler family relationships during those times. When Fred is asked about which shows he dislikes the most, he replies:

Fred: Umm . . . yeah, there are a lot . . . there are shows that I dislike but I probably watch them as well. So, on one hand I can say this is base, lewd and crude and stupid BUT I'm also attracted to it. So, I think the Howard Stern show is absolutely abhorrent. It is awful. NO redeeming value at all but occasionally I'll watch it just because it is lewd and crude and has no redeeming value. But, a show like *Jackass* on TV. It is just . . . absolutely crude and there is no redeeming value and I think it's awful but I'll occasionally watch that as well.

Interviewer: Do you watch these because they sort of alert you to what's out there in the whole world, or. . . .

Fred: No. It's just people doing stupid things and sometimes there is an attraction to people doing stupid things, I guess.

Interviewer: Is there any relationship between your likes and dislikes here and what you consider to be your spirituality?

Fred: Umm . . . well not with *Jackass* but certainly with *Andy Griffith*. There is an innate sense that there is goodness in everyone and that there is value in personal relationships and you know, things were much simpler and the problems we see now. It may just be a fairy tale in my mind, but there is an attraction in that for me, especially with kids growing up now and worrying about what is going on in the world.

Fred is uncommonly self-revealing about his viewing and listening habits. His motivations for these "guilty pleasures" are far from clear. All he can say is that he simply watches them. In a way he is a bit like Jay Milliken in Chapter 6, who seemed to make some of his viewing choices simply on the basis that things "were on" the two channels he could receive. When given the opportunity to ascribe another motive, Fred rejects it, returning again to the simple notion that he is attracted to viewing people doing "stupid things." Like Megan Sealy, he interprets a question about spirituality and media to refer to values and ethics, and then describes his favorite program, *The Andy Griffith Show*, as conveying a sense of positive values and a simpler time, something that he sees as positive for children today.

We met David Mueller in Chapter 7. He is in his twenties, the father of three, and a devout Mormon. He and his wife, Kathy, take their roles as parents in the media age very seriously. Unlike some parents we've interviewed, they seem very aware of the range of television and other media available to their children, and stress the importance of kids learning to make their own moral and spiritual judgments in their media choices. The Interviewer follows their lead, asking at one point,

Interviewer: . . . do you ever find media that actually sort of support . . .
like, say these movies, do they ever have messages that reinforce you
know, strong morals or. . . .

David: Yeah, I think, that's one of the things we try to point out, a lot of
them, it's a . . . God, just a . . . trying to think of an example here right
off the top of my head, it's like . . . we were watching *Bug's Life* where
all the ants stand together and help each other, they're happy and
work together, they all clean up the mess afterwards, nobody
complains, you know, and stuff like that and that's something you try
to . . . and even on . . . you know, whether it's cartoons or anything
that you see, it's like, you'll point an article out in the paper or something that says, "You know, this little kid did this and this and
this . . ." and, you know, I look at it this way, you can find whatever
you want to look for. Even, you know, some people say, "The news is
so depressing, you know, all they have is just who died and who got
shot up," whatever. But then again you can always make whatever
positive, whatever you're looking for. And that's a lot of what we do is
just look for the more positive type things. You know, and we're pretty
choosy, it's gonna be real hard to find good things when all you have
is . . . it was like, *Silence of the Lambs*. What was good [laughs] about
that show? The only funny part about that was there was . . . the
second one, this *Hannibal* one. The gentleman who plays the bad guy
in there, it was on the . . . I was reading this little script thing about
the movie that was coming out and . . . I think it was the *New York
Times*. And it was saying that that first week it opened, he did a tour
of the United States and every night he went to a different theater in a
different town and there was a particular scary part and was in the
theater and he would whisper that same line to the people in front of
him [laughs]. And they were reporting back about what had happened
and he was like, he says, "The only place that people did not run out
of the theater screaming was in LA and they turned around and they
go, 'Cool dude.' [laughs] That's him! Hey man, can I get your auto-
graph?'" He said that everybody else was so into the show that they
just left the theater, you know. . . .

Interviewer: So you're saying that point is that even in something like that
you can sometimes find something humorous there or uplifting.

David: But that was . . . a . . . yeah, that's something that we're trying to
instill in our kids is that . . . that there is good things out there and if
you look at the good things, or look for the good . . . that's what you
need to be looking for. I mean, you can find, I was just telling you
about the bad things about all these shows and stuff, but, and there's
good . . . in the same amount there's as much good and things that
way. I'm not as, you know, as far as *The Simpsons*, I . . . I'm like, you
can find good there too if you really look hard enough. I mean, they're

cartoons, if you don't take them to heart [laughs] you know, but they're not kids' cartoons. A lot of cartoons are not.

There is a struggle here that we've seen before. David seems to be pulled between his own attraction to a range of film and television, "experiences in," and his sense, as a parent, that there are troubling things found there (an "account of"). Like most of the parents we've interviewed, David feels strongly that his most basic role as a parent in this regard is to help his children come to the place where they can make their own judgments about the media they consume. The media do provide opportunities for object lessons, discussions, and interactions. Importantly, it seems to be these opportunities for interpretation and understanding that can turn what might be thought of as negative media to positive media. Good can be found in anything, David and others contend, and it seems to be the parents' role to find those nuggets and highlight them. This is of course rooted in the widely shared idea that the appropriate role for parents *vis-à-vis* media is to help children come to make their own (appropriate) choices. As we have seen, it is much more common to encounter "pedagogical" as opposed to "prophylactic" approaches to media and parenting among our interviewees. By this I mean that most of the individuals we've interviewed place a premium on being seen to make their own choices about media, both in terms of what they watch, and the kinds of conclusions and lessons they draw. Few want to be thought of as someone who cannot make their own judgments about media or who cannot control media in their own lives. At the same time, they want to think of their children in the same way, particularly as they develop to young adulthood. Therefore, few of them want to be seen to be "protecting" their children (particularly older children and teens) from "bad media." Instead, they want to be thought of – and for their children to be thought of – as individuals who can make their own autonomous choices.

It remains intriguing that we have found it to be so difficult for most interviewees to make direct connections between their media lives and their values lives. That is compounded in this chapter by the relative infrequency of easy connections between media and religious or spiritual lives. In spite of what we might have thought (and many others have said) there is little evidence in our interviews of direct religious, or religious-like, functions and effects of media. If the media sphere is able to provide opportunities for religious or spiritual inspiration in a way that is homologous to, or even replaces (much less contests), conventional practice, we would have expected to find much more direct evidence of this in our interviews. More importantly, we would have seen the ways that this is made possible in media culture. By expanding this to look at a range of possible functions or effects of media, from inspiration to identity-building, we might have hoped to have found the media coming to provide clear and straightforward resources to religious and spiritual practice. What we found instead were examples in these categories of function and effect, but that were at the same time far from straightforward or directly evocative of traditional religious or spiritual forms.

We've seen evidence previously that helps explain this to a certain extent. People are, as we've seen, unlikely to want to think of media as religiously or spiritually valid. The received "accounts of media" in this regard are clear and forceful. In a postmodern world shaped by enlightenment principles, the idea that something like religion or spirituality could be contained in something like "the media" is seen on some level as preposterous. But, there is a more fundamental explanation as well. As we've gradually begun to see through these interviews, media practice and spiritual or religious practice reside in quite different places in the life-world. There is a self-consciousness about each, and a reflexive engagement with each that keeps each in its place. This is not to say that they are not related, because they are, and in some fundamental ways. There is a sense in these interviews that the claims and ideas of the broader culture, as represented in media, are the larger and more encompassing claims, at least as regards cultural meanings and representations. As much as it might seem likely that individuals and families who identify themselves with focused religious or spiritual beliefs or claims would base their interactions with the culture on those claims, this seems not to be the case. Instead, they seem to want to describe their faith and spirituality in ways that articulate with the mediated ideas and values of the larger culture. Or they see them as separate and separable, as in the case of morally conservative households that nonetheless consume media as "guilty pleasures."

In any case, the idea at the root of this chapter – that the media sphere provides material and experiences that either contest or replace traditional religious or spiritual influences, practices or behaviors – was not convincingly supported. As we have seen, we clearly need to look elsewhere and in different ways for evidence of the contribution of media to religion and spirituality or vice versa. A more persuasive picture of these relations emerged in Chapters 5, 6, and 7; something we will return to as we sum up and conclude in Chapter 10.

Chapter 9

Media and public religious culture post-09/11/01 *and* post-11/2/04

We have now developed a sense of the ways that individuals and families work in relation to media culture. We've also thought about similarities and differences in media experience among various social and religious locations. In all, we've seen a kind of stability in the practices of media consumption at the household level in our interviews, and can now begin to describe some of the outlines of that stability. In Chapter 3, we considered the range of media genres and institutions related to religion: news, religious broadcasting, religious publishing, and entertainment. I argued there that the significant modern phenomenon is the way that these various contexts are intermingling, but, at the same time, that it seems more likely that the "nonreligious" contexts of media would influence religion, than vice versa. In part as a confirmation of that notion, we've found ourselves so far concentrating on entertainment media and the ways that our interviewees can be seen to interact with entertainment programs. In most cases it has seemed that the entertainment media are the common, taken-for-granted context that they think and talk the most about. But, I've made the point that the real question is not how people succeed or fail in relation to predicted and presumed viewing and consumption of particular genres of media but instead how people move across genres, programs, channels, and contexts in their reception of resources that are meaningful to them.

Religion and media intersect on a number of social and cultural planes, many of which I introduced in Chapter 2. Because much of this book has concentrated on the everyday and lived experiences of people in their homes, we've followed their experiences and interests. These conversations have thus quite naturally moved in the direction of the popular or entertainment media, and the commodified experiences of religion and spirituality that are negotiated and made sense of there. But, I've also argued for a view of media that is large and encompassing, claiming that by so doing we can enter the media/religion landscape in a number of ways and from a number of perspectives.

In Chapter 3, I argued for a redefinition of media and religion away from a number of the received analytical categories we've used in the past.

As I said there, this was a kind of postmodern argument, holding that it is important to deconstruct some of those understandings in order to reconstruct a view of religion and media from "inside" the experiences and interactions of audiences. One implication of such an approach, of course, is the notion that there are thus no systematic or overarching readings, meanings, or responses possible. If the logic implicit in media texts and messages does not define the nature or frameworks of knowledge and value, then where would such frameworks be found? As we've seen in the interviews in the last several chapters, there are, in fact, broad, consensual, and systematic readings of media texts. There is a degree of commonality, common experience, and consensus on the nature of media, on the kinds of religious and spiritual messages and meanings encountered there, and on the ways that those readings and meanings come into play in the lives of viewers. Many of these emerge from common experiences, such as shared demographies or points in the lifecourse. As we saw in Chapters 5, 6, and 7, there seemed to be a great deal of commonality among parents based on their roles *as parents* in relation to media in their households. Other such readings emerge from shared or common values or ideas.

In this chapter, we'll consider a set of systematic readings and discourses that have emerged from contemporary historical experience. The turn of the twenty-first century brought media and religion to the fore in unprecedented ways. I would like to argue that what we will look at in this chapter is a kind of "bookend" to the discussions we undertook in Chapters 2 and 3 about "medium theory" and the positioning of religion, religious institutions, and religious authority in terms of their positioning in the media. As we saw there, the latter part of the last century witnessed the gradual erosion of some of the settled relations in the religious public sphere. Religious institutions in general began to lose their authority and legitimacy. This was in part a function of the emergence of a media sphere that could increasingly define the nature of religion, spirituality, and religious meaning in late modernity. The place that religion finds and can find in media discourse thus became problematic, and the century ended with these questions in a good deal of dispute. Our inquiries into how people, in their homes and private lives, consume and make meaning with regard to religion and spirituality served to describe the processes and grounds on which religion and spirituality are understood in relation to media culture. We also could see there that the pervasiveness and ubiquity of media experience as such a grounding gives the media sphere a particular role and significance in these regards. What we may see here, then, is the beginnings of an analysis that can help us again describe, in larger and more holistic terms, the place and stature of religion in late modernity, this time in relation to the media that have become articulated in fundamental ways into that modernity.

There are meaningful themes and values and symbols and tropes in media texts and messages. Our interviewees seemed very much to want to be part of a larger dialogue or set of dialogues in the culture. They found satisfaction and salience in being part of larger conversations. We'll now turn to an exploration of ways that those larger conversations can come to be themed by historical events. What we have seen and learned here about the way people read media religiously and spiritually can help us see the extent to which these events that are, on their face, about religion are also about media and about the interaction between religion and media. In fact, as we will see, the kinds of explorations we have undertaken allow us to address such large themes in new ways.

Change at the millennium

The new millennium has ushered in a new conversation both *at the intersection* between religion and media, and *about* religion and media. Religion has seemingly re-entered public life and public (and thus *media*) discourse at a whole new level in the years since the September 11, 2001 terrorist attacks. As we will see, 9/11 was in large measure a media phenomenon. It unleashed a set of global, cultural, and media trends that have yet to be fully worked out. But we can already see that it changed the landscape by altering the frameworks and contexts within which religion and religious ideas seem to be active in history, culture, and media. In a way, the events of 9/11 brushed aside ongoing debates about the place of religion in the public square. Before that day, it was not uncommon to hear skepticism from people in the news business about how and where religion should be counted in overall coverage of domestic and international politics. Afterwards, that issue was settled, and the only question was how best to account for religion when looking at those "larger" questions.

Not unrelated to post-9/11 considerations and discourses, religion began to play a larger and larger role in domestic politics in the US, culminating (in a sense) in the November 2, 2004 election, which in some ways seemed to be all about religion. Before the election, opinion polling pointed to an emerging "religion gap," with frequent religious-service attenders more likely to vote Republican by a wide margin. Exit polling at the time of the election indicated that the key constituency group that made the difference in electing George Bush was a group that came to be called "values voters," people who were motivated at the polls more by religious and cultural *values* than by questions of foreign or domestic policy.[1]

Both the events of 9/11 and the US general election in 2004 call our attention away from the private sphere of meaning-making that we've concentrated on up to this point, and redirect it to the larger national and international public sphere. What can the narratives of self and practices of meaning-making we've been looking at here tell us about the significance of these larger events for religion, society, and culture? More importantly, perhaps, what can they tell us about the future of relations between religion and media, and the future of the religion/media interaction in the forming and shaping of religious, social, and cultural life? As we've seen here, meaning-making in relation to media culture involves both formal and received resources and resources that are emergent and in dispute. As we will see, important events and trends such as 9/11 and the role of religion in the election easily (and rather unproblematically) flow into the inventory of symbolic resources out of which we make religious and spiritual sense in the media age. And, in so doing, they point to the extent to which the interaction between religion and media in late modernity has become an increasingly profound and far-reaching one.

Religion and media in 9/11 and its aftermath

It is trite to say that the events of September 11, 2001 were unprecedented in their scope and effect. No major city in the "Group of Eight" industrialized countries had experienced such a major loss of life from an intentional act of violence in peacetime.[2] A strike at the heart of American commerce and media with such surprise galvanized the world and the nation. Throughout the world, at least the Western world, it is now conventional to use the term "9/11" to describe the events, and to think of international relations and global politics in "pre-9/11" and "post-9/11" terms. A great deal of public and scholarly comment has followed, focusing on everything from the security implications of the attacks to their impact on public consciousness, locally, nationally, and internationally.

The religious subtext of the attacks has also been an important, if problematic, element of discussion and debate. The barbarism of the events scandalized the world, and there has been an ongoing effort to reconcile them with their claimed roots in religion. A much-feared anti-Arab or anti-Islamic backlash did not materialize to any great degree,[3] but it could be argued that, in a more subtle way, smaller-scale reactions against Islam and against people of Middle-Eastern and/or Muslim descent continues, and underlies certain political debates and repercussions that continue to gather force both in the US and elsewhere.[4]

In keeping with the theme of this book, however, it is important to understand the attacks as significant for the interaction between religion and media that they represented and continue to represent. They simply would not have had the same force or effect without the media. At the same time, they brought religion to the fore in new and unprecedented ways, ways that have forever shaped the way we see its contributions to politics, public discourse, social change, and political struggle. Further, the fact that religion and media *interacted* in these events is also significant.

The media, religion, and religion and media together were important in the events and their aftermath in four ways. First, *the media were the source of national and global experience of the events.* They were for all intents and purposes *media events.* Second, the media were and are *the source of "our" knowledge of "them" and "their" knowledge of "us."* Third, American media exports such as films are an important basis *for the Islamist moral critiques of US and Western Culture.* And finally, 9/11 illustrated and confirmed the role of the media as central to a new "civil religion" based in *public rituals of commemoration and mourning.* Let's look at each of these in turn.

The media as the source of the experience

One of the most unprecedented things about the 9/11 attacks was when and where they occurred. Subsequent political and security analyses of the strategy behind them noted that Bin Laden had a penchant for choosing targets for their political and symbolic value, and for sticking with targets once they were chosen. On one level, then, the 9/11 attacks on the World Trade Center were nothing more than a second attempt following the less "successful" 1992 bombing there.[5] On another level, though, the 9/11 events were exponentially more significant in that they were so spectacular. Their spectacle was an effect of their timing. The two airplanes arrived at their targets approximately eighteen minutes apart. In the most media-saturated city in the world, hundreds of cameras were trained on the smoldering north tower when the second airplane struck the south tower, ensuring that millions of people throughout the world saw that strike live on television.[6]

What the city, the nation, and the world saw, in living color, was a horrible spectacle. Victims of the attack waved from windows above the smoldering floors, and, in acts of unimaginable desperation, many of them flung themselves to their deaths to avoid the flames. And then, the most unimaginable sight of all: two 110-story buildings – the very symbols of the modern triumph of metropolitan civilization – crumbling to rubble. All of this was captured, shown live, repeated, and commented upon by media observers during hours and days of coverage. Every reader of this book no doubt has these images forever imprinted in memory. The immediacy, and more important, the visuality of the spectacle defined it and continues to define it. Other incidents of violence and horror before and since have also been visualized. War, genocide, natural disasters, and accidents are visually documented. In the case of 9/11 we all *participated* in the events, knowing that these things were happening, in real time, to real people, in a place where – our intellect told us – such things should not happen, as we were watching them.

In her thoughtful work on the role that visualization and depiction plays in the process of "bearing witness," media scholar Barbie Zelizer points out that the ability to picture and represent events such as the

Holocaust has changed the way witnessing is seen and done in modernity.[7] Visual records play an ever more significant role in our collective experience of our common humanity, and in our personal and political relation to suffering. It has been widely observed that those events that are pictured achieve a place in public consciousness not shared by events that are merely reported upon by other means. For example, the Boxing Day Tsunami of 2004 galvanized world attention to the plight of hundreds of thousands of casualties and millions of survivors while unpictured events going on at the same time, such as the massacres in the Darfour province of Sudan, received less attention.

I contend that, in addition to the visuality of 9/11, there was also its instantaneity. We all knew that these things we were watching were happening at that very moment. I do not want to ignore a more troubling aspect of these matters that has also been widely observed as a reason for the relative prominence of the 9/11 events. That is that, while disasters and catastrophes have come to be coded as commonplace in the developing world – something that happens to "those" unfortunate people "over there" – events such as 9/11 (where the total number of victims was in fact only around one one-hundredth the number who died in the Boxing Day Tsunami) become news because they are happening to white people in the developed world.[8] On one level, it can be said that in the global media landscape not all human lives are of equal worth. On another level, we should also remember that in the conventional journalistic calculus, things are news because they are unusual or unprecedented, and a major terrorist attack, within the borders of the United States, was unusual and unprecedented.

The instantaneity of the 9/11 depictions and reception did serve to draw viewers into a common experience in a new and galvanic way. It became an event and an experience that was widely shared on a moral and emotional level, as evidenced by the global outpouring of sympathy and support. It thus had the makings, at least, of a binding experience that transcended its immediate surroundings. Many communities and contexts and interests have tried to "claim" it, leaving aside the unquestioned claims of the victims and their families. Did it "belong" to New York (hundreds also died at the Pentagon and in a field in western Pennsylvania)? To the firefighters and police on the scene? To America and patriotic American ideas about justice and right? To the West? To the Christian world?[9] The right to define its moral, political, and religious meaning continues to be an issue of great debate to this day, and will no doubt be so for decades to come.[10] The point of interest to our discussion here, though, is the nature of the event and the experience. The attacks of 9/11 were a turning point in history that was experienced in a deep and profound way because they were mediated in real time. Their relationship to religion is perhaps less obvious, but, as we proceed to reflect on them, religion will become a more and more important dimension of the story.

Our knowledge of "them" and their knowledge of "us"

The afternoon of September 11, 2001 was a regularly scheduled lecture day in an introductory course in mass media and society. Like many of my colleagues, I chose to offer the 200-odd students in the class an opportunity to process the events of the morning, and opened the floor for questions, responses, and discussion. One of the first questions asked was, "Why didn't we know someone hated us that much?" Other students chimed in with similar wonder that we could have been so blind to such sentiments about the US. Implicit in these questions was the assumption that, in a modern, mediated world, saturated with journalism, we should be more knowledgeable about "others" out there, and their attitudes about "us." This was compounded in subsequent days by the growing sense that immigration, globalization, and global social and cultural change was making it ever more important to know about the rest of the world, to try to understand it, and (in the case of the US foreign policy establishment, at least) to try to project a more favorable impression of the US to the rest of the world.

These discourses are rooted in one of the most significant functions of media in modernity: their role in transcending geography, bringing once vastly separated individuals, groups, and communities into closer contact with one another. Marshall McLuhan's widely noted aphorism that the media age would usher in a "global village" is now thought to be over-drawn and overly optimistic. The media do have the capacity to cross space and erase time, and, as geography becomes less of a barrier, we do increasingly know more about the "others" from whom we are separated by great distances. The instantaneity of the electronic media has made it possible for us to know much more about events across the world as they happen, and to have a contemporaneous grasp of events abroad. The visuality of the electronic media has added a sense of credulity to this knowledge, as pictures are taken to be more real and credible than oral or written accounts.[11]

Whereas McLuhan is taken to have expected that this mediated connection would bind disparate communities and peoples closer together, things don't seem to work quite that way. There is evidence, for instance, that increasing knowledge about others can lead as readily to mistrust and misunderstanding as to trust and understanding.[12] A major reason for this has to do with the context and framing of reception of media messages. In a classic international and cross-cultural study, Tamar Liebes and Elihu Katz showed that viewers of the 1980s US soap opera *Dallas* read the show in ways that were more dependent on those viewers' own contexts and life situations than on the central themes and messages of the program.[13] Viewers can and do make new meanings out of the things they view from "other" contexts, meanings that are as dependent on their own situations as on the manifest values or messages in those media materials.[14]

More specific to the challenges of 9/11 and its aftermath, though, is the particular way the East is represented in the West, and vice versa. My students expressed the feeling that they had not been well served by media that have been shown by their nature to be inordinately focused on the developed world and myopic about international news beyond a few key areas of US special interest, such as Israel.[15] Also significant is the obverse, the issue of how American and Western lives, interests, and values are portrayed in the other direction. At the root of these concerns, of course, is an issue near to McLuhan's concerns, that is how global understanding is or is not served by the media we consume. There is no doubt that, in all respects, the events of 9/11, their precursors, and their consequences were rooted in a mediated knowledge base. This makes 9/11 a media issue in a fundamental way, to the extent that we are concerned about its roots in ideology and values, and about ways it might have been avoided or its causes and consequences ameliorated. That so much of its motivation and its reception were *framed by religious ideas* makes it by definition an issue of media and religion, something that we'll look at in more detail next.

Media as the source of Islamist critiques

In their early coverage of the attacks, the so-called "mainstream media" of North America and the West attempted to describe for the first time in a comprehensive way the roots of Islamist ire against American and Western culture. While we should not forget that, for most critics, fundamental political realities of US foreign policy and historic international behavior are at the root of the problem,[16] there is no denying that a cultural/moral critique also motivated the 9/11 attackers.[17] Press reports of Al-Qaida and its motivations stressed this moral critique. Simply put, Al-Qaida and Islamist movements more generally identify their challenge to the West in historic terms, and identify Western values, particularly Western *moral* values, as an important underlying motivation for their particular *jihad*. A press report at the time of the attacks quoted a young Islamist seminary student from Pakistan, "We are happy that many *kaffirs* (infidels) were killed in the World Trade Center. We targeted them because they were *kaffirs*, unbelievers."[18]

This was echoed in the instructions given to the attackers themselves. Referring to the passengers they would encounter – and ultimately kill – on the planes, the instructions carried by Mohammed Atta and others referred to them as sacrificial animals. "You must make your knife sharp and must not discomfort your animal during slaughter," they said.[19] There was of course concern that some of the attackers might have become encultured during their time in the US, and Atta felt it necessary to remind them that their basic struggle was against the apostate and depraved West. It was essential to think of the victims of the attacks in these terms, and these terms were rooted in a sense that the overall struggle was between the moral claims of the two worlds: Al-Qaida's particular (and to most Muslim authorities heretical) claims about Islam – morally superior to the depraved West.

Where do these ideas about the West come from? As has been widely noted, the media are of course the primary context within which "they" could know about "us." In an analysis of the influence of satellite broadcasting in the Arab world, Middle East scholar Fouad Ajami describes an advertisement for a Western product appearing on Al Jazeera, the satellite network widely viewed across the Arab world.

> One ad offered a striking counterpoint to the furious anti-Westernism of the call-in program. It was for Hugo Boss "Deep Red" perfume. A willowy Western woman in leather pants strode toward a half-naked young man sprawled on a bed. "Your fragrance, your rules, Hugo Deep Red," the Arabic voice-over intoned. I imagined the young men in Arab-Muslim cities watching this. In the culture where the commercial was made, it was nothing unusual. But on those other shores, this ad threw into the air insinuations about the liberties of the West – the kind of liberties that can never be had by the thwarted youths of the Islamic world.[20]

As anyone who has observed the media scene in non-Western contexts knows, this is but one example of the kind of anachronism one regularly encounters there. The political economy of Hollywood-based media production is such that foreign distribution is often the most profitable outlet for films or videos that would never make it in their home markets.[21] Most often, these films – along with the major features that have a life both at home and abroad – contain large amounts of sexuality and violence, things that sell well globally.[22] What this means is that in much of the developing world – and significantly in the Middle East – what is seen of the West is a picture that few people in the West would wish to have identified as emblematic of Western values of either sexuality or violence. The ubiquity and instantaneity of global media mean that we are no longer able to have a private conversation, or to keep our national cultural material to ourselves. Others are looking in, and they are drawing their own conclusions. This plays into the events of 9/11 in a profound and fundamental way, in that Al-Qaida's critique of the West is less theoretical and more concrete to its followers and potential followers. Combining the Islamist reading of history in terms of a global struggle between two worlds[23] with a moral critique that provides followers and supporters with concrete and galvanic images of the West, clerics and other leaders have given their masses some powerful ideas and motivations.

These trends should not be difficult for those of us in the West to understand, parallel as they are to our own reactionary and Fundamentalist movements. However, the moral critique should not be seen in terms of its consumption by followers "in the street" as an ephemeral matter. Mark Juergensmeyer, author of a definitive work on religious terrorism, observes, of the images of the West consumed in the Islamic world, "It is difficult for those of us in the West to appreciate how these people [Islamists] feel *shamed* by what they know of the West. They feel *personally* responsible to do something about it."[24] This echoes of course the kind of moral critiques that frequently erupt in the US, and to a lesser extent elsewhere in the West, over "immoral" film, television, books, or other media. Religiously inflected critics here are seemingly highly motivated to address such things. That people several steps removed from this context are also watching, are also similarly offended, and are moved to action is a new and unprecedented reality of the media age. Islamists also share in common with certain of their Christian Fundamentalist counterparts a sense of persecution. Religion scholar Elizabeth Castelli's recent work on the so-called "Persecuted Christians" movement has demonstrated how legitimate cases of persecution have been conflated in some Christian circles with presumed "oppression" of Christians in the *Christian* West.[25] For Islamists and Christian Fundamentalists alike, claims to oppression and persecution can be powerful in building common purpose and solidarity.

In both cases, the media can be powerful contexts for the realization of the condition of oppression. Fouad Ajami quotes an Islamic preacher, Sheik Muhammad Ibrahim Hassan, commenting on the connection between this sense of oppression and 9/11:

> "Oppression leads to an explosion," he said angrily. "Under the cover of the new world order, Muslims in Chechnya and Iraq have been brutalized. . . . Any Muslim on the face of the earth who bears faith in God and his Prophet feels oppression today. If a believer feels oppression and thinks that no one listens to him and that power respects only the mighty, that believer could be provoked to violent deeds. We saw things – horrors – in Bosnia that would make young people turn old. . . . Where were the big powers and the coalitions and the international organizations then? Where are they now, given what is going on in Palestine? The satellite channels have spread everywhere the knowledge of this oppression."[26]

What is most significant about this situation is not, of course, the politics and balance of power, things that are immemorial and universal. Nor is it surprising to hear such a critique of US and Western policies and practices from a religious figure in the Muslim world. What is just beneath the surface is the reality that the media age has made these symbols and these issues real in a way that brings them directly to the fore in the lives of individuals and movements. As the Sheik notes, the media have made these images, symbols, and struggles available everywhere. The two valences of this situation – the knowledge of the exercise of real power by the West in political contexts in the Muslim sphere of influence and the spreading through entertainment media of images of the West that shame conservatives there – work together, and worked together in the bill of particulars carried by Al-Qaida in 9/11.

The "new civil religion" of commemoration and mourning

No one who watched the coverage of the events of 9/11 on US television could escape the sense that this was more than a mere "news" story. Admittedly it was, and one of the most significant and striking of all time. Like earlier moments in television history, "being in the right place at the right time" made the careers of some previously less well-known reporters and anchors. What soon emerged, though, was a kind of rhythm of representations, narratives, accounts, and remembrances.[27] The nearly incessant replaying of the images soon became problematic for some, especially children.[28] But, there is a sense in which such coverage, and conventions of coverage that emerged with 9/11, were part of a larger media landscape.

That landscape is a long tradition of mediated public experiences stretching back at least to the Kennedy assassination in 1963. That event was a major turning point in American media and journalistic history. Occurring at a time when television was just coming to its own as a news medium, the events in Dallas provided an unprecedented opportunity for the visual, real, and instantaneous power of the medium to emerge. As with 9/11, there were technical and logistical reasons for this, including the presence of so many media to cover what was a politically significant event, the recently perfected ability to send television images back and forth across the country, the eventual emergence of actual amateur film of the shooting itself, the live-on-camera shooting of the assassin himself, and the fact of the "media-friendliness" of the Kennedy administration. Also as with 9/11, the overarching reality of the event played the key role. A young, popular, charismatic president, known to the public because of television, was killed so unexpectedly and publicly. The shooting occurred on a Friday. The American (and indeed, the world) public thus had a whole weekend to watch and to try to come to terms with the events. And, as they unfolded, there was continuing drama. The search for the killer, his eventual arrest and then killing. The hurried inauguration of the new president. The return of the body to Washington the same night, with live images from the tarmac as the casket and the young widow, still wearing her blood-soaked clothing, entered the hearse. The statement from President Johnson attempting to reassure the public of a stable transition. And then later, the lying-in-state, the state funeral, and the burial. Few who were alive at the time can forget the images and the emotions.

And, significantly to our considerations here, it was all televised. Television reporters and anchors struggled to find their footing in this new reality. Anchors such as Walter Cronkite served to guide the viewing world through the events, offering words of sorrow, comfort, hope, and consolation. It forever changed the way we think about television news, and imprinted on a generation of television news people (and on succeeding generations) the expectation that at certain times, and with certain events, their role would be to step up and act in real time and with real emotion. There are simply those times when emotional detachment is difficult, particularly when journalists are experiencing the same events at the same time as their audiences. The years since 1963 have seen many debates in professional circles about "personality journalism" and about the tendency for television journalists to become entangled with their stories. Behind many of these debates is a cultural memory of the JFK assassination.

It is my argument that this event ushered in the beginnings of a new form of public ritual linked to collective national and international processes of commemoration and mourning. In the years since 1963, there has been a series of such events. These include the tumultuous year of 1968, which saw the assassinations of Martin Luther King and Robert F. Kennedy, as well as the Chicago Democratic Convention. Television of course played an important role in public experiences of the Vietnam War and its aftermath, and some of the same issues and trends might be seen in the coverage of Watergate. But, commemoration of loss is the key ingredient of the rituals I have in mind, linking the JFK assassination with subsequent events such as the Challenger explosion, the shootings at Columbine High School, the bombing of the Murrah Federal Building, and of course 9/11.

Cultural scholars Daniel Dayan and Elihu Katz have described the role of television in the emergence of global forms of what they call "media events." These collective events are "real" in the sense that they are rooted in actual political, religious, or civic processes, but they are also important and unique because they are televised and interrupt the flow of television. Television, say Dayan and Katz, has introduced new contexts, processes, and conventions to these forms, seeing in them an underlying taxonomy composed of contests, conquests, and coronations. They would not be structured in the same way without television, they argue, and television makes them national, even global, in scope and character. Religion may play a role in the events described by Dayan and Katz, but its presence or absence is not a central feature of their analysis.[29]

I wish to take things in a different direction than Dayan and Katz, looking more directly at how 9/11 can be seen as an expression of a kind of "civil religion" of commemoration and mourning. This differs from Dayan and Katz's view in two key ways. First, I see in events such as the Kennedy Funeral, the Challenger explosion, Oklahoma City, and 9/11 the dimension of mourning, of contention with shared fear and loss. Critical questions about the legitimacy of the state, not just about the status of a leader such as Kennedy, are in play, and the whole question of the function of such an event in support of social order is also in question. Second, whereas Dayan and Katz tend to sidestep the implicit religiosity of these events (while very persuasively describing the role that explicit religious form plays in them), I want to look more directly at the way that religious sentiments, sensibilities, and meanings come into play in them.[30] Dayan and Katz tend to see the role of religion in such events as either a legitimating authority or as a source of formal elements that are brought into play in the structuration of the events. So the approach here is at some distance from their analysis, following instead Robert Bellah's influential ideas about the function of civil religion. To Bellah, civil religion is something that, while existing in secularized public contexts, nonetheless seeks to infuse those contexts with deeper and more profound meanings. Bellah notes: "American civil religion is not the worship of the American nation but an understanding of the American experience in the light of ultimate and universal reality."[31] Bellah's own work outlined ways in which formal and informal contexts of public ritual have traditionally been infused with such themes and values.[32] Often these have been seen as somewhat denatured, including things such as seemingly rote prayers and invocations at sporting and political events. A vibrant debate has continued in popular culture over whether and what kind of popular-cultural materials might be serving such civic piety, and whether it would be delegitimated by its commodification or diluted by its over-application.[33] I want to contend that, in events like 9/11, the media have come to play a central role in civil religious practices that are authentic to critical moments in national self-understanding.

This argument rests, of course, on the notion that media can be significant in providing the context for the crafting of novel ways of making such meanings. Many have suggested such an organic role for media and for media rituals. A formal argument to this effect relies of course on the notion that significant ritualization can take place beyond specifically religious contexts and, further, in media contexts. Ritual scholar Catherine Bell has noted that evolving understandings and practices of ritual have in fact broken some of the key boundaries of religious sanction, leading to "new styles of ritualization."[34] Ronald Grimes has explored at some length the notion that the media can be at the center of such ritualization. Noting that ritualization may or may not be "religious" in some fundamental way, he observes that media can function as ritual. At the same time, he cautions that there is nothing necessarily ritually significant about media. Consistent with Geertz's ideas about religion, it depends, to Grimes, on the particular moments, meanings, and practices.[35]

Powerful political and national narratives and sentiments, such as those that might be invoked by an event like 9/11, have been traditionally thought of as stable, firm, and consistent. Newer ways of thinking about culture have begun to question such assumptions. We now think of fundamental cultural ideas as evolving and as significantly rooted in contemporary experience. Reflecting on the way commemoration invokes significant memories of the nation and its values, historian John Gillis observes,

> we are constantly revising our memories to suit our current identities. Memories help us make sense of the world we live in; and "memory work" is, like any other kind of physical or mental labor, embedded in complex class, gender and power relations that determine what is remembered (or forgotten), by whom and for what end.[36]

It is interesting to note that it has only been relatively recently in American culture, at least, that ideas about the kinds of meanings, rooted in consensual understandings of where we've come from, have concerned the broad swath of public discourse. Traditionally, only the cultural elites cared. Gillis notes that, in addition to this sort of democratic uninterest in the past, the American project was originally conceived of as very much about the future, with figures such as Jefferson specifically eschewing the idea of narrativizing a national "past."[37]

Yet there are some received notions available to us from the earliest days of the republic, ideas that can be seen to still be in play (though not necessarily determinitive) in the way that tragic events such as 9/11 are remembered, interpreted, and understood. In his comprehensive study of the *physical* sites of American violence and tragedy, cultural geographer Kenneth Foote cites an early expression of American ideas of civil religion in a quotation from Joseph Galloway published in 1780.

> The fundamental and general laws of every society are the lessons of instruction by which the subject is daily taught his duty and obedience to the State. It is the uniformity of these lessons, flowing from the same system of consistent polity, which forms the same habits, manners, and political opinions throughout the society, fixes the national attachment, and leads the people to look up to one system of government for their safety and happiness, and to act in concert on all occasions to maintain and defend it.[38]

The fundamental idea that collective interest underlies a sense of duty and obligation to public order is nearly generic in American civic education. One way of thinking about civil religion, then, is through ideas like these, where the religion is not sectarian, but underlies a sense of duty to a state whose legitimacy is both underscored and justified by its relationship to public sentiments, duties, and obligations. The system is in a way self-justifying when it works smoothly. That is why it is so fundamentally unsettling (and might so readily invoke ideas of – and defense through – civil religion) when catastrophes seem to befall the nation and its people. Both its provision of security and its legitimacy are under assault.

It late modernity, it seems, this theme of legitimacy is paired with questions of unity, of shared and common purpose. In an era defined by self and self-identity, our relations and senses of empathy with other "selves" become a prominent issue and concern. Such unity is also under siege in events like the JFK assassination or 9/11. It becomes necessary to rebuild a sense of commonness and unity out of a sense of disruption and loss. As Foote points out, there is a malleability to the social practices that address such concerns. Citing Eric Hobsbawm's notion of "invented tradition," he echoes Wade Clark Roof's invocation of the same idea, and thus allows a linkage to ideas of religious practices that are constituted by such invention.[39] The overarching project of commonness or common purpose is, as I said, under assault in events like those described by Foote, the bombing of the Murrah building, and, of course, the September 11 attacks.

Edward Linenthal has provided the definitive reading of the Oklahoma City events, and he directly addresses the question of what can be salient about events that focus on American victimization rather than American triumph. Clearly, in both Oklahoma City and 9/11, there were attempts to craft a narrative of triumph. As Linenthal notes, however, such attempts rang hollow in a situation where a "traumatic vision" was more connected with the actual experience.[40] Instead of a narrative or tradition of "patriotic sacrifice," Linenthal argues that a narrative of victimization actually functions better to bind communities – and the nation – together.

> Perhaps one of the greatest attractions of a nationwide bereaved community is that it is one of the only ways Americans can imagine themselves as one; being "together" with millions of others through expressions of mourning bypasses or transcends the many ways in which people are divided – by religion, by ideology, by class, by region, by race, by gender.[41]

How commemoration is done has also undergone change over time, change that is significant to questions of the integration of media into these processes. The Vietnam veterans' memorial in Washington ushered in a new set of practices of memorialization. First, it specifically memorialized all of those killed, and, second (perhaps in conjunction with that level of personalization), the practice evolved of visitors leaving memorial objects at the wall. In her account of the meaning of the wall, Kristin Haas notes that these objects reflect a blended mixture of secular and civic traditions of commemorating death. "Many, many people carrying things to the wall are working to come to terms with particular losses and with their

troubled patriotism," she notes.[42] As Haas's analysis demonstrates, objects
have the capacity to carry complex meanings and associations, connecting
with the malleability of meaning-making we considered earlier. Miles
Richardson suggests that the reason for this is that objects have a permanence that words lack. "In all cases, the objects left are more powerful
than the words that their givers might have spoken . . . [they] continue to
speak . . . long after we are gone," he observes.[43]

The September 11 events thus occurred in a historical trajectory
defined by prior mediatization of commemoration and mourning, by
prior experience with a similar event of victimization and loss, and by an
evolving set of practices that Linenthal calls a "memorial vocabulary,"
including the sending or leaving of objects including cards, poems,
flowers, and stuffed toys, particularly teddy bears. Linenthal further notes
the interesting phenomenon experienced at Oklahoma City as well as at
Columbine, the tendency for certain people to develop a "presumed intimacy" with victims and their families.[44] It is inescapable that this sense of
intimacy is related in some way to the mediated experience of the events.
Linenthal and Foote also note the emergence of a kind of "democratiza-
tion" of such events as individuals are able to come to their own ideas
about how best to participate, and are motivated by the mediated close-
ness of the events to do so.

In late modernity, such democratic practice necessarily involves individual autonomy and personal initiative. Gillis connects this rather
self-consciously to the media age.

> We are more likely to do our "memory work" at times and places of
> our own choosing. Whereas there was once "a time and a place for
> everything," the distinctions between different kinds of times and
> places seem to be collapsing. As global markets work around the clock
> and the speed of communications shrinks our sense of distance, there
> is both more memory work to do and less time and space to do it in.
> As the world implodes on us, we feel an even greater pressure as indi-
> viduals to record, preserve, and collect.[45]

This addresses concerns such as those we attributed to Kenneth Gergen in
Chapter 2. Gergen holds that in modernity the self has become "saturated," with limited prospects for constructive or redemptive action.
Gergen sees the kind of practices we're considering here, where people act
in concrete ways to participate in collective experience, as one source of
optimism about modernity.

> The capacity to give life to words, and thus to transform culture, is
> usefully traced not to internal resources but to relatedness – which
> serves as the source of all articulation and simultaneously remains

beyond its reach. We confront, then, the possibility of a new order of sublime – suited to the technoworld of the postmodern – a relational sublime.[46]

Events of common suffering and vicitimization are, as we've seen, dramatic moments of relatedness, with connection and commonality the whole point. This is a dimension of the "new civil religion" that separates it from received notions. On a level more related to the media, though, is the simple fact that the experience is, in the first instance, one that is experienced through the media. 9/11 was instantaneous, real, and visual. In a long and established line of such events, a "priesthood" of media figures, including reporters and anchors, held important roles in the experience, conveying important ideas about its meaning and providing a narrative of its unfolding across time. As Dayan and Katz point out, this is a well-established and long-accepted role, where conventional practices and expectations are suspended for the sake of a larger purpose.[47] The ritual vocabularies through which the media narrate events like 9/11 have become complex, routine, and conventional. While a detailed study from this perspective remains to be done, there is evidence of one important element of these conventionalized media narratives in Linenthal's accounts of the Oklahoma City bombing. Too quickly, he notes, voices in the media began to speak of "healing" and "closure." Whereas it can be argued that such violence can never truly be healed, Linenthal contends, newspaper columnists, television anchors and reporters all began talking of closure for the events.[48] "Closure" and "the healing process" (a term heard frequently in the local television coverage of the Columbine massacre) are concerns of a priesthood oriented toward conventionalized rituals more than they are concerns of journalists covering a process that might never (as Linenthal argues) come to closure.

In Oklahoma City, at Columbine, and near the World Trade Center, Pentagon, and Western Pennsylvania sites, the "democratic" claiming of a role in commemoration involved the physical claiming of a location, typically a fence.[49] Fences surrounding the World Trade Center site and a nearby church became the sites of spontaneous shrines filled with the objects of the "vocabulary of memorialization." Flags, poems, teddy bears, news clippings, posters, banners, clothing, and more conventional paraphernalia including candles and wreaths covered the site. Many of these came from outside the US, a testament to the global nature of the events.

The notion that there is an evolving trajectory of such commemoration is supported by the seeming emergence of such practices in smaller, more localized events. For example, a tragic murder of a young shop attendant in my home town stimulated a familiar response. Within hours of the news, a spontaneous shrine appeared at the storefront where the killing occurred. It grew and developed over the coming days, and contained many of the familiar elements of the "public vocabulary of mourning" we've been talking about: flowers, teddy bears, poems, etc.[50]

The intermixture of the media-experienced and the direct relationship to the events invokes ideas about the nature of media experience that ring true with the evolving perspective we have been describing here. Media sociologist John Thompson speaks of "mediated quasi-interaction" where communication mediates between audience experience and events. Thompson intends to refer to the experience of day-to-day life more than to such singular events as 9/11, but his description is still apt.

> For many individuals whose life projects are rooted in the practical contexts of their day-to-day lives, many forms of mediated experience may bear a tenuous connection to their lives: they may be intermittently interesting, occasionally entertaining, but they are not the issues that concern them the most. But individuals also draw selectively on mediated experience, interlacing it with the lived [direct] experience that forms the connective tissue of their daily lives.[51]

Mediated civil rituals of commemoration and mourning can be described as a particular case of what Thompson describes. Seeing events like 9/11 as powerful and systematic themes and texts ordering media content and practice, we can see their reception, consistent with the picture Thompson paints, as a negotiation between their interests and experiences on the one hand, and events that almost demand response on the other. These must be, at the same time, integrated into their daily lives. The outpouring of objects and actions that followed 9/11 is evidence of such motivations and negotiations, and in a way just the "tip of the iceberg" of ritual actions tied to the mediated events. As an example, a local reporter wrote of her family's experiences and reactions to 9/11 very much in ritual terms, and in terms that speak to the existence of evolving, consensual, and larger modes of ritualization surrounding the event.

> In the past few weeks, there have been many more folded hands and bowed heads around the nation's dinner tables. I know that has been the case at our house. We've clasped hands and stumbled through prayers because we aren't sure what else to do. The horror of the terrorist attacks in New York City and Washington is beyond our scope. Our words are feeble, but they tumble out along with our tears. I lit two candles, one to represent the families torn apart by violence, the other to remind us that God mourns with us. I explained the significance of the candles to my son and husband and took myself by surprise. How did I know that? What was I thinking about? Yet, I kept going, pushed by faith I often question.[52]

It is significant in this account that conventional religion and religious doctrine is nearly absent. Moved to action, this family finds solace in references to God in the context of a more fundamental invented ritual of commonality and oneness with victims and the rest of the nation. As with many, this writer found herself pushed in the direction of religious faith, but at the same time moved to engage in ritualization directed toward coming to terms with the tragedy as a civil, not a religious, event. The mediated experience brought the power and the horror and the loss of the events home, and people in their homes were moved to respond.

Some of our interviewees described their experiences around 9/11 in similar terms. Paula Wilcox lives in a major western city with her mother, Molly, and her daughter, Denise.[53] When interviewed soon after the attacks, they initially express a sense of distance from the events.

Paula: We watched the beginning of it and now I just think it's gotten to the point where it's too much.
Interviewer: Too much, how so, in what way?
Molly: Well, they're repeating everything. So you've already seen everything. If something new happens, then I want to watch it. But I don't want to watch all the repeat[ing].
Paula: I personally don't like to hear – I mean if it happened to me, I wouldn't want to be on TV. I wouldn't want to have anyone watching me and hearing about my sorrow and stuff. And I don't enjoy watching other people suffer. And so watching everybody talk about how bad they're suffering is just not something for me to watch. There's so much suffering in the world and I don't want to sit and watch it over and over again. I mean it's not that I don't feel for them. It's not something that I want to watch.

We might expect, then, that the Wilcox family would avoid the kind of integration into ritual surrounding 9/11 that we've been talking about. They have seen a great deal of coverage (indeed, this interview took place within a week of the events) and have well understood the level of suffering experienced by those directly involved. When asked if they did participate in any ritualizations, it turns out they did.

Paula: Denise and I did some stuff. Like on the Internet, some people sent stuff about it. Like, at this time you're supposed to go out and light a candle. We did that. School – I don't think the grammar school that they do current events and stuff like that. They don't make a big deal of it.

The Wilcox family then commemorated the event in their own way. They were not overly involved; they did not travel to New York or send gifts or objects to victims. They seemed rather unconnected, yet, at the same time, they did invest some time and energy in a specific ritual act – lighting a candle at an appropriate time and – significantly – in conjunction with a larger shared ritual co-ordinated through the Internet. This seems like a small and insignificant thing. But against the larger backdrop, they participated in a direct way in a ritualization, on their own time, in their own home. Older traditions of civil religion never contemplated a level of private action of that order. Another of our interviewees, Megan Sealy, who we met in Chapter 8, reported a similar motivation to action. She and her son, Dell, put a flag on their car and donated money to the Red Cross. In addition, Megan recalled,

> Well, I went to church because they would have noontime prayers for people in New York and for their families. . . . I went just to feel that I was doing something, trying to make things better.

Jim Vowski illustrates the extent to which the lived and mediated experience of 9/11 is imprinted both across time, and as a moment that interrupted time and has led to new ways of thinking and acting – a definitive moment. Jim lives in the suburbs of a large western city with his wife, Sarah, age 41, and their son, Jake, 18, and daughter, Brenna, 13.[54] They attend an Evangelical megachurch regularly, and it is their main place of social contact and engagement. Both Jim and Sarah are employed full-time. As this interview was taking place in the fall some years after 9/11, the Interviewer asked Jim in his individual interview about his and his family's commemorations of the attacks. Jim and his family did participate in a small way in the one-year anniversary commemorations, but did little else. At the same time, he seems to have been moved by the events in the same way that Paula Wilcox and Megan Sealy were.

Interviewer: Yeah. After 9/11 there were a lot of media commemorations. Did you do anything to commemorate the one-year anniversary?
Jim: Only the minute of prayer. We did it. The whole nation was supposed to do it on the anniversary. That was the only thing.
Interviewer: Did you watch any of the coverage?
Jim: No.
Interviewer: Have you done anything to commemorate since?
Jim: No.
Interviewer: Okay.
Jim: If you really want to know, that [9/11] was, again, God's hand. We did a lot afterwards, praying for those families, and what a heinous thing. I get up and go to work in the morning, and all the sudden, I'm just gone. So, that way, we prayed for the families and try to lean in for the family and kept them in our hearts for quite a while and that sort of idea. . . .

While Jim does not specifically wish to dwell on it spiritually or religiously, or think that the nation should, he does see it as an incident that carried important "lessons" for the nation, thus confirming a sense that it was a defining event, even for Jim. And, Jim clearly sees it to be in a line of mediated events stretching back to the JFK assassination.

> So, no, that day will always live with me, but no different than probably than – I can remember being a very small boy and my mother running in to the room and telling John Kennedy had been shot. Even at that time, I didn't know who JFK was, but then later, seeing all the stuff on TV, then as a small boy, I realized who he was then. So, that will be another mark in time that way, and, again, the Lord, personally, I just thought . . . and this is the way I believe, and I told Sarah after 9/11, we're going to see much more feel good movies. And that's a natural reaction, and so is that so bad? I mean it's bad those people in that situation, but God took them to heaven, so they're in a better place than we can ever imagine, and back here is where we've got to learn from this act and how to grow and how to be better people.

Interestingly, Jim's sense of the significance of the 9/11 events echo some of the religious critiques domestically and from "abroad."

> Osama bin Laden did it and organized it, but God allowed him to do it. Did he allow them to do it, so this nation could be humbled, and say, enough of this sickness on TV, enough of this raping and pillaging, CEOs getting paid 2 billion dollars and the employees can't get a 30 cent raise, you know, to all this heinous unevenness that we seem to think we are above and beyond, that we don't have any of that in this country, and, personally, I think our country is running rampant

Thus, Jim's experience of the 9/11 attacks describes its outlines as a definitive ritual of commemoration and mourning. The event and the experience were unique and galvanic, and are something that he cannot put out of his mind. He links them with the trajectory of such events and experiences, stretching back through history. He felt motivated to commemorate them with his family, and evoked reflection on the meaning of those relationships. The events evoked ritual acts, even a year later, but more importantly were a liminal moment of reflection and criticism. They were also linked very much to a set of common discourses and debates about their political and moral significance.

If I am right, the components of this emerging civil religion of commemoration and mourning involve both media practice and "real-life" practice. A set of conventions of media coverage of events like 9/11 has emerged, with journalists taking roles that link them personally and morally to the events, and at the same time function to narrate the experience for the broader public. The mediation of the events connected people to them in ways that gave the events a sense of reality and instantaneity. The unique horror of the events gave them a particular power to motivate action. The actions moved in the direction of finding commonality and connection rather than of crafting narratives of triumph or transcendence. The unique facticity of the experience further motivated people in disparate locations remote from the events to take ritual action, even actions as trivial as lighting candles and attending prayer services. The nature and extent of the evolution of these cultural forms will no doubt continue to evolve. What is clear, though, is that the events of 9/11 provided a unique and particular moment of interaction between ideas of religion and practices of the media.

The other component of this evolving tradition of course involves the formal structuration of the coverage of such events. While, as I have said, it is beyond the scope of this book to undertake a detailed analysis, there is much evidence that those responsible for providing and narrating such events do, in fact, move to a level of participation, almost a priestly role. As Dayan and Katz note, they "suspend their normal critical stance and treat their subject with respect, even awe."[55] They certainly did in 9/11. A particularly profound example, and one that connects the context of production with the context(s) of consumption by erasing the proscenium that is usually interposed between production and audience, comes from Public Broadcasting's flagship evening news program *The Newshour with Jim Lehrer*. On their 19 September 2001 program, they covered a photographic exhibition mounted in Greenwich Village called "Here is New York." The exhibition was composed of photographs of the events of 9/11 and its aftermath, and the gallery where it appeared was selling prints as a fund-raising project to support relief and rebuilding efforts in the city.[56] At the end of the news report, anchor Jim Lehrer introduced a photomontage of images from the exhibition, accompanied by the haunting vocal "Evening Falls . . . " by the New Age diva Enya.

The result was an intensely moving meditation on the meaning of the events. The implicit spirituality and religiosity could not be avoided. At a key moment in the montage, where the Enya track modulates and swells, with an organ becoming the featured instrument, the images showed first a picture of a blown-out window, cropped so that a cruciform shape revealed a scene of destruction behind, and that faded to an image of a cemetery with the smoldering city behind, and other formal funerary scenes. I have shown this video during lectures on a number of occasions, and it never fails to bring an emotional response. It is very powerful, and is deeply linked to the events in a way that only the medium of television can be. That it was also powerful to the *Newshour* audience was evidenced by the fact that the program replayed it, over a month later, introduced by Lehrer this way: "And now, an encore presentation. We first aired this report on September 19. We've had many requests to see it again, and so we are re-airing it tonight. Ray Suarez has the story."[57] The story ended again with the video elegy. It stands as a powerful example of the way that media and media experience can connect with audiences and publics through events like 9/11, and that an expectation now exists, on the part of both media professionals and audiences, that practices of commemoration are part of the business of the media.

The shared experiences of the 9/11 events are a marker in cultural and media history not just because of the sheer significance of the events, but also because they brought into relief the ways that media experience is integrated into both public and daily life. As we saw, they were huge and transcendent in their significance, but also small and local in their consequence and in what they called individuals to do and to think. They served to erase the proscenium that is presumed to exist between audiences and media. They were not a watershed in this regard because, as we have seen and I have argued, that barrier has long since become negotiable in reflexive late modernity. But they did motivate us to new ways of thinking and acting. It is possible to speculate that the fact that Glenn Donegal, who we met in Chapter 4, was motivated to move outside his own frame of reference to seek out information or material about "other faiths" signals a new post-9/11 consciousness of otherness and difference. We have seen that many of our informants (and other studies have shown[58]) turn to media for information and ideas that transcend their traditional sources and contexts of religious and spiritual meaning. That is the essence of the seeking sensibility as applied to media. In a post-9/11 world, such practices support the possibility of awareness and possibly understanding, something that many felt they lacked before the tragic events.

In a larger sense, though, it is important to understand that the media do carry the implication that some kinds of common experiences and common ideas can be and are made available. On a fundamental level, it may be a condition of mediated modernity that the question is not so much how discrete communities understand each other, but about how the global mediascape presents both difference and commonality to us all.[59]

Media, religion, and politics

The November 2004 US General Elections were widely anticipated and subjected to more scrutiny than any in recent memory. The facts of a closely divided electorate, the emergence of digital media as important in political discourse and coverage, an ongoing and controversial war, and the contested nature of the 2000 election, all served to heighten interest in the contest. As I noted earlier, though, the election was also unique in the attention devoted to religion by the campaigns and the media. Early in the cycle, stories about the "religion gap" began to surface, and a seemingly confused press had some difficulty moving beyond a rather superficial reading of the situation. Clearly, Evangelicalism found a place at the table in the second Bush administration in an unprecedented way. Press coverage, however, showed a tendency to emphasize Evangelical influence in a kind of self-fulfilling way, concentrating on some of the most powerful "social issues" that linked Evangelicals and conservative Catholics, primarily abortion and gay marriage. In a National Public Radio commentary eight months before, Daniel Schorr had predicted the significance of religion in the upcoming contest, and illustrated the range of ways, from concrete to metaphoric, that "religion" might be read as an element of political discourse.

> "I believe in an America where the separation between church and state is absolute." That was presidential candidate John Kennedy before an association of Protestant ministers in Houston in 1960 assuring them that being a Catholic would not affect his policies. I doubt whether a candidate would speak with such secular absolutism today when religion has become a familiar part of campaigning. President Bush has spoken of his religious journey starting in 1986, when he gave up drinking and committed his heart to Jesus Christ. Before him, there had been President Reagan, who spoke in almost prophetic terms of the Soviet Union as "the evil empire."[60]

Consistent with many commentators, Schorr referred to a time when religion was assumed to be outside the bounds of political discourse. An "elephant in the room," in the 1960 election, it had been taken off the table by Kennedy's strong affirmation of secularism. To Schorr and many others, the 2004 election had changed that, and religion would more and more be part of the mix.

In the end, religion was not just part of the discourse; it was taken to have made the difference in the election. While any of the various components of the Bush coalition could be said to have played the critical role, a higher turnout of Evangelicals and voters who listed "moral values" as their primary motivation for voting was widely looked to as the most significant difference between the 2000 and 2004 plebiscites. Twenty-two percent of those responding to exit polls identified values as their top concern, compared with 20 percent who listed the economy. The prominence of religion and values may have been an artifact of the polling, but the underlying reality of a deepening and strengthening relationship between religion and politics seems to have become a fact of political life in the US.

Nicholas Kristof summed up some of the prevailing concerns about this turn of events in a *New York Times* Column.

I'm not denigrating anyone's beliefs. And I don't pretend to know why America is so much more infused with religious faith than the rest of the world. But I do think that we're in the middle of another religious Great Awakening, and that while this may bring spiritual comfort to many, it will also mean a growing polarization within our society.

But mostly, I'm troubled by the way the great intellectual traditions of Catholic and Protestant churches alike are withering, leaving the scholarly and religious worlds increasingly antagonistic. I worry partly because of the time I've spent with self-satisfied and unquestioning mullahs and imams, for the Islamic world is in crisis today in large part because of a similar drift away from a rich intellectual tradition and toward the mystical. The heart is a wonderful organ, but so is the brain.[61]

Implicit in much of the debate about the religiosity of the American electorate in 2004 are two notions that are significant to our concerns here. First is the idea that religion is somehow irreconcilable with the rational processes of politics, and, second, that the particular religiosity that is typical of the new emerging segment of the electorate responsible for Bush's victory was conservative and, in Kristof's terms, reactionary and self-satisfied. I don't wish to engage in a moral argument here about the nature of the religious politics that seem to be emerging. Rather, I want to reflect on some of the claims being made by proponents and critics of this emerging religious politics in light of the role that media may play. It may be that neither view is fully descriptive of the situation as people make political choices in the contexts of their private lives. Each view contemplates a normative role for religion in politics, with those who celebrate the conservative turn on issues like abortion and gay marriage seeing this as a return to morality, and those who lament the trends concerned about the emergence of a "theocracy" that will necessarily overwhelm the diversity of opinion contemplated by a constitution that sought to be neutral on the question of religion.

One conservative voice raised a concern about these trends in the aftermath of the election. Joe Loconte of the Heritage Foundation pointed to an earlier tradition in American politics where religious leaders like Reinhold Niebuhr and Martin Luther King, Jnr, stood above the political fray. Current religious leadership seems to have lost that distance, he contends:

today, much of the religious right marches in lockstep with the Republican Party, while the religious left functions like an echo chamber for the Democrats. Christian conservatives join Republicans to mobilize against gay marriage, but don't muster great interest in families at risk in the inner city. They seem to like the Bush administration's economic policies, but offer little criticism of corporate scandals or President Bush's record on affordable health care. Before the election, Pat Robertson even claimed that God told him President Bush would win handily. "It doesn't make any difference what he does, good or bad," Robertson said, "God picks him up because he's a man of prayer."[62]

Loconte levels similarly specific criticism at religious leaders on the left who seem unable to distance themselves from Democratic Party politics. Pointing to examples of religious voices that vex politics because they do not easily fit into one camp or the other, Loconte concludes,

> Jewish philosopher Abraham Joshua Heschel once described a prophet as "a person whose life and soul are at stake in what he says, who can perceive the silent sigh of human anguish." Many of today's religious leaders don't discern that silent sigh because they can't seem to escape the din of political rhetoric. They camouflage their partisanship with piety, and like the Biblical character Esau, sell their birthright for a bowl of soup.[63]

The election post-mortems thus described an emerging public script hypothesizing a trend in relations between religion and politics. The momentum out of the election clearly seemed to be with the religious conservatives, who helped the Republicans retain the White House (though, as in 2000, by a small percentage margin). Their influence was thought to be rooted in conservative leaders' supposed power to control large swaths of the electorate and hold the keys to power for the Republican Party. At the same time, though, there were and are doubts on the left and the right about this scenario, and, in an important way, the media are at the center of some of these doubts. Many of the most prominent conservative religious leaders are prominent because of their media presence. *Christianity Today*, the influential Evangelical magazine, raised questions about this situation in an article in the spring of 2005. Wondering who influences the Evangelicals that are now influencing politics, the author, Ted Olsen, noted that the most influential leaders were not necessarily the ones who are most prominent in the media.

> *New York Times* columnist David Brooks came early to the fight, challenging fellow journalists to stop quoting Jerry Falwell and Pat Robertson. "There is a world of difference between real-life people of faith and the made-for-TV, Elmer Gantry-style blowhards who are selected to represent them," he said.
> Evangelicals agree. A spring 2004 poll from PBS's *Religion and Ethics Newsweekly* found that only 23 percent of self-described evangelicals had "warm or positive feelings" toward Falwell – the same

percentage they gave "pro-choice groups." Robertson scored higher, at 34 percent, but still lower than labor unions (36%) and far below Pope John Paul II (44%) and James Dobson (40%).

The real spokesperson for evangelicalism, said Brooks, is John Stott, who is "always bringing people back to the concrete reality of Jesus' life and sacrifice."[64]

Olsen laments the situation of undue influence by figures like Robertson and Falwell, echoing long-standing elite ideas about the nature of authority in the media age.

> But the kind of gospel that Joe Disciple follows, how he communicates his faith, what emphases he puts in his life are increasingly determined by a media diet of both sacred and secular victuals.
>
> In a sense, Robertson and Falwell get quoted in papers and booked on talk shows because they get quoted and booked on talk shows: Rolodexes don't get cleaned out very often. But they also get booked because they're quick with the quote: they help to feed an omnivorous media machine hungry for thoughts (or lack thereof) condensable into a dozen words that will make one side or another angry.[65]

The interviews we've seen here can help address these concerns raised about the emerging role of religion in American politics. We began the project of this book by intending to test a notion very like the concern raised by Olsen over the way that the media diet might relate to religious and spiritual understanding. In the process, we've heard from people from across the religious and spiritual spectrum about the ways they integrate their spiritual, religious, and media lives. We've wanted to view these relationships in a way that contrasts with Olsen's assumptions. While he, and others, are quick to assume that media can influence the way people are religious and spiritual, we've wanted to be open to the possibility that media and religion/spirituality can influence each other in the making of the meanings and identities through which we live our lives. Media celebrity may be pragmatic, even capricious, but should we fear that those logics (or lack thereof) become the determining factor?

In a larger sense, too, Olsen's concerns deserve some analysis and reflection (and not just because they are so widely shared). If, indeed, the current religious/political alignment is skewed in the direction of conservative (Evangelical and conservative Catholic) ideas, should we be concerned with the seeming entropic circularity implicit here? That is, is it a problem that the source of religious authority that is influencing important aspects of public policy is itself authoritative because of its public mediation, not because of its rootedness in fundamental and consensual ideas that are authentic to the religious cultures for which it seems to speak? In a sense, this is a moral, ethical, and religious question that must be answered in other ways and contexts. But, because media are involved and mediation is thought to be such an important part of the equation, there are some things we can say, based on our explorations in this book.

First and foremost, there seem to be more commonalities than there are differences among various religious biographies in the way they use media. So, what we say of Evangelicals we are likely also to say of Catholics and metaphysical seekers and liberal Protestants in these regards. Second, one of the most consistent things we have found about the way people use media in their religious and spiritual self-narratives is that they treat the media as a resource in relation to other aspects and influences in their lives. I quoted John Thompson earlier on this point. The people we've heard from selectively integrate media into the warp and woof of their lives. This was true, we saw, even of the households that thought of themselves as motivated by religious or spiritual values in their media consumption. Third, it is clear that the decline in the authority of religious institutions pervades what we have seen. The historic claims of church, sect, doctrine, and history no longer hold the sway they once did. Instead, they are part of the array of symbols, traditions, and values that people bring together in their own way into narratives that make sense for them, located as they are.

Fourth, perhaps the most powerful and consistent thing we've seen is the nearly universal belief among our interviewees that it is they, themselves, who must be the final arbiter of belief and value in their own lives. They do not wish to be seen to surrender to the media, or indeed to any external authority, the right to make decisions for them. This is most obvious as they talk about how to make decisions about media rules. Behind rules is the sense that it makes a difference what kind of things they and their children watch, listen to, and do. The values in those things are important to our interviewees, and they want to make decisions about what is right and proper. But, they do not look to others to make those decisions for them. They must make them themselves. More tellingly, perhaps, it is nearly universal among our interviews that children must be brought to make those decisions for themselves, as well. Few of our parents wanted to be seen to be restricting their older children's viewing to protect them from things they should not see (younger children were a different matter). The appropriate way to think of media, if I can sum it up simply, is as a cultural resource that is inevitable, even necessary, and that it is up to us to make our own decisions about it.

Fifth, what I have said about relations between "religious" and "secular" media and the potential for "crossing over" is also important here. Many of our born-again interviewees lived on both maps. They consumed both religious and secular material, and there is a sense in which the secular is the definitive media context. As we observed in many of those cases, there is a salience, even attraction, to such media, including things that are thought of as "guilty pleasures." Thus, it might not particularly matter to our born-again believers what a Robertson or Falwell thinks or says. In fact, it was common among our interviewees to regard televangelism with some derision. Religious authority seemed to yield to a range of mediated sources that people use and integrate. This tends to extend to clerical authority in general. Few of our interviewees wanted to leave it even to their own pastor or priest or rabbi or imam or shaman to decide these things for them.

Ultimately, it is, as we assumed in our earlier chapters, the "self" that is the place where things are authoritatively brought together. It is up to the individual, our interviewees believe, to make sense of the world, to draw on resources of memory, tradition, belief, family, school, place-of-worship, and media culture to craft a sense of themselves that works and functions in contemporary life. We saw very little in our interviews that would suggest the kind of ideologically determining role implicit in some of the concerns and criticisms we've heard and seen. The linkage between media, belief, and behavior (political or otherwise) is not as direct and instrumental as we might fear, at least based on our inquiries here.

What we may be seeing is a situation much closer to the normative one called for by Joe Loconte. At least in terms of their intentions and ideal selves, our interviewees do not see necessary linkages between religion and authority in either the social or political spheres. They lead complicated lives, where a variety of pressures, influences, sources of insight, values, and symbols come into play on a daily basis. The world around them changes and they must find ways to evolve with it. They do not think of themselves as "blank slates" onto which religious or political discourses are written. Instead, they are consumers and users of such discourses, contending with the competing claims of various contexts and voices.

An example of the complex negotiation between belief, politics, media, culture, and values that ensues comes from our interview with Doreen Richards. The issue of gay marriage (and gay rights more generally) came to rival abortion as the fundamental-values issue in the 2004 election. Most observers and commentators, looking at the big picture, would assume a rather easy and facile connection between conservative religiosity and attitudes about gay rights, which would be reflected, or even influenced, by media reception. Doreen showed us that things are not nearly so simple. She is a 55-year-old who lives in the suburbs of a major midwestern rust-belt city with her husband, Marvin, and the last of their five adopted children. She describes herself as a devout and traditional Catholic.[66]

During the interview, Doreen revealed that, while she does not generally like reality shows, she has seen a number of them, and she and the Interviewer engaged in a discussion of the genre. The one reality program she does like and watch regularly is *Queer Eye for the Straight Guy*, where five gay men perform a "makeover" on a straight man, including clothing, personal grooming, and general living arrangements and lifestyle. The Interviewer asks:

Interviewer: Okay. How do you reconcile *Queer Eye for the Straight Guy* and your Catholicism?

Doreen: Oh, I have a hard time with this. You know we all have Catholic guilt and I'm a . . . not like a fallen-away Catholic. I'm not shaken in my faith by the priests and their little go-arounds with young boys and I think they should be punished and the Church was wrong in hiding it. My actual Catholic faith has kept me going. My God, look at all I've been through with the kids I had, my heart, my cancer. So my Catholic faith is the foothold of my life. I'm not too sure, though. Boy, this is hard. Homosexuality is a hard thing for me because in my professional life I've known several homosexuals and in my personal life. And I have never met one that has been offensive, abusive to me, ummm . . . anything but up and up. None of the ones I know have ever tried to hide it and they have all been very good people doing all very good things in their lives. Now, I know there are some really pathetic queers around but fine, there are pathetic human beings who are straight people. So, I have a hard time for the homosexuals I know, I have a hard time believing that God will condemn them to Hell and so . . . I have to put that. . . . There are several points in my life that I have to put into a little pocket somewhere and not try to justify it because I can't. But I just don't feel that I should, I don't know, gays don't bother me. They never have.

On one level, this is an intriguing demonstration of how social change occurs. The gradual connection Doreen has had with gay co-workers and others in her own life has begun to erode some of the suspicions she may once have held. It also demonstrates how the interview moment often brings people to articulations of senses of themselves and their place in the web of social relations that may be new or evolving. She clearly struggles with received preconceptions (derived both from social and religious contexts) about acceptance of homosexuality, and at the same time realizes the ways that such conceptions run up against what may be a more basic value – that of acceptance and tolerance.

On another level, it shows how the media do function to express (and perhaps enforce) trends and values in the larger culture. Doreen's expressed ideas about homosexuality may derive in some measure from her direct and personal experience, but *Queer Eye* may provide her with a broader context and more to think about. Alongside the more formal contexts of discourse about gay rights, such as in the political sphere, her interaction with the program provides important resources for understanding and action. It is not yet a settled matter for her, obviously, but she clearly wants to come to terms with an interpretation of things with which she is comfortable, one that accounts for competing claims and experiences.

Doreen's experience illustrates an important way that concrete and fundamental issues in the political sphere may enter lived experience through the media. It also demonstrates how people in various social and cultural locations and of certain values "types" can interact with these interventions. The larger picture of religion and politics in the post-9/11 and post-2004 election worlds may seem firm, determined, and predictable. We need to remember, though, that that picture is made up of people like Doreen, and our other informants, who through their motivations and their actions may not behave in the predicted ways. In particular, the easy assumptions that are often made about the relationship between politics, religion, and media need to be thought through more carefully.

I started this chapter by suggesting that we needed to address some questions in the larger social and political context. In a way, I could not present a study of religion and media, at this point in history, without looking into the events of 9/11 and the new and evolving relations between religion and politics. The study did not, of course, intend to address these issues; they occurred while the research interviews were underway, and people's reactions to 9/11 and to religious/political debates became part of our conversations. The fact that they did occur enables us to see some things about how the larger system of relations between media culture and political culture works in the lives and experiences of audiences. I've argued that we need to understand the relationship between religion and media culture in the context of media practice and, consistent with important theoretical resources in the media field, the ways that media practice interacts with and relates to other aspects of people's lives and experiences. We've seen how the experience of 9/11 and the questions of religious politics entered these narratives of self and did so both through the media and through non-media experiences and contexts. Further, we've seen that the way these things were made sense of involved a negotiation on behalf of the self of meanings and narratives directed at that task. Some of these are more successful than others. Some make more sense to us, as observers, than others. What is clear, though, is that we need to understand these things as complex negotiations worked out in these lives as much as determined or fixed values or claims that determine belief or action. We'll consider these issues again, along with a more general assessment of the prospects of religion and religious meaning-making in the media age in the next chapter.

Chapter 10

Conclusion

What is produced?

We began this study of the relations between religion and the media intending to address the ways that the media age has come to condition the practice and meaning of religion in late modernity. From that rather broad-sounding mandate, we narrowed our focus to what I argued was a question prior to the many others that might have been asked. Before we could look at the big picture of religious meaning, spiritual symbolism, religious and spiritual traditions, religious institutions, religious education, and the relationship of religion to national and global politics, it seemed to me that we should first look at how people, as media consumers and media audiences, access, interact with, and make sense of mediated religion. In this concluding chapter, I'd like to sum up the major things we've found, and, in a tentative way, suggest some of the implications of what we've found for these, and other, "larger" questions.

In part, this exploration has been based on narrowed expectations. To get to the (presumably) "fundamental" level of actual media practice, we've had to adjust our perspective away from the global to the local, and from the broad spectrum of potential "effects" of media and religion on one another to the more precise means, moments, and ways by which "the media" become important or meaningful in religious and spiritual ways. The reasons for this narrowing involve both the conceptual challenges of defining when and where we think this might be happening, and the methodological challenges of actually studying these interactions. For reasons we discussed in detail in Chapter 4, we have moved to detailed discussions with a range of individuals, families, and households, the fruits of which I've presented in the previous four chapters. We've looked at those accounts for evidence of the ways people are integrating media experience into what I've called their "plausible narratives of the self," conceiving of the question of identity as being an important marker of the relationships we're interested in. These "narratives," as I've said, have not been the goal of our inquiries, but instead part of the "raw material," or data, out of which we have developed evidence of the relations we are interested in.

As a fundamentally *sociological* project, our study has wanted to look to the contexts, influences, and consequences of the relationship between media and religion in the material spheres of cultural and social life. It has been my argument that, to do so, we must look at things very concretely and directly in the social sphere. Fortunately, a set of methods of social and cultural analysis is available that has aided us in our inquiries. As we begin to assess what we have found, we will discover that our findings are more directly relevant to some questions than they are to others. Meanings, consequences, or effects in the social spheres where we have been looking will of course be the most directly implicated by what we have found. That does not prevent us, though, from informed speculation about other spheres as well. What follows, then, is a discussion of what we have seen and heard in our inquiries. Some of what we will say directly addresses issues and concerns that we considered as part of the justification for this study. Other things – and they are some of the most provocative and intriguing things we've found – emerge from the study itself.

The ubiquity of media

Across all the interviews and observations, from a variety of contexts and perspectives (social, religious, ethnic, and otherwise), no other single thing seems so universal as the sense of the ubiquity, pervasiveness, or inescapability of the media. From household to household and interview to interview, all share in common an assumption – even an expectation – that the media are universal and "taken for granted." They are the *lingua franca* and the common ground of contemporary social and cultural experience and practice. Numerous previous studies have arrived at the same conclusion, showing, among other things, that the media condition the structuration and tempo of daily life, and the norms, languages, and contexts of social and cultural discourse.

The pervasiveness of media is, further, something that is often reflexively engaged in the accounts we have seen. For an example, in Chapter 7 Jan Van Gelder lamented the power and pressure that the media seem to exert on her home life, in spite of hers being a family that has taken concrete steps to limit their role. Across our interviews, parents have felt this pervasiveness and ubiquity most keenly. The media, including television, film, popular music, and – increasingly – personal media and hand-held devices, are at the center of youth culture today, and their influence seems to stretch across a range of social domains, from the structuring of time, to the provision of common cultural idioms and the topics of conversation through which broader social discourse takes place.

What is most significant to our explorations here is that the media are also pervasive in the homes of those who – for religious or other reasons – we might have expected to exercise the most "control" over them. In fact, in such homes (the Millikens in Chapter 6, for example) what is distinct is their sense that they have to *do something* about the media, not the fact of the presence of media in the home in the first place. This is the important point here. It is commonplace to think of contemporary US cultural and social life as "media saturated." We all know how prominent media have become in our lives, and the range of media available in the home continues to grow exponentially. What is interesting here is that those families who we would expect to be the "outliers" in terms of their relationship to the media seem instead to accept this reality almost tacitly. We might ask, "What else are they to do?" Well, they could separate themselves, as others have done.[1] By and large they do not. Instead, they seem to accept the pervasiveness of media as a given, a "fact of life," and they proceed to negotiate with the situation. They do what John Thompson (quoted earlier) suggests that people do with media: they treat their relationship to media as a *mediation,* an interaction of ideas and experiences from media and ideas and experiences from daily life.

Further, they experience "the media" both as individual programs, services, and experiences, and as a "package." They understand on an experiential level the fact of life at this point in the development of media in the West – the concentration and cross-media interaction of these industries. On another level, however, they have a tendency to see "the media" as a kind of monolithic force. They relate to individual programs individually, and often with a degree of personal pleasure or salience, but see "the media" as a whole as a different matter.

This sense of the ubiquity and pervasiveness of media is consistent, as we noted earlier, with ideas from David Gauntlett and Annette Hill, and from Sonia Livingstone, among others, about the ways that the media are now integrated into daily life. They are, in a way, a settled matter. No matter what we might want to think about their implications or effects, they are now an accepted part of domestic space, and have become, in a way, "transparent," to use Livingstone's term. As I said earlier, there is a sense in which the "accounts of media" we have encountered here are a measure of this process of integration. I would argue that the fact that such "accounts" still exist and hold sway – that they are in fact important publicly shared normative ideas – is a measure of their as-yet-incomplete integration. While we must accept on some level (as our interviewees nearly universally do here) that the media are now part of the fabric of daily, private, domestic (as well as public) life, we still lack the symbols and language we need to describe their role in anything like the normative terms that we use to describe the *gemeinschaft* of the idealized past. This is significant, apparently, as the past and ideas and symbols from the past play so prominently as our interviewees struggle to describe their ideals of values, spirituality, faith, family life, and the inter-relationships between these domains. The language of the past is powerful language, and the vocabularies of the past have yet to have been successfully adapted to incorporate the reality of the pervasive media.

This pervasiveness further seems to have achieved a kind of *continuity* in most of these homes. There is a "flow" to life as it has been described here, and the media play their role. They are markers of the patterns of daily life, and important markers of key moments (conversations) in the developing "moral economy" of the household.[2] They are the stuff of conversations within the family and beyond it. Media technologies are important markers and resources, part of the social and cultural inventory that helps establish the family's place in the web of social relations. At the same time, the media are not determinative of all that goes on. Unlike some previous work that assumed a central role for media in directing the flow of experience in private life,[3] in the households we've heard from here, the relationship between media and the rest of daily experience seems more *interactive*. As I have said, it is not an easy or a settled matter, but it is not a situation where the "flow" of life is in many ways the *media* "flow."

Media as "the common culture"

The media are not pervasive or ubiquitous only because of their physical or sociostructural location. They are also important in these accounts for what they convey: a "common culture" that is at one and the same time both challenging *and* alluring.[4] Its attraction arises from its presumed location at the center of the culture. The media are assumed to (and found to) represent symbols, events, and ideas that are both important and lodged in a broader social and cultural context. These interviewees seem to want to be part of that discourse. For the time being, at least, it seems that television, more than other media, is the embodiment of that cultural space. It remains to be seen whether this will continue to hold sway as the media evolve.[5]

Television's role as a conveyor of this common culture seems to work on three levels in these interviews. First, a number of our interviewees, as we noted in Chapters 6 and 7, treat the media – particularly television – *as a kind of "right" or "expectation."* As a particular example, we noted Jay Milliken's explanation for his television choices, "I can only get two or three channels" and he watches what is on *them*. This notion of "expectation" is evident in subtle ways across a wide range of the interviews. For example, parents who articulate clear ideas about the problems with the media and concerns about their children's attraction to media, un-selfconsciously report curling up to Jay Leno or David Letterman each night at another point in the interview.

The second level on which television, in particular, seems to function as a "common culture" lies in its capacity to convey *a common set of symbols, ideas, and languages*, elements that become part of a common cultural "currency."[6] The latest fads, trends, idioms, and icons can be found there, and through its news and entertainment programs – and increasingly through its "infotainment" – television increasingly tells us not necessarily "what to talk about," but "what is *being* talked about." Our interviewees expressed a sense of these relations as going on "out there," and of being important both for what they can tell us about what is going on, but also to keep us current on what everyone else is talking about, too. This notion of media as a set of "cultural currencies of exchange" is not a new idea, of course, but in the context of interviews that probed religion and spirituality as potential alternative contexts of meaning and value we might have expected to encounter views at some distance from the norm. We really did not. Instead, what we found was a *negotiation* between these assumed and taken-for-granted media-centered discourses and alternative values and ideals. The question is whether the "momentum" seems to be more with the media discourse or with the alternative (i.e. the religious or spiritual context). We'll return to this matter shortly.

The third level on which the "commonness" of media culture seems to operate is related to the capacities of the media to present *culturally relevant material in powerful and attractive ways*. In our discussion of interviewees' "experiences in" media, we noted that the motivations for a wide range of media choices among them were explainable simply by the tactile, sensorial, or other attractiveness of certain media. The media work in part because they are well-crafted, salient, and fitted to their time and place. We've tended to focus on the "guilty pleasures" we've encountered here in terms of the sources of the "guilt," but we need to remember that the real story is the "pleasure." Rachel Albert, a "born-again Christian" we met in Chapter 6, watched *X-Files* and *Star Trek*, programs that she clearly knew were at odds with her expressed religiosity. But, they were attractive, compelling, and absorbing for her in the same way they were for millions of others. These programs (and most others) work because they articulate and express important ideas and values that are in play in the culture. Rachel, and nearly everyone else we interviewed, was well aware of those discourses, and found some measure of involvement in them through her participation in television representations of them. Her willingness to include accounts of this practice in her narrative of self may be a measure of her quest to integrate ideas from both sources – the broader culture and her religious faith – into a coherent whole.

Among the ideas we considered in the early chapters was the notion of "dualism," and the idea that we could helpfully think of "religion" (or "faith" or "belief" or "spirituality") and "media" as separate and separable spheres. I speculated that we needed to move beyond such an idea because it was likely that, in the media age, media would be increasingly taking the role of providing religiously and spiritually meaningful resources. While there is evidence that that line is being crossed (discussed in more detail below) there may be ways in which separate spheres appear to exist, based on these interviews. One of those ways has to do with this idea of the "common culture." Some of our interviewees (particularly the "metaphysical believers and seekers" and "secularists") were readily able to conceive of religiously or spiritually significant things in the media. Some traditionalists felt this way, too. For others, though, such as Rachel, there is more of a "bright line" between cultural resources related to her faith and resources of the "broader culture." What is significant is that, even in cases like Rachel's, the resources of the "broader culture" hold sway, or are even in a way determinative. Once again, what seems to be happening is something that we predicted, based on our theoretical ruminations: that people would negotiate a plausible sense of self out of a range of resources.

Across many of our interviews, though, we got the sense that "the media" are, in a way, more "culturally" than "religiously" or "spiritually" meaningful. Most of them seemed to be able to reflexively position themselves, their faith, their values, the media, and the claims of the broader culture, and make decisions and choices accordingly. The media are religiously significant, but do not "replace religion," in this sense, for everyone in every case.

We should also note that this "common cultural" discourse plays a role in interactions within the household as well as beyond it. Just as individuals found value in the cultural currency they could access and express in interactions with friends, co-workers, and others, many of the families here also interacted around, and used, these resources for their own discourses in the household.

The practices we've been talking about here, rooted as they are in the logics of individual "selves" making sense out of a range of cultural resources, look very much like a kind of "postmodern" moment, where the fixed and determinative forms and shapes of society have given way to idiosyncrasy and solipsism. There is a lot of invention, play, and negotiation in these interviews. Interviewees seem to draw on a range of domains and ideas as they make sense of themselves and their lives. In some ways, it is difficult to find systematic themes, motivations, or outcomes in these accounts. Clear reference to social or cultural "truths" do not seem to determine meaning outcomes. Fundamental social or class interests are not readily on display (though they clearly lie behind much of what we've seen). Religious history or doctrine do not seem to play a major determinative role in the process. Clerical authority is not much of a factor. So, what are the central logics? What kind of systematic conceptions and ideas and values claims can we see?

This cultural-meaning level is one of the places where we can see the contrast we discussed earlier, between Giddens's ideas about the way that autonomous "selves" make systematic meanings directed at their perfection in the context of postmodernity, and Gergen's concerns about a cultural context that seems overwhelming and out of control. From what we've seen here, it may be that Gergen is overly pessimistic. The range of sources of cultural meaning experienced by these interviewees is, indeed, wide, even in the less advantaged households. The proliferation of television channels, the increasing ubiquity of the Web and Internet, and a range of other changes in the media marketplace have put the media at the center of this cacophony. At the same time, though, there is a certain logic and organization to what these "selves" are up to. And, the mediated "common culture" is an important element of this. Certainly, there is a lot that these people have to confront, contend with, and sift through. But they do make choices and do find ways of describing themselves to themselves and to us that make sense in their contexts, and a good deal of this is oriented toward what the broader culture looks at and values. At the same time, for many of these households ideas and resources out of the domain that has interested us the most – religion and spirituality – also provide markers and grounding. Whether this is adequate to stabilize the situation Gergen laments is beyond the scope of this study.

We can look at this situation from a different perspective by returning to one of our theoretical sources, pragmatism/Interactionism. I proposed that an Interactionist approach would conceive of these "narratives of self" as negotiations intended to make sense in certain contexts, but also to make sense in relation to broader claims, values, idioms, and meanings in the culture. Almost by definition, such accounts orient themselves to things that are common to the cultural context where they reside. A good deal of the material related to media in our narratives here is understandably in the category we've been calling "accounts of media" – that is, claims and conceptions about the role and positioning of the media and of media practice in the wider context of social and cultural values. At the same time, though, our interviewees clearly contend with important ideas that come to them *through* the media. The passage from Doreen Richards at the end of Chapter 9 is an example. In spite of what might have been a settled sense of social values concerning homosexuality, she connects with a salient program that has helped her (along with direct personal experience, of course) to begin to rethink some of these basic values.

Doreen's account could perhaps be read as an example of how the media in late modernity are serving to undermine fundamental social and cultural structures and values. At the same time, it seems more clearly to be an example of the evolution of values about an important social issue, expressed in the central location of the media, articulating with Doreen's own social experience and thus serving as a kind of grounding for her evolving beliefs. This is an example of how the "common" might be built out of the seeming "cacophony" of the culture. Doreen's interaction with her social context, and with the media, are serving to provide a standpoint through which she can come to understand her evolving self.

The unresolved issue here, of course, is whether we should be optimistic or pessimistic about this situation. There is reason to believe – against the argument that the postmodern condition lacks centers and standpoints and organizing logics – that there is a *centering* in the "common cultural" aspects of media experience. Among the lamentations about the late-modern condition is a concern about the emerging "identity politics" that increasingly define the political age. Religion has been identified as a major player in this regard. Religion, the argument goes, serves increasingly to provide alternative centers and sources of interests and insights, supporting an increasing atomization of the cultural center. The evidence here would suggest an alternative reading. Religion can and does provide such sources of centering and meaning, and our interviewees readily referred to its lessons and its value for them. At the same time, though, they also saw themselves as part of a larger mediated cultural discourse. This does not, of course, necessarily mean that there is a consensus (Glenn Donegal in Chapter 4 comes to mind), but it cannot be said that the religious conservatives among our interviewees, for example, are isolated at the margins of the culture. Like everyone else – as media audiences – they *participate* in that culture.[7]

Negotiations with media and culture

In Chapter 4, I argued for the narrative approach in this study, contending there that such narratives would provide a kind of heuristic through which we could see the interacting relations of media, religion, spirituality, and context as cultural resources to meaning-making. I further argued that there was value in making the question of "identity" the central organizing idea of this inquiry, because it would provide an occasion through which we could see these various elements coming together in the self-presentation of identity. As we've seen along the way, it has made sense to describe the process of meaning-making in these domains as a "negotiation" between often disparate ideas, contexts, and claims. And, in some ways, "disparate" is not quite the right word. In many cases, what we encountered was evidence of *contradictions* in these lives and these narratives, along with the ways that our interviewees were working to resolve them.

These negotiations are among the most interesting and helpful things we've encountered in our interviews. To a greater extent than we perhaps expected, our interviewees, in their narratives, express a level of *reflexive autonomy* in the way they construct these narratives of self. We clearly expected a level of reflexivity in these accounts. Giddens contends that this sense of positionality *vis-à-vis* culture is one of the most significant things about late-modern life. Further, based both on Giddens and on the "new-paradigm" religion scholarship, we'd anticipated that a level of autonomy would also be a factor.

Distinctions

Distinction seemed to be central to many of these accounts and negotiations. Positionality *vis-à-vis* the media is naturally an issue of distinction, and there is a good deal of literature in media studies focused on difference and distinction, and their social value. A number of significant distinctions were common among our interviewees.

Many of our interviewees, across a range of social and religious categories, agreed with the dominant "account of" media that the "screen media" are of lesser, or more questionable, value than other media.[8] Priscilla Castello, as we'll recall, made this explicit in Chapter 5. Television in particular, but all the "visual" media as well, are somehow suspect in a way that other media, such as books, are not. The one exception, of course, is film, with "serious" film being among the media that many of our interviewees found particularly meaningful spiritually and morally. There was a tendency in our interviews for those we called "metaphysical seekers," "mainstreamers," and "secularists" to hold this view of screen media. At the same time, though, there was broad agreement on books and the printed word being by far the preferred medium, particularly for children, in the opinion of parents.

Another interesting distinction is that, at the same time, most of our interviewees seemed to want to connect with what we might call "authentic" religious or spiritual sentiments and experiences when we raised the question of the media. We've observed how difficult it was for interviewees to make easy and unproblematic connections between these things. We used a variety of means to "get at" questions of spiritually meaningful media. Often, it was only after extended conversations that interviewees were able to describe such experiences. Most often, when they did it was music that they referred to, though there were also examples of films, books, and other resources. Examples from television were harder to come by, but some of the ones where television did come up were particularly interesting, such as the meaningfulness of *Andy Griffith* for at least two of our male informants reported here.[9]

Undoubtedly the distinction about "screen media" is, like other of these distinctions, a received "account of media" that is widely shared in the culture. As has been noted elsewhere,[10] it is common in educational and parenting discourse to derogate television and the visual media. It is not surprising that such opprobrium would also be applied to spiritually or religiously relevant media. The significance of film is a related "account of." Film has long since achieved a status in most elite circles as at least potentially a kind of "art," and is therefore assumed to be relevant to deeper levels of meaning. Music is not similarly situated, but it may be that music may actually be a mode that is simply particularly meaningful religiously and spiritually. Clearly one of the "repressed modes" of expression I noted earlier, music has long had a formal role in religious ritual and practice, but is also negotiable into nonformal and "implicit" settings. At least, that is the way it looks from the perspective of our interviews. An additional significant element, of course, is the fact that a political economy of popular religious music has arisen in recent years in the form of Contemporary Christian Music (CCM). As we saw, CCM was a very important source for many of our interviewees, particularly for young people in "born-again" households. The significance of music was not limited to them by any means, however.

Another important set of distinctions made by our interviewees was between themselves and "others out there." Not unlike the classic "third-person effect" in media studies,[11] many were able to identify themselves in regard to these questions by virtue of who they were *not*. Most parents, for example, saw themselves as distinct from other parents who did not exercise the right kind of influence over their children's media lives. More significant to our project here, though, were distinctions made with reference to religious values and attitudes regarding media. The most common of these were those among our "mainstream," "metaphysical seeker," and "secularist" cohorts who saw attitudes about media as an important marker of *religious* identification. Clearly referring to the commonly understood tendency for religious conservatives to be moralistic in their approach to media, and to be more concerned about "sex" than about "violence" in the media, a number took great pride in distinguishing themselves in this way. "We're not moralists," they seemed to be saying with pride, "and that is a way that we differ from religious conservatives." Some of our interviewees were particularly keen to make it clear that they cared more about "violence" on television than they did about "sex," again a way of clarifying where they reside on the religious-cultural turf. Interestingly, and consistent with what I said earlier about the "common culture" of the media, it did seem that both the "born-again Christians" or the "dogmatists" (the two categories that would presumably be the most conservative in this regard) were perhaps more concerned with "sex" than "violence," though not markedly so. One of the commonalities among the interviews in Chapters 6 and 7 was the seemingly shared parental concern with both sex *and* violence. But the interesting issue, in any case, is that the inferred attitude about media serves as a commonly understood marker of religious difference.

One of the most unexpected and fascinating of the distinctions we've seen is the almost universal derogation of "religious broadcasting" in these interviews. It was very common, in the first instance, that when interviewees found that we were interested in the relationship between media and religion, they'd assume that televangelism was the point. As the interviews progressed, we'd find that, in spite of knowing a good bit about some kinds of religious television, even our born-again and Evangelical interviewees would seek to distance themselves from that kind of media. Clearly, there is a level of social opprobrium attached to televangelism in the culture in general. It is interesting to see that that sense also stretches to those audiences that should be most likely to be viewers and listeners. With the partial exception of radio programs from the Focus on the Family organization and children's media such as the *Veggie Tales* series, we found very few examples of self-consciously religious media being very important in these narratives. Specific televangelism ministries were identified and criticized. While some ritualistic mention of religious TV occurred in some interviews, religious television never rose to the surface as the kind of interesting, attractive, or meaningful programming that even the Evangelicals found in "secular" media.

Some found an occasional religious program meaningful, but the PAX network and sentimental and inoffensive programs on the Hallmark network were clearly preferred, even for them. This is an important finding, taken together with what we've seen about the relationships between religious identity and the media of the broader, "secular" culture. It is of course commonplace to think of there being a syllogistic relationship between conservative religious values and conservative religious broadcasting. This is connected, of course, with the rise of televangelism and its role in the emergence of the neo-Evangelical movement. The evidence here would suggest a different reality, however. Those with longer memories might suggest that televangelism does not fare well, even with its "core" potential audience, because of the scandals that rocked the industry in the late 1980s. There is little evidence of that here. Rather, what people object to about televangelism are specific things about the form of the genre as they understand it. Jay Milliken and Karl Callahan, for example, found the programs too much devoted to "hocus-pocus" and the "health and wealth" gospel.

The view of televangelism encountered here is consistent with sentiments attributed to mainstream Evangelicals by *Christianity Today*'s Ted Olsen in Chapter 9. Olsen decried the tendency for televangelism figures Pat Robertson and Jerry Falwell to get disproportionate attention from the secular media because they *are* television figures. He contended that they are not looked to as authorities by mainstream or majority Evangelical opinion. Consistent with this, when televangelism did occur in our interviews, it was most often *Trinity Broadcasting* or *Benny Hinn* that were mentioned. Neither Robertson nor Falwell figured in any of our interviews with "born-again" or "dogmatist" interviewees in Chapters 6 and 7.

A "symbolic inventory"?

There are other issues beyond the distinctions made that are significant of the negotiations we've encountered. One of the expectations I'd set up at the outset concerned the role that media may play in providing a kind of *"symbolic inventory"* to the practice of religiously infused meaning-making. As we'll discuss in more detail later, there are many examples of media working in this way. However, it is important to note that, in the means or style of negotiation we've seen, the media seem to be important on two levels. In addition to a *"symbolic inventory,"* they are also a *context*. Much of what we said earlier about the media conveying the "common culture" is rooted in this sense of context. Processes and practices of legitimation of various ideas and values in the media involve a negotiation between these two senses of media. Judy Cruz, in Chapter 4, was a good example of this as she assessed mediated discourses about science and fantasy fiction.

Judy is also a good example of another dimension we see in these negotiations, that the kinds of things that are taken to be religiously and spiritually meaningful in these narratives are often quite surprising. A good deal of the material mentioned is predictable, starting with the range of programming we've been calling "sentimental" and "inoffensive," things like *Little House on the Prairie*, *Christy*, and *Seventh Heaven*. Some programming, like specifically "religious broadcasting," was notable for its absence from these discussions. But a wide range of material beyond these was talked about, everything from science and fantasy fiction, to mystical gothic dramas, to violent films like *Braveheart*, to *The Simpsons*, to *Monty Python and the Holy Grail*. In a way, the selection of material to talk about was one of the modes of distinction we talked about earlier. A significant point of social distinction between Terry Albert, the "born-again" father who mentioned *Braveheart*, and the "secularist" mother Sheryl Murphy, who identified *Gandhi*, is in those choices. This underscores the notion of autonomy discussed at the outset. Rather than circulating around a set of ideas about what is or should be meaningful in media, the logic of these interviews has centered on autonomous choice.

"Playful" practice

At the heart of the questions of autonomy and choice is another issue in these negotiations, an expectation rooted in much of the "received discourse" about the media. Cultural authorities of a variety of kinds, including teachers, clergy, religious educators (and university professors), have conceived of the practice of media consumption, particularly at the level of viewing choices, to be something of a *deliberative* process. A wide range of lay discourse about media, as well as many of the ideas at the heart of the so-called "media literacy" movement, assume that people bring a range of ideas and values to play in their decisions about what to watch and what to do in the media sphere. In contrast, much of what we have seen here seems to be more *playful* than it is *deliberative*. We've already noted the tendency for people here to think of the media as something that they simply "do." Their mode of practice in this "doing" seems to follow its own logics, not the sort of cognitive, deliberative course that we might have wanted or expected.

Children and autonomy

Another matter of negotiation emerges when we look at how people in our interviews thought of themselves as parents and the appropriate relationship between media and religion/spirituality in relation to children.[12] As we noted in Chapter 7, many of those households we might expect to take the most moralistic stance toward media, the "born-agains" and "dogmatists," did not universally do so. Born-again believers, in particular, tended to shy away from the sense that it was up to them to protect their children from "bad" media. Even Glenn Donegal, who we declared a "dogmatist," expressed the view we might call "pedagogical" as opposed to "prophylactic" when it comes to media and children. "We want them to know that life is full of choices," Karl Callahan said in Chapter 6. The notion that parenting should be about helping children make autonomous media choices on their own fits with the overall theme of autonomous choice we've seen develop throughout these interviews. It makes sense that adults who feel autonomous and empowered to make their own decisions and draw their own conclusions would see their role as helping their children develop the same skills.

We might have expected such a view from the "mainstream believers" and "metaphysical seekers" among our interviews, due to received assumptions about the relationship between social class and ideas about parenting. We might also then have expected our more "conservative" parents to be more moralistic and controlling with their children. Instead, nearly all of our parents here, across Roof's categories, expressed an "account of media" that the proper role of parents *vis-à-vis* media is to equip their children with the skills and values they need to make their own choices, not attempt to protect them from things they should not see. This was true even for parents who otherwise expressed the most moralistic "accounts of media." It seems that, in the context of the ubiquitous "common culture" of the media, where few parents have chosen to avoid media altogether, most have concluded that the appropriate response is to prepare their children to interact with it, rather than attempt to avoid it.

Social class

We have not, to this point, discussed questions of *social class* in any detail. While issues of class and class interests underlie a good deal of culturalist media studies, I've argued for an approach here that looks beyond questions of the kind of class tastes and practices that have been the focus of other efforts, to establish some sense of how resources based in religious and spiritual commitments and experience are brought into play. Questions of class and other social categories clearly play a role. While a thorough analysis of class issues is beyond the scope of this study, one area where class may well play an important role has to do with the expressed media tastes and choices we've seen. We've seen how interviewees' media choices in some cases defy a logical connection to their religious values. But, in the case of Jay Milliken or the Muellers, for example, it could be argued that their approach to media expresses rather well the tastes and interests of their social class, perhaps better than it expresses their religious commitments. We asked at one point, "What is essentially 'religious' about their media choices?" We answered, "Nothing." The same can be said, conversely, for some of the taste preferences among our "metaphysical seekers" and "secularists." This of course relates to the issue of the media as a "common culture." As I said earlier, there is a sense in which the practices we see here are more "culturally" than "religiously" oriented. As class tastes are embedded in that broader "culture," they play a role in connecting many of our interviewees to it.

In Chapter 7 we considered the utility of Roof's taxonomy to our analysis here. While we found much of value in the comparisons we were able to do there, we nonetheless observed that the commonalities between the various categories in some ways were more interesting than the differences. This has led, as we've seen, to the development of a sense of the media being connected to notions of a "common culture" (as I've phrased it) to which people across the categories of "religion" and "spirituality" are oriented. There are some ways in which Roof's ideas have been fully supported in this analysis, though. Chief among these is in his notion of "seeker" or "quest" culture. As we noted, Roof has suggested that the mode of "seeking" is rooted in fundamental social realities of late modernity. In particular, he points to Giddens's ideas about the self and its reflexivity and quest for perfection. In a way "seeker" religiosity is Giddens applied to late-modern religion. What we've seen here supports these ideas. Nearly all of our interviewees express some form or level of "seeking" sensibility. This is even the case among those of Roof's categories who should presumably be the most oriented to institutional, doctrinal, or clerical authority. "Born-agains" and even some "dogmatists" here describe themselves as at the center of their religious meaning-making, and few if any wish to surrender to anyone the authority to make decisions for them.

What's in the "symbolic inventory"?

One of the important questions here is the nature of the religiously and spiritually meaningful material present in the media. In an earlier chapter, I argued that one of the things that these narratives would do would be to enable us to position ourselves with these interviewees, "looking back" with them toward the media, and get a sense of what they see and experience there. We've already established the logic of this as a way of understanding what is in the inventory of symbols, ideas, and values present in the media relevant to these questions. If we'd instead taken a more inductive approach – a formal "content analysis" for example – we'd have missed much of what we've been discussing here. For example, we'd have missed the array of programs and other media materials that have been identified as meaningful by informants here, but which we otherwise would have missed because they seemed not to be "religious" in any formal way. We also would have missed the playful and indirect and nondeliberative way that they engage with the media they find significant and salient.

One major category of material in the media sphere is, of course, "media events" such as the 9/11, Oklahoma City, and Columbine incidents. There is an array of ways and times that the media "break in" on the flow of daily life and daily experience, bringing news and other events that may be spiritually or religiously significant. There is evidence here that people understand and respond to such interruptions, though their level of orientation to them might be lower here than we would have expected based on the scholarly literature that has been devoted to media events, media ritual, and "enchantment" through the media.

At the same time, though, a very wide range of media are religiously and spiritually meaningful to our interviewees. In addition to the somewhat idiosyncratic examples given by people like Judy Cruz, there are a number of television programs that are widely viewed as important across our interviews. The two series that stand out are the family drama *Seventh Heaven* and the animated farce *The Simpsons*. While they were seen broadly as important examples of religion in the media, there was clearly no consensus among our interviewees about these programs. Most would seem to agree that *Seventh Heaven*'s sentimentalism is an important element of its importance, while noting the formal element that the program is about the family of a minister, and thus – on some level – must be taken as self-evidently "religious." But, as many have noted, the religiosity of the family is not a major dimension of the program; what seems more important to the interviewees here who identified it positively is its self-conscious "goodness" and "good-heartedness."

The Simpsons, by contrast, is much more controversial. While only the more conservative households ("born-agains" and "dogmatists") here seemed to refer to *Seventh Heaven* positively, both "conservative" and "liberal" (that is, "mainstreamers," "metaphysical seekers," and "secularists") had seen – and had opinions about – *The Simpsons*. There is an interesting range of views among the conservatives, though, with some describing the program as embodying all that is bad about television, and others enjoying it as regular viewers.[13] In a way this program served to define some of the differences and contrasts between our households. Those who were the most interested in the "broader culture," as well as those who could think of the program in terms of its irony and metaphor rather than seeing it as realistic, were understandably the most likely to speak approvingly of *The Simpsons*.

Other programs also appeared in our interviews for their obvious and self-conscious "religious" implications. These included *Touched by an Angel*, and more intriguing examples such as *Buffy the Vampire Slayer* and *Crossing over with John Edward*. Combined with the range of "unexpected" sources of symbolic resources in the media (such as *The Terminator, Andy Griffith, To Kill a Mockingbird, X-Files, Star Trek*, etc.), there appeared to be a good deal of evidence that the notion that the media do function as a kind of "symbolic inventory" is justified. Once again, in keeping with the research approach taken here, things in this inventory that are significant are those that are *seen to be* significant in the context of interviewees' expressed narratives. That something like *Seventh Heaven* is taken to be religiously significant because of formal characteristics of its plot is a judgment that is based on its being taken that way in our interviews.

In the theory of religion and media I developed in Chapter 3, I suggested that we might find the media a particularly fertile source of symbolic resources expressed through modes of religious experience that have been "repressed" by clerical authority over the course of the mid-to-late twentieth century. These modes include *"the visual," the body, objects, ritual, music, and "experience" itself*. I suggested there that, if the media were moving to a place of centrality in contemporary religious experience and expression, we might find evidence of these modes of experience playing a role in binding individuals to that evolving process. As we've seen, the picture at the household level is a bit more subtle and complicated than that. Certainly, the media are integrated in important ways into meaning-making at the household level, and the media do provide a range of symbolic resources to contemporary "religious" and "spiritual" questing. There isn't a lot of evidence here, though, that the media *per se* are interposing themselves in these processes. Thus a "transformationist" idea of the role of media in late modernity, that mediated modes of experience might well be allowing media to take on some of the core roles and functions of religion – to *become* "religion" – is not clearly supported here.

There are a number of examples in our interviews of various of the "repressed modes" playing important roles in religious and spiritual meaning-making. In Chapter 5, for example, Butch Castello talks about a number of media experiences, making reference to "the visual" and "experience," in particular. As we've noted, many of our interviewees have also identified music as an important mode of experience for them religiously and spiritually. There is a way in which we can see the list of "repressed modes" as in some ways more potentially significant to "metaphysical seekers" like Butch than to others (the most common modes mentioned in our interviews were "the visual," "music," and "experience"). At the same time, though, Glenn Donegal – who is very decidedly *not* into the "New Age" – expresses a great interest in the "repressed mode" of "experience" (in his discussion of rites-of-passage). As we've seen, the mode of autonomous "seeking" seems to cut across many of the received categories here, and to the extent that "seeking" and "questing" move outside legitimated centers and sources (as we've seen that it does), we'd also expect to see these "repressed modes" play a role. Instead of a "transformationist" notion of media and religion, what we've seen is more of a "constructivist" idea: that the media are significantly involved in providing contexts and resources to the negotiation and construction of meanings that can be seen to "make sense" in certain ways and certain places. The "action," as it were, is in the hands of the individuals making these meanings. That the media make accessible modes of experience and expression that may have been repressed in earlier times is significant, but not the center of the story.

If the "metaphysical seekers" seemed to be most oriented toward film, the printed word, and "experience," the only other category that seemed also to have characteristic tastes in terms of media or modes of expression was the "born-again Christians" who identified religiously themed audio and videocassettes and CCM as important to them. It is this latter area – we should mention – that is the only place we see an unequivocal role here for specifically and self-consciously "religious" media.

What is achieved?

If our primary concern here has been to find that place (the "where" I spoke of in Chapter 2) where significant interactions between media and religion occur, a secondary – but perhaps equally important – question concerns what happens there. What is the outcome? What is achieved? The negotiations we've seen between the media sphere and the spheres of daily life seem clearly to support certain kinds of outcomes.

One of the most significant achievements is in the way that media practice interacts with and enables the individuals here to be, in Roof's words, "fluid, yet grounded." In a way, this seems to be the overall lesson of these interviews. Contemporary meaning practice is rooted in the individual, in individual experience, and in individual processes and practices of meaning-making. They do not look to others – in media or in institutional or clerical authority – for overarching answers and explanations. Instead, they see the claims and propositions from such sources as input into their own quest for a meaningful answer. The model, notes Roof, is Lifton's idea of the "protean self." The "fluidity" is in the *process*, whereby it is possible to always be on the lookout for new insights and resources. At the same time, "grounding" is important, and the resources of tradition, history, doctrine, "shared memory" and "imagined community," as well as resources from unconventional places and of unconventional types, such as those available in and through media, are important touchpoints to this "grounding." We should remember as well that the media are also a *source* and a *context* through which more traditional symbols, ideas, and values are made available.

It also appears that the model of meaning-making we developed earlier, that of narratives of self serving the construction of "ideal selves" (*pace* Giddens), describes rather well the picture we've seen in these interviews. While it can't be said that we necessarily know and know of all the other locations and modes of interaction through which meanings are made, there is much evidence available here of cultural and social resources being brought to the service of self and identity.

There is less evidence here of direct religious, spiritual, or quasi-religious or quasi-spiritual functions and effects of media. True, we did not set out to identify places where media were being transformed into religion or were transforming religion in a fundamental way, but we did conduct our interviews in places where evidence of this happening would be available to us. Questions of the role of the formal characteristics of media presentation in making media experience "real" in religious or spiritual terms[14] seem beside the point to the processes of negotiation we've seen here. The same could be said for notions such as the "archetypal" and other "formal" theories we noted in Chapter 3.

The same could also be said for a range of ideas rooted in the Durkheimian notion of "enchantment" or "effervescence." On some fundamental level, there is thought to be a set of religious motivations or functions that are transcendent, mystical, magical, and beyond the scope of rational meaning and action.[15] It has been widely assumed that formal and *genre* characteristics of specific media place them in a position to be able to make those modes problematic in late modernity, either by interposing media experience for "real" experience, or by confusing and complexifying commonly understood ways of understanding and inhabiting these modes. The result, as I've said, would be a "transformation" of the nature and practice of religion and spirituality.

This study is not precisely fitted to addressing these questions, both for conceptual and methodological reasons. At the same time, it is hard to detect even traces of such "effects" of the media age in the interviews here. As described by our interviewees, media experiences of a range of kinds, including "events" such as 9/11 (experienced through the media), do not carry with them a level of meaning or facticity that would accrue were any such experiences responsible for "re-enchanting the world" for them. Admittedly, it could be that what the media have done – and there *is* potential evidence for this in our interviews – is undermine the *capacity for "enchantment"* by bringing into question the bases of belief in such things. There is enough evidence here of moments and locations where individuals do place themselves in the position of *being enchanted* (through, for example, "music" and "experience") to suggest that people retain this capacity in the media age.

Further, as we saw in Chapter 8, there is not a lot of evidence, either, of media unequivocally serving more rudimentary functions such as inspiring or providing moral or religious role models. Could such functions be occurring on some more subtle, or even subliminal levels? Of course, and our method might not be sensitive to those and might have missed them. Still, we'd expect some kind of evidence here.

The few exceptions we have here are telling. Once again, let's look at Judy Cruz, for whom it could be said that a kind of media-centered religious meaning-making is significant. The intriguing feature of Judy's case is that her struggle over religious symbolism and religious authority in the context of media concerns her sense that media-centered representations of science and fantasy fiction should be *more* authentic than they are. She sees mediated fantasy genres in the mystical/mystery tradition as overly commodified and domesticated.

But Judy is nearly unique along this dimension. For the vast majority of our interviewees, the issue is not the interposition of media into fundamental religious "functions." Instead, media culture serves as a broad context within which they can and do find ways of negotiating meanings that relate to greater or lesser extents to their own "authentic" ideas and meanings. In a fundamental way, what we've seen here are practices of meaning-making that are authenticated much more on the level of the "systemworld" than the level of the "lifeworld" (to refer back to a point we made in Chapter 4). Due in great measure to the nature of the method we have used – depending on our interviewees to engage with us in a cognitive, and on some level rational, process of description – what we have found is evidence of the way that media materials are integrated on a more or less *rational* level into the warp and woof of daily life. At the same time, these accounts detail ways that media materials can be and are "deeply meaningful." It is not all about rationality, even in these accounts.

Even if we had found convincing evidence that nonrational or "mystical" meanings were accruing to media practice, we might still have the overarching sense that the real "action" is with the broader "common" culture, and not with specific or "enchanted" religious or spiritual "cultures."

What is achieved then? It seems that individuals use the range of resources available to them, including media resources, to make sense of themselves in religious, spiritual, and social terms. The underlying logic of this tends to be one of fitting these resources, symbols, claims, and values into the broader context of a common culture to which they wish to relate on some level. This aspired involvement is, of course, differentially realized "on the ground," in lived lives. Many of those we've interviewed seem to inhabit particular locations, often defined by their religious and spiritual ideas and commitments. There are two troubling questions that deserve further exploration but are beyond the scope of this study.

The first of these unresolved questions is the one raised by the ongoing scholarly and public discourse concerning "social capital" and participation in civil society including the whole question of civic engagement. For our interviewees, it does seem that the media continue to present a broader "common" context of ideas and values to which they must on some level relate. To the extent that they are living in disparate communities of commitment, as we noted above, what are the possibilities for them to engage in that broader context socially and politically, rather than to orient primarily to their "group"? This has large and profound implications for democracy and democratic participation in an era marked – as we noted in Chapter 9 – by increasing interactions between media, religion, and politics.

The second unresolved question is related to the first, but is somewhat more esoteric, rooted as it is in ongoing debates in social theory. It is the persistent question of whether what seems to be (and is subjectively taken to be) "empowerment" of these individuals to make sense of their own lives and take autonomous control over the way that they integrate ideas of religion, spirituality, culture, and values is, in fact, "empowering." It could be, as many have argued, that practices of audience meaning-making in the media age are, on a fundamental level, a chimera.[16] The resources, after all, are derived from a media culture that operates under its own logics, is economically situated in such a way that it must continue to ensure its own legitimacy, and has therefore evolved into a context of content and audience practice that establishes a sense of autonomy and empowerment, but within a very narrow range of options for action in the social sphere as a consequence.

The evidence from our explorations to address each of these residual concerns is mixed. Many of our interviewees seemed to move from meaning to action in their interactions with media culture. Many also engaged at a broader social level to bring their ideas and values to the fore in community and civic contexts. At the same time, many did neither of these things. In many of the latter cases, there were concrete social and economic reasons for their "retreat" from civic engagement and action. One learning from the kinds of field research we've seen here is the complex nature of contemporary life with its competing conditions, demands, and pressures. There is little evidence here that the media are important *impediments* to such action. But, these are explorations for another day and another study.

The relationship of "media" to "religion"

There is much evidence here that the media have come to define the terms through which religious and spiritual interests and ideas are formed, shaped, and conveyed. Dayan and Katz described this, with reference to the way that the media can transcend the social spaces and contexts once controlled by clerical authority, as "disintermediation."[17] By this they also mean that, in the media age, audiences reflexively transcend traditional boundaries, and are now brought nearer "the action" in the public sphere. On a more pervasive level, though, the "common culture" represented by the media has today become determinative of the contexts, extents, limits, languages, and symbols available to religious and spiritual discourse. For religious institutions, to exist today is to exist in the media, and they have continued to struggle with that reality.[18]

In the relations between "religion" and "the media," the latter are, in many ways, in the driver's seat. We see that, as I said, with reference to the whole sense of "common culture" accessible through, and experienced in, the media. That culture, and those ideas and discourses, are the themes and topics of everyday social discourse. To the extent that religious and spiritual ideas and motivations enter in, they must do so within the limits and constraints established there. Even for the households we'd expect to be the most resistant to this, media culture and its ideas and values set the terms of debate in great measure.

Further, as we noted in Chapter 3, few examples exist of media rooted in religious culture actually "crossing over" to prominence in secular culture. It is much more common for things to go the other way. There, we had looked at the specific cases of Evangelically rooted film, television, and music, and noted that little historical evidence existed for those media moving outside the boundaries of that culture (in spite of being widely expected to do so by people *within* that culture). The evidence from our interviews deepens this analysis by saying that it is not just the case that there are few non-Evangelicals in the audience for Evangelical media, but that it seems there may be a great number of Evangelicals in the audience for non-Evangelical media. The dualism of that statement, though, is misleading. It is more accurate to say that all of our informant households shared a common interest in "secular" media. For the Evangelical households, there were, in addition, materials from Evangelical sources in the form of television, film, and (most importantly) music. For all of our households, people could be said to be in the process of negotiating between the claims and values of the mainstream or "common" culture they encountered in the media and more particular claims and values, among them the claims and values of their religious or spiritual commitments.

The dynamics of the relationship between religion, media, and Evangelical identity might be well illustrated by Ted Olsen in the last chapter. In the case of televangelists and their relationship to Evangelical culture, it appears that the primary implication of their being in the media is in establishing a kind of credibility in media culture as being part of that media culture. Thus, some kinds of leadership may well come from media presence and prominence. As Olsen points out, though, that prominence can be ephemeral. For secular journalism, being a prominent Evangelical media figure may lend credibility. It does not necessarily do so for Evangelicals "in the pew," as it were.

This suggests one of the things we've been noting all along, but that is very significant to our interests in relations between religion and media: the issue of *reflexivity*, and the sense that most of our interviewees on some level understand their place in these relations. Most of our interviewees readily talked about these things in terms of "accounts of media" through which they positioned themselves on the media landscape. As we noted above, it worked for a number of our more "liberal" interviewees to make explicit reference to ideas such as the commonplace that conservatives are more concerned about "sex" than they are about "violence." Across the board, most interviewees saw themselves as engaging in a set of audience and discursive practices that were self-conscious and aware of the histories, motivations, meanings, and commitments represented by the various media.

As I said above, it would not be quite correct to talk about practices here as *deliberative* with reference to *viewing choices*. At the same time they are cognitive, even rational, in their approach to meaning-making once they get to the media and reflexive about the whole process later on. Once again, this tends to undermine the idea that it is an important implication of the media age that media are – through their mechanical or formal characteristics – able to insert themselves into the process of religious practice or religious consciousness, and therefore to fundamentally transform the nature of religious experience. The connections seem more subtle and complex than that. Most of our interviewees and interview households have established patterns of evolved religious and spiritual meaning and practice. They regard their media lives with reference to those domains and regard those domains with reference to their media lives. What results is a negotiated conditional settlement, one that is open to revision as they continue to seek that feeling of being "fluid, yet grounded."

Certainly, their relationship to the "common culture" of the media as a shared set of ideas and experiences will guide and condition their interactions and sense-making in other contexts of their lives, including their religious and spiritual lives, both formal and informal. There may also be a way that the reflexively engaged media age has served to change and perhaps "disenchant" these informants and the Western media audience as a whole. In *Religion and Media*, Hent De Vries (2001) wonders whether the removal of the capacity of "the magical" and "the miraculous" from daily life is a fundamental function of the media age.[19] He suggests that the power of religion has always resided, in part, in the essentially technical ability to manipulate experience in such a way as to establish authority.[20]

In these interviews, neither "magic" nor "authority" loom large. Few informants use media in such a way as to invoke this idea of "the miraculous." Those who do – Judy Cruz's interest in science fiction and mystery comes to mind – do so with unconventional programs and materials. The relationship to "authority" is also an issue. For Judy, "authority," even over the implicit theodicy of science fiction, is beside the point. The issue of religious authority in the media age may well be located beyond the question of individual experience such as Judy's. Instead (and De Vries's and others' arguments on this point still may be well taken[21]) Judy's relationship to authority may be evidence that the media age may have so destabilized formal religious authority on a general level that it is no longer on the social or cultural "radar screen" on particular levels.

There is, at the same time, an argument from the other direction – as articulated by journalist Nicholas Kristof in Chapter 9 – that the media age has seen the evolution of a "mystical turn" in the world of religion, thus reversing the trend toward secular rationality in late modernity. The evidence here is also mixed on this point. Clearly, the media context seems to be one in which people can make a range of conceptual and moral and spiritual connections, often in ways that, to the post-Enlightenment mind, defy reason. And the notion that the times are defined by a decline in general in the legitimacy of traditional cultural authority also has been claimed to be connected to the influence of the media age.[22] But, at the same time, there is evidence in these interviews of a continuing, reflexively engaged autonomy in meaning-making and action. It could be, of course, that it is a function of the media age that people feel increasingly empowered because of the instrumentality they feel through their private "knowledge work" as media consumers, that this is a false sense of empowerment and autonomy, and that this extends as well to the domain of "religion" or "spirituality." In the end, neither of these consequences of the media for religion – too little mystery or too much – can be established without historical scholarship. The "slice in time" we engaged in here is not appropriate to the task.

The decline in authority and the rise in autonomy – if that is what we are seeing – seem from these interviews also to be a cross-class and cross-religious phenomenon. As we saw in Chapters 5 and 6, "born-agains" were in many ways as much "autonomous seekers" as were the "mainstream believers." As we saw, no one wanted to leave it to anyone else to make media decisions for them. And, as we saw, there was a tendency for the media sphere to have a normative authority that religious institutions do not. Glenn Donegal in Chapter 4 was a good example of this. Committed to a faith that he feels has saved his life, he nonetheless sees that as something within *him*, not something that is stored in "religion." And, the media sphere – both "secular" and "religious" – provides him with the values and symbolic and discursive resources he needs to act out his faith in his daily life.

In this way as well, the so-called "secular" media sphere may be the normative and determinative sphere. For many of these interviewees, their attraction to the "common culture" of the media sphere places them in a dialectical relationship to what they see to be some of their fundamental values. Yet they continue to participate and negotiate ways of making this all make sense. All agree on there being some distance – some contradiction – between the media sphere and the normative bases of their lives and values. While this is once again beyond the scope of this study to establish, it may well be that the "effect" is a kind of inexorable "secularization," if by that term we mean a shift away from religious authority as a basis of knowledge and action.

Backing up a bit, it is also important to note again that what seems to drive media practice is not in most cases a process of deliberation over appropriate and normative values – including religious values – but the salience of the media experiences themselves. Actual reasons for viewing given television programs are hard to articulate, beyond a level best expressed as "I like it." For some, as we have seen, the reasons are even less well-articulated than that.

This helps explain a major ongoing controversy in the American "culture wars." For decades there has been a seeming contradiction between the expressed moralist attitudes of religious authorities and parents on the one hand and actual media behaviors on the other. In spite of widespread condemnation of the sex, violence, profanity, and irreligion of the "secular media," including opinion poll results establishing these views as widely shared, the media have continued to enjoy large audiences with this same fare. As an example, it was revealed in 2004 that the controversial potboiler *Desperate Housewives* was achieving impressive audience ratings in the Bible Belt.[23]

As media executives have repeatedly pointed out, "if no one watched, we wouldn't show it." So, many have wondered, how is it that people say one thing and do another? These data provide some insight. It seems clear that people actually occupy more than one "map" as regards their media lives. Media are highly salient and attractive, and tend to be watched almost as a matter of right. On another level, however, there is a whole array of "accounts of media" rooted in broad social conceptions as well as more focused religious and spiritual ones. People seem, as we've seen, to be able to occupy both of these self-understandings with some ease. And, there are socially-acceptable ways to do so. In private and interpersonal life there is wide social acceptance of watching, and talking about, a range of salient media experiences. And the media themselves, including the "news" media, support those discourses with increasing coverage of entertainment and show business news. At school, at church, synagogue, or mosque, in formal settings, and – perhaps most importantly – when answering questions on opinion polls, "accounts of media" come easily into play.

Some residual questions still nag. Primary among these is something we have not noted until now – the question of whether the model of religious evolution we've been relying on here is one that will pertain into the future. Roof's work on "Baby-Boom religiosity" is provocative and compelling, and fits well with evolving "new-paradigm" religion scholarship. In fact, the "Boom" may turn out to be a generational "tipping point" of some kind in the evolution of American religion. Certainly, dimensions of Boom religiosity that have been most important – the dimension of "fluidity vs groundedness," the centrality of the self, and, most importantly, "seeking" or "questing" – seem to be important and indicative of the times. It of course remains to be seen whether succeeding generations will follow the same path. And, as has been widely noted, the tendency for younger people to be even more media-involved than their parents means that some of the phenomena we've seen here may well become more characteristic as time goes on. Among our interviews, the children of the household do seem to share with their parents ideas and beliefs such as the centrality of the self, suspicion of external authority, and the importance of being open to new experiences and insights. As they become more and more integrated with their media, things could change further. Youth culture has always been, in important ways, media culture as well. It is hard to separate these two, and that should also continue to be the case as we move into the future.

A final thought about the relation of this inquiry to debates and questions in the broader field of media studies takes us back to some of the discussions at the beginning of this book. As I noted there, there has been a tendency for media studies to eschew a focus on formal or even informal religion. A range of scholars in media studies (we've considered James Carey, John Fiske, Daniel Dayan, Elihu Katz, and Nick Couldry here, among others) have sought to undertake studies of media and things related to religion (ritual in the cases of Dayan, Katz, and Couldry). In most cases, they have sought to "denature" the implicit or explicit religion in the domains under study. Other culturalist scholars have simply not looked at religious or religion-like domains very closely. We can now see through the lives and reflections of our interviewees a kind of synthesis of work on religion or spirituality *per se* and these broader literatures.

Our interviewees seem very much to live on the same kind of map of domestic practice described by other research in the fields of media studies and cultural studies. They live in a post-Enlightenment, secularized (using a conditional definition of that term, of course), late-modern world, defined by personal autonomy, the self, and rational and reflexive modes of cultural practice. At the same time, though, they can be said to be involved in a process of "re-naturing" the religiosity or spirituality of these practices, building religion and spirituality into things through their redis-covered interest in invigorating social and cultural experience with these dimensions. This most probably does not constitute a "re-enchantment" of the world in an age of "magical media." It could be described, however, as a social and cultural development rooted in negotiative meaning practice in the media age.

The evolution of the media has brought about major changes in social and cultural life. There is good historical evidence that the media and religion have evolved together. This is particularly the case in the periods following the development of printing and the subsequent devel-opment of the mass media. This co-evolution has not been smooth and mutually beneficial. In the context of everyday experience, we still struggle to integrate media into our lives in ways that satisfy our values and senses of self. We are suspicious of their influence. They seem objec-tively to convey values and ideas that we find troubling. In the broader contexts of schooling, public and civic life, and politics, there are similar senses of disquiet. Much of this disquiet continues to be articulated with and around ideas derived from religion. Even as Europe and North America continue to secularize (in the sense that religious authority, at least, is in decline in both contexts[24]), religion continues to play a role in discourses about normative values. Thus, "religion," and "the media," contend with one another and will continue to do so well into the future.

On another level, the relationship is defined by the fact that the media are now the context through which social and cultural relations occur and repre-sentations are made. Religion, both formal and informal, explicit and implicit, is now fully subject to this fact. As religion increasingly contends with politics and seeks to find a role in civil society, it will be under the conditions of medi-ation that it will do so. Beyond these issues, there is the tendency for religion and media to *interact* in important ways. Media exposure serves as a kind of *accelerant* to religious discourse, providing the "oxygen of publicity" to ideas and movements that may not have been able to achieve prominence before. Religion also acts as a kind of *accelerant* to media, acting as something outside the realm of normal media discourse that exists, intervenes, and contradicts that discourse with a kind of portentous possibility.

These relations are unlikely to change markedly in the future. What we know after our inquiries here, though, are some things about how individuals, families, and groups in the media audience work to make sense of all of this on a day-to-day basis. We now know more about what media experience is capable of in those contexts. Audiences seem to know more about what is going on in relations between religion and media than they are often given credit for. They are engaged with media in a variety of ways, and are able to position themselves with some ease with reference to the claims of the media sphere. It is another step to move beyond this level – where we have been looking at the integration of media, religion, and spirituality in daily media experience – to a level where more focused questions of value and action are brought to bear. The "where" of our inquiries here has been the "where" of domestic life and the social network relations that immediately surround it. What is needed next are more focused, "located" studies of those times, places, and occasions where questions of value and action are brought to bear in the lives of people such as the ones we've seen here.

That task, and the range of intriguing questions we've considered in this chapter, but found to be beyond the scope of this study, still await. Among these are studies that will pursue questions of how varying religious and spiritual perspectives and attitudes interact with media in ways that *do* reflect those commitments. This would shift the perspective away from the broad analysis of audience practice (and how religion and spirituality figure into it) to more focused questions of how specific groups differentially use media to make meanings and representations. It is clear from this study that the media are important, even determinative. The ways they are determinative, and for whom, under what circumstances, and with what consequences, remain to be shown.

It was the purpose of this book to look in depth at one important set of questions in a way that would provide groundwork for other inquiries into the broad and complex implications of religion in the media age. There is important and provocative groundwork here. What is more exciting, though, is to look forward to the reflections, reactions, inquiries, and new insights that will follow.

Appendix
Notes on method

The interviews in this book were conducted during an ongoing study of meaning-making in the media age. An extensive account of that project, along with in-depth discussions of its approach and methodology, were published in 2004 as *Media, Home, and Family*.[1] I will not repeat that material here, but will provide a brief overview. Readers interested in more detail should consult the earlier volume.

In the main, the theoretical and methodological approach of the overall study is intended to address a gap in the media studies literature identified by Lila Abu-Lughod in 1997. Assessing the "ethnographic turn" in media theory, Abu-Lughod observed – to that point at least – much more theoretical reflection on the value of this approach than actual field research had taken place.[2] The situation today is, of course, far different, and this study joins a growing literature in media studies that is rapidly developing a substantive record in ethnographic and interpretive audience research.[3]

The approach taken in this book is linked to the development of the overall research project as detailed in *Media, Home, and Family*. Briefly put, the project began with the notion that the significance of media to meaning (including religious or spiritual meaning) would be rooted in key moments or "passages" of life. The approach was "post-positivist," stressing the need to shift the terms of analysis away from notions of the instrumental power of the media to the moments and locations in life where media are consumed. It soon became clear, however, both as the result of field experience and evolving theoretical reflection, that this approach was too limited. The field experience showed that the interaction of media and religion clearly was taking place somewhere beyond those key moments of crisis and transition. Theoretically, we were coming to realize that our method necessitated a rethinking of our positions as researchers and our complicity in the construction of the narratives we were developing.[4] My colleague Lynn Schofield Clark articulated for us the notion that we were going beyond the "post-positivism" of our initial phase to a "constructivist" position that moved to the center the question of the status and meaning of the narratives we were developing from our interviews.[5]

We were gradually moving away from an implicit paradigm that conceived of the project in rather traditional terms (looking for "effects" of media on religion or vice versa) to an interpretive paradigm that centered the meaning-making process in a form and context that was available to us: the accounts and narratives of interviewees as they reflected with us on their experience of media in daily life. This was articulated more clearly as the study moved into a second phase, which placed a particular focus on the digital media. In conjunction with these studies, Lynn Clark has developed an extensive project looking at teens and youth media practice in general, and a good deal of our interview attention also moved in those directions.

The interviews reported here stretch across a number of the phases of the overall project, which has developed a "sample" that now includes 144 families. The majority of interviews have taken place in the Denver metropolitan area. No interviews have been conducted in the city of Boulder (where our university is located) itself. In addition to these, a number of interviews have been conducted in other regions of the US, including in the upper midwest, the northeast, and in southern and northern California. One group of interviews involves families that are related to one another, allowing analysis of that type of social network.

In each of these household-level studies, we conduct in-depth, semi-structured interviews with all household members as a group, and then follow up with individual interviews with each of them. In keeping with the protocols of our university's human subjects panel, all individual interviews are conducted with an assurance of anonymity. Names reported in this book and elsewhere are therefore not actual names, and other efforts are made to shield identities. These household interviews are followed up, when appropriate and promising, with additional interventions that might include observations, focus group interviews, and other projective techniques. Only interview material is reported in this volume.

As is detailed in *Media, Home, and Family*, an important feature of our method has been the ongoing collaboration of the field research team in regular weekly meetings where interview transcripts are discussed. In addition, these meetings function as an ongoing field research seminar, with assigned readings from current theoretical and methodological literature. These meetings then become the context within which we reflect together on the nature of the research, develop ideas for ultimate publication, and review and refine our methods and instrumentation on an ongoing basis.

It was from these meetings that a number of the most important ideas emerged. I have attempted to credit some of the contributions of individual members of our research team in the foregoing chapters of this book. I do want to acknowledge here, though, some contributions to the analyses reported here that were more general influences on my thinking. Lynn Schofield Clark has played a major role in the form and shape of all phases of this project for over ten years now, and her influence on my work has been profound. I have already mentioned her important theoretical work on the "constructivist" orientation of our project, but also must credit her with a range of nuanced and sophisticated insights into the nature of religious practice as it relates to media culture. In addition, she has always kept issues of class, ethnicity, and difference in general in the forefront of our thinking, and therefore of my work here.

Henrik Boes was the second field researcher on the project, and contributed a ground-breaking master's thesis in religious studies based on his interview work with us. Henrik focused, at an early stage, on the essentially *ludic* nature of the media practices we were seeing. Whereas the literatures had us looking for religiously inflected media practices that would be sober and deliberative, Henrik saw in his own studies, and in others, that much of this activity is better described as "playful," rather than "deliberative." As can be seen in this book, this continues to be the case in many of our households.

One of the most challenging things in initial phases of the study was to analyze the claims being made by parents – particularly fathers – about media policies and practices in the household. Joe Champ was the interviewer in a number of the initial households where this became a theme, and it was Joe who helped us see past the explicit claims being made by these fathers toward the implicit structuration of ideas about fatherhood and manhood in those contexts. Joe's influence helped me to move to an analytic position that interpreted the social meaning of these claims.

The theme of fatherhood and manhood continues to be an interest of mine, and of our ongoing work, and Monica Emerich has been particularly helpful in continuing to think about issues of gender in relation to parental authority, and the symbolic meaning of that authority. Monica's own interests in spirituality and social change in the context of media practice has helped us focus on the ways that media – as commodities – function or may function in daily practice. Curtis Coats has also conducted some important field research in this area.

Diane Alters was influential in helping us see that the "implicit" religiosity of programs needs to be analyzed along with the "explicit" as a package. Her interest in *The Simpsons* attuned her to the challenging question of how we might socially legitimate or authenticate media experiences and practices that might not – on their face – seem "religious." Diane's sophisticated reading of the humanities literature on meaning and identity helped me (and us) articulate what we are seeing with larger themes in the culture. In addition to her intellectual skills, Diane was and is an excellent and persuasive writer, and those gifts have given great form and shape to the project and my thinking here.

Lee Hood wanted us always to keep in mind that these were family systems we were looking at, after all, and that the relations within the household around meaning and identity needed to be kept at the forefront. She was also an advocate for listening to the children in the households. Particularly in the early stages of our work, we did extensive interviews with younger children, and Lee was particularly accomplished at interpreting that material.

Anna Maria Russo took a particular interest in family systems as well, and her own work on single-parent families problematized for me questions of how family dynamics might shift in relation to differing media practices between households. Anna Maria also was very helpful in analyzing material related to media events and to the 9/11-related material that appears in Chapter 9, and helped us see that, while our interviewees seemed not to be overly involved in post-9/11 ritual, they nonetheless were profoundly – if subtly – affected and involved.

Christof Demont-Heinrich, Scott Webber, Michelle Miles, and Denice Walker were not centrally involved in analysis of questions of religion *per se*, though they did participate in many of the interviews reported here. To my thinking, they contributed a good deal of skepticism about the centrality of religion or spirituality in these interviews. Their healthy challenging of the notion that religion was explicitly present in the first instance allowed us to rethink some unstated assumptions in our method and approach. Later, we were able to rearticulate a sense of relations between religion and media that accounted for what appeared on the surface to be less evident as a result of those conversations.

Jin Kyu Park has been of inestimable help in the process of reconceptualization and rethinking that has typified our methodological journey. Jin is particularly good at identifying patterns and taxonomies of practice in interview material. He brings an exceptionally sophisticated grasp of cultural theory to these tasks, and his ability to make sense out of the narratives in interview material is doubly impressive in that he is not working in his native language. Jin was particularly helpful in the analysis in Chapter 8. He joined Lynn, Diane, and Joe in helping me see that the analysis in Chapters 6 and 7 represent, in addition to findings about the way that media practice transcends those categories, an implicit critique of the taxonomy itself. Jin struggled to fit various tentative taxonomies and structures to the data, and, through his efforts, we came to the kind of interpretive voice that would most helpfully express what we have seen and found.

In addition to these major turns, our meetings have provided literally scores of other insights, many of which we have attempted to record in weekly minutes. As we said in *Media, Home, and Family*, no analysis coming out of this project can be seen as entirely individual or novel. In both theoretical and methodological terms, what I have been able to report here is the result of a collaborative effort, and that is the key methodological point I would emphasize here.

I'll conclude with a few reflections on some of the unique approaches in our collaborative work represented in this book. First, it does appear that the narrative approach underlying our analysis was helpful and productive. Second, the notion of identity as the objective of the practice of meaning-making proves useful heuristically, and did prove to be a good way of describing and analyzing the interactions between various elements and domains. Third, the approach of treating media materials as a kind of "material culture" also proved useful. Interviewees were able to articulate their relations to media with a kind of objectivity that helped us see their relations to other domains of their lives. In sum, the method seemed to work well, and provided substantial material for interpretation and analysis.

The most interesting and challenging part of this study – implicit in much of what I've said above about our theoretical and methodological challenge and evolution – is the phenomenon that most of our interviewees had such a difficult time making clear and straightforward connections between their media lives and their religious/spiritual lives. I (and we) did not expect this to be as big a challenge as it turned out to be. Much of our reflection and rethinking was driven by the need to come to grips with this situation. What resulted, both here and in our earlier work, has been a more subtle, nuanced, and – in our view – sophisticated view of relations in these critical areas. As qualitative/interpretive work, this transition has been substantive in both methodological and theoretical terms. We leave it to readers and colleagues to help us judge the breadth of its significance.

Notes

Introduction

1   A film released in 2004 that intermixes philosophy, mysticism, and science in an exploration of the meaning of life. It was widely seen in the US as an antithesis to Gibson's more traditional or dogmatic work.
2   But not, as we will see, from the scholarly discourse, where a provocative and fruitful set of directions, influenced by culturalism, have evolved.
3   These can be seen at http://www.paikstudios.com/ [accessed March 1, 2006]
4   Hoover, Stewart M. (1988) "Television myth and ritual: the role of substantive meaning and spatiality," in James W. Carey (ed.) *Media, Myths and Narratives: Television and the Press*, Newbury Park: Sage, p. 176.
5   Hoover, Stewart M., Lynn Schofield Clark, and Diane F. Alters with Joseph G. Champ and Lee Hood (2004) *Media, Home, and Family*, New York: Routledge.

I What this book could be about

1   Of course, there is ample evidence that the process was developed first in the Far East centuries before.
2   Eisenstein, Elizabeth (1979) *The Printing Press as an Agent of Change*, New York: Cambridge University Press, pp. 22–34. There were, of course, other implications of the rise of printing including contemporaneous changes in modes of religious knowledge and understanding. See, for example, Schneider (2001).
3   And of course it faced an emerging threat to its authority in the form of a movement – the Reformation – that profited from and embraced this new media technology.
4   McLuhan was suggesting, on a micro-level, what had previously been claimed for media on a macro-level by his fellow Canadian, Harold Innis – that the structure of media of an age can be seen to have structured the religious sensibilities of that age (Innis 1950). Successors to McLuhan in the "Toronto School" have continued this line of thought (see, in particular, de Kerckhove and Dewdney (1995). Other work on the perceptual characteristics of television include: Reeves and Nass (1996) and Sturken and Cartwright (2001). For a review of this in the context of psychological theories of the flow of everyday life, see Kubey and Csikszentmihalyi (2002).
5   Ong (2002).
6   Jacques Ellul (1967) provides one of the most complex arguments to this effect, lodged very much in modernity. See also Babin (1970).

7   I am aware of the contradiction between my use of the term "organic" here and the classic Durkheimian formulation. What I refer to as "organic" is actually more related in context and meaning to his notion of "mechanical" solidarity.

8   The primogenitor of all such work is the classic study of the audience for broadcast religion (Parker *et al.* 1955).

9   Bruce (1990), Frankl (1987), Hadden and Shupe (1988), Schultze (1990), Hadden and Swann (1981), Horsfield (1984), Hoover (1988), Peck (1993).

10 Silk (1995), Stout and Buddenbaum (1996), Hoover (1998), Badarracco (2005).

11 This leaves aside the fact that the same tendency can be seen in media scholarship that might reasonably have looked at religion. See, for example, my arguments in later chapters about the work of Dayan and Katz (1992) and Fiske (1987) in particular.

12 In Hoover (1988), for example, I outlined the beginnings of an argument about televangelism that resonates with culturalist media scholarship today: that the significance of these ministries might well reside in the relation they bore to the context and history of their viewing more than in some instrumental "effect." See also Peck (1993).

13 There is, of course, an important argument that media and religion have never been separated, that all religions are mediated to some extent. Important and influential scholarship has also demonstrated that, even in modernity and late modernity, Protestantism, for example, has continued to be a prodigious producer of media of its own (see, in particular, Morgan 1998) and aggressive about projecting its images into the "secular" media as well (Hendershot 2004). These issues will be discussed in more detail in later chapters. In sum, though, the powerful received idea that the realms of "religion" and "media" have been or should be present is more a function of the commitments of theological and ecclesiastical authorities on the one hand and leading thought in the field of media studies on the other, than it is a fundamental reality. This will be discussed in more detail in the next chapter.

14 For a more thorough discussion, see Hoover and Venturelli (1996).

15 For the classic statement, see Innis (1950), but see also Silverstone (1991) and Moores (1993), pp. 70–116.

16 Much of this literature is rooted in the early persuasive work of Berger and Luckman (1966).

17 For an influential collection focusing on the case of youth culture, see Hall and Jefferson (1976). See also Grossberg (1992). For a discussion in relation to religion, see Clark (2003), pp. 3–23 and 224–36.

18 Medved (1992), Meyers (1989), and Postman (1986).

19 Kubey and Csikszentmihalyi (1990). For a more recent statement, see Kubey and Csikszentmihalyi (2002).

20 Silverstone (1994), Moores (1993), and Couldry (2003).

21 Newcomb and Hirsch (1983).

22 For a critical discussion of this literature, see Hoover *et al.* (2004).

23 For a review of this literature, see Seiter (1999). See also Clark (2003).

24 Clark (2003).

25 Dayan and Katz (1992), Rothenbuhler (1998). For a critical review and analysis, see Couldry (2003).

26 Hoover and Russo (2002). Hoover and Russo argue, additionally, that this role is one that has evolved over time, originating with the Kennedy assassination, but gradually developing through more recent crises such as the Challenger explosion, the Oklahoma City bombing, the Columbine School Shootings, the funeral of Princess Diana, and of course the events surrounding 9/11. See also Chapter 8, this volume.

27 For a culturally nuanced view, see Appadurai (1991).
28 See, for example, Eck (2001).
29 There has been particular progress in the field of anthropology. See, e.g., Ginsburg *et al.* (2002).
30 The tradition loosely based on Marshall McLuhan, but more recently identified with works such as Meyerwitz (1985).
31 Giddens (1991).
32 See Gergen (1991) for the articulation of the view that such knowledge is, in fact, disempowering and problematic. Giddens takes a different view, that we must simply understand this as a condition of contemporary life.
33 I much prefer "late modernity" to "postmodernity" as a description of the contemporary era. Not only am I somewhat skeptical that the claimed elements of "postmodernity" might have been able to reach far and wide enough in the culture to achieve any totalizing or epochal status, but I am also skeptical that these elements (in particular, claims about the status of symbols and ideals) can be found to be in flux anywhere outside the terms of academic, postmodern discourse. I am convinced, with Giddens and others, that we do live in a time of "late modernity," where fundamental social, conceptual, cultural dimensions are typical of an "age."
34 Jameson (1992), Harvey (1989).
35 Baudrillard (1983).
36 For a complete discussion, see Carter (2000). See also Neuhaus (1986).
37 Hunter (1992).
38 McLuhan of course suggested that film and television, while sharing visuality, also differed, in that one was more absorbing (cool) than the other. For a psychological discussion of visuality, see Messaris (1994). See also Sturken and Cartwright (2001), pp. 45–69. For a discussion of issues of the visual with relation to contemporary American religion, see Morgan and Promey (2001) and Morgan (1998).
39 I am indebted to one of my teachers, Ray Birdwhistel, for drumming into us, "the first question should not be 'what is happening?' but 'where is this happening?'"
40 Gerbner and Connolly (1978).
41 Muggeridge (1977).
42 Myers (1989).
43 Schultze *et al.* (1991).
44 Schultze (2002).
45 Postman (1986).
46 Fore (1987). See also Fore (1990).
47 Medved (1992).
48 Bennett (1993).
49 Gerbner *et al.* (1984). See also Gerbner *et al.* (1989).
50 Buddenbaum and Stout (1996).
51 See survey work by Robert O. Wyatt reported in Dart and Allen (1993), pp. 21–7. Hoover *et al.* (1995).
52 Dayan and Katz (1992).
53 Rothenbuhler (1998).
54 Marvin (1999).
55 Couldry (2003).
56 Durkheim (1995).
57 Carey (1975).
58 For a recent critique of Carey's use of the term ritual, see Saebø (2003).
59 For a prominent and influential example, see Bird (2003). See also Ginsburg *et al.* (2002).

60 For a definitive review of Cultural Studies theory, see Turner (1990). I do not wish to ignore a very significant dimension of much of Cultural Studies: its historical-materialist roots. While the anthropological approach I will follow in this book focuses on practice and on the agency of audiences in determining meanings and outcomes, the question of determination is far from settled, and an important continuing question for Cultural Studies (see next note).

61 See the debate published as Garnham (1995) and Grossberg (1995).

62 Lila Abu-Lughod has assessed this turn from an anthropological perspective in an essay focusing on some of the initial efforts by media scholars, which she found too theoretically, and not enough anthropologically, driven. Abu-Lughod (1997).

63 For a complete discussion, see Moores (1993) and Bird (2003).

64 Albanese (1998).

65 For literature reviews of these trends, see Clark and Hoover (1997) and Clark (2002).

66 Winston (2000).

67 Clark (2003).

68 Rosenthal (2004).

69 Hangen (2002).

70 Schmalzbaur (2003).

71 McCloud (2004).

72 Mitchell (2000).

73 Hendershot (2004).

74 Morgan (1996).

75 Of course, the same can be said for some earlier "classics" in media and religion studies, including Horsfield (1984), Hoover (1988), Schultze (1990), Frankl (1987), and Peck (1993).

76 Herberg (1983).

77 For the classic statement, see Lerner (1964). In one chapter, Lerner describes the worldview of a traditional tribal elder, conveying with some sensitivity the fact that such people would soon find themselves caught up in the relentless march of modernity, something that they would struggle to understand and account for. The implicit message: such worldviews would soon be a thing of the past as modernity brushed aside such (religiously modulated) ideas and values. Ironically, that passage referred to Iran.

78 For a more complete discussion of the emergence of religion into journalistic discourse, see Hoover (1998).

79 As is obvious from the discussion in the introduction, this is not necessarily a new phenomenon. However, it does seem to be more and more common. On the US side of the Atlantic, for example, much has been made of the involvement of prominent actors such as John Travolta and Tom Cruise in the Church of Scientology. There was a good deal of press attention in 2003 to the story that the Australian actor Mel Gibson is involved, along with his father, in the development of a conservative Catholic movement. Meanwhile, British newspapers reported in the summer of the same year that the singer Madonna, her husband, and a number of other American and British celebrities were involved in founding a new London headquarters for a center devoted to the teachings of the Kabbalah (*Observer*, Sunday, 23 May 2003, p. 3).

80 I described them as 1) a concern with ideology and power; 2) a concern with the "effects" of media on religion or vice versa; and 3) a concern with media as a center of Durkheimian social meaning and solidarity.

81 I would argue, by the way, that these limitations are also present in other approaches, including more positivist, empiricist, and quantitative ones.

82 A curious anecdote relevant to our discussions here is that when television broadcasting did arrive in Fiji in 1995 there were already a number of television sets there, supplied – along with VCRs and tapes – by Australian supporters of a US televangelism ministry.

83 For a complete account of this project, including an extensive discussion of the methodology also used here, see Hoover *et al.* (2004).

84 Geertz (1973), p. 90.

2 From medium to meaning

1 "Reception" as a term of art in media and cultural studies refers to the processes, practices, and contexts wherein people consume and use media.

2 Habermas (1989). There has been, of course, a vibrant debate over Habermas's work, particularly in relation to questions of who was or is included in discursive civil society rooted in such reception. Cf. Fraser (1993).

3 Nord (2004), Underwood (2002).

4 Moore (1995). See also McDannell (1998) and Morgan (1998).

5 De Tocqueville (2000). See also Bellah (1986).

6 This distinction continues to be seen in such things as the separate "lists" of book sales kept by the publishing industry. Even though "religious" books have been among the best-sellers in volume, they don't appear on the *New York Times*'s best-seller list, but on a separate "religious" list.

7 Fischer (1994).

8 For a synthetic recent account, see Schudson and Tifft (2005).

9 Ibid., pp. 22–3.

10 Thompson, John B. (1995) *The Media and Modernity*, Stanford: Stanford University Press, in particular Chapter 1.

11 See Promey (1996) and Rosenthal (2001), for more complete discussions of these debates within American Protestantism (discussed further below). Two prominent streams of thought are represented by Bennett (1993), a moralist reading of contemporary culture, including media, and Robert Putnam (1996), who contends that the content and cultural location of much of television is counter-productive to social and civic engagement. NB, as well, that the so-called "Leavisite" approach to culture, against which contemporary cultural studies lodges itself, conceives of such "popular" media and "popular" culture as something to be overcome by "high" or "refined" culture.

12 Advertisers of course became directly and unabashedly involved in the production of early broadcasting, for example, a situation that only came to an end with the "quiz show scandals" of the 1950s (for a complete discussion, see Barnouw 1990). Others argue persuasively that the commercial basis of American media, far from freeing those media from influence, integrate them into structures of dominant economic influence. See McChesney (1995) and Alterman (2003).

13 McChesney (1995). This was also a trend in British broadcasting and in other "public service" systems as well.

14 For an account of this phenomenon in youth-oriented marketing, see Goodman, Barak and Dretzin, Rachel, *PBS Frontline Video* "The Merchants of Cool," WGBH, 2001.

15 Popular history and popular discourse recognizes, for example, the role of William Randolph Hearst and his newspapers in the Spanish–American War. See Sloan *et al.* (1989). See also Schudson and Tifft (2005), pp. 20–4.

16 So named because of the formation in the years 1930 to 1965 of a scholarly project devoted to social theory and research that was based at the Institute for Social Research at the University of Frankfurt, Germany. Major figures in this

"school," including Theodor Adorno, fled the rise of Nazism and, along with their students, continued to play a role in social theory about media.

17 Tönnies (1957).
18 Horkheimer and Adorno (1972), pp 120–67; Adorno (1991). For a critical analysis, see Kellner (1989), chapters 5 and 6.
19 A comprehensive review is beyond the scope of a footnote, but several accounts of this research are available, including Liebert and Sprafkin (1988). For a critical appraisal, see McGuire (1986).
20 See Kubey and Csikszentmihalyi (1990) as an example, and for a thorough review of the literature. See also Gunter and McAleer (1997), Bryant and Zillmann (1994), and Huesmann and Malamuth (1986).
21 See Jamison (2002), Jamison (2000), and McDevitt and Chaffee (2000).
22 See, for example, Arnett (1992), Arnett (1991).
23 Cf., for example, the collection in Andersen and Collins (2004). See also, as an example, Morgan (1987).
24 Charters (1933).
25 I do not intend to argue that these media do not have effects or that previous research in this direction is invalid. There is, in fact, convincing evidence of direct effects of various media on various audiences under various circumstances. The problem is that we know little of other media, other audiences, or other circumstances as a result of many of these studies. Further, as I introduced in Chapter 1 and will discuss in more detail later, some questions are simply not amenable to study in terms of their supposed "effects."
26 Habermas (1985). To Habermas, "lifeworld" is the expressive, natural, and organic sphere of authentic experience, the place into which we are born and in which we grow, raise our children, and pursue our individual quests for meaning and value. "Systemworld" is our experience of the rationalization, routinization, and bureaucratization of modern life.
27 For a complete discussion, see Hoover *et al.* (2004).
28 Thompson (1995), pp. 7–8.
29 Katz and Lazersfeld (1955).
30 Blumer (1975); see also McQuail (1970).
31 This was expressed, for example, in debates between the churches of the Protestant establishment and the emergent Evangelical movement that was seen as far more interested in such "directly effective" messages. For a discussion of these perspectives, see Ellens (1974). For a defense of the Evangelical approach, see Armstrong (1979).
32 Quoted in Carpenter (1985), p. 15. See also Dorgan (1993).
33 Parker *et al.* (1955).
34 Parker *et al.* (1955).
35 Schultze (1987).
36 Horsfield (1984).
37 Hoover (1988).
38 Peck (1993).
39 Martin-Barbero (1997).
40 Moore (1995).
41 McDannell (1998).
42 Morgan (1998); Morgan and Promey (2001).
43 Schmidt (1995).
44 Winston (2000).
45 Hendershot (2004).
46 Admittedly, "media" can be understood as artifacts. See, for example, Moores's (1993) discussion of media technologies as objects in the context of private and domestic spaces. The difference here is a matter of nuance perhaps. Thinking of

religious artifacts also allows us to begin thinking of the religious and spiritual practices that integrate those artifacts into individual experience, a very different view than attributing the autonomy in the process to the medium.

47 De Vries (2001), p. 28. While I agree with DeVries (and others in that volume) that questions of the "enchantment" or the mystery traditionally associated with religion, and the implications of technology in that regard, are important, they may not fundamentally address what is done when people encounter or interact with media materials. I will discuss this in more detail in the final chapter.

48 For a complete discussion, see Warner (1993) and Yamane (1997).

49 Williams (1977).

50 Giddens (1991).

51 Giddens (1991), in particular pp. 19–35.

52 On the "positive" side, an increased level of personal autonomy, while on the "negative" a higher level of cynicism about social institutions, including politics.

53 Gergen (1991).

54 This contrasting view of the self and media culture is an issue we will return to in later chapters, assessing the extent to which there is evidence in our interview data that supports one or the other perspective.

55 For a comprehensive discussion, see Moores (1993).

56 Denzin (1992), p. 26. This will be discussed in greater detail in later chapters.

57 For a complete discussion, see Clark (2003), pp. 3–23.

58 Warner (1993).

59 Roof (1999).

60 This has been most clearly expressed in the so-called "culture wars" that have emerged at the boundary between Neo-Evangelical and old-line religious traditions. For a definitive discussion, see Hunter (1992).

61 Roof (1999), p. 124.

62 For more detailed accounts of interactionist theory in relation to culture, see Denzin (1992). Erving Goffman (1959) developed the most elaborate theory of self-presentation in relation to interactionist ideas.

63 Denzin (1992), pp. 27–8.

64 "Seeking a focus on joy in field of psychology," *New York Times*, 28 April 1998, section F, p. 7.

65 Csikszentmihalyi and Rochberg-Halton (1981).

66 Spiegel (1992), Sieffert (1994), and Marc (1996).

67 Herberg (1983).

68 For more complete discussions, see Rosenthal (2001) and Hoover and Wagner (1997). In the US, the instrumentality was the so-called "sustaining time" system through which the dominant religions were given access to local and national airtime on commercial television. A parallel system emerged in the UK, with the BBC establishing both its own internal religion unit and terms through which other religions would receive airtime. Later, the authority moved outside the BBC itself, but the fundamental dynamic remained the same: broadcasting authorities were in the position of deciding which were legitimate religious voices and which were not. For a critical view from a movement "left out" of the British system, see Quicke and Quicke (1992).

69 Fore (1987).

3 Media and religion in transition

1 Much of the following discussion can be compared with received or classic definitions of mass communication, such as that offered by Charles Wright (1974).

2 As was discussed to some degree in Chapter 1, these questions, in fact, form the basis of the field of cultural studies and its approach to media studies. The work of Richard Hoggart and Raymond Williams (in particular) raised the important question of whose cultures were valid and normative. For a substantive discussion, see Turner (1990).

3 There is good reason, as well, to think of processes of reception generally in terms of what they *produce* rather than simply what they *consume*.

4 Enzensberger (1974).

5 Bagdikian (1997); McChesney and Nichols (2002).

6 Jhally (1990).

7 In the US, the "newer" Fox, UPN, WB, and PAX networks have each emerged within the last fifteen years, benefiting from regulatory incentives that link the prospects of over-the-air broadcasters to the cable and satellite services in local market areas.

8 A good deal of scholarship has been devoted to Web-based religion in recent years. See, for example, Hadden and Cowan (2001), Zaleski (1997), Brasher (2004), Hoover and Park (2005), and Miller and Slater (2000).

9 Of course, this had existed for decades in radio, with such major players as the Moody Bible Institute domestically and Trans World Radio internationally, running religion-only networks and services from the 1930s onward (Ellens 1974).

10 For an early account of the phenomenon, see Hadden and Swann (1981) and Horsfield (1984).

11 Hendershot (2004).

12 For a more complete discussion, with reference to journalism in particular, see Hoover (1998).

13 ABC employed a religion reporter, Peggy Wehmeyer, with much fanfare in 1993 and she continued for several years, but the network no longer has anyone in that post.

14 Aside from the work of some prominent exceptions such as the production team of Bill and Judith Moyers, public television has been an even less salubrious environment for religion than commercial television in the US.

15 It followed the network airing of a less self-consciously religious (but nonetheless religiously identified and supported) series called *Christy* the year before (Garron 1998).

16 Garron (1998).

17 For a complete discussion of the *Touched* phenomenon, see Clark (2003).

18 Alters (2003). See also Lynch (2005), pp. 149–56.

19 These trends were in some ways even more evident in programs targeting the youth audience. For a complete discussion, see Clark (2003). These trends were greeted with skepticism in some quarters. Media scholar John Fiske, for example, observed, "It's all turning into some sort of sloppy spirituality, characterized by the New Age movement and by a lot of this sentimental Christianity that's going on" (Zerbisias 1997).

20 This sort of challenge to established religion by recording stars is, of course, nothing new; the Beatles' widely noted claim to be "more famous than Jesus" is a prominent example. However, the 1990s arguably saw a new boldness and directness in prominent artists taking on religion – or the mantle of religion – in popular media and popular culture.

21 There is a prodigious bibliography of scholarly and popular work relating to religion and film, too large to list comprehensively here. Of particular note, however, have been Nolan (2003), Mitchell (2005), Miles (1997), and Martin and Ostwald (1995). An interesting development along these lines is the

emergence of a successful new commercial educational and encounter movement, called "Spiritual Cinema Circles," devoted to supporting, viewing, and discussing spiritually significant films.

22 Similar trends were underway, over the same period, in the UK and in Europe in general. In the case of the UK, see, in particular, Tracey (1998).

23 This debate flares from time to time. In the winter of 2004, it arose over an incident involving the singer Janet Jackson during the Super Bowl halftime show. She exposed too much skin for traditional tastes, and a series of investigations, hearings, and threats by the FCC ensued. In the same time period, the Commission also cracked down on popular radio "shock jock" Howard Stern and levied fines for what they saw as on-air indecency and profanity.

24 Lattin (2003).

25 Poovakkattu (2003). In some ways, though, American religious evolution differs significantly from that on the other side of the Atlantic. For example, a 2001 survey published in the *Scotsman* reported that while nearly 37 percent of Scots have had a supernatural experience, 55 percent never attend religious services, and only 28 percent believe clergy contribute to society (Kerevan 2001). The *New York Times* reported in 2003 on the situation of a priest in the Danish Lutheran Church who was suspended from his parish for saying he did not believe in God. Members of his parish and his local community rallied to his defense (Alvarez 2003).

26 Evans (1999).

27 The most influential work related to religious restructuring was Wuthnow (1990). In the area of religious practice, Roof (1992) was particularly influential, as has been his more recent *Spiritual Marketplace* (1999), which we will discuss in more detail presently.

28 Giddens (1991), pp. 179–80.

29 This is, of course, a contradiction to traditional social theory, which would hold that the decline of religious differentiation would lead to a decline in interest in religion. As religion scholars such as Roof and Warner (who we will discuss presently) point out, this idea of secularization relied on the assumption that religion was a property of religious institutions and structures. This new, more individualized religion is instead thought by its adherents to be something for which they are responsible instead.

30 Hammond (1992).

31 Roof (1992).

32 Roof (1992), p. 195.

33 Roof (1992), p. 256.

34 Wuthnow (1998).

35 Roof (1999), p. 9.

36 Roof (1992), p. 247.

37 Roof (1999), pp. 67–8.

38 Giddens (1991), pp. 32–4.

39 Roof (1999), p. 41.

40 For complete discussions, see Silk (1995) and Hoover (1998).

41 Detailed examples of media decision-makers' impressions of religion can be found in Silk (1995) and Hoover (1998), as well as in John Dart and Jimmy Allen, *Bridging the Gap*, Nashville: The Freedom Forum First Amendment Center, 1993.

42 Silk and Hoover both detail James Gordon Bennett's early introduction of religion coverage into the pages of the *New York Times* as a competitive strategy. The *Times* continued to cover the sermons of prominent New York City pulpits well into the 1960s. *Time Magazine* was distinctive for its attention to religion

over the years, a trend followed by the other newsmagazines. *Time*, for example, featured prominent religious leaders on its cover during the 1950s and 1960s, including Protestant theological icons Reinhold Niebuhr and Paul Tillich. In fact, by the 1980s, most major newsmagazines and metropolitan daily papers, as well as the Associated Press and United Press International, had dedicated religion reporters or staffs, though relatively few at any one outlet (Silk 1995).

43 There were, of course, precursors of these events. CNN's Jeff Greenfield, for example, has noted that as the US Civil Rights Movement was rooted so deeply in religion, its early stages largely occurred "under the radar" of the mainstream press. This is ironic in that of the major television news outlets, CNN has been among the most resistant to introducing religion reporting as a beat, though there has been a good deal of self-criticism there (CNN 1993).

44 For helpful descriptions and analyses, see Quebedeaux (1974), Wuthnow (1990), Roof (1999), Marsden (1983).

45 See Marsden (1983).

46 It has been argued that, for a variety of reasons, Evangelicalism has been particularly attuned to media and popular culture, and prone to see the media as likely contexts for the doing of religious "good." See, for example, Hendershot (2004), Clark (2003), McCloud (2004), and Schultze (1987).

47 Wilson (2005). The ad was particularly striking because it violated the unspoken rule that religious messages must always be inoffensive. Making its point with regard to openness, it portrayed "other" faith groups as exclusionary, using the symbol of black-shirted "bouncers" denying people access to church. The church reports a remarkable response to the ad, with large numbers of hits on its websites, calls to local congregations, and new attenders directly attributed to its message of openness.

48 While this description relates most closely to the situation in the US, some similar trends are obvious in the context of the UK. For example, in an interview in the (London) *Times*, the then new Head of BBC Religious Broadcasting, Alan Bookbinder, noted that among the effects of the September 11 attacks and some other recent events in Britain was a renewed profile for religion in news and programming (Snoddy 2002). An interesting footnote to this story, and one relevant to our discussions here, is that Bookbinder is a self-avowed agnostic. His appointment raised quite a few eyebrows as a result, but his argument that media coverage of religion must by definition be rational and oriented to ideas rather than the promotion of faith illustrates the terms of the problem of religion.

49 An April 2004 study by the Media Research Center confirmed an increase in coverage of religion by the major US networks, finding that the number of stories had more than doubled over the previous ten years (Bauder 2004).

50 Hadden and Cowan (2001).

51 Kornblut (2000).

52 *Broadcasting and Cable Yearbook, 2002–2003.*

53 *Broadcasting and Cable Yearbook, 2002–2003.* A note on claimed "subscribers" to these services is in order. In all cases, these figures represent the total number of subscribers to the basic cable services on which these channels appear as an option. They do not necessarily represent subscribers, supporters, or regular viewers of these services. In fact, the actual levels of viewing are much smaller, probably in the hundreds of thousands for each rather than in the millions. For a thorough discussion of the issue of televangelism audience size during the heyday of the form, see Hoover (1987).

54 Hinsliff (2000). Interestingly, one of the major reasons for the reluctance of British authorities to allow religious broadcasting has been fear of the excesses of the US model.

55 For a thorough discussion of this history, see Hoover (1988).
56 Moore (1995), Winston (2000), Morgan (1996), Nord (2004), Underwood (2002).
57 Borden (forthcoming).
58 Nord (2004).
59 Blake (2004).
60 Borden (forthcoming).
61 Ali (2001).
62 Hendershot (2004), p. 209.
63 *Christianity Today* Magazine Rates and Data (www.christianitytoday.com/help/advertising/print/ct.html) [accessed 3 August 2005].
64 Which folded in 1993.
65 Alsdurf (forthcoming).
66 Hoover (1988).
67 Hoover *et al.* (2004), Chapter 3.
68 See Hoover (1988) for a discussion of this process with regard to religious broadcasting, and Hendershot (2004) in relation to Evangelical and prophecy films. In both cases, an impulse to make media that would move into the secular marketplace faces the problem of accommodating to the demands of that marketplace, and, in both cases, the record is clear that it is a nearly insuperable challenge to make such "crossing over" work. The same situation has been widely noted in regard to the "crossover" potential of the Christian music industry.
69 Hendershot (2004), particularly the discussion of the film *Left Behind*, pp. 200–9. Hendershot quotes a number of Evangelical informants asking, "Why can't Christians make better movies?"
70 Zerbisias (1997).
71 Zerbisias (1997).
72 Hendershot's review of Christian marketing and contemporary Christian music concludes that this kind of programming – generically "wholesome" – is understood to be the successful approach for "crossing over" from the "other direction" as well (Hendershot 2004, Chs 1–2 and p. 199).
73 No fewer than three scholarly volumes dealing with the film were announced within weeks of its premier.
74 Apostolos-Cappadona (1997); see also Korp (1997).
75 Goethals (1982).
76 Morgan (1999).
77 For a discussion of realism in the Gibson *Passion*, see Morgan (2004).
78 Best and Kellner (1991).
79 Wildmon (1989); Medved (1992).
80 Bellah (1986), pp. 279–81.
81 Carey (1989), p. 18.
82 Culturalist media theory has long articulated a powerful critique of such totalizing understandings of mass media. See, in particular, Moores (1993), pp. 1–10.
83 Harvey (1989).
84 McLuhan (1994).
85 Ellul (1967).
86 Ong (1986).
87 DeVries and Weber (2001).
88 I limit my criticism of deVries and Weber's (2001) efforts because, in other respects, many of the contributions to their volume are insightful, even masterful, accounts of various aspects of the implications of the media age for religion. Curiously lacking among their contributors (aside from some anthropologists) are any social scientists whose work focuses on religion and media.

89 For a critique of McLuhan and Ong in this regard, see Underwood (2002), pp. 209–14.
90 For a complete discussion with reference to media studies, see Hoover and Venturelli (1996).
91 Rothenbuhler (1998); Couldry (2003). While there is good reason to be clear about the distinction between ritual practices that are primarily social or practical in orientation, and those that are more self-evidently "religious," the boundary between the two realms is not nearly so clear. For a critique of the media studies literature's invocation of the concept of ritual, see Grimes (2001).
92 Fiske (1987), p. 22.
93 Dayan and Katz (1992).
94 Couldry (2003).
95 Thomas (2005). For a more complete account of his perspective, see Thomas (1998).
96 Albanese (1998).
97 Warner (1993).
98 Warner (1993).
99 Warner (1993).
100 Roof (1999), pp. 126–7.
101 Paul Heelas and Linda Woodhead described religiosity in Britain in similar terms. Heelas and Woodhead (2000).
102 Warner (1993), p. 1,078.
103 Roof (1999), p. 132.
104 Roof (1999), p. 137
105 Hoover (2003). Among these "modes," the *visual* mode has received a great deal of recent attention among art historians interested in reception and material culture. These new perspectives stress that, in spite of what has seemed to be an official derogation of popular visual imagery among Protestant authorities (in particular), nineteenth- and twentieth-century Protestant cultures in fact produced a profusion of visual materials (Morgan 1999). The seeming contradiction between the perspectives of theological authority on the one hand, and a prodigious production of popular imagery on the other, is partly addressed by Sally Promey's analysis presented in this chapter.
106 Roof (1999), p. 144.
107 For a discussion of these criticisms in relation to youth culture, and a particularly interesting example in an analysis of the trend toward teen-oriented films and television with satanic or Wiccan themes, see Clark (2003). With regard to the effects of media on audiences in general, see Medved (1992) and Meyers (1989).
108 Rosenthal (2001).
109 Promey (1996). For a nuanced discussion of critical theory and its relation to visual objects in general, see Koch (2001).
110 Promey (1996), pp. 156–60.
111 Bellah (1986).
112 Warner (1993), p. 1,076.
113 Roof (1999).
114 Hendershot (2004), pp. 5–7. An interesting anecdote is the report from 1999 that an Evangelical group called "Daystar" was planning a webcam trained on Jerusalem's eastern gate so as to capture Christ's Second Coming were it to occur in conjunction with the new millennium (Silverman 1999).
115 Morgan (1999).
116 Stark and Bainbridge (1985).

117 Hendershot (2004); and Clark (2003) (specifically with regard to teen culture, pp. 229–31).
118 A judgment that is undergoing change in the context of US religious politics post-2004. See Chapter 8 for a discussion.
119 Roof (1999).
120 Roof (1999), p. 197.
121 Rosenthal (2001).

4 Articulating life and culture in the media age

1 Ultimately, of course, the process of theory-building in most areas of media studies has always involved an interaction between the "quantitative/empiricist" and "qualitative/interpretivist" camps. As should be obvious from the discussions in this book, the field of media and religion studies is no different.
2 Christopher Lasch (1977) *Haven in a Heartless World: The Family Besieged*, New York: Basic Books.
3 David Gauntlett and Annette Hill (1999) *TV Living: Television Culture and Everyday Life*, London: Routledge and the British Film Institute, particularly pp. 283–93. For an important and substantive study in the US context focused specifically on television and children, see Ellen Seiter (1999).
4 Stewart M. Hoover, Lynn Schofield Clark, and Diane F. Alters, with Joseph G. Champ and Lee Hood (2004) *Media, Home, and Family*, New York: Routledge.
5 Hoover *et al.* (2004), p. 172.
6 Hoover *et al.* (2004), p. 22.
7 Hoover *et al.* (2004), p. 27.
8 James Lull (1991) *Inside Family Television*, London: Routledge.
9 David Morley (1992) *Television, Audiences, and Cultural Studies*, London: Routledge.
10 Elihu Katz and Tamar Liebes (1985) "Mutual aid in the decoding of *Dallas*: preliminary notes from a cross-cultural study," in Phillip Drummond and Richard Paterson (eds) *Television in Transition: Papers from the First International Television Studies Conference*, London: British Film Institute.
11 This is most provocatively understood in relation to Pierre Bourdieu's ideas about taste and class, and the way in which taste can and does act as marker in social relationships. (Pierre Bourdieu (1984) *Distinction: A Social Critique of the Judgment of Taste*, trans. Richard Nice, Cambridge, MA: Harvard University Press.)
12 Gauntlett and Hill (1999), p. 128.
13 James Carey (1989) *Communication as Culture*, Boston: Unwin-Hyman, pp. 28–9.
14 Ellen Seiter (1999). *Television and New Media Audiences*, Oxford: Oxford University Press, p. 58.
15 Hoover *et al.* (2004), op cit.
16 Festinger (1957); see also Neighbour (1992).
17 Gauntlett and Hill (1999), p. 291.
18 I am indebted to Roger Silverstone for an early influence on my thinking about the utility of narrative in media research, though his work focused on text rather than audience. See Roger Silverstone, "Television myth and culture," in James Carey (ed.) (1998) *Media, Myths and Narratives, Television and the Press*, Newbury Park, CA: Sage, pp. 32–3.
19 Wade Clark Roof (1999) *Spiritual Marketplace: Baby Boomers and the Remaking of American Religion*, Princeton: Princeton University Press, p. 217.

20 As an example, see J. Overcash (2004) "Narrative research: a viable methodology for clinical nursing," *Nursing Forum* 39(1) (January–March): 15–22.

21 Notable examples are Dan P. McAdams (1993) *The Redemptive Self: Stories Americans Live By*, New York: Oxford University Press; Catherine Kohler Riessman (1993) *Narrative Analysis*, Newbury Park, CA: Sage; and Amia Lieblich, Rivka Tuval-Mashiach, and Tamar Zilber (1998) *Narrative Research: Reading, Analysis, and Interpretation*. Newbury Park, CA: Sage.

22 A particularly interesting discussion of this approach is Megan Blumenreich (2004) "Avoiding the pitfalls of 'conventional' narrative research: using post-structural theory to guide the creation of narratives of children with HIV," *Qualitative Research* (4)1: 70–90.

23 See, in particular, Deborah Reed-Danahay (1997) *Auto/Ethnography*, New York: Berg. For a notable variation, see Sherry Ortner (1993) "Ethnography among the Newark: the class of '58 of Weequakic high school," *Michigan Quarterly Review* 32: 411–29. Ortner embeds her own biographical ethnography within an exploration of her high-school class. Another variation is the field of "interpretive biography," which uses narrative/interpretive techniques in relation to biography (Norman K. Denzin (1989) *Interpretive Biography*, Newbury Park, CA: Sage).

24 Paul Ricoeur (1991) *From Text to Action*, trans. Kathleen Blamey and John B. Thompson, Evanston: Northwestern University Press, p. 15.

25 Paul Ricoeur (1992) *Oneself as Another*, trans. Kathleen Blamey, Chicago: University of Chicago Press, pp. 141–5.

26 Ricoeur (1992), pp. 165–8.

27 For a complete description of the methodology, see Lynn Schofield Clark, "The Journey from Postpositivist to Constructivist Methods," Chapter Two in Hoover *et al.* (2004).

28 Charles Taylor (1989) *Sources of the Self: The Making of the Modern Identity*, Cambridge, MA: Harvard University Press, p. 27.

29 Erving Goffman (1959) *The Presentation of Self in Everyday Life*, Garden City, New York: Doubleday.

30 The foundational theorist here is George Herbert Mead (George Herbert Mead (1934) *Mind, Self and Society*, Chicago: University of Chicago Press, pp. 138–40).

31 I should acknowledge here the existence of a literature that is critical of the notion of narrative, in particular Galen Strawson's (2004) thoughtful contribution in the *Times Literary Supplement*. While I don't want to side-step the important issues Strawson has raised, I would argue that the use of the concept I am proposing here is a conditional one that resides *within* his "psychological" category. It is the kind of thing that he accepts as narrative, but declares "trivial." The notion that, when asked, people construct presentations of themselves that have a certain consistency and narrativity is not directly addressed by Strawson's arguments. Neither does it directly confront those arguments.

32 Robert William Kubey and Mihaly Csikszentmihalyi (1990) *Television and the Quality of Life: How Viewing Shapes Everyday Experiences*, Mahwah, NJ: Lawrence Erlbaum Associates.

33 Kenneth Gergen (1991) *The Saturated Self: Dilemmas of Identity in Contemporary Life*, New York: Basic Books, p. 16.

34 Anthony Giddens (1991) *Modernity and Self-Identity: Self and Society in the Late Modern Age*, Stanford: Stanford University Press, pp. 52–3 (emphasis in original).

35 As with all interviews in this book, these are not these interviewees' real names. This interview was conducted by Monica Emerich.

36 See, in particular, Diane F. Alters, "At the Heart of the Culture: The Hartmans and Roelofs," Chapter Seven in Hoover *et al.* (2004).

37 Heather Hendershot (2004) *Shaking the World for Jesus: Media and Conservative Evangelical Culture*, Chicago: University of Chicago Press.

38 This program aired on the US CBS network from 1960 to 1968. It featured a small-town southern sheriff, played by Griffith, who lived with his son and an aunt, who was his housekeeper. It was never revealed whether he was divorced or widowed, but there was no wife present. The absence of a wife, and the absence of any people of color on the program, are generally pointed to as examples of the show's catering to a time of social anxiety about changes in race and gender relations.

39 Howard has directed such notable films as *Grand Theft Auto, Backdraft, Splash, Apollo 13, A Beautiful Mind, Cinderella Man,* and *The Da Vinci Code.* While some of his earlier work was of the potboiler variety, his more recent work has received substantial critical acclaim.

5 Reception of religion and media

1 This is a term used by one of my professors, Ray Birdwhistel, to describe social research that unknowingly generates the results it seeks by tautologically investigating issues that are so "taken for granted," that it is not really possible to find informants who would answer in the negative.

2 All interview material here, unless otherwise identified, is from interviews conducted as part of the "Media, Meaning, and the Lifecourse," and "Religion, Meaning, and the New Media@Home" projects of the Center for Media, Religion, and Culture at the University of Colorado, supported by grants from the Lilly Endowment, Inc. For more information, see www.mediareligion.org. This interview was conducted by Dr Joseph G. Champ. Interviews here will always be identified in endnotes by the researcher who conducted them. All informant names are fictitious in keeping with standard protocols of human subjects research.

3 Lynn Schofield Clark, "Being Distinctive in a Mediated Environment: The Ahmeds and Paytons," Chapter Six in Hoover *et al.* (2004)

4 Clark, ibid, p. 96.

5 As my colleagues and I noted in *Media, Home, and Family*, there does not appear to be a systematic pattern, based in religious belief, predicting who will reject media and who will not.

6 The interview with the Fallons was conducted by Christof Demont-Heinrich.

7 My colleagues and I discuss this in detail in *Media, Home, and Family* as well. See Chapter 6, in particular, where the Payton family is discussed. David Gauntlett and Annette Hill (1999) make a similar point in *TV Living*, particularly around the use of television by many as a "friend" or "companion." See also the notion of the "transparency" of media in Livingstone (2002).

8 Interviews with the Johnsons were conducted by Christof Demont-Heinrich.

9 Such rules are one of the most tangible and salient elements of family identity. For a further discussion of this, see Hoover *et al.* (2004).

10 These are all half-hour programs on the Cartoon Network. *Dexter*, at least, has extensive tie-ins to gaming, with an X-Box version of *Dexter* available, and an online *Dexter* game available on the Cartoon Network's website for free.

11 A game available for free download.

12 A website devoted to computer games, music, videos, graphics, and other things. It is not a children's website, and advertises alcohol, among other products for older audiences.

13 Though, at least one of our interview families, the Callahans, who we will meet in Chapter 6, objected to *Wishbone* on religious grounds, finding it too "politically correct" for their tastes.

14 This raises a question, of course, about their expressed limit of an 8 o'clock bedtime for the boys, as *ER* is on at 9 in the market where they live.

15 The interviews with the Cruz family were conducted by Dr Scott Webber.

16 From www.scifi.com/johnedward/: "John Edward reunited people in the physical world with their loved ones who have crossed over." *Crossing over with John Edward* airs on the Sci-Fi Network Monday through Thursday at both 11 and 11:30 p.m. and also airs Sunday at 8 and 8:30 p.m. The show features John Edward interviewing people who are interested in contacting loved ones who have crossed over.

17 The interview with Judy Cruz supported another major analysis growing out of this research (Clark 2003). Our interest in aliens and the supernatural at the time of this interview was, in part, stimulated by that project. While Clark was interested in Judy as an example of "fantasy" versus "real" representations of religion and their popularity, my point here is to show how Judy does not fit neatly into received categories of belief and behavior.

18 As I've suggested before, it is enlightening to think of how Judy would answer standard survey questions about her religiosity and her media behaviors. She would be classified as a fairly devout Catholic, and someone who does not watch much televangelism. We might be expected to assume that her religiosity is the reason for her rejection of religious broadcasting. Instead, it is a much more complex picture "on the ground."

19 The Castellos' home is decorated in Japanese style, with low tables, cushions on the floor, and a variety of Asian decorative artifacts. The interview with the Castellos was conducted by Monica Emerich.

20 Gayuna Cealo is a Burmese Buddhist monk who has an extensive following in the US (www.cealo.net).

21 Aeng (1996); Fiske (1987).

22 Jenkins (1992).

6 Cultural objects and religious identity among born-agains and mainstream believers

1 Roof (1999), p. 7.
2 Roof (1999), p. 9.
3 The term "lived religion" emerged from a longer-term scholarly discourse that brought an anthropological perspective to bear. Much of this thought is presented in Hall (1997).
4 Roof (1999), p. 41.
5 Roof (1999), p. 44.
6 Roof (1999), p. 132, citing Lifton (1993), p. 9.
7 Roof (1999), p. 132.
8 The Milliken family was interviewed by Scott Webber and Michelle Miles.
9 For a more detailed discussion of this style of viewing and a critique of its stereotype, see Joseph G. Champ's discussion of these issues in Hoover *et al.* (2004), Chapter 9.
10 The Callahans were interviewed by Lee Hood.
11 The Alberts were interviewed by Lee Hood.
12 The Alberts' one television set is in the parents' bedroom so as to more easily monitor and control the household's viewing.
13 The Boswells were interviewed by Lee Hood.

14 The Allens were interviewed by Scott Webber.
15 Diane F. Alters, "In the Heart of the Culture: The Hartmans and the Roelofs," Chapter Seven in Hoover *et al.* (2004),.
16 Ibid, p. 116.
17 Ibid, p. 128.
18 Ibid, p. 117.

7 Cultural objects and religious identity among metaphysical believers, dogmatists, and secularists

1 The Stevens-Van Gelder family was interviewed by Lee Hood.
2 For a complete discussion of the Stevens-Van Gelder family's consumption of local news, see Hood (2001).
3 The Tabor-Collins family was interviewed by Anna Maria Russo.
4 This reveals a lacuna in Roof's taxonomy, and our understanding of the nature of "seeker" religiosity. It is commonplace to think of US-born former Christians, who convert to Buddhism or other non-Western religions, as having clearly demonstrated a "seeker" practice, when we would not necessarily say the same thing about Protestants converting to Catholicism, Christians to Judaism, or vice versa.
5 The Price-Benoit family was interviewed by Lee Hood. They are discussed with reference to their media and parenting practices in Lee Hood, "Fitting in with the Media: The Price-Benoits and the Franzes," Chapter 8 of Hoover *et al.* (2004).
6 Hoover *et al.* (2004), p. 144.
7 The Castellos were interviewed by Monica Emerich.
8 Kim Anderson was interviewed by Denice Walker.
9 The Muellers were interviewed by Joseph G. Champ.
10 I should stipulate here that it is not their Mormonism, *per se*, that qualifies the Muellers as "dogmatists," but rather their approach to their faith. We also have among our interview families Mormons who fit in the "mainstream believer" category, for instance.
11 The Murphy-Gordon family was interviewed by Lee Hood.
12 It is interesting, though, that one of the three films in question was *Animal House*, hardly a paragon of avant-garde film-making.
13 The Abrahams were interviewed by Lynn Schofield Clark.
14 . . . with the exception of a number who used alternative media such as books and videocassettes produced for children by religious organizations.

8 Representing outcomes

1 Conservative critics such as Medved (1992), but even voices that present more nuanced readings, such as Warren (1997), still assume that the momentum, as we have said, is with the media.
2 For a suggestive and persuasive example of the idea of there being religious or religious-like functions of media in audience experience, see Gregor Goethals (2000). Goethals has been a consistent and influential voice in support of a Durkheimian reading of religion in media, focusing therefore on outcomes and functions, though focusing on a mass audience, rather than an individual reception level.
3 Roxanne Connor was interviewed by Denice Walker
4 Chris Chandler was interviewed by Anna Maria Russo.
5 Rayna Hancock was interviewed by Joe Champ.

6 Judy Cruz was interviewed by Scott Webber.
7 The Milliken family was interviewed by Scott Webber and Michelle Miles.
8 The Baylors were interviewed by Christof Demont-Heinrich.
9 The Sealys were interivewed by Christof Demont-Heinrich.
10 For a fuller account of Web-based religious information-seeking, see Hoover, Clark, and Rainie (2004).
11 The Steins were interviewed by Anna Maria Russo.
12 In order to protect Jeff's anonymity, it is necessary that I not name the specific "New Age," "self-help" movement he has become involved in.
13 Hoover *et al.* (2004).

9 Media and public religious culture post-09/11/01 and post-11/2/04

1 It is beyond the scope of this book to address this matter in detail, but we should not overlook that such an understanding of the relationship between religion and politics in the 2004 election cycle is entirely too superficial and limited. For example, the so-called "religion gap" should be understood to be a gap related to type or style of religion rather than to religion *per se*. Evangelicals, for example, are both more conservative politically and more likely to attend religious services more frequently. Non-Evangelicals may be no less fervent about their faith, but tend to attend formal religious services less frequently. Thus, the presumed association between "religion" and "politics," measured by attendance alone, is spurious.

2 The signal precedent for a time was the bombing of the Murrah Federal Building in Oklahoma City in 1995. In a haunting passage, Edward Linenthal wrote of that event in 2001, "Will a future terrorist act that inflicts even more death consign Oklahoma City to a less prestigious location on the landscape of violence?" (Linenthal 2001, p. 234).

3 Ismail (2001). While no systematic study exists, anecdotal and press accounts do detail a large number of incidents of "backlash."

4 Said (1997). Political struggles over immigration in Western Europe seem to have drawn some of their force and effect from post-9/11 understandings of the dangers of immigration from Islamic countries, and from the widespread notion that 9/11 represented a resurgent confrontation between Islam and the West.

5 Juergensmeyer (2001).

6 The planners could not have anticipated that film footage of the first plane strike would also surface, shot by a French cameraman working on a documentary about New York firefighters, and that a security camera also would capture the crash at the Pentagon. But, in an increasingly media-saturated world, we have come to expect that, somehow, pictures of such things are more and more routinely available, either from surveillance cameras or from the ubiquitous amateur videographer.

7 Zelizer (2005).

8 Mitchell (2006). See the chapter on "reframing news" in particular, where Mitchell asks, "why is it that when about 3000 people died on September 11 most news broadcasters and newspapers around the world provided saturation coverage for days and sometimes weeks afterwards, while when over 3 million die in the D.R.Congo it is largely ignored by the media?"

9 Of course, these are only the claims rooted in the normative view of the events. In addition to these, there are the claims of Al-Qaida itself, and of those who see the events as a justified attack on the US or the West generally.

10 At the risk of a seemingly gratuitous reference, my own institution found itself embroiled for most of 2005 in a controversy brought on by a faculty colleague's

definition of the event as an example of justice meted out by the dispossessed of the "South" against the exploiters of the "North."

11 This is, of course, a problematic notion. For a thoughtful discussion, see Sturken and Cartwright (2001), Chapter 8.

12 Kellner (1992). See in particular pp. 1–11.

13 Liebes and Katz (1990). See also Lull (1988) and Mandel (2002).

14 Ginsburg *et al.* (2002), pp. 14–16.

15 Said (1979); Said (1997); Gans (1979); Tuchman (1980); Epstein (1972).

16 Ajami (2001).

17 Singer (2001).

18 Singer (2001).

19 "Focus special: the Atta document in full," (London) *Observer*, 30 September 2001, p. 17.

20 Ajami, op. cit.

21 Sturken and Cartwright (2001), p. 319.

22 Mattalart *et al.* (1994).

23 We should not overlook that this "clash of cultures" interpretation of the West's confrontation with Islam (widely credited to historian Bernard Lewis) is echoed by influential voices in the West as well. Hirsch (2004).

24 Juergensmeyer (2001).

25 Castelli (2004).

26 Ajami (2001).

27 For a description of this form of broadcasting, see Dayan and Katz (1992), pp. 4–7.

28 Linenthal (2001) cites a study by psychiatrists at the University of Oklahoma which found that children were depressed by the images, and that pre-schoolers "thought that each time they saw the ruins of the Murrah Building a new building had been destroyed" (p. 75). Anecdotal reports at the time of 9/11 suggested similar effects on children. A colleague of mine recounted that she'd realized that her young son had concluded that each time he saw the 9/11 footage, another building had been attacked.

29 Dayan and Katz (1992). For a discussion of their taxonomy, see pp. 25–39. I am indebted to Nick Couldry for his thorough and thoughtful critique of Dayan and Katz's work. On the whole, I agree with his analysis, and, to the extent that what I have to say about the rituals of commemoration and mourning need to be seen in the sort of totalized terms he problematizes, I see no problem with calling them, to paraphrase Couldry (2003), "event-based narratives where the claims of a central set of concerns are particularly intense" (p. 67). I further acknowledge here the consonance between Couldry's tentative analysis of the 9/11 events (pp. 72–4) and my own.

30 This difference may of course be rooted in differing scholarly paradigms. Dayan and Katz's analysis is historical and formal, whereas I am speaking here as an audience researcher.

31 Bellah (1974), p. 40.

32 Therefore, my approach also differs significantly from Bellah's in that he did not envision popular culture as playing a role, focusing, like Dayan and Katz, on the formal elements of the events and practices.

33 See, for example, Forbes and Mahan (2000), particularly pp. 1–20, Chidester (2000). See also Chidester and Linenthal (1995).

34 Bell (1998), p. 220.

35 Grimes (2001).

36 Gillis (1994), p. 3.

37 Gillis (1994), pp. 7.
38 Foote (1997), p. 267.
39 Foote (1997), p. 267 n.10.
40 Linenthal (2001), p. 234–5.
41 Linenthal (2001), p. 111.
42 Haas (1998), pp. 95–6.
43 Richardson (2001), p. 266.
44 Linenthal (2001), p. 74.
45 Gillis (1994), p. 14.
46 Gergen (1996), p. 166.
47 Dayan and Katz (1992), p. 7.
48 Linenthal (2001), pp. 94–5.
49 See, with regard to the Columbine site specifically, Pike (2001).
50 There also seems to be a growing and developing public practice of memorialization at sites of highway fatalities, requiring state highway departments to institute new rules regulating them. Linenthal and Foote note that, while there has been a longer-standing Catholic practice underlying this, it appears to be spreading more broadly in the culture.
51 Thompson (1995), p. 230.
52 Keeler (2001).
53 The Wilcox family was interviewed by Christof Demont-Heinrich
54 The Vowski family was interviewed by Curtis Coats.
55 Katz and Dayan (1992), p. 7.
56 Smith (2001).
57 *The Newshour with Jim Lehrer*, 12 November 2001.
58 See, for example, Hoover, Clark, and Rainie (2004). A significant percentage of religiously oriented Internet use was devoted to finding out about "other religions."
59 For a helpful discussion, see Ginsburg *et al.* (2002), "Introduction."
60 Schorr (2004).
61 Kristof (2003).
62 Loconte (2004).
63 Loconte (2004).
64 Olsen (2005).
65 Olsen (2005).
66 Doreen Richards was interviewed by Monica Emerich.

10 Conclusion

1 One informant, it will be recalled, identified the "Amish" as an example of such separation. However, there are families who do separate themselves in less radical ways, but do, nonetheless, separate themselves from media. See Hoover *et al.* (2004), Chapter 6, for the example of Corrine Payton.
2 This is, of course, a term from Silverstone (1981).
3 Cf. Kubey and Csikszentmihalyi (1990).
4 Horace Newcomb's (1987) proposal that we think of television as a "cultural forum" is very much related to what we've seen here.
5 For younger interviewees, it seems that the Internet and Web may be gradually taking television's place in this regard.
6 There is an extensive literature focused on this issue, most of it rooted in Bourdieu's (1984) ideas about taste as a currency of cultural exchange. See also Thompson (1995), p. 16.

7 My colleague Diane Alters contributed a thoughtful discussion on these questions. See Diane F. Alters, "In the Heart of Culture: The Hartmans and the Roloefs," Chapter Seven in Hoover *et al.* (2004).
8 My colleague Jin Park was the first to argue that this notion about screen media is an important area of distinction.
9 And others we've interviewed who are not included in this book.
10 Lee Hood, Lynn Schofield Clark, Joseph G. Champ, and Diane F. Alters, "The Case Studies: An Introduction," Chapter Five in Hoover *et al.* (2004).
11 Cf. Davison (1983).
12 For an extensive discussion of parenthood in relation to this research and some of these same informants, see Hoover *et al.* (2004).
13 *The Simpsons* is, in fact, one of the most interesting programs in terms of religious or spiritual ideas, of the last decade or so (cf. Pinsky 2001). My colleague Diane Alters (2003) has devoted a good deal of scholarly attention to the program and my colleague Lee Hood includes a discussion of the program in Chapter 8 of Hoover *et al.* (2004), pp. 135–7.
14 For example, see Goethals (1997).
15 For a relevant statement, see Murdock (1997). See also De Vries and Weber (2001), and Derrida (2001).
16 For classic statements, see Garnham (1995) and Grossberg (1995).
17 Dayan and Katz (1992), p. 215.
18 For a historical description of these relations, see Underwood (2002), particularly Chapters 4 and 7.
19 De Vries (2001), pp. 24–7.
20 De Vries (2001), p. 25.
21 Cf. Derrida (2001), pp. 56–93.
22 Postman (1986).
23 Carter (2004). Carter quotes a spokesman for the Evangelical Focus on the Family organization on the subject: "History has shown that even people who could be described as values voters are prone to sinful behavior and watching representations of sinful behavior," Mr. Schneeberger said. "Is it shocking that people would be enticed by it? It's not shocking, but it is tragic." It is also ironic that many controversial programs, such as the 2004 hit *The O.C.*, and *The Simpsons*, were aired on the conservative Fox Network.
24 Leaving aside, of course, the "de-secularization" of both Europe and North America that is underway as the result of immigration.

Appendix

1 Hoover *et al.* (2004).
2 Abu-Lughod (1997).
3 Cf. Seiter (1999), Gauntlett and Hill (1999), Bird (2003), and Clark (2003).
4 In *Media, Home, and Family*, we credit, in particular, the influence of Guba and Lincoln (1994), pp. 105–17.
5 Clark (1999) "Learning from the Field: The Journey from Post-Positivist to Constructivist Methods," paper presented to the International Communication Association, San Francisco, May.

Bibliography

Abu-Lughod, Lila (1997) "The interpretation of culture(s) after television," *Representations* 59: 109–33.

Adorno, Theodor (1991) *The Culture Industry: Selected Essays on Mass Culture*, ed. J.M. Bernstein, London: Routledge.

Aeng, Ien (1996) *Living Room Wars: Rethinking Media Audiences for a Postmodern World*, London: Routledge.

Ajami, Fouad (2001) "What the Muslim world is watching," *New York Times Magazine*, November 18, p. 48.

Albanese, Catherine (1998) *America: Religions and Religion,* Florence, KY: Wadsworth Publishing.

Ali, Lorraine (2001) "The glorious rise of Christian pop," *Newsweek,* July 16, p. 40.

Alsdurf, Phyllis (forthcoming) "Evangelicalism and the presidential election of 1960: the 'Catholic Question' in *Christianity Today Magazine*," in Lynn Schofield Clark (ed.) *Religion, Media, and the Marketplace*, New Brunswick: Rutgers.

Alterman, Eric (2003) *What Liberal Media? The Truth about Bias and the News*, New York: Basic Books.

Alters, Diane F. (2003) "'We hardly watch that rude, crude show': class and taste in *The Simpsons*," in *Prime Time Animation: Television Animation and American Culture*, eds Carol A. Stabile and Mark Harrison, London: Routledge.

Alvarez, Lizette (2003) "Fury, God and the pastor's disbelief," *The New York Times*, July 8, p. A4.

Andersen, M.L. and Collins, P.H. (eds) (2004) *Race, Class, and Gender: An Anthology*, Belmont, CA: Wadsworth/Thomson.

Apostolos-Cappadona, Diane (1997) "Vamps and tramps: the persistence of Eve in popular culture." Paper presented to the Eighth International Colloquium on Theology and Communication, Rome, September.

Appadurai, Arjun (1991) "Global ethnoscapes: notes and queries for a transnational ethnography," in Richard Fox (ed.) *Recapturing Anthropology*, Santa Fe: School of American Research Press, pp. 191–210.

Armstrong, Ben (1979) *The Electric Church*, Nashville: Thomas Nelson.

Arnett, Jeffrey (1991) "Adolescents and heavy metal music: from the mouths of metalheads," *Youth and Society* 23: 76–98.

——(1992) "The soundtrack of restlessness – musical preferences and reckless behavior among adolescents," *J. Adolescent Research* 7: 313–28.

Babin, Pierre (1970) *The Audio-visual Man*, Dayton: Pflaum Press.

Badarracco, Claire (2005) *Quoting God: How Media Shape Ideas about Religion*, Waco: Baylor University Press.

Bagdikian, Ben (1997) *The Media Monopoly*, Boston: Beacon Press.

Barnouw, Eric (1990) *The Sponsor: Notes on a Modern Potentate*, Oxford: Oxford University Press.

Bauder, David (2004) "Religious fervor resulting in more coverage by networks," *The Denver Post*, 9 April, p. D1.

Baudrillard, Jean (1983) *Simulations*, New York: Semiotext(e).

Bell, Catherine (1998) "Performance," in Mark C. Taylor (ed.) *Critical Terms for Religious Studies*, Chicago: University of Chicago Press.

Bellah, Robert (1974) "Civil religion in America," in Russell E. Richey and Donald G. Jones (eds) *American Civil Religion*, New York: Harper Forum Books.

——(1984) *The Broken Covenant: American Civil Religion in Time of Trial*, San Francisco, CA: Harper.

——(1986) *Habits of the Heart: Individualism and Commitment in American Life*, Berkeley: University of California Press.

Bennett, William (1993) *Book of Virtues*, New York: Simon & Schuster.

Berger, Peter and Luckman, Thomas (1966) *The Social Construction of Reality: A Treatise in the Sociology of Knowledge*, Garden City, New York: Anchor Books.

Best, Steven and Kellner, Douglas (1991) *Postmodern Theory: Critical Interrogations*, London: Macmillan.

Bird, S. Elizabeth (2003) *The Audience in Everyday Life: Living in a Media World*, New York: Routledge.

Blake, John (2004) "Christian wares expand in scope: holy socks, faith hero cards, tattoos on market," *Atlanta Journal-Constitution*, 3 July, p. 1B.

Blumenreich, Megan (2004) "Avoiding the pitfalls of 'conventional' narrative research: using poststructural theory to guide the creation of narratives of children with HIV," *Qualitative Research* (4)1: 70–90.

Blumer, Jay (1975) *The Uses of Mass Communications: Current Perspectives on Gratifications Research*, Beverly Hills: Sage.

Borden, Anne (forthcoming) "What would Jesus buy? Christian booksellers negotiate ministries and markets," in Lynn Schofield Clark (ed.) *Religion, Media, and the Marketplace*, New Brunswick: Rutgers.

Bourdieu, Pierre (1984) *Distinction: A Social Critique of the Judgment of Taste*, trans. Richard Nice, Cambridge, MA: Harvard University Press.

Brasher, Brenda (2004) *Give Me That On-Line Religion*, Piscataway, NJ: Rutgers University Press.

Broadcasting and Cable Yearbook, 2002–2003 (2003) New York: Broadcasting & Cable Publications.

Bruce, Steve (1990) *Pray TV: Televangelism in America*, London: Routledge.

Bryant, J. and Zillmann, D. (eds) (1994) *Media Effects: Advances in Theory and Research*, Hillsdale, NJ: Lawrence Erlbaum Associates.

Buddenbaum, Judith and Stout, Daniel (1996) "Religion and mass media use: a review of the mass communication and sociological literature," *Religion and Mass Media: Audiences and Adaptations*, London: Sage, pp. 12–34.

Carey, James W. (1975) "A cultural approach to communication," *Communication* 2(2): 1–25.

——(1989) *Communication as Culture*, Boston: Unwin-Hyman.

Carpenter, Joel (1985) "Tuning in the gospel: fundamentalist radio broadcasting and the revival of mass evangelism, 1930–45," paper delivered to the Mid-America American Studies Association, University of Illinois, Urbana, 13 April.

Carter, Bill (2004) "Many who voted for 'values' still like their television sin," *The New York Times*, 22 November, p. A1.

Carter, Stephen (2000) *God's Name in Vain: The Wrongs and Rights of Religion in Politics*, New York: Basic Books.

Castelli, Elizabeth (2004) "Presentation to the Conference Media, Religion, and Culture," New York University, 8 May.

Charters, Werrett Wallace (1933) *Motion Pictures and Youth*, New York: Macmillan.

Chidester, David (2000) "The church of baseball, the fetish of Coca-Cola and the potlach of rock 'n' roll," in Bruce Forbes and Jeffrey Mahan (eds) *Religion and Popular Culture in America*, Berkeley: University of California Press.

Chidester, David and Linenthal, Edward (eds) (1995) *American Sacred Space*, Bloomington: Indiana University Press.

Clark, Lynn Schofield (2002) "The Protestantization of research in media and religion," in Stewart M. Hoover and Lynn Schofield Clark (eds) *Practicing Religion in the Age of the Media: Explorations in Media, Religion, and Culture*, New York: Columbia University Press.

——(2003) *From Angels to Aliens: Teenagers, the Media, and the Supernatural*, New York: Oxford University Press.

Clark, Lynn Schofield and Hoover, Stewart M. (1997) "At the intersection of media, culture, and religion: a bibliographic essay," in Stewart M. Hoover and Knut Lundby (eds) *Rethinking Media, Religion, and Culture*, Thousand Oaks, CA: Sage.

Couldry, Nick (2003) *Media Rituals: A Critical Approach*, London: Routledge.

Csikszentmihalyi, Mihaly and Rochberg-Halton, Eugene (1981) *The Meaning of Things: Domestic Symbols and the Self*, Cambridge, UK: Cambridge University Press.

Dart, John and Allen, Jimmy (1993) *Bridging the Gap*, Nashville: Freedom Forum First Amendment Center.

Davison, W. Phillips (1983) "The third-person effect in communication," *Public Opinion Quarterly* 47 (spring): 1–15.

Dayan, Daniel and Katz, Elihu (1992) *Media Events: The Live Broadcasting of History*, Cambridge, MA: Harvard University Press.

de Kerckhove, Derrick and Dewdney, Christopher (1995) *The Skin of Culture*, Toronto: Somerville House Publishing.

De Tocqueville, Alexis (2000) *Democracy in America*, Chicago, IL: University of Chicago Press.

De Vries, Hent (2001) "In media res: global religion, public spheres, and the task of contemporary comparative religious studies," in Hent De Vries and Samuel Weber (eds) *Religion and Media*, Stanford: Stanford University Press.

De Vries, Hent and Weber, Samuel (eds) (2001) *Religion and Media*, Stanford: Stanford University Press.

Denzin, Norman K. (1989) *Interpretive Biography*, Newbury Park, CA: Sage.

——(1992) *Symbolic Interactionism and Cultural Studies: The Politics of Interpretation*, Oxford: Blackwell.

Derrida, Jacques (2001) "Above all, no journalists!" in Hent De Vries and Samuel Weber (eds) *Religion and Media*, Stanford: Stanford University Press.

Dorgan, Howard (1993) *The Airwaves of Zion: Radio and Religion in Appalachia*, Knoxville: University of Tennessee Press.

Durkheim, Emile (1995) *Elementary Forms of the Religious Life*, trans. Karen E. Fields, New York: The Free Press.

Eck, Diana (2001) *A New Religious America: How the World's Most "Christian Country" Has Now Become the World's Most Religiously Diverse Nation*, San Francisco: HarperCollins.

Eisenstein, Elizabeth (1979) *The Printing Press as an Agent of Change*, New York: Cambridge University Press.

Ellens, J. Harold (1974) *Models of Religious Broadcasting*, Grand Rapids: Eerdmans.

Ellul, Jacques (1967) *The Technological Society*, New York: Vintage.

Enzensberger, Hans Magnus (1974) *The Consciousness Industry: On Literature, Politics, and the Media*, New York: Seabury Press.

Epstein, Edward Jay (1972) *News from Nowhere: Television and the News*, New York: Random House.

Evans, Clay (1999) "A church for all seasons," *Boulder Daily Camera*, 8 May, p.1E.

Festinger, Leon (1957) *A Theory of Cognitive Dissonance*, Evanston, IL: Row Peterson.

Fischer, Claude (1994) *America Calling: A Social History of the Telephone to 1940*, Berkeley: University of California Press.

Fiske, John (1987) *Television Culture*, London: Routledge.

Foote, Kenneth (1997) *Shadowed Ground: America's Landscapes of Violence and Tragedy*, Austin: University of Texas Press.

Forbes, Bruce David and Mahan, Jeffrey (2000) *Religion and Popular Culture in America*, Berkeley: University of California Press.

Fore, William F. (1987) *Television and Religion. The Shaping of Faith, Values and Culture*, Minneapolis: Augsburg/Fortress.

——(1990) *Mythmakers: Gospel, Culture and Media*, New York: Friendship Press.

Frankl, Razelle (1987) *Televangelism: The Marketing of Popular Religion*, Carbondale, IL: Southern Illinois University Press.

Fraser, Nancy (1993) "Rethinking the public sphere: a contribution to the critique of actually-existing democracy," in B. Robbins (ed.) *The Phantom Public Sphere*, Minneapolis: University of Minnesota Press, pp. 1–32.

Gans, Herbert (1979) *Deciding What's News*, New York: Pantheon.

Garnham, Nicholas. (1995) "Political economy and cultural studies: reconciliation or divorce?" *Critical Studies in Mass Communication* 12: 62–71.

Garron, Barry (1998) "Touched by an angel," *Hollywood Reporter*, April 20.

Gauntlett, David and Hill, Annette (1999) *TV Living: Television Culture and Everyday Life*, London: Routledge and the British Film Institute.

Geertz, Clifford (1973) *The Interpretation of Cultures*, New York: Basic Books.

Gerbner, George and Connolly, Kathleen (1978) "Television as new religion," *New Catholic World*, March/April: 52–6.

Gerbner, George, Gross, Larry, Hoover, Stewart, Morgan, Michael, and Signorielli, Nancy (1989) "Response to 'Star Wars of a Different Kind: Reflections on the

Politics of the Religion and Television Research Study,'" *Review of Religious Research* 31(2) (December): 111–24.

Gerbner, George, Gross, Larry, Hoover, Stewart, Morgan, Michael, Signorelli, Nancy, Wuthnow, Robert and Cotugno, Harry (1984) *Religion and Television: A Research Report by the Annenberg School of Communications*, Philadelphia: The Annenberg School.

Gergen, Kenneth (1991) *The Saturated Self: Dilemmas of Identity in Contemporary Life*, New York: Basic Books.

——(1996) "Technology and the self: from the essential to the sublime," in Debra Grodin and Thomas R. Lindlof (eds) *Constructing the Self in a Mediated World*, Thousand Oaks: Sage.

Giddens, Anthony (1991) *Modernity and Self-Identity: Self and Society in the Late Modern Age*, Stanford: Stanford University Press.

Gillis, John R. (1994) "Memory and identity: the history of a relationship," in John R. Gillis (ed.) *Commemorations: The Politics of National Identity*, Princeton: Princeton University Press.

Ginsburg, Faye, Abu-Lughod, Lila, and Larkin, Brian (eds) (2002) *Media Worlds: Anthropology on New Terrain*, Berkeley: University of California Press.

Goethals, Gregor (1982) *TV Ritual: Worship at the Video Altar*, Boston, MA: Beacon Press.

——(1997) "Escape from time: ritual dimensions of popular culture," in Stewart M. Hoover and Knut Lundby (eds) *Rethinking Media, Religion, and Culture*, Thousand Oaks, CA: Sage.

——(2000) "The electronic golden calf: transforming ritual and icon," in Bruce Forbes and Jeffrey Mahan (eds) *Religion and Popular Culture in America*, Berkeley: University of California Press.

Goffman, Erving (1959) *The Presentation of Self in Everyday Life*, Garden City, NY: Doubleday.

Goodman, Barak and Dretzin, Rachel (2001) *PBS Frontline Video* "The Merchants of Cool." WGBH.

Grimes, Ron (2001) "Ritual and the media," in Stewart M. Hoover and Lynn Schofield Clark (eds) *Practicing Religion in the Age of the Media: Studies in Media, Religion, and Culture*, New York: Columbia University Press.

Grossberg, Lawrence (1992) *We Gotta Get Out Of This Place: Popular Conservatism and Postmodern Culture*, New York: Routledge.

——(1995) "Cultural studies vs. political economy: is anyone else bored with this debate?" *Critical Studies in Mass Communication* 12: 72–81.

Guba, Egon and Lincoln, Yvonne (1994) "Competing paradigms in qualitative research," in Norman Denzin and Yvonne Lincoln (eds) *Handbook of Qualitative Research*, Thousand Oaks: Sage.

Gunter, Barrie and McAleer, Jill (1997) *Children and Television*, 2nd edn, London: Routledge.

Haas, Kristin Ann (1998) *Carried to the Wall: American Memory and the Vietnam Veterans Memorial*, Berkeley: University of California Press.

Habermas, Jürgen (1985) *The Theory of Communicative Action, Volume Two: Lifeworld and System: A Critique of Functionalist Reason*, Boston, MA: Beacon Press.

——(1989) *The Structural Transformation of the Public Sphere*, Cambridge: MIT Press.

Hadden, Jeffery K. and Cowan, Douglas E. (2001) *Religion on the Internet*, Vol. 8, London: Elsevier Science and Technology Books.

Hadden, Jeffrey and Shupe, Anson (1988) *Televangelism: Power and Politics on God's Frontier*, New York: Henry Holt.

Hadden, Jeffrey K. and Swann, Charles E. (1981) *Prime-Time Preachers: The Rising Power of Televangelism*, Reading, MA: Addison-Wesley.

Hall, David (ed.) (1997) *Lived Religion in America: Toward a Theory of Practice*, Princeton: Princeton University Press.

Hall, Stuart and Jefferson, Tony (eds) (1976) *Resistance through Rituals: Youth Subcultures in Post-War Britain*, London: Hutchinson.

Hammond, Philip (1992) *Religion and Personal Autonomy: The Third Disestablishment in America*, Columbia, SC: University of South Carolina Press.

Hangen, Tona (2002) *Redeeming the Dial: Radio, Religion, and Popular Culture in America*, Chapel Hill, NC: University of North Carolina Press.

Harvey, David (1989) *The Condition of Postmodernity: An Enquiry into the Origins of Cultural Change*, Oxford: Blackwell.

Heelas, Paul and Woodhead, Linda (eds) (2000) *Religion in Modern Times: An Interpretive Anthology*, Oxford: Blackwell Publishers.

Hendershot, Heather (2004) *Shaking the World for Jesus: Media and Conservative Evangelical Culture*, Chicago: University of Chicago Press.

Herberg, William (1983) *Protestant – Catholic – Jew: An Essay in American Religious Society*, Chicago, IL: University of Chicago Press.

Hinsliff, Gaby (2000) "Evangelists may spread the word by radio," [London] *Observer*, 27 August, p. 7.

Hirsch, Michael (2004) "Bernard Lewis revisited," *Washington Monthly*, November, www.washingtonmonthly.com/features/2004/0411.hirsh.html [accessed 5 February 2006].

Hood, Lee (2001) "The Local News Audience and Sense of Place: A Home in the Global Village," Ph.D. dissertation, University of Colorado.

Hoover, Stewart M. (1987) "The religious television audience: a matter of size or significance?" *Review of Religious Research* 29: 135–51.

——(1988) *Mass Media Religion: The Social Sources of the Electronic Church*, London: Sage.

——(1998) *Religion in the News: Faith and Journalism in American Public Discourse*, Newbury Park: Sage.

——(2003) "Meaning, faith and spirituality in the media world," in Jolyon Mitchell and Sophia Marriage (eds) *Mediating Religion: Conversations in Media, Religion and Culture*, Edinburgh: T. & T. Clark/Continuum.

Hoover, Stewart M., Clark, Lynn Schofield, and Alters, Diane F. with Joseph G. Champ and Lee Hood (2004) *Media, Home, and Family*, New York: Routledge.

Hoover, Stewart M., Clark, Lynn Schofield, and Rainie, Lee (2004) *Faith Online*. A report of the Pew Internet and American Life Project. www.pewinternet.org.

Hoover, Stewart M. and Park, Jin Kyu (2005) "Religion and meaning in the digital age: field research on Internet/Web religion," in Eric Rothenbuhler and Mihai Coman (eds) *Media Anthropology*, Thousand Oaks: Sage.

Hoover, Stewart and Russo, Anna Maria (2002) "Ritual, representation, and media in public commemoration." Paper presented to the American Academy of Religion (AAR) Annual Meeting, Toronto, Canada, November.

Hoover, Stewart M. and Venturelli, Shalini S. (1996) "The category of the religious: the blindspot of contemporary media theory?" *Critical Studies in Mass Communication* 13: 251–65.

Hoover, Stewart M. and Wagner, Douglas K. (1997) "History and policy in American broadcast treatment of religion," *Media, Culture and Society* 19(1) (January): 7–27.

Hoover, Stewart, Venturelli, Shalini, and Wagner, Douglas (1995) *Final Report: Religion and Journalism*, Boulder: University of Colorado.

Horkheimer, Max and Adorno, Theodor W. (1972) *Dialectics of Enlightenment*, trans. John Cumming, New York: Seabury Press, pp. 120–67.

Horsfield, Peter (1984) *Religious Television: The American Experience*, New York: Longman Press.

Huesmann, L.R. and Malamuth, N.M. (eds) (1986) "Media violence and antisocial behavior" (special issue), *Journal of Social Issues* 42(3).

Hunter, James Davidson (1992) *Culture Wars: The Struggle to Define America*, New York: Basic Books.

Innis, Harold (1950) *Empire and Communication*, Toronto: University of Toronto Press.

Ismail, Faezah (2001) "Showing the true face of Islam," *New Straits Times (Malaysia)*, 18 November, p. 1.

Jameson, Frederic (1992) *Postmodernism, or, the Cultural Logic of Late Capitalism*, Durham: Duke University Press.

Jamison, Kathleen (2000) *Everything You Think You Know about Politics . . . and Why You're Wrong*, New York: Basic Books.

——(2002) *The Press Effect: Politicians, Journalists, and the Stories that Shape the Political World*, New York: Oxford University Press.

Jenkins, Henry (1992) *Textual Poachers: Television Fans and Participatory Culture*, New York: Routledge.

Jhally, Sut (1990) *Codes of Advertising: Fetishism and the Political Economy of Meaning in the Consumer Society*, New York: Routledge.

Juergensmeyer, Mark (2001) Remarks to the annual meeting of the Society for the Scientific Study of Religion, Columbus, OH, November.

Katz, Elihu and Lazersfeld, Paul (1955) *Personal Influence*, Glencoe, IL: Free Press.

Katz, Elihu and Liebes, Tamar (1985) "Mutual aid in the decoding of *Dallas*: preliminary notes from a cross-cultural study," in Phillip Drummond and Richard Paterson (eds) *Television in Transition: Papers from the First International Television Studies Conference*, London: British Film Institute.

Keeler, Janet K. (2001) "Amazing grace: thanking God helps in times of sadness," *Boulder Daily Camera*, 29 September, p. 1D.

Kellner, Douglas (1989) *Critical Theory, Marxism and Modernity*, Cambridge: Polity Press, chs 5 and 6.

——(1992) *The Persian Gulf TV War*, Boulder: Westview Press.

Kerevan, George (2001) "Faithful cynics of a new nation," *Scotsman*, 30 April, p. 3.

Koch, Gertrud (2001) "Mimesis and the ban on graven images," in Hent DeVries and Samuel Weber (eds) *Religion and Media*, Stanford: Stanford University Press, pp. 151–62.

Kornblut, Anne (2000) "Changes are voted for public television bill, gives air time to religious groups," *The Boston Globe*, 21 June, p. A3.

Korp, Maureen (1997) "Teaching from the headlines: myth and the media coverage of Diana's death," *Religious Studies News*, 20 November, p. 20.

Kristof, Nicholas (2003) "Believe it, or not," *New York Times*, 15 August, p. A6.

Kubey, Robert William and Csikszentmihalyi, Mihaly (1990) *Television and the Quality of Life: How Viewing Shapes Everyday Experiences*, Mahwah, NJ: Lawrence Erlbaum Associates.

——(2002) "Television addiction is no mere metaphor," *Scientific American*, February, www.simpletoremember.com/vitals/TV_Danger_SCIAM.htm [accessed 5 February 2005].

Lasch, Christopher (1977) *Haven in a Heartless World: The Family Besieged*, New York: Basic Books.

Lattin, Don (2003) "Surveys show jump in people who belong to church of 'none'," *Boulder Daily Camera*, 6 December, p. D1.

Lerner, Daniel (1964) *Passing of Traditional Society*, New York: Simon & Schuster Adult Publishing Group.

Liebert, Robert L. and Sprafkin, Joyce (1988) *The Early Window: The Effects of Television on Children and Youth*, New York: Pergamon.

Liebes, Tamar and Katz, Elihu (1990) *The Export of Meaning: Cross-Cultural Readings of "Dallas,"* New York: Oxford University Press.

Lieblich, Amia, Tuval-Mashiach, Rivka, and Zilber, Tamar (1998) *Narrative Research: Reading, Analysis, and Interpretation*, Newbury Park, CA: Sage.

Lifton, Robert Jay (1993) *The Protean Self: Human Resilience in an Age of Fragmentation*, New York: Basic Books.

Linenthal, Edward (2001) *The Unfinished Bombing: Oklahoma City in American Memory*, New York: Oxford University Press.

Livingstone, Sonia (2002) *Young People and New Media: Childhood and the Changing Media Environment*, London: Sage.

Loconte, Joe (2004) Commentary, *All Things Considered*, National Public Radio, Friday, 5 November.

Lull, James (1988) *World Families Watch Television*, Beverly Hills: Sage.

——(1991) *Inside Family Television*, London: Routledge.

Lynch, Gordon (2005) *Understanding Theology and Popular Culture*, Oxford: Blackwell.

McAdams, Dan P. (1993) *The Redemptive Self: Stories Americans Live by*, New York: Oxford University Press.

——(1998) *Narrative Analysis*, Newbury Park, CA: Sage.

McChesney, Robert (1995) *Telecommunications, Mass Media, and Democracy: The Battle for the Control of US Broadcasting, 1928–1935*, Oxford: Oxford University Press.

McChesney, Robert W. and Nichols, John (2002) *Our Media, Not Theirs: The Democratic Struggle against Corporate Media*, New York: Seven Stories Press.

McCloud, Sean (2004) *Making the American Religious Fringe: Exotics, Subversives, and Journalists, 1955–1993*, Chapel Hill: University of North Carolina Press.

McDannell, Colleen (1998) *Material Christianity: Religion and Popular Culture in America*, New Haven, CT: Yale University Press.

McDevitt, Michael and Chaffee, Steven (2000) "Closing gaps in political communication and knowledge: effects of a school intervention," *Communication Research* 27(3): 259–92.

McGuire, William J. (1986) "The myth of massive media impact: savagings and salvagings," in George Comstock (ed.) *Public Communication and Behavior*, Vol. 1, London: Academic Press, pp. 175–257.

McLuhan, Marshall (1994) *Understanding Media: The Extensions of Man*, Cambridge, MA: MIT Press.

McQuail, Denis (1970) *Towards a Sociology of Mass Communication*, New York: Macmillan Publishing Co.

Mandel, Ruth (2002) "A Marshall Plan of the mind: the political economy of a Kazakh soap opera," in Faye Ginsburg, Lila Abu-Lughod, and Brian Larkin (eds) *Media Worlds: Anthropology on New Terrain*, Berkeley: University of California Press.

Marc, David (1996) *Demographic Vistas: Television in American Culture*, Philadelphia, PA: University of Pennsylvania Press.

Marsden, George (1983) "Preachers of paradox," in Mary Douglas and Steven Tipton (eds) *Religion and America: Spiritual Life in a Secular Age*, Boston, MA: Beacon Press.

Martin, Joel and Ostwald, Conrad (1995) *Screening the Sacred: Religion, Myth, and Ideology in Popular American Film*, Boulder: Westview Press.

Martin-Barbero, Jesus (1997) "Mass media as a site of resacralization of contemporary cultures," in Stewart Hoover and Knut Lundby (eds) *Rethinking Media, Religion and Culture*, Newbury Park, CA: Sage.

Marvin, Carolyn (1999) *Blood Sacrifice and the Nation: Totem Rituals and the American Flag*, Cambridge, UK: Cambridge University Press.

Mattalart, Armand, Emmanuel, Susan, and Cohen, James (1994) *Mapping World Communication: War, Progress, Culture*, Minneapolis: University of Minnesota Press.

Mead, George Herbert (1934) *Mind, Self and Society*, Chicago: University of Chicago Press.

Medved, Michael (1992) *Hollywood vs. America*, New York: HarperCollins Publishers.

Messaris, Paul (1994) *Visual Literacy*, Boulder, CO: Westview Press.

Meyers, Kenneth (1989) *All God's Children and Blue Suede Shoes: Christians and Popular Culture*, Wheaton, IL: Good News Publishers.

Meyerwitz, Joshua (1985) *No Sense of Place: The Impact of Electronic Media on Social Behavior*, New York: Oxford University Press.

Miles, Margaret (1997) *Seeing and Believing*, Boston: Beacon Press.

Miller, Daniel and Slater, Don (eds) (2000) *The Internet: An Ethnographic Approach*, Oxford: Berg.

Mitchell, Jolyon (2000) *Visually Speaking: Radio and the Renaissance of Preaching*, Louisville, KY: Presbyterian Publishing Corporation.

——(2005) "Theology and film," in David Forth (ed.) *The Modern Theologians*, Oxford: Blackwell.

——(2006) *Media and Christian Ethics*, Cambridge, UK: Cambridge University Press.

Moore, Laurence R. (1995) *Selling God: American Religion in the Marketplace of Culture*, New York: Oxford University Press.

Moores, Shaun (1993) *Interpreting Audiences: The Ethnography of Media Consumption*, London: Sage.

Morgan, David (1996) *Icons of American Protestantism: The Art of Warner Sallman*, New Haven, CT: Yale University Press.

——(1998) *Visual Piety: A History and Theory of Popular Religious Images*, Berkeley: University of California Press.

——(1999) *Protestants and Pictures: Religion, Visual Culture, and the Age of American Mass Production*, New York: Oxford.

——(2004) "Catholic visual piety and *The Passion of the Christ*," in Brent S. Plate (ed.) *Re-Viewing The Passion: Mel Gibson's Film and Its Critics*, New York: Palgrave Macmillan, pp. 85–96.

Morgan, David and Promey, Sally (eds) (2001) *The Visual Culture of American Religions*, Berkeley and Los Angeles, CA: University of California Press.

Morgan, Michael (1987) "Television, sex-role attitudes, and sex-role behavior," *Journal of Early Adolescence* 7(3) (fall): 299–314.

Morley, David (1992) *Television, Audiences, and Cultural Studies*, London: Routledge.

Muggeridge, Malcolm (1977) *Christ and the Media*, London: Hodder & Stoughton.

Murdock, Graham (1997) "The re-enchantment of the world: religion and the transformation of modernity," in Stewart M. Hoover and Knut Lundby (eds) *Rethinking Media, Religion, and Culture*, Thousand Oaks, CA: Sage.

Neighbour, Roger (1992) *The Inner Apprentice*, Plymouth, UK: Petroc Press.

Neuhaus, Richard John (1986) *The Naked Public Square: Religion and Democracy in America*, 2nd edn, Grand Rapids, MI: Wm. B. Eerdmans Publishing Company.

Newcomb, Horace (1987) *Television: The Critical View*, New York: Oxford University Press.

Newcomb, Horace and Hirsch, Paul (1983) "Television as a cultural forum: implications for research," *Quarterly Review of Film Studies* 8: 48–55.

Nolan, Steve (2003) "Towards a new religious film criticism: using film to understand religious identity rather than locate cinematic analogue," in Jolyon Mitchell and Sophia Marriage (eds) *Mediating Religion: Conversations in Media, Religion, and Culture*, London: T.&T. Clark.

Nord, David Paul (2004) *Faith in Reading: Religious Publishing and the Birth of Mass Media in America*, New York: Oxford University Press.

Olsen, Ted (2005) "Who's driving this thing?" *Christianity Today Online*, 21 February, www.christianitytoday.com/ct/2005/108/12.0.html [accessed 26 June 2005].

Ong, Walter (1986) *The Presence of the Word: The Prolegomena for Cultural and Religious History*, Minneapolis: University of Minnesota Press.

——(2002) *Orality and Literacy*, New York: Routledge.

Ortner, Sherry (1993) "Ethnography among the Newark: the class of '58 of Weequakic high school," *Michigan Quarterly Review* 32: 411–29.

Overcash, J. (2004) "Narrative research: a viable methodology for clinical nursing," *Nursing Forum* 39(1) (January–March): 15-22.

Parker, Everett C., Barry, David W., and Smythe, Dallas W. (1955) *The Television–Radio Audience and Religion*, New York: Harper's Publishing.

Peck, Janice (1993) *The Gods of Televangelism: The Crisis of Meaning and the Appeal of Religious Television*, Lexington, MA: Greenwood Press.

Pike, Sarah (2001) "After Columbine: demonic teens on the Internet, God's martyrs in the headlines," presentation to the Religion and Popular Culture Division, American Academy of Religion, Denver.

Pinsky, Mark L. (2001) *The Gospel According to The Simpsons: The Spiritual Life of the World's Most Animated Family*, Louisville: Westminster/John Knox.

Poovakkattu, Varghese (2003) Letter to the editor, *Time* [European Edition], 14 July, p. 8.

Postman, Neil (1986) *Amusing Ourselves to Death: Public Discourse in the Age of Show Business*, New York: Penguin Books.

——(1993) *Technopoly: The Surrender of Culture to Technology*, New York: Vintage Books.

Promey, Sally (1996) "Interchangeable art: Warner Sallman and the critics of mass culture," in David Morgan (ed.) *Icons of American Protestantism: The Art of Warner Sallman*, New Haven: Yale University Press.

Putnam, Robert (1996) "The strange disappearance of civic America," *The American Prospect* 24 (winter), www.prospect.org/print/V7/24/putnam-r.html [accessed 5 February 2006].

Quebedeaux, Richard (1974) *The Young Evangelicals: Revolution in Orthodoxy*, New York: Harper & Row.

Quicke, Andrew and Quicke, Juliet (1992) *Hidden Agendas: The Politics of Religious Broadcasting in Britain, 1987–1991*, Virginia Beach, VA: Dominion Kings Grant Publications, Inc.

Reed-Danahay, Deborah (1997) *Auto/Ethnography*, New York: Berg.

Reeves, Byron and Nass, Clifford (1996) *The Media Equation: How People Treat Computers, Television, and New Media like Real People and Places*, Cambridge, UK: Cambridge University Press.

Richardson, Miles (2001) "The gift of presence: the act of leaving artifacts at shrines, memorials, and other tragedies," in Paul Adams, Steven Hoelscher, and Karen E. Till (eds) *Textures of Places: Exploring Humanist Geographies*, Minneapolis: University of Minnesota Press.

Ricoeur, Paul (1991) *From Text to Action*, trans. Kathleen Blamey and John B. Thompson, Evanston: Northwestern University Press.

——(1992) *Oneself as Another*, trans. Kathleen Blamey, Chicago: University of Chicago Press.

Roof, Wade Clark (1992) *A Generation of Seekers*, San Francisco: HarperCollins.

——(1999) *Spiritual Marketplace: Baby Boomers and the Remaking of American Religion*, Princeton: Princeton University Press

Rosenthal, Michele (2001) "Turn it off: TV criticism in the *Christian Century Magazine*, 1946–1960," in Stewart M. Hoover and Lynn Scofield Clark (eds) *Practicing Religion in the Age of the Media: Explorations in Media, Religion, and Culture*, New York: Columbia University Press.

——(2004) *Satan and Savior: American Protestants and the New Medium of Television*, Basingstoke, UK: Palgrave Macmillan.

Rothenbuhler, Eric (1998) *Ritual Communication: From Everyday Conversation to Mediated Ceremony*, Thousand Oaks, CA: Sage Publications.

Saebø, Gunnar (2003) "Media, Ritual and the Cultivation of Collective Representations," Doctoral Thesis, Faculty of Arts, University of Oslo, pp. 272–5.

Said, Edward (1979) *Orientalism*, New York: Vintage.

——(1997) *Covering Islam: How the Media and the Experts Determine How We See the Rest of the World*, New York: Vintage.

Schmalzbaur, John (2003) *People of Faith: Religious Conviction in American Journalism and Higher Education*, Ithaca, NY: Cornell University Press.

Schmidt, Leigh E. (1995) *Consumer Rites: The Buying and Selling of American Holidays*, Princeton: Princeton University Press.

Schneider, Manfried (2001) "Luther with McLuhan," in Hent De Vries and Samuel Weber (eds) *Religion and Media*, Stanford: Stanford University Press, pp. 189–215.

Schorr, Daniel (2004) Commentary, *Weekend Edition Sunday*, National Public Radio, 11 January.

Schudson, Michael and Tifft, Susan (2005) "American journalism in historical perspective," in Overholser, Geneva and Hall Jamieson, Kathleen (eds) *The Press*, New York: Oxford University Press.

Schultze, Quentin (1987) "The mythos of the electronic church," *Critical Studies in Mass Communication* 4(3): 245–61.

——(ed.) (1990) *American Evangelicals and the Mass Media: Perspectives on the Relationship between American Evangelicals and the Mass Media*, Grand Rapids: Zondervan.

——(2002) *Habits of the High-Tech Heart*, North Dartmouth, MA: Baker Books.

Schultze, Quentin J. *et al.* (1991) *Dancing in the Dark: Youth, Popular Culture, and the Electronic Media*, Grand Rapids: Eerdmans.

Seiter, Ellen (1999) *Television and New Media Audiences*, Oxford: Oxford University Press.

Sieftert, Marsha (1994) "The audience at home: the early recording industry and the marketing of popular taste," in James Ettema and D. Charles Whitney (eds) *Audiencemaking: How the Media Create the Audience*, Thousand Oaks: Sage.

Silk, Mark (1995) *Unsecular Media: Making News of Religion in America*, Champaign, IL: University of Illinois Press.

Silverman, Rachel Emma (1999) "Ministry vows to beam Second Coming via Internet," *The Denver Post*, 20 June, p. 21A.

Silverstone, Roger (1981) *The Message of Television: Myth and Narrative in Contemporary Culture*, London: Heinemann.

——(1988) "Television myth and culture," in James Carey (ed.) *Media, Myths and Narratives, Television and the Press*, Newbury Park, CA: Sage.

——(1991) "Television and everyday life: towards an anthropology of the television audience," in Margorie Ferguson (ed.) *Public Communication: The New Imperatives*, London: Sage, pp. 173–89.

——(1994) *Television and Everyday Life*, London: Routledge.

Singer, Saul (2001) "Unbelieving West," *Jerusalem Post*, 30 November, p. 9A.

Sloan, William David, Sloan, David, and Startt, James D. (1989) *The Media in America: A History*, Worthington, OH: Publishing Horizons.

Smith, R. (2001) "Snapshots of September 11, 'A Gathering of Witnesses'," *New York Times*, 11 October, p. E1.

Snoddy, Raymond (2002) "A man of ideas but not of faith," *The Times*, 24 October, Section 2, p. 9.

Spiegel, Lynn (1992) *Make Room for TV: Television and the Family Ideal in Postwar America*, Chicago: University of Chicago Press.

Stark, Rodney and Bainbridge, William S. (1985) *The Future of Religion: Secularization, Revival and Cult Formation*, Berkeley: University of California Press.

Stout, Daniel and Buddenbaum, Judith (eds) (1996) *Religion and Mass Media: Audiences and Adaptations*, Newbury Park, CA: Sage.

Strawson, Galen (2004) "Against narrative," *Times Literary Supplement*, 15 October.

Sturken, Martia and Cartwright, Lisa (2001) *Practices of Looking: An Introduction to Visual Culture*, Oxford: Oxford University Press.

Taylor, Charles (1989) *Sources of the Self: The Making of the Modern Identity*, Cambridge, MA: Harvard University Press.

The Newshour with Jim Lehrer, 12 November 2001.

Thomas, Günter (1998) *Medien, Ritual, Religion: Zur religiösen Funktion des Fernshens*, Frankfurt: Suhrkamp.

——(2005) "Religious forms on television," in Eric Rothenbuhler and Mihai Coman (eds) *Media Anthropology*, Thousand Oaks, CA: Sage.

Thompson, John B. (1995) *The Media and Modernity*, Stanford: Stanford University Press.

Tönnies, Ferdinand (1957) *Community and Society (Gemeinschaft und Gesellschaft)*, East Lansing, MI: Michigan State University Press.

Tracey, Michael (1998) *The Decline and Fall of Public Service Broadcasting*, Oxford: Oxford University Press.

Tuchman, Gaye (1980) *Making News*, New York: The Free Press.

Turner, Graeme (1990) *British Cultural Studies: An Introduction*, London: Unwin-Hyman.

Underwood, Doug (2002) *From Yahweh to Yahoo!: The Religious Roots of the Secular Press*, Urbana: University of Illinois Press.

Warner, R. Stephen (1993) "Work in progress toward a new paradigm for the sociological study of religion in the United States," *American Journal of Sociology* 98(5) (March): 1044–93.

Warren, Michael (1997) *Seeing through the Media: A Religious View of Communications and Cultural Analysis*, Harrisburg: Trinity Press International.

Wildmon, Don (1989) *Don Wildmon: The Man the Networks Love to Hate*, Anderson, IN: Bristol House Ltd.

Williams, Raymond (1977) *Marxism and Literature*, New York: Oxford University Press.

Wilson, David (2005) "The US church that sold itself without selling its soul," *United Church (Canada) Observer* (June), pp. 32–5.

Winston, Diane (2000) *Red-Hot and Righteous: The Urban Religion of the Salvation Army*, Cambridge, MA: Harvard University Press.

Wright, Charles (1974) *The Sociology of Mass Communication*, Chicago: University of Chicago Press.

Wuthnow, Robert (1990) *The Restructuring of American Religion: Society and Faith since World War II*, Princeton, NJ: Princeton University Press.

——(1998) *After Heaven: Spirituality in America since the 1950s*, Berkeley: University of California Press.

Yamane, David (1997) "Secularization on trial: in defense of a neo-secularization paradigm," *Journal for the Scientific Study of Religion* 36 (March): 107–20.

Zaleski, Jeffrey P. (1997) *The Soul of Cyberspace: How New Technology Is Changing Our Spiritual Lives*, San Francisco: HarperCollins.

Zelizer, Barbie (2005) "Finding aids to the past: bearing personal witness to traumatic public events," in Eric Rothenbuhler and Mihai Coman (eds) *Media Anthropology*, Thousand Oaks, CA: Sage.

Zerbisias, Antonia (1997) "Hallelujah! TV sees the light: spiritually inspired series are going forth and multiplying in God's country," *Toronto Star*, 7 December, p. B1.

Index

"healing" 249
Heidegger, Martin 35
Hendershot, Heather 18, 35, 64, 78–79, 306n.68, 306n.72, 307n.114
Herberg, Will 18, 43, 51
Heritage Foundation 257
Heschel, Abraham Joshua 258
hierarchy of acceptable media 76, 199, 202, 272
high art 76
Hill, Annette 86, 88, 89–90, 266
history of the media 7–8
history, revising 246
Hobsbawm, Eric 40, 247
Hoggart, Richard 303n.2
Hollywood vs. America (Medved) 15
Home Box Office 43
Home Improvement 163, 196
Hood, Lee 188
Hoover, Stewart M. 5, 227, 297n.12, 297n.26, 302n.68
Horsfield, Peter 33
Howard, Ron 106
humanism 16, 159, 196

I Love Lucy 171–72
Icons of American Protestantism (Morgan) 18
idealism 30, 93, 214
identity: describing myself 222–24; families 103; I want to identify with it 217–19; and meaning 39–44; and narrative 91–92; "others" 273; presented identities 21; and self 97; theories of 15; *see also* self, project of
ideology 14–15, 39–40, 76
individualism 2, 3, 152–53
Industrial Revolution 30–31
informing media 213–17
infotainment 268
Innis, Harold 296n.4
inoffensive programming 275
inspiring media 209–12, 282
instantaneity 238
institutional-structural approaches 7–9, 39, 40
instrumentalism 67–68, 75
integration of media 41, 260, 266
interactionism 40–41, 93–94, 302n.62
interactions about the media: disentangling 207; expectations about 227; explanation of 88; I describe myself 222–24; Internet 217; significance of 205; youth 115–16
International Association for Media and Communication Research 18
Internet: access to 119–21, 138–39, 168–69; Buddhism 138; church sites 192; diversification 48; endorsing media 225; interactions about the media 217; news 194; withdrawal of access 153
interpretations, open/closed 2–3
interviews: methodology 291–95; narratives and 98–112; preparation for 86–91, 208; summaries of 141–46
invented tradition 247
Iranian revolution 1979 18–19, 58
Iraq 242
Islam 59, 240–43
Islamic Revolution 1979 18–19, 58
It's a Miracle 126–28, 173, 211
It's a Wonderful Life 160

Jackass 229
Jackson, Janet 304n.23
Jan interview: *see* Stevens-Van Gelder interview
Japanese Doomsday Cult 19
Jay interview: *see* Milliken interview
Jeff interview: *see* Stein interview
Jenkins, Henry 145
Jenkins, Jerry 62
Jesus Christ Superstar 116–17
Jesus, concepts of 178
Jewish Renewal Community 177–79
jihad 240
Jill interview: *see* Fallon interview
Jim interview: *see* Vowski interview
Joan of Arcadia 50
Johnson interview 118–26, 145
Joseph interview: *see* Abraham interview
journalism 15, 26, 57–60
Judaism 177–78, 198–99
Judy interview: *see* Cruz interview
Jurgensmeyer, Mark 242

Kathy interview: *see* Mueller interview
Katz, Elihu: disintermediation 284; interactions about the media 88; media events 244–45; "others" 239; post-9/11 249, 254; ritual 15; voting behavior studies 32, 69–70